GLOBAL INVESTING

Also by Julian Walmsley

*THE MACMILLAN DICTIONARY OF INTERNATIONAL FINANCE
THE FOREIGN EXCHANGE HANDBOOK
NEW FINANCIAL INSTRUMENTS

**Also published by Macmillan*

Global Investing

Eurobonds and Alternatives

Julian Walmsley

MACMILLAN

First published 1991

Published by
MACMILLAN PRESS LTD
Houndmills, Basingstoke, Hampshire RG21 2XS
and London
Companies and representatives
throughout the world

Typeset by Footnote Graphics,
Warminster, Wiltshire

Printed in Hong Kong

British Library Cataloguing in Publication Data
Walmsley, Julian
Global investing: Eurobonds and alternatives.
1. International money markets
I. Title
332.4′5
ISBN 0–333–51023–2

To Jane

Contents

Appendices

List of Acronyms

International finance has unfortunately spawned a bewildering array of acronyms. I have tried to keep them to a minimum but they are something of a necessary evil in this field. The following is a list of most of the acronyms used in the book.

A1	Top rating for commercial paper by Standard & Poor's
AAA	Top rating for bonds by Standard & Poor's
ACE	Joint trade matching system set up by Cedel and Euroclear
ADR	American Depositary Receipt
AFBD	Association of Futures Brokers and Dealers (of the UK)
AIBD	Association of International Bond Dealers
AIM	Amsterdam Interprofessional Market (Dutch OTC bond market)
AKV	Auslandskassenverein (German securities depository)
AMBAC	American Bond Assurance Corporation
APT	Automated Pit Trading (screen-based futures trading on LIFFE)
ASX	Australian Stock Exchange
BBB	Lowest Standard & Poor's rating that is 'investment grade'. Below BBB are 'junk bonds'.
BIG	Salomon Brothers Broad Investment Grade bond index
BPC	Bearer Participation Certificate
BTAN	Bons du Tresor à Taux Fixe et Interêt Annuel (French government bonds of under 5 years maturity)
CAC	Compagnie des Agents de Change (French equity index: CAC-40)
CATS	Certificates of Accrual on Treasury securities (US zero-coupon bonds)
CATS	Computer Assisted Trading System (used in Toronto, Brussels and Madrid)
CBOE	Chicago Board Options Exchange
CBOT	Chicago Board of Trade (futures exchange)
CD	Certificate of Deposit
CDS	Canadian Depository for Securities Ltd
CEDEL	Centrale de Livraison de Valeurs Mobilières (Eurobond clearing centre based in Luxembourg)
CFTC	Commodity Futures Trading Commission (of the USA)
CI	Certificat d'investissement
CME	Chicago Mercantile Exchange
CMO	Collateralized Mortgage Obligation

COB	Commission des Opérations de Bourse (French stock market regulator)
COP	Continuously Offered Payment rights (issued by World Bank in Switzerland)
COLTS	Continuously Offered Long Term Securities (issued by World Bank in Eurobond market and US)
CONSOB	Commissione Nazionale per le Società e la Borsa (Italian stock market regulator)
CORES	Computer-assisted Order Routing and Execution System (used on Tokyo Stock Exchange)
CUBES	Coupons Under Book-Entry Safekeeping (US system for trading stripped bond coupons)
DAX	Deutsche Aktienindex – German 'real-time' equity index
DOT	Designated Order Turnaround system (used on New York Stock Exchange)
DTB	Deutsche Termin Börse (German futures exchange)
DTC	Depository Trust Company (of New York)
EC	European Community
ECGD	Export Credit Guarantee Department (UK)
ECP	Euro-commercial Paper
ECU	European Currency Unit
EEC	European Economic Community
EMS	European Monetary System
EUCLID	Euroclear Computer Link to its members
FAZ	Frankfurter Allgemeine Zeitung (German equity index)
FELIN	Fonds d'État Libérés d'Interêt Nominal (French government zero coupon bonds)
FFCB	Federal Farm Credit Bank (of the US)
FGIC	Financial Guaranty Insurance Corporation (US bond insurer)
FHLB	Federal Home Loan Board (of the US)
FHLMC	Federal Home Loan Mortgage Corporation (US housing agency)
FICO	Financing Corporation (US agency rescuing thrifts)
FIMBRA	Financial Intermediaries, Managers and Brokers Regulatory Association (of the UK)
FNMA	Federal National Mortgage Association (US housing agency)
FRCMO	Floating Rate Collateralized Mortgage Obligation
FRN	Floating Rate Note
FSA	Financial Security Assurance (US bond insurer)
FTA-GS	Financial Times/Institute of Actuaries/Goldman Sachs international equity indices
FTSE	Financial Times-Stock Exchange index of 100 shares

GNF	Global Note Facility
GNMA	Government National Mortgage Association (US housing agency)
GSCC	Government Securities Clearing Corporation (of the USA)
IBF	International Banking Facility (USA)
IBIS	Inter Banken Informations System
ICON	Indexed Currency Option Note
IDR	International Depositary Receipt
IET	Interest Equalization Tax
IID	International Institutional Delivery system (of the DTC in New York)
IMF	International Monetary Fund
IMM	International Monetary Market (Chicago)
IO	Interest-Only (stripped bond)
IMRO	Investment Management Regulatory Organisation (of the UK)
IOSCO	International Organisation of Securities Commissions
IPMA	International Primary Market Association (of the AIBD)
ISDA	International Swap Dealers' Association
ITS	Intermarket Trading System (links US stock exchanges)
JASDEC	Japanese Securities Depository Centre
JGB	Japanese Government Bond
JSCC	Japanese Securities Clearance Corporation
LAUTRO	Life Assurance and Unit Trust Regulatory Organisation (of the UK)
LBO	Leveraged Buy-Out
LIBID	London Inter-bank Bid rate
LIBOR	London Inter-bank Offer rate
LIFFE	London International Financial Futures Exchange
LIMEAN	London Inter-bank Mean Rate (average of bid and offer)
LTOM	London Traded Options Market
MATIF	Marché à Terme des Instruments Financiers (Paris futures exchange)
MBIA	Mortgage Bond Insurance Association (US bond insurer)
MLP	Master Limited Partnership
MMP	Money Market Preferred
MoF	Ministry of Finance (Japan)
MOFF	Multiple Options Financing Facility
MONEP	French options exchange
MSCI	Morgan Stanley Capital International equity indices
MTN	Medium Term Note
NASD	National Association of Securities Dealers (USA)
NASDAQ	National Association of Securities Dealers Automated Quotation system

NIF	Note Issuance Facility
NK225	Nikkei index of 225 Japanese shares
NPV	Net Present Value
NSCC	National Securities Clearing Corporation (USA)
NYFE	New York Futures Exchange
NYSE	New York Stock Exchange
OAT	Obligation Assimilable du Trésor (French government bond)
OM	Optionsmaklarna (Swedish options and futures exchange with branches in Paris and Helsinki)
OTC	Over-The-Counter
OPEC	Organisation of Petroleum Exporting Countries
PC	Participation Certificate
PCC	Primary Capital Certificate
P/E	Price-Earnings ratio
PIBOR	Paris Inter-Bank Offered Rate
PO	Principal-Only (stripped bond)
RUF	Revolving Underwriting Facility
S&P 500	Standard & Poor's index of 500 US equities
SDFS	Same Day Funds Settlement system (run by the New York DTC for money market securities)
SEAQ	(UK) Stock Exchange Automated Quotation system
SEC	Securities and Exchange Commission (USA)
SEK	Swedish export credit body
SEPON	Stock Exchange Pooled Nominees (UK company used in stock exchange settlements)
SIB	Securities and Investments Board (of the UK)
SICOVAM	Société Interprofessionelle de Compensation de Valeurs Mobilières (French securities settlement system)
SIMEX	Singapore International Monetary Exchange (futures exchange)
SLMA	Student Loan Marketing Association (US agency)
SNIF	Short-term Note Issuance Facility
SOFFEX	Swiss Options and Financial Futures Exchange
SRO	Self-Regulatory Organisation
STARS	System for Transfer and Registration of Securities (Australia)
STRIPS	Separate Trading of Registered Interest and Principal (US system for trading zero coupon Treasury bonds)
SVT	Spécialiste en Valeurs du Trésor (market-maker in French government bonds)
SWIFT	Society for Worldwide International Financial Transactions (payment system linking international banks)
TAURUS	Transfer and Automated Registration of Uncertificated Stock (UK securities settlement system)

TIFFE	Tokyo International Financial Futures Exchange
TIGRs	Treasury Income Growth Receipts (US zero-coupon bonds)
TLC	Transferable Loan Certificate
TLI	Transferable Loan Instrument
TOPIX	Index of Tokyo Stock Exchange first section equities
TRAX	Trade registration system for Eurobonds run by the AIBD
TSA	The Securities Association (of the UK)
TSE	Tokyo or Toronto Stock Exchange
TWRR	Time-Weighted Rate of Return
USU	Unbundled Stock Unit
VRC	Voting Rights Certificate
YCAN	Yield Curve Anticipation Note

Preface

The prime object of this book is to put the Eurobond market – and its recent offshoot, the Euroequity market – in the context of the range of markets open to the international investor. Before 'globalisation' was a fashionable term, the Eurobond market (despite the misleading 'Euro' prefix) was global. Now it is having to fit into a new pattern, where other markets have joined it in the global market-place. This book aims to describe that new pattern, which is bound up with the revolution in global communications and trading that has taken place over the last decade. It also describes briefly the major domestic equity and bond markets which are the global investor's alternatives to the Euromarkets.

Since this book was written while working for an offshore investment institution investing without restrictions in equities, bonds, futures and options on a global basis, but with some need for ongoing liquidity and sensitive to international tax regimes, the focus reflects that bias. Where appropriate the viewpoint aims to reflect particular domestic constraints such as applied by the major domestic investor regulation bodies.

The book is written from the viewpoint of an investor needing to understand the markets in which he or she operates, rather than as a technical manual. But I hope that enough detail has been included on calculations, new issue mechanics, clearing systems and the like that it will serve as a useful introductory reference source for those needing to get to grips with nuts and bolts. Where technical detail is included it is generally in the Appendices rather than cluttering up the main text.

I have been greatly helped by being able to draw on the knowledge of a number of people in the investment field, and have gained a great deal from discussions with, in particular, Chris Greetham and the other Board members of Oil Investment Corporation, Ken Cholerton and Paul Abberley at Lombard Odier Investment Services, Richard Foulkes at Schroder Capital Management International, Adrian Lee at J. P. Morgan Investment, Jim Muzzy and Frank Rabinovitch at Pacific Investment Management Company, Michael Linsell at Warburg Investment Management International and Richard Abramson and Frank Trainer at Sanford C. Bernstein & Co. I must also thank Jim Watt at the Royal Bank of Canada in Toronto for reviewing the draft text, and Ken Ayers and Rob Hall at Frank Russell Co., and Vivienne Miller at the WM Co. for reviewing Appendix 6 on performance measurement. My thanks to all of them, and the many others too numerous to name who have spent time answering my many enquiries. It goes without saying that responsibility for any errors is mine alone.

JULIAN WALMSLEY

Preface

Part One
Background

1 The Global Spectrum

It is fashionable to talk of a global market for securities. Such a market has begun to be born. But, to borrow a phrase, between the idea and the reality falls the shadow – of settlement problems, national legal and regulatory systems, and other constraints. Still, a number of changes have made markets less regional. They include:

(a) better telecommunications and information flows;
(b) growing acceptance of the benefits of international diversification by investors;
(c) the creation of the interest rate and currency swap market, which means that a borrower can search the globe for the cheapest securities market;
(d) the resulting tendency to switch from banks to global securities markets for funding;
(e) which impelled securities firms to follow the example of the banks during the 1970s, when they moved to create a global network of branches;
(f) the resulting need for capital led a number of securities firms to seek partners, leading to the creation in London of combinations of commercial and investment banks (following the German and Swiss pattern of universal banks) and the arrival of large Japanese financial institutions as shareholders in US investment banks.

Because of all these things, the issuers and intermediaries in the markets have begun to become much more accustomed to think on a global scale. This in turn has influenced the investing community. Certain investors by their nature – supranationals, pension funds of multinational companies – have for some time looked at the world as one world for investment purposes. But during the 1980s, influenced by the changes mentioned above, this point of view was adopted by many more investing institutions. The process continues, albeit at a slower pace, after the Crash of October 1987, which called a brief halt. Investors sought the comparative safety of their home markets. But it seems certain that these trends are irreversible.

The purpose of this book is to give a simple outline of some of the choices facing someone planning to invest on a global basis. Its coverage is necessarily broad rather than deep. It should be thought of more as a road map, a sketch, than an authoritative manual; but it may be of some use in describing the terrain to the traveller.

We begin with a short outline of the development of some of the markets: understanding where we are today is perhaps helped by knowing where we came from. Then we look in Chapter 4 at the range of basic instruments – bonds, warrants, convertibles and equities – available to the investor in some of the important markets. Next we look at some of the newer instruments: zero coupon and asset-backed bonds, and some of the so-called 'synthetic' instruments. This is followed by a short outline of the so-called 'derivative' markets for futures, options and swaps, which discusses how these markets can impact on investment decisions. Then in Chapter 8 we focus on the important subject, for the international investor, of foreign exchange risk.

The largest single homogeneous international market is the Eurobond market, with its attendant sub-markets – Eurocommercial paper, Euro-deposit markets, and Euro-equities. Chapters 9–12 discuss the growth of the market, its issuing and trading practices, its regulation, and the various instruments and sectors of the market, including Euroequities. Chapters 13–16 consider the major alternatives – Eurodeposit markets (Chapter 13), national money markets, commercial paper and medium-term notes (Chapter 14), major government and corporate bond markets (Chapter 15), and national equity markets (Chapter 16).

None of these markets would work without settlement systems. Chapter 17, therefore, looks at the crucial, if mundane, questions of settlement, clearing and custody. The importance of this issue was highlighted recently by the Group of Thirty, which produced a report under the chairmanship of John Reed, the Chairman of Citicorp, commenting:

> The world's securities markets are of increasing importance to all who are involved with modern day business ... At the same time, it is clear that the operational characteristics of these markets – particularly the trading, clearing and settlement procedures – are of uneven quality ... [which] ... inhibits international investment flows, while the intersection between local practice and growing volumes and values could, under adverse circumstances, represent a very serious risk to the world's financial network.
>
> (*Clearance and Settlement Systems in the World's Financial Markets*, March 1989, p. iii)

Lastly, Chapter 18 takes a look into a cloudy crystal ball and assesses some of the major issues facing the global investor and the markets in which he or she will operate, both regulatory and otherwise.

THE GLOBAL SPECTRUM

The purpose of this first chapter is to give a broad overview of the spectrum of choices as they present themselves to the international investor.

As a first cut, Figure 1.1 presents a very crude picture of the money value

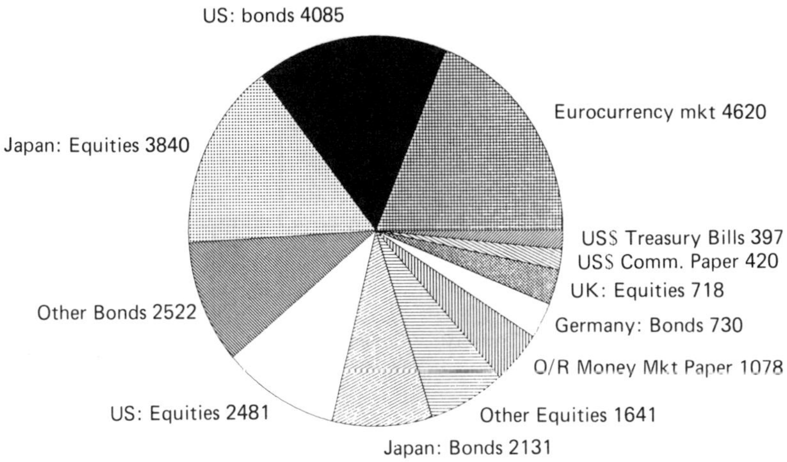

FIGURE 1.1 Global investment choices December 1988 ($bn) Bonds include domestic and Euro

SOURCES: Morgan Stanley Capital International (MSCI), Bank of England, Merrill Lynch

of some of the major markets. Because there is no one good source of international financial data, the numbers used here are of variable quality and are from different sources, so they should not be relied on too much. A better title for the chart might be 'Impressions of a Market' – something like a Whistler Nocturne, rather dim and hazy.

The diagram oversimplifies, of course: there is a huge, complex range of markets and instruments available to the global investor. In the beginning, things were fairly straightforward: you had the choice of fixed-rate bonds, equities or cash. Now, though, the pattern is more complex. To the three basic categories need to be added at least two more: floating-rate instruments, and derivatives. Within each category is a range of alternatives that over the last two decades has greatly widened.

The most basic group is cash. This can be divided into bank deposits (repayable at call, or time deposits) and tradable paper. The lowest-yielding instrument of this group is the Treasury bill. Next in safety is the certificate of deposit (CD) issued by a top-class bank from a major developed country such as the USA, Japan or UK. Such a CD will usually carry the implied backing of the central bank of the country concerned. Next comes the banker's acceptance (bill of exchange) for it carries two promises to pay (that of the issuer and that of the accepting bank), though it is less certain that a central bank would bail out holders of a bank's acceptances.

Next comes commercial paper, where the main safety comes in the fact

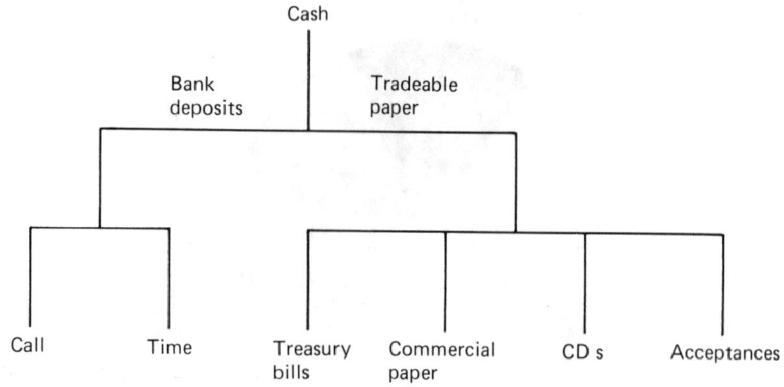

FIGURE 1.2 Cash

that it is usually very short term. Commercial paper issued in the USA is invariably rated by Moody's or Standard & Poor's (see Chapter 14), but this in and of itself is not a guarantee. Kloeckner & Co.'s paper was still rated A1 the week before the company collapsed (although the rescue arranged by Deutsche Bank bailed out holders). Apart from their limited credit risk, all these instruments are rather safe in terms of market risk: interest movements will have relatively little effect and holders need not wait long to have their full principal returned.

Next in terms of safety from market risk comes the floating-rate note (FRN). The classic FRN pays six-month London Inter-Bank Offered Rate (LIBOR) – the effective cost to banks in London of borrowing for six months – plus (or, for very good credits, minus) a margin of ⅛ per cent or more. So, every six months, its value should return close to par – assuming the issuer's quality is unchanged. Thus the risk from interest rate movements is small.

More recently, however, the Euromarkets have embroidered a number of different themes on the classic FRN (discussed in more detail in Chapter

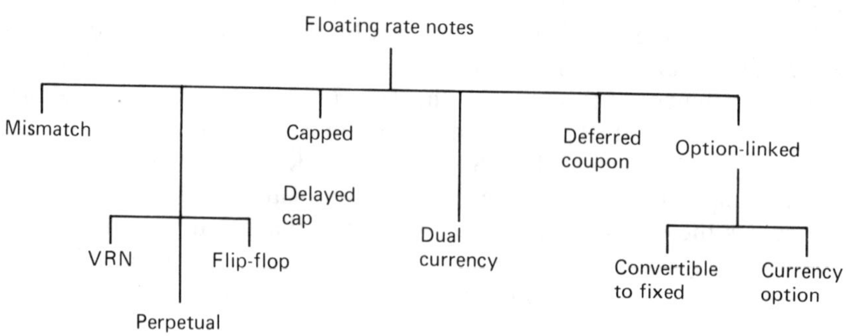

FIGURE 1.3 Floating rate notes

6). The mismatch FRN resets the six-month LIBOR every month; capped FRNs set a limit on the LIBOR payable; deferred coupon FRNs pay large coupons in some years and little or none in others (mainly a tax play); variable rate notes allow the margin to vary; perpetuals take your money but never give it back; flip-flops allow the investor to flip from a perpetual into a dated FRN and back; dual currency FRNs allow the redemption value to vary with an exchange rate; while option-linked FRNs give the investor various options whose value supposedly compensate for lower coupons.

It is in the bond arena that we see the widest global range of choices. The chart oversimplifies the full range and omits a number of important variations in the interest of clarity. Choices include the investor's domestic government bond market; bonds issued by a wide range of other governments in their own domestic markets; mortgage-backed securities in the USA, UK and certain other countries such as Denmark and Germany; together with, in the US, more exotic variants such as collateralised mortgage obligations (CMOs) and CMO residuals; medium-term notes; privately placed bonds of many descriptions; domestic corporate bonds and corporate Eurobonds; and a range of Eurobond exotica such as indexed currency option notes (ICONs), heaven and hell bonds, synthetic FRNs and other instruments. These are discussed more fully in Chapters 5 and 6.

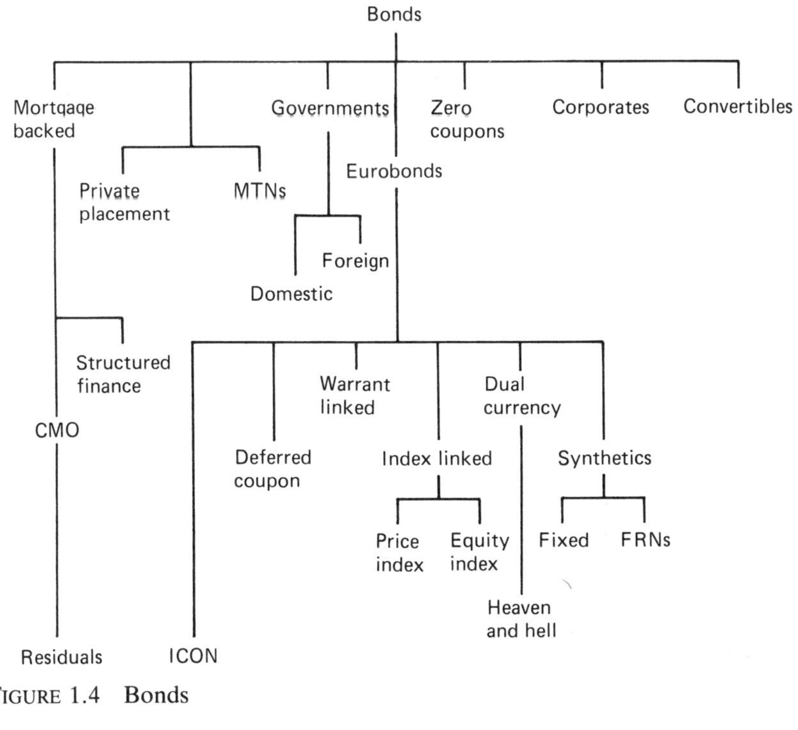

FIGURE 1.4 Bonds

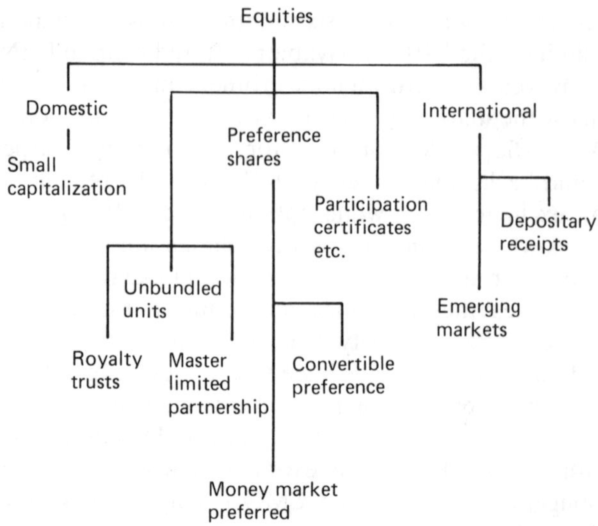

FIGURE 1.5 Equities

Next along the spectrum come the large domestically and internationally traded equities – such as those which form the components of the Morgan Stanley Capital International World Index. Here, there is a huge diversity of credit risk, earnings potential and currency exposure. What these stocks do generally have in common, though, is that they can be traded in at least moderate size on an international basis. Often they can be traded in the investor's home market through depositary receipts (discussed in Chapter 4).

The international investor will come across participation certificates, allowing participation in profits but no votes, in a number of countries; preference shares are particularly important in the USA for tax reasons, which led to the invention of money market preferred. More recent innovations in the USA have seen a number of different concepts – master limited partnerships, royalty trusts and unbundled units – which are touched on in Chapter 4. Finally, at the far end of the risk/return spectrum come the markets which are generally referred to as 'emerging' – Thailand, Korea, Brazil and other such places. Clearly, some of these have immense potential. Equally clearly, the investor needs good understanding of the risks before venturing into these waters.

Most recently, a number of derivative securities have been introduced. Futures and options contracts on bonds, and interest rate and currency swaps, allow the investor to transform assets from one currency to another, and even to produce equity returns from cash or vice versa (see Chapter 7). These derivative securities can affect the underlying assets – witness the effect of equity futures in the Crash of 1987.

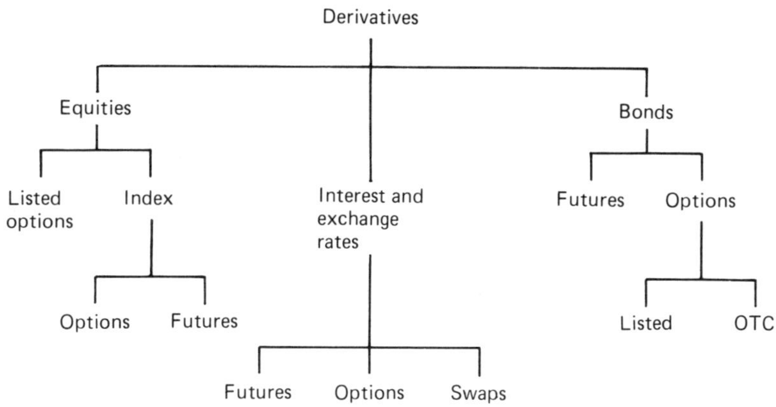

FIGURE 1.6 Derivatives

They also create a new split between the ownership of rights to an equity return from the ownership of equity voting rights, an issue which is of growing importance in the international context. Even where full voting rights are available, the global investor will find problems in exercising them. Institutions in some countries – notably the UK and the USA – are used to exercising actively the voting power implied by their shareholdings when appropriate. Indeed the US ERISA regulations require corporate pension funds to do so. But this is much more difficult in the international arena.

In Japan, for example, companies require the physical presence of the shareholder, and most companies hold their annual general meeting on the same day. In some countries, custodians cannot vote as proxy for the beneficial owner; in others, the beneficial owner must be physically present to vote. In several countries, companies are not required to notify shareholders of forthcoming meetings as long as they are advertised in a local newspaper. Thus, the spread of global investing may imply the growth of 'absentee owners': institutions with ownership rights but effectively deprived of voting power.

Still, the rewards of international investment can be substantial – albeit variable. A brief summary (Table 1.1) of the international investor's experience over the last decade will show how much returns have varied – and hence how crucial it has been to be in the right markets. It also confirms the pattern that longer-run studies of the USA and UK have shown, and that theory would lead us to expect. Equities consistently produce a higher return than bonds, which in turn normally produce a higher return than cash (though the abnormally volatile conditions of 1979–81, which produced a sharply inverted US yield curve, affected the US returns).

Table 1.1 Total return 1979–88

	Average annual increase (%) in local currency terms *Equities*	*Bonds*	*Cash*	*Exchange rate vs $*
USA	16.3	10.0	10.6	–
Japan	19.6	7.7	6.5	4.5
UK	21.4	14.6	12.7	−1.2
Germany	13.0	7.3	6.6	0.3
Switzerland	10.1	3.6	2.8	0.8
France	22.5	12.1	11.6	− 3.6
Netherlands	19.9	9.6	7.4	− 0.2
Canada	28.3	15.1	13.1	− 0.1
Australia	13.9	10.9	11.7	− 2.9
World average	19.9	10.4	10.1	–

Source: UBS Phillips & Drew, *World Capital Markets*, March 1989.

Thus, for example, a US investor in Japan, on an unhedged basis, would have earned 19.6 per cent per annum from equities and experienced a currency gain of 4.5 per cent per annum on average for a total return of over 24 per cent per annum; conversely, a Japanese investor in the USA would have averaged 16.3 per cent equities gain with a loss of 4.5 per cent on the currency for a net 11.8 per cent.

A longer-term perspective on the equity risk/return comparison can be seen from Table 1.2, showing the evolution over a quarter-century in some of the major markets.

GLOBAL TRADING

It is very difficult to get good statistics on who is doing what internationally. It is clear that there is a good deal more international trading than there was: but it is not clear how much. We have fairly good figures for Eurobond trading, and equity trading in national markets – Figure 1.7 shows developments in the four largest markets, and highlights the explosive growth of Japan – but our figures for cross-border trading are limited. The events of October 1987 had one benefit: they triggered a number of official studies of the markets, which give a snapshot of how the global securities market had evolved by that date. The data is by no means complete since it does not really cover bonds, but, for example, the Federal Reserve Bank of New York gave the estimates listed in Table 1.3 for international equity flows.

At its peak, just before the October 1987 crash, foreign share trading on the most active international market, the International Stock Exchange in

Table 1.2 Annual equity returns and volatility in US$ 1960–85

	Compound return	*Standard deviation*
Australia	7.4	24.9
Austria	9.9	35.9
Belgium	11.6	17.4
Canada	9.6	17.3
Denmark	10.9	27.8
France	7.6	25.2
Germany	11.2	29.9
Italy	4.4	34.6
Japan	16.2	28.9
Netherlands	11.2	19.4
Norway	10.8	48.1
Spain	8.6	21.7
Sweden	11.5	20.6
Switzerland	11.1	27.9
UK	10.5	31.2
US	9.6	16.9

Source: R. G. Ibbotson and G. P. Brinson, *Investment Markets*, McGraw-Hill, 1987.

London, had grown 70 per cent over the previous twelve months to a daily volume of £525 ($850) million. It accounted for almost one-third of the volume of trading in the London market. In addition, London had a widespread off-exchange market in international equities, estimated to be about as big as the volume traded on the Exchange. Over half the trading was estimated to be done by non-residents.

During 1988, as equity investors world-wide retreated into their home markets, trading by foreigners in London fell back to around 17 per cent, according to International Stock Exchange estimates as listed in Table 1.4.

The bulk of London's trading is in French and German equities, with an active market also in US and Japanese stocks. By contrast, trading on the

Table 1.3 Net purchases of foreign equities ($bn) residents of various countries

	1985	*1986*	*(Jan. Sept.) 1987*
Canada	0.4	1.6	0.3
Germany	1.6	2.4	– 0.6
Japan	1.0	7.0	13.5
UK	5.6	10.5	5.3
USA	1.9	2.4	1.6

Source: Federal Reserve Bank of New York, *Quarterly Bulletin*, Summer 1988.

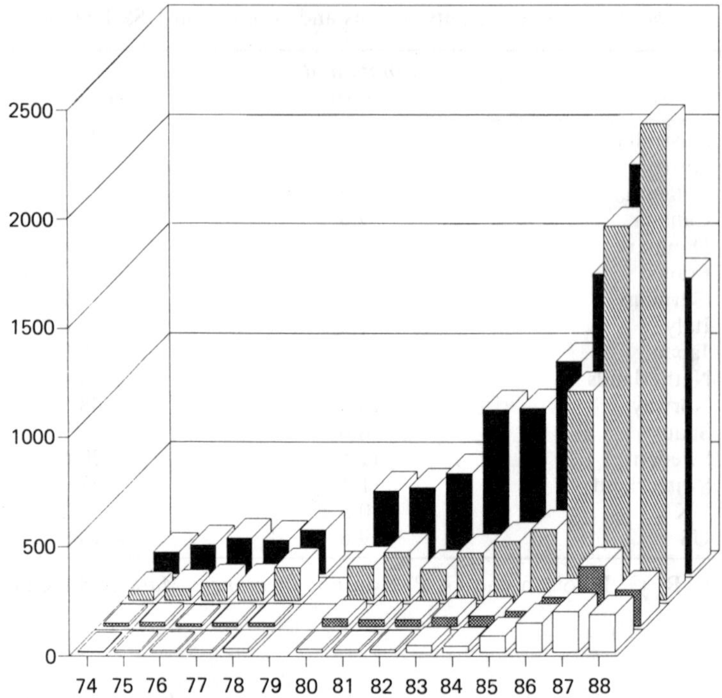

FIGURE 1.7 Stock market turnovers 1974–88 (US$bn)

SOURCE: Morgan Stanley, Capital International

New York Stock Exchange is largely confined to ADRs (American Depositary Receipts – certificates evidencing ownership of shares) of UK companies, while at the time of the Crash only 1.5 per cent of Tokyo's volume was in foreign shares.

The Federal Reserve's study concluded that:

> In summary, by September 1987, the activities of cross-border investors had grown considerably in most major equity markets, but the foreign share of total stocks outstanding and of transactions volume remained fairly low in the largest markets ... compared to cross-border investment, 24-hour trading (of stocks on exchanges outside their home country) represented a more limited and specialized channel for the transmission of disturbances from one equities market to another. As a general phenomenon, it had not developed to the point where it could easily spread a stock market decline around the globe ... The principal

Table 1.4 ISE trading by country of customer (£bn)

UK	162.3
Continental Europe	11.9
USA	8.8
Japan	1.4
Other	5.6

international linkage between national stock markets appears to be the unobservable and indirect one created when sharp price declines in overseas markets contribute to a panicky market psychology.

In response to the events of October 1987 international investors inevitably cut back. Estimates from Salomon Brothers (International Equity Flows, August 1989) suggest that the total world value of cross-border equity trading fell by 10 per cent in US dollar terms in 1988 (with a 25 per cent fall in volume terms). As the chart drawn from their figures shows (Figure 1.8) the major centre for cross-border trading is the UK, which during 1988 was a net investor in Europe (excluding the UK) and Japan, and a net seller of shares in the USA and the rest of the world. Japan was a net seller of rest of the world stocks and a small net buyer of US, UK and continental European stocks.

Global equity trading is a relatively new phenomenon, and as the Federal Reserve's comments show, it is not yet fully established. But

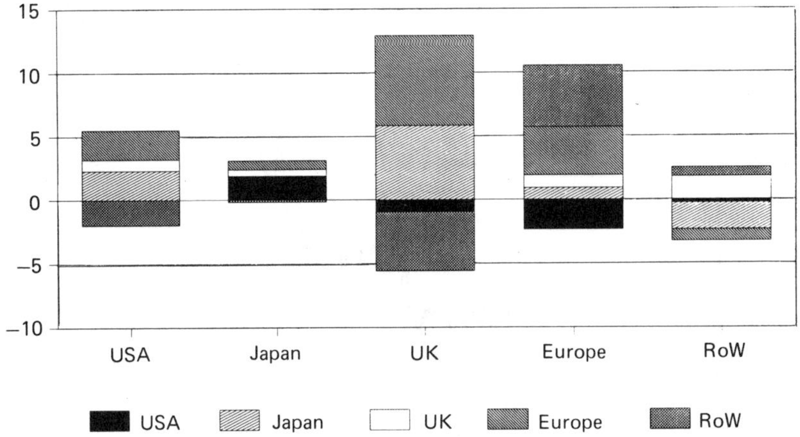

FIGURE 1.8 Cross-border equity flows: UK is leading investor, followed by Europe, and USA

SOURCE: Salomon Brothers

global trading in Eurobonds is fully established, and has been for years: for this was the first true global securities market.

EUROBONDS: THE FIRST GLOBAL MARKET

The Eurobond market is huge. By some measures it is the biggest capital market in the world. Yet it seems obscure to many people. A notorious example occurred when the British government produced a White Paper on regulating London securities markets. No mention whatever was made of the Eurobond market. This despite the fact that the scale of Eurobond trading in London dwarfed that of the Stock Exchange by a factor of 20. The chart in Figure 1.9 shows the rapid growth of trading in Eurobonds during the 1980s. Monthly turnover running at $300–500 billion compares with total 1988 turnover of the London stock market of $165 billion.

Many investors, however, still feel that Eurobonds are a shadowy, foreign market. Traditionally, investors in the Eurobond market were of ill

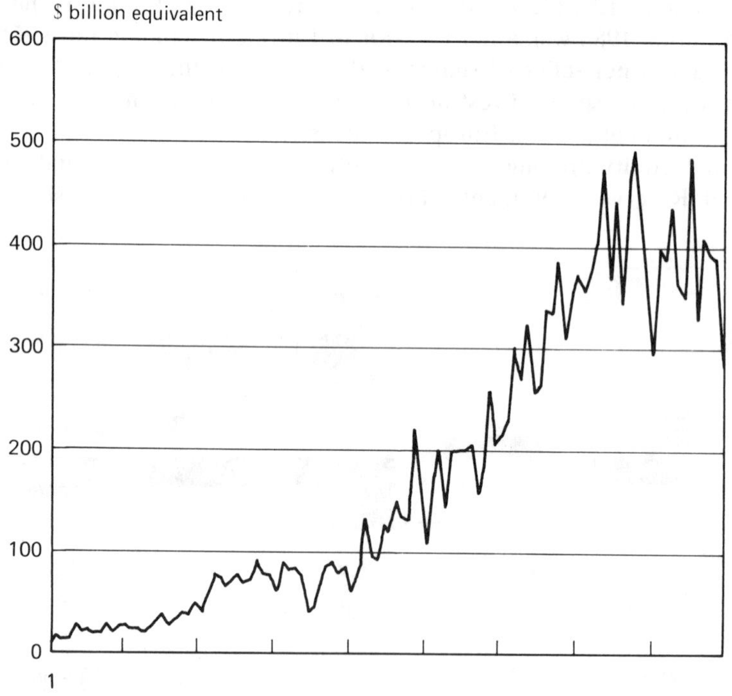

FIGURE 1.9 Total Eurobond turnover: monthly, primary and secondary
SOURCE: AIBD

repute. Legend had it that they were either Belgian dentists, intent on preserving their savings from the attentions of the tax-man, or dictators from developing countries, who would arrive occasionally in their private jet to fondle their ill-gotten gains.

As the market has grown, though, this raffish image has come to be replaced by a more mundane, but more important, mix of investors. The market is now the province of a very wide range of international investors, ranging from institutions such as the World Bank, international insurance companies, banks and large corporations down to the wealthy individual so beloved of market mythology.

Eurobond practitioners are themselves partly to blame for the extent of misunderstanding of the market. There has been a tendency to cultivate the mystique of the market. Recently, particularly in London, the frenetic expansion of Big Bang followed by the inevitable painful contraction have led to suggestions of the market's demise. Like Mark Twain's premature obituary, such statements are greatly exaggerated. While not yet perhaps healthy, the market in 1988 handled a record volume of new issues in a wide range of currencies, and it remains a central source of funds for a range of institutions and corporations around the globe.

Figure 1.10 shows turnover through Euroclear and Cedel from 1985–8 and illustrates another important feature of the market, its growing diversity. Intermediaries and investors who in the past confined themselves to floating-rate notes – a market recovering only gradually from the crisis of 1986 (see Chapter 4) – and the classical straight Eurobond, have begun trading a range of other instruments. The largest part of the phenomenal growth in the 'other' category reported by the AIBD comes from trading in government bonds. The AIBD figures, drawn as they are from Euroclear and Cedel, exclude US Treasuries and UK gilt-edged stock which do not clear through those bodies, but include activity in German Bunds, French OATs, and Dutch government bonds. (The figures will also include turn-over in Eurocommercial paper and some of the warrant activity associated with equity-warrant-linked Eurobonds.)

More recently, attempts have been made to integrate international equity trading into the transnational framework of the Euromarkets. At the most basic level, Euroclear announced in April 1989 that it was accepting 400 of the most important Japanese equities for clearance through its systems, and now between Euroclear and Cedel about 2,000 equities from a dozen or more countries can be cleared through a single transnational clearing system.

The emphasis placed on the Euromarkets in this book flows from the belief that the international markets will flow through the easiest channels, and that over time the equity markets will follow their bond counterparts in flowing through the Euromarket networks. The process will be much more complex. Governments are much more sensitive to the internationalisation

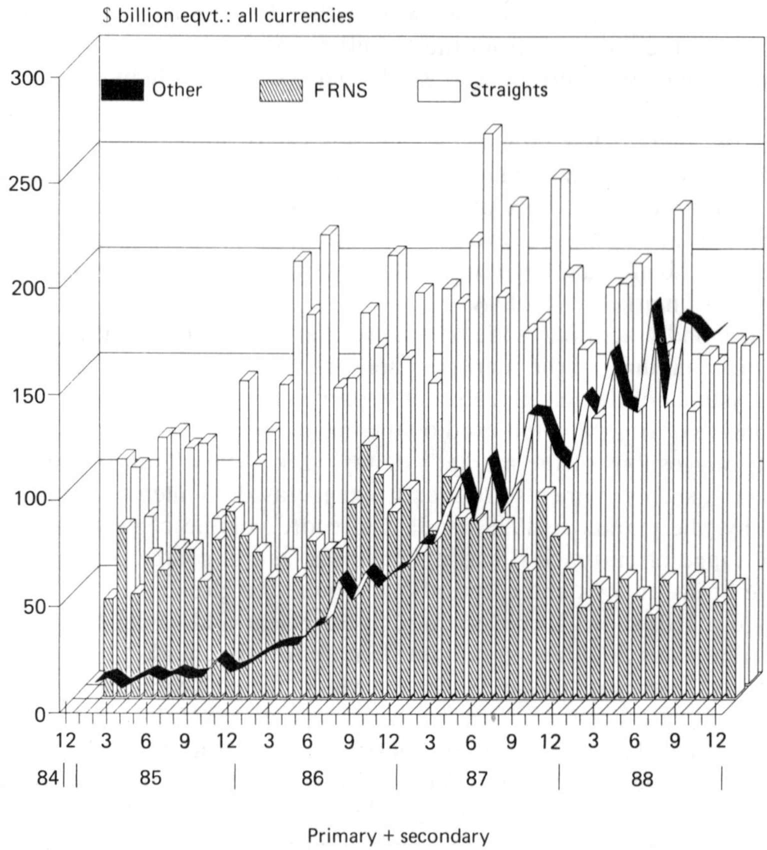

FIGURE 1.10 Eurobond turnover: by instrument
SOURCE: AIBD

of the ownership and control of major corporations than to the trading of debt. Also, stock exchanges have a vested interest in keeping control of the trading of 'their' equities. The basic difference between global trading through a network of exchanges and through the transnational network of the Euromarkets (or an electronic system linked, say, to Reuters) is that in the former case the number of market-making participants is limited to those allowed to buy seats on the national exchanges. In the latter case, market-makers need only people, hardware and creditworthiness. The value of stock exchange seats, which lies in privileged access to a trading monopoly, would decline, and with it the position of their holders.

A countervailing force is that the exchanges themselves are coming to realize that they are in competition: the New York Stock Exchange has begun to gear up for 24-hour trading in an effort to win back international market share from the International Stock Exchange in London. In June 1989, NASDAQ announced it would begin trading two to three hundred over-the-counter stocks from 4.00 a.m. Eastern Standard Time in order to compete with London. They are also coming to realise – most notably in London – that they themselves must integrate with the global electronic systems that are emerging. It may be that the stock exchanges will blend into the Euromarket approach; it remains my view that the latter model is the most likely for the development of global securities trading. In any event, the rest of this book is an attempt to survey the current pattern of global investment opportunities and how the Eurobond and Euro-equity markets fit into them, beginning in the next two chapters with a brief description of how we got there.

2 Early Years: 1963–1979

Equity markets go back at least to 1555, with the foundation of the Muscovy Company; bond markets can be traced back even further. But life is short, so we will skip the first four hundred years, and concentrate on the last quarter of a century. Suffice it to say that by the early 1960s most of the world's major stock exchanges were functioning again after the traumas of the Second World War. But in Europe – although convertibility was generally restored in 1958 – there remained in place of a wide network of exchange controls inhibiting international flows of funds. British investors wanting to buy overseas equities, for example, had to pay a premium for foreign exchange, called the investment premium. This fluctuated widely, hitting 50 per cent or more at times of crisis. Some institutions were already investing on a global basis (for example, Capital International opened their Geneva office in 1969, and Swiss and Scottish investment firms also had a long tradition of international investment) but they were isolated exceptions. Government bond markets remained the province of domestic investors, and the international bond markets were effectively non-existent. The first step to globalisation was the development of the Eurocurrency market (see Chapter 13) around 1958–9, followed in 1963 by the emergence of the Eurobond market.

FOUNDATION OF THE EUROBOND MARKET

Contrary to market legend, the Eurobond market did not spring fully armed out of the head of Julius Strauss and Siegmund Warburg. It grew from an older usage. There had been a long tradition of foreign bonds launched on various domestic markets, from the Frfr100 million Baring indemnity loan to finance French preparations after Napoleon in 1817 through French loans to Czarist Russia, British financing of the Argentine rail system, and the Dawes and Young Plans of 1924 and 1930 to finance German reparations. The key difference lay in the fact that the Eurobond market by its very nature was multinational in scope. It was a 'turntable' market by which funds came from many countries to go to many countries.

The exact starting date of the market is itself the subject of argument. Although by common consent the Autostrade issue in July 1963 marked the birth of the market, as a market, issues were made earlier which might technically be considered Eurobonds, or at least to have some of their features. Philips, for example, issued dollar bonds in the Netherlands in 1949 and 1951, for a total of $25 million; the Portuguese entity SACOR issued in 1961 a bond denominated in the seventeen-currency European

Unit of Account. In May 1963 Samuel Montagu privately placed a three-year $20 million bearer bond issue for the Belgian government with the Bank of London and South America, the Bank of Nova Scotia, Kleinwort Benson and Schroder Wagg.

Single issues, though, do not a market make. The Autostrade issue of 1 July 1963 began a sequence of issues that developed into a true market. The true significance of Autostrade was that for the first time a dollar issue was lead managed by a non-US syndicate (SG Warburg, Banque de Bruxelles, Deutsche Bank and Rotterdamsche Bank). Hitherto it had been unthinkable that a public US$ issue would not be led by a US syndicate. The Philips and Belgian deals were private placements and the SACOR deal, being denominated in a unit of account, had no natural domestic syndicate.

The major difficulties to putting the issue in place were regulatory – arranging for the issue to be listed on the London and Luxembourg Stock Exchanges, persuading the Bank of England to accept the concept – and tax: overcoming the hurdle of UK stamp duty on bearer bonds, for example.

Once the deal was done, the concept of a dollar bond market in Europe began to emerge, with the encouragement of Douglas Dillon, President Kennedy's Secretary of the Treasury. He was urging Europeans to raise finance in their own markets rather than borrow in New York, which added to US balance of payments problems. Indeed, two weeks after the Autostrade deal, President Kennedy announced the imposition of the Interest Equalization Tax, designed to discourage foreign bond issues in the USA. The IET was a powerful driving force in the early growth of the Eurobond market.

The market quickly opened up to non-European borrowers: in December 1963 Canon Camera offered US$5 million of 6.25 per cent convertible debentures maturing in 1978. Norway in May 1964 launched the first government loan, a large issue – by the standards of the day – in the form of a $25 million twenty-year bond. The first Eurobond with equity warrants in June 1964 was issued in the form of $25 million for Istituto per la Ricostruzione Industriale (IRI) with warrants attached for shares in its subsidiary, Società Finanziaria Siderurgica (FINSIDER).

STOCK MARKET DEVELOPMENTS

In the early 1960s stock markets were less internationally open than the Eurobond market, which even then was a fairly freewheeling multinational market. The UK stock market, as already mentioned, was a largely domestic animal owing to exchange controls (although the existence of the 'sterling area' at this stage meant that those countries included in the

	Eurobond market	Stock markets	Financial environment
1961		Sony ADR	
1963	Jul: Autostrade issue Dec: Canon convertible		IET imposed
1964	Norway issue IRI equity warrant issue	Japan: Collapse of stock market. Rescue of Yamaichi	
1965	Mobil L 10 m. L/DM issue $20 m. Cyanamid issue	Germany: VEBA privatisation	US Voluntary Foreign Credit Restraint
1967	Total new issue volume reaches US$1 billion	Japan Securities Clearing Corp. set up France: COB set up	Arab/Israeli war Devaluation of pound sterling
1968		UK Takeover Panel	Mandatory US investment controls
1969		US 'back-office' crisis builds up	US credit squeeze
1970	ENEL FRN IOS collapses	US SIPC set up	
1971	First $100m. issue	NASDAQ set up	US$ devalued

FIGURE 2.1 The 1960s

sterling area such as Australia were able to float issues in London). Investors could buy foreign stocks and did so. But the penalty cost imposed by the 'investment currency premium' charged for the sale of foreign exchange to the investor was such as to discourage substantial outflows into foreign equities (as of course it was designed to do). Likewise at this stage Japanese investors were forbidden to invest abroad (and indeed the country's current account situation, like that of the UK, was such as to limit the scope for this). The New York stock market was unrestricted, but such was the scope for domestic investment that little interest was paid to foreign stocks. Foreign firms – except from Canada – were forbidden to become members of the Exchange until 1977 (as was also the case in London and Tokyo until 1986).

An early move towards internationalisation of the Japanese market was made by Sony in 1961, with the issue of the first American Depositary Receipt (see Chapter 4) by a Japanese company. However, in 1963 the imposition of the Interest Equalization Tax by President Kennedy stifled what little interest there was in international investment by US institutions (even though it did not in fact apply to ADRs). Also, in 1964–5 the Japanese market hit a severe crisis which would have discouraged foreign investors in any event. Tightening credit and an emerging recession combined to produce a crack in an overbought market. The 1961 creation of the Second Section had been combined with heavy pressure by the Stock Exchange on the major securities firms to buy large blocks of stock in the new market. Yamaichi Securities, then the largest firm, held the largest blocks during the 1964 collapse and had to be rescued by the Bank of Japan. Of 600 Japanese securities firms in 1960, 430 remained in 1965.

EARLY GROWTH OF THE EUROBOND MARKET: 1965–9

By the start of 1965, the Eurobond market could be said to have been established. But it was a fledgling market. A very small number of issues had been made, and there were no real secondary markets. It was entirely possible that the whole affair might simply die away.

That this did not happen is mainly due to the Vietnam war. Vietnam put heavy pressure on the American balance of payments. So President Johnson announced in February 1965 the Voluntary Restraint Program. This aimed to hold back American companies from investing overseas, unless there was a gain to the US balance of payments. At the same time, US commercial banks were told not to make new loans to international borrowers, including overseas subsidiaries of US firms. These firms were encouraged to tap local markets overseas for funds.

This created a new group of high-quality borrowers seeking capital from the Eurobond market. An example was Mobil Oil, which in June 1965 issued a fifteen-year bond in the amount of £10m. It was redeemable in 1980 in sterling or Deutschmarks at an exchange rate of DM4.16 per pound. On the other side of the market, the fact that Italy, for example, was supplying substantial dollar funds to the Euromarket via swaps between the Italian Exchange Office and commercial banks meant an ample supply of funds. As the BIS commented at the time: 'That the Eurodollar market and the Eurobond market should grow together is no coincidence ... The European banks that underwrite these bond issues need to maintain a pool of dollars in case they have to take up securities that the market cannot promptly absorb.'[1]

In September 1965 came the first US dollar denominated straight US bond for a US corporation: US$20 million for American Cyanamid. The market grew steadily, and for the first time in 1967 the value of new issues succeeded US$1 billion equivalent.

But 1967 was also a year of severe international currency pressures. The June Arab–Israeli war set off a crisis which peaked with the devaluation of sterling in November 1967. This triggered a fresh round of pressure on the US dollar, which caused great strain on the gold 'pool' run by the central banks (aimed at holding the US dollar price of gold fixed). In March 1968 the pool collapsed and a two-tier fixed/floating gold price was created. In response to these pressures, in January 1968 President Johnson imposed mandatory controls on outflows from the United States. The previous voluntary guidelines were abandoned. US firms were severely restricted in overseas investments: the pressure on them to borrow abroad became much more severe. US corporate borrowing in the Eurobond market trebled during 1968 (to US$1.96 billion, compared with US$0.53 billion in 1967).

The Vietnam war, as well as putting pressure on the US balance of payments from 1965 on, drove the American economy into high gear as resources were committed to the war. As a result, Wall Street was bullish. Other stock markets also benefited from the strength of international economic activity, led by the USA. In Japan, the market began to recover from the 1964–5 crisis: the Nikkei 225 rose from 1,588 in January 1966 to 2,534 in June 1970. An important step towards automating the operations of the market was taken in 1967 with the setting up of the Japanese Securities Clearing Corporation. The German stock market was boosted in 1965 by the partial privatisation of VEBA (following a similar operation for Volkswagen in 1959). In France stock market reforms included the setting up in 1967 of the Commission des Opérations de Bourse to supervise market activity. The UK stock market also responded to regulatory problems in 1968 by setting up the Panel on Takeovers and Mergers.

MARKET PROBLEMS 1969–70

During the first part of 1969 the USA imposed a credit squeeze, which flowed through to the Eurodollar market, pushing rates up sharply to almost 12 per cent and incidentally leading to a 50 per cent growth in the Eurocurrency market (from $30bn to $45bn). This failed to prevent heavy upward pressure on the Deutschmark, however, which was allowed by the German authorities to float before being fixed at a new higher level.

This squeeze combined with rising settlements problems in New York to create severe problems for US broking firms. Goodbody & Co., one of the largest brokers in the country, went under and had to be rescued by Merrill Lynch. During 1967–70 the New York Stock Exchange had to take a hand in the affairs of more than half its members, because of the firms' operational deficiencies. This crisis spilled over into the Euromarkets, where settlement difficulties arising from the clearing of dollar bonds in New York led to the foundation of Euroclear (see Chapter 17). The crisis also led to the Securities Investors Protection Act of 1970 which set up the Securities Investors Protection Corporation to protect investors from broker default. In London, also, the need to reform the settlements system was recognised and the Stock Exchange began working on Talisman, its computerised settlements system. Ambitious plans were announced in 1971 but only partially implemented in 1979 (see Chapter 17).

Another problem at this time was that boom conditions in the US economy had led to excessive optimism by intermediaries and investors. A number of Eurobond issues floated at this time later went into default. In

Table 2.1 Eurodollar FRN issues ($m)

1970	300	1980	4,163
1971	0	1981	6,370
1972	60	1982	11,802
1973	40	1983	14,776
1974	170	1984	31,653
1975	215	1985	46,818
1976	1,070	1986	38,354
1977	1,730	1987	7,339
1978	2,340	1988	6,899
1979	3,898		

Sources: G. Ugeux, *Floating Rate Notes*, Euromoney Publications, London, 1985 (Eurodollar FRNs 1970–84); Salomon Brothers, *Floating-Rate Financing Quarterly*, December 1986; *International Financial Review*, January 1988 and January 1989.

particular, a number of issues were floated by companies associated with Investors Overseas Services. IOS was an aggressively managed mutual fund sales organisation which pyramided its operations to the point where in 1968 it managed funds exceeding $2 billion. During 1970, however, the extent of its manipulations became apparent and the company crashed. It was subsequently bought by International Controls Corporation, controlled by Robert Vesco, who was in due course accused of fraudulently converting US$224 million to his own account, and is still actively sought by a number of police forces.

During the course of 1970, in addition to the default problems mentioned earlier, the markets were made more nervous by the collapse of the Penn Central Transportation Company in the USA, which at that time had large amounts of commercial paper outstanding. US rates began to edge up, and with this background, instruments bearing fixed rates became less attractive. In response to this interest rate volatility, the floating-rate note was introduced to the Euromarkets in May 1970 with an issue by ENEL (Ente Nazionale Per L'Energia Elettrica).

The ENEL notes paid interest at a rate of 0.75 per cent above six month LIBOR (London Inter-Bank Offered Rate – the effective borrowing cost of banks in London). They could be redeemed if the interest rate payable exceeded 13 per cent. The ENEL issue was US$50m; the following month a US$75 million issue for Pepsico used a similar formula. Thus was born a large segment of the Eurobond market. (See Table 2.1.)

THE ARRIVAL OF FLOATING EXCHANGE RATES

The next few years were ones of violent upheaval in international financial markets. At various points various bond markets were effectively closed to foreign investors in an effort to prevent currency flows disrupting domestic financial markets:

Germany	1972–4
Japan	1978–9
Holland	1971–4
Switzerland	1964–6, 1972–4, 1978–9

In 1970–1, pressure on the US dollar began to build intensively, to the point that in August 1971 President Nixon announced a devaluation of the dollar, its removal from the gold standard, and domestic US price and interest rate controls. During this unprecedented international financial instability, securities markets and particularly the Eurobond market endured hard times. However, the latter continued to grow and 1971 saw another milestone in the market, the first US$100 million Eurobond issue, for Esso Overseas Finance NV.

In the US domestic market at this period an important step forward was taken with the setting up in 1971 of the National Association of Securities Dealers Automated Quotation System (NASDAQ). This allowed electronic trading of over-the-counter equity issues on a national basis. Previously dealers in the market could never be sure if they were getting the best price since there was no quick, centralised way of checking for it. April 1971 saw the Securities and Exchange Commission (SEC) bringing about the first steps in the USA towards freely negotiated commissions, with the deregulation of commission rates on orders over $500,000.

In December 1971, the central banks of the world met in conclave with the United States and hammered out the Smithsonian Agreement, so-called because it was negotiated on the premises of that august institution in Washington. The Agreement enshrined a 13.6 per cent revaluation of the Deutschmark against the US dollar, and during 1972 confidence was temporarily restored, helped in part by the foundation of the EEC 'snake' (forerunner of the European Monetary System set up in 1979) linking EEC currencies together with the aim of greater stability.

US interest rates began to fall and the Eurobond market benefited accordingly. New issue volume rose from US$3.28 billion equivalent in 1971 to US$5.5 billion equivalent in 1972. Conditions continued favourable into 1973. In January of that year the Carnation company was able to offer a US$25 million fifteen-year convertible bearing a record low coupon of just 4 per cent. However, pressure on the dollar began to build, leading to a new 10 per cent devaluation of the dollar in February 1973, followed in March by the joint float of EEC 'snake' currencies. The era of floating exchange rates had begun.

An innovation perfectly timed to take advantage of this was the creation in 1972 of a financial futures market by the International Monetary Market

	Eurobond market	Stock markets	Financial environment
1972	New issue volume reaches $5 billion		EEC 'snake' set up IMM Financial futures market set up
1973		CBOE set up US DTC set up UK SE merges Japan Securities Dealers Assoc. set up	$ devalued Oil crisis Japan forbids capital exports
1974	Many market-makers withdraw	Collapse of Burmah Oil	Collapse of Herstatt, Franklin National IET removed
1975	First $100m. issue by a sovereign	US May-Day UK stock market recovers	World recession
1976	EEC 'jumbos' $300m. + $500m.	NYSE DOT system set up	UK forced to borrow from IMF
1977	First $500m. corporate issue	US NSCC created First foreign NYSE member	Germany, Japan impose exchange controls
1978	Deutsche Bank 'steals' Norway mandate	US ITS system created	

FIGURE 2.2 The 1970s

(IMM) in Chicago (see Chapter 7). The first contracts were on foreign exchange and were reasonably but not outstandingly successful; the big breakthrough came later with the creation of interest rate futures. At about this time another major step forward was the creation in 1973 of the Chicago Board Options Exchange, which allowed for the first time a liquid secondary market in options on individual stocks. Around the same date, the New York Stock Exchange's clearing arrangements were improved by the foundation of the Depository Trust Company, which by centralising holdings of stock certificates cut down the need for physical transfer. Meanwhile, in the UK, 1973 saw the unification of five regional stock exchanges, together with the Dublin Exchange, into one unit, The Stock Exchange. In Japan, the Securities Dealers Association was set up and as part of the liberalisation of the market the first issue of equity by a foreign company (General Telephone and Electric Co. – GTE) took place, to be followed by issues by Paribas and IU International.

THE OIL CRISIS

In October 1973, the world's economy took a drastic turn for the worse. The Yom Kippur war broke out and, as part of the Arab–Israeli conflict, the price of oil was raised sharply by the Organisation of Petroleum Exporting Countries (OPEC). The impact on international financial markets was devastating. The impact on Japan, 99 per cent dependent on imported energy sources, was particularly serious and Japanese banks, desperate for US dollar funding, were forced to pay a 'Japan premium' on inter-bank borrowings. This state of affairs led the Bank of Japan to ban foreign investments by Japanese investors. The prohibition lasted until 1977 and did much to hold back the internationalisation of Japanese investors' approach.

The result of this set of events was a crippling loss of international confidence in financial markets, which badly hurt all stock markets and the Eurobond market. It was compounded by the collapse in the summer of 1974 of the Herstatt Bank in Germany, which severely disrupted foreign exchange trading. The Franklin National Bank in California also collapsed because of unwise foreign exchange speculation. The atmosphere became apocalyptic. To quote one investment manager who went through the 1973–4 bear market: 'None of us who went through two years when anything we bought in the morning was available at a more attractive level by the afternoon can forget it . . .' (Alistair Ross Goobey in *The Money Moguls*). In the UK the final blow was the collapse over Christmas of the Burmah Oil Co. A group of five insurance companies – Legal & General, Equity & Law, Sun Alliance, Commercial Union and the Prudential – combined to invest on a concerted basis at the end of that year, and January 1975 saw a spectacular recovery.

The difficulties in the Eurobond market arising from this period were compounded by the US decision to abolish the Interest Equalization Tax and remove capital controls in early 1974, partly thanks to enormous inflows into the US dollar caused by the huge financial flows associated with the quadrupling of the oil price. It has been said[2] that by the end of 1974 there were only four market-makers left in the Eurobond market: Kidder Peabody, Credit Suisse White Weld, Merrill Lynch and Kredietbank (Luxembourg). But after the severe pressures of 1973–4, 1975 saw the start of a recovery. Against the background of falling interest rates and a gradually recovering world economy, the growth of the Eurobond market continued steadily.

In the US domestic stock market the bear market was followed by another drastic event, the abolition of negotiated commissions in May 1975 at the behest of the SEC. There was a rapid shrinking in the number of brokerage firms. But overall the outcome was by no means the disaster that had been predicted. In the equities markets – as distinct from the debt markets, where negotiated commissions had been the rule anyway – commissions were cut on average by 40–50 per cent and then stabilised around 1979, which in turn boosted trading volume. Between 1974 and 1980, aggregate share trading volume on US securities more than tripled (although it should be borne in mind that the base year, 1974, was depressed). Trading volume was also helped by the introduction of more efficient computer systems, notably the Designated Order Turnaround (DOT) system, introduced in 1976. This lets a NYSE member firm transmit orders electronically direct to the NYSE floor, speeding execution of small deals.

THE ERA OF 'JUMBO' EUROBOND ISSUES

In the happier atmosphere of 1975–9 as the world economy recovered from the first oil crisis, two important Eurobond developments took place: the growth of large, liquid issues and the invention of the 'pre-priced' deal. In August 1975 came the first US$100 million issue for a non-corporate entity, New Zealand. This was shortly followed by much larger issues. January of 1976 saw a remarkable period of activity with $1.9 billion in issues (more than the entire 1974 total). The European Economic Community (EEC) led the way. It aimed to borrow heavily to help its member states finance the balance of payments pressures caused by the oil crisis. In January, the European Coal and Steel Commission broke the $125 million mark with a new bond issue. In turn this was rapidly dwarfed by two jumbo issues for the EEC of US$300 million and US$500 million in March and April 1976 respectively.

Arguably the first pre-priced Eurobond issue came to market in October 1975, US$50 million for New Zealand. (There is some controversy over the meaning of the term pre-priced. The most widely used definition would be that a 'pre-priced' deal is a commitment to buy a whole issue, but with a co-management group already in place, while a 'bought deal' is the commitment of one single house to buy a whole issue.)

The latter part of 1976 saw increasing international financial turmoil, with sterling particularly in the firing line. In November there was a major sterling crisis, in which the pound fell to the new record low of $1.55, forcing the British Chancellor of the Exchequer, Denis Healey, to cancel his trip to the International Monetary Fund (IMF) and dash back from Heathrow airport to be at the centre of affairs. The UK announced that it would borrow $3.9 billion from the IMF, and when this was put in place, sterling recovered sharply. As after the 1967 devaluation, sterling's removal from the firing line left the dollar exposed, and during 1977 pressure began to build up.

Despite this, US interest rates were not really moving up sharply and the bond market continued active. In May 1977 the EEC again raised a US$500 million bond issue through a dual tranche 5/7 year offering. This was managed, despite the nervousness in markets caused in April by the news of Credit Suisse's disastrous losses at its branch in Chiasso. In December 1977 a new milestone was reached with a US$500 million twelve-year offering for Shell International Finance NV. This was a classic pre-priced issue, with the three major Swiss banks making a joint proposal to Shell and then forming a syndicate once the proposal had been accepted.

In domestic securities markets, 1977 saw the foundation in the USA of the National Securities Clearing Corporation jointly by the NYSE, the American Stock Exchange, and NASDAQ. The NSCC handles trade comparison and reconciliations, trade netting, and marking to market of open trading positions, linking in to the DTC for actual settlement of securities trades. Also in this year the internationalisation of the NYSE was enhanced by the arrival of its first non-North American member firms.

The year 1978 saw gradually increasing pressure on the US dollar. In February, central banks announced a joint package of intervention. Many non-US central banks imposed exchange controls, seeking to defend their currencies against inflows from the dollar. The Bundesbank, for example, imposed a 100 per cent marginal reserve requirement on inflows from abroad. The Bank of Japan imposed a 50 per cent requirement on 'free yen' deposits, i.e. yen deposits held by foreigners. It had already, in the previous year, relaxed the restrictions which had been imposed in 1973 forbidding Japanese investment overseas. Germany banned foreign purchase of domestic bonds.

As always, dollar weakness cut back the flow of dollar Eurobond issues. The volume of new US dollar bonds in 1978 totalled only US$5.53 billion, compared with Deutschmark bonds totalling US$4.92 billion. Competitive pressures on the new issue houses began to build. April 1978 saw the aggressive use of a pre-priced bid by the Deutsche Bank to wrest the Kingdom of Norway from its traditional lead managers, Hambros Bank, by making a pre-priced bid for a proposed US$250 million five-year note offering. This is one of the early instances of the aggressive tactics which were later to become commonplace in the market.

Pressure on the dollar increased gradually throughout the year, becoming intense in October, forcing the Federal Reserve to raise its discount rate by 1 per cent on 1 November. It also imposed reserve requirements on domestic deposits in an attempt to slow the growth of money supply, activated US$30 billion of currency swap packages with other central banks and at the same time issued US$10 billion of foreign currency bonds – dubbed Carter bonds by the market.

By 1978, while the various domestic stock markets remained rather domestic in orientation, the Eurobond market was an established global market. It had demonstrated its freewheeling innovativeness and its vitality through some testing years. In contrast, the New York Stock Exchange had just admitted its first foreign members – still forbidden in the UK and Japan. The UK's international investment skills were still hampered by exchange controls, which had only just been lifted in Japan. Operators in all these markets might be forgiven for feeling that they had passed through a turbulent period: but nothing had prepared them for the explosive volatility of the next decade.

NOTES

1. *Annual Report 1966*, p. 142.
2. H. C. Donnerstag, *The Eurobond Market*, *Financial Times Publications* 1975.

3 The Coming Together of the Markets: 1979–1989

THE ROLLER-COASTER YEARS: 1979–81

Events at the turn of 1978–9 were dominated by the crisis in Iran, which led to the flight of the Shah in January 1979. International securities markets were not at first affected by the turbulence in the Middle East, and the summer of 1979 was busy. However, at the end of June OPEC raised oil prices by 24 per cent. This put pressure on the US dollar, since the United States continued to be a heavy importer of oil. The decision by President Carter to reshuffle his cabinet rather abruptly mid-July further eroded confidence in the currency, which was only temporarily boosted when Mr Paul Volcker was appointed Chairman of the Federal Reserve at the end of July.

In September, the US discount rate was raised to 11 per cent, and by a further 1 per cent on 6 October as part of the famous 'Saturday night special' package introduced by Mr Volcker. As well as the rise in the discount rate, an 8 per cent marginal reserve requirement on increase in bank liabilities was imposed. Mr Volcker also announced a 'New Monetary Policy' aiming to focus henceforth on reserve levels rather than interest rates. The impact on the bond market was immediate. The most famous casualty was a US$500 million issue for IBM, the first for that borrower, which had been announced just before the package. When released for sale on 10 October, it fell to a discount of 5 points, causing massive losses.

The next month, Iranian militants seized the US Embassy in Tehran and took its staff hostage. The United States in retaliation froze Iranian assets. Tension in the Middle East rose sharply. In December OPEC raised oil prices by another 30 per cent. At the turn of the year the Soviet Union invaded Afghanistan. All of these tensions contributed to an explosive rise in the price of gold; from a level of US$397 per ounce at the end of September, it had risen to US$512 per ounce on 31 December. The invasion of Afghanistan triggered a truly sensational rise in the price, which on 25 January peaked at US$850 per ounce.

Meantime, in the wake of these turbulent events, the structures of the global markets had been developing apace. In 1978 the UK followed the lead of Chicago, and introduced traded options on equities, albeit in a limited fashion to begin with (only calls – the right to buy at a pre-fixed price; puts – the right to sell – were not traded until 1981). A key event, as it turned out in retrospect, was the abolition of exchange controls in the United Kingdom. This allowed London capital markets to compete internationally unfettered by capital restrictions. Already, despite exchange controls, a remarkably sophisticated financial structure existed in London. But it effectively excluded the stock market, which remained limited and parochial because of its exclusion from the free international flow of capital.

In the US domestic market, an important step towards a truly national securities market came with the adoption of the Intermarket Trading System in 1978, at the behest of the SEC. This linked the NYSE with regional exchanges. It let specialists and floor brokers on one exchange floor transmit buy or sell orders to market-makers on another. If there were a better price on another exchange, the ITS allowed a specialist or floor broker to transmit a 'commitment to trade' to the market-maker on that exchange. The latter could accept or decline. It is possible that the ITS may form the nucleus of international linkages between exchanges, rather than the NASDAQ-type electronic linkage approach being propounded by institutions such as Reuters.

The Eurobond market, in early 1979, saw a development which would have major significance for the primary market (see Chapter 9). This was the coming of the 'grey market'. In many respects, this was due to the personal determination of Stanley Ross, Chairman of Ross & Partners (Securities) Limited. Against the united opposition of traditional syndicate managers, he decided to display the 'real' price for newly issued bonds before they had completed the syndication process. That is, market professionals would trade among themselves at prices showing what they felt the bond was really worth. Meanwhile, the bonds were still being offered to the lead manager's clients at the syndicate price. If the professionals felt the issue was over-priced and marked it down, the result was much embarrassment for the lead syndicate manager. Ross began by showing a grey market on his Reuters monitor screen for the US$200 million Dow Chemical 9.625 per cent loan which was announced on 14 February 1979. In later years, the concept became accepted as part of the normal issue process.

The pressure on financial markets continued unabated in 1980. Indeed it was reinforced in March when President Carter announced a further tightening of credit policy. The Federal Reserve raised its marginal reserve requirements to 10 per cent and imposed a 3 per cent surcharge on excessive discount window borrowings. In response, short-term money market rates soared to 20 per cent. An article published at about this date was entitled 'Please sir, may we have our $200 million back?' (The sum represented the estimated losses in the Eurobond market during the previous month.)

The enormous volatility of interest rates during this period greatly boosted trading in financial futures which allowed investors and borrowers to hedge their interest rate risk, and it contributed to the invention of the

	Eurobond market	Stock markets	Financial environment
1979	Emergence of 'grey market'		Oil crisis UK exchange controls abolished US 'Saturday night special' Iranian crisis
1980	First bought deal	UK USM set up US NYFE set up	Afghanistan invaded US credit squeeze Liberalization of exchange controls in Japan
1981	Zero coupon bonds IBM/World Bank swap IBFs set up	Nomura joins NYSE MoF allows equity warrant bonds	US prime 20.5%
1982		TSE CORES set up US equity futures NASDAQ/ITS link	Falklands Mexico, Drysdale crises LIFFE founded

FIGURE 3.1 The early 1980s

interest rate swap (see Chapter 7). This period of dollar weakness also encouraged the Japanese authorities to take a key step: exchange control was drastically liberalised. Previously, what had not been specifically permitted was automatically forbidden. The new law laid down that in principle Japanese investors were free to do what they wished, unless it was specifically forbidden. As the Japanese economy recovered from the second oil shock to produce huge export surpluses, the long-term consequence was to release a flood of investment money on to other markets, especially the USA.

Another liberalising move took place in the UK, where in 1980 the Unlisted Securities Market was set up to allow access to public capital for smaller firms with shorter track records than would be permitted on the main Exchange. In New York, August 1980 saw the setting up of the New York Futures Exchange (NYFE) – after a shaky start, the NYFE introduced a contract based on the NYSE composite index, but it has never really matched the Chicago exchanges' strength.

THE FALSE DAWN

The fixed-rate Eurodollar bond market was reopened on 24 March 1980 with the announcement of a US$500 million issue for the Kingdom of Sweden. The coupon was fixed at 15¼ per cent. Over the next six weeks, conditions rapidly improved on the back of a spectacular fall in the US

Federal funds rate, which collapsed from 20 per cent in March to 8 per cent at the end of April. The rally continued until June, when the AAA-rated Canadian borrower Export Development Corporation offered US$150 million of six-year notes carrying a coupon of just 9.5 per cent compared to the 15¼ per cent paid by the Kingdom of Sweden less than three months earlier.

These strongly bullish conditions were the ideal background for the genesis of the 'bought' deal. In April 1980, the firm Credit Suisse First Boston committed themselves to buy US$100 million of 13.375 per cent five-year notes from General Motors Acceptance Corporation (GMAC) without having formed any co-management group, as would be customary with a pre-priced issue.

The bull market conditions, coupled with the strongly rising oil price, led to a boom in issues for second-line oil or energy-related companies. A number of these, such as Blocker Energy, Galaxy Oil Company, Pengo Industries and MGF Oil Corporation, all defaulted on Eurobonds after two or three years.

During the second half of 1980, interest rates began to edge upwards again. The rally had been a false dawn: the problems of the US economy remained unsolved. In September, the Iraq–Iran war broke out, and against this background the Federal Reserve raised the discount rate by 1 per cent. The discount rate was raised again in November to 12 per cent, together with a 2 per cent surcharge for heavy use of the discount window. The US dollar began to strengthen, helped by tension in the Middle East and also the general strike in Poland and the emergence of Solidarity. The latter put pressure on the Deutschmark, which was weakened by worries over the exposure of German banks to Poland.

The dollar began to rise strongly against all currencies, helped by the arrival of President Reagan. In February 1981 the Bundesbank had to take action to defend the Deutschmark; German call money soared to 20 per cent. Despite the strength of the dollar, long-term interest rates in the United States remained stubbornly high. Ford Motor Credit paid 16 per cent in February 1981 for a three-year US$150 million issue. By April, the prime rate in New York had risen to 20.5 per cent.

In these conditions, with high US dollar interest rates, the zero coupon bond became attractive to investors, because of the fact that it protects the investor against the risk of rates falling later. That is, a zero coupon has no 'reinvestment risk' (see Chapter 5). In June 1981 the first zero coupon Eurobond was brought to the market for Pepsico Capital Corporation NV. This followed closely on the first ever publicly syndicated zero coupon issue for JC Penny in April 1981 in the US domestic market. (The very first Eurobond zero coupon issue, in June 1966 for BP Tanker Company Limited was effectively a private placement, in view of its small size, US$6.21 million producing net proceeds to the borrower of US$4.46 million.)

GENESIS OF THE SWAP MARKET

Market conditions in the summer of 1981 were extremely difficult; by 1 July the European Investment Bank was forced to withdraw an eight-year bond offering because the 15 per cent coupon was considered to be unrealistically low. In August, the World Bank paid 16 per cent for a five-year issue. After this issue an announcement was made which at first seemed a curiosity but which was to have momentous implications for global bond markets. It was announced that the bond had been used for a swap between the World Bank and IBM. The World Bank traditionally borrowed in Swiss francs, to the extent that its paper was becoming less welcome in the Swiss market. IBM had issued Deutschmark and Swiss franc bonds. Due to the great rise in the dollar since the bonds were issued, IBM had unrealised currency gains, which it wished to crystallise. The solution to these problems was for the World Bank to take over IBM's liabilities in respect of servicing its Swiss franc and Deutschmark bonds; in exchange, it issued the US dollar bond and passed the dollar proceeds on to IBM. (See Appendix 5.)

This first public announcement of a swap deal linked to a bond issue, together with the extremely high standing of the parties concerned, legitimised the swap technique. Over the next few years this led to a spate of bond issues which were openly 'swap-driven', that is the overall terms of the issue were dictated by conditions in the swap market rather than the bond market. In some cases, this led to issues which were badly mispriced, but which ended up profitable for the investment bank concerned because of the private swap deal undertaken behind the bond issue. (The swap market is discussed further in Chapter 7.)

During 1981 three events of importance for the Japanese market took place: the Ministry of Finance eased restrictions by issuers on warrant-linked bonds, which later grew to a very important segment of the Eurobond market; Japanese banks were allowed to sell government bonds (challenging the traditional monopoly of the securities houses in this field); and in the international arena, Nomura Securities became the first Japanese member of the New York Stock Exchange. In the Eurocurrency markets, the event of the year was the opening in December of International Banking Facilities (IBFs) in New York – an attempt to 'bring the Eurodollar market back home'. US banks were allowed to run Eurodollar operations in New York, exempt from Federal Reserve reserve requirements – provided they were confined to off-shore business. In the event, IBFs did not remove the Eurodollar market from London to New York, but they did reduce the amount of activity booked in the Caribbean and also London by US banks. They also, inevitably, increased the international flavour of business done out of New York.

The failure of OPEC to agree on an oil price in August 1981 and the general weakness of the oil market led to a fairly sustained decline in interest rates in the last quarter of the year. In January 1982 there was a huge surge in zero coupon issues intended for Japanese investors. In January alone borrowers issued zero coupon bonds with a face value of more than US$3 billion. In some instances almost 100 per cent of individual issues were pre-placed in Japan; at that time, Japanese investors in zero coupons were effectively tax-exempt.

Apart from this, early 1982 proved difficult for the Eurobond market. The Reagan Administration in February admitted that a previous Budget deficit estimate of US$40 billion might now be closer to US$100 billion. The US economy was clearly in severe difficulties, and interest rates remained stubbornly high. Over the spring and summer, hostilities in the Falklands, the collapse of Drysdale Securities, major problems at Banco Ambrosiano, and the emerging Mexican crisis successively tested confidence. The latter proved to be the trough for the bond market. A spectacular rally followed. By November, General Electric Credit was able to offer US$200 million of eight-year bonds with a coupon of ten per cent using the partly-paid technique.

The instability of rates was a good omen for at least one institution: in September 1982 the London International Financial Futures Exchange opened its doors for business with, amongst others, a financial futures contract based on Eurodollar deposits which benefited from the rapid swings in US dollar interest rates. An important development in the USA was the introduction in April/May 1982 of equity index futures on a number of futures exchanges, with the Chicago Mercantile Exchange's S&P 500 contract being the most successful. Another important development was the introduction by the SEC of its Rule 415, the so-called 'shelf registration' rule. This allowed firms to pre-register their intent to issue bonds, giving time to comply with the formalities, so that the actual issue could be launched with a day or two's notice, in the light of prevailing market conditions. This allowed the introduction of the Euromarket 'bought deal' to the US market.

The year also saw a further development in the US national securities system, when the SEC forced the stock exchanges to permit a link between NASDAQ and their communications link, the Intermarket Trading System. Similar systems developments occurred in Japan, where the Tokyo Stock Exchange introduced its Computer Assisted Order Routing and Execution System (CORES) adapted from a similar system developed in Toronto (which has also been exported to Paris). The system is a development of NASDAQ and similar to DOT in that it allows orders to be channelled electronically straight to the trading floor.

During 1982, the Eurobond market passed a very severe test with flying colours: total primary market new issues equalled US$43.64 billion equivalent, in a year when coupons on AAA bonds fell from 16.5 per cent to

10 per cent. The groundwork had been laid for a spectacular growth in jumbo issues; in January 1983 the Kingdom of Sweden made the first US$1 billion issue, a floating rate note. In June the EEC issued US$1.5 billion of seven-year FRNs. Both of these issues demonstrated successfully that very large single issues could be placed in the floating rate note sector, and also that considerable liquidity could be attained in secondary market trading for such issues. In October 1983 the Kingdom of Sweden returned with a second US$1 billion, another floating rate note whose main features were its very narrow spread – 0.25 per cent over LIMEAN – and its final maturity of twenty years. (LIMEAN is the average of London inter-bank bid and offer rates.) The great strength of the FRN market was in part due to weaker conditions in the straight bond sector, where interest rates had been steady earlier in the year and had now begun to edge upwards.

During 1983 Mikuni & Co., an independent firm which had been founded in 1975, began to provide independent credit rating of Japanese corporate bonds: a first step towards developing the kind of credit assessment long taken for granted in the USA. For the international capital markets a more momentous development occurred in that year in London – one whose significance was not clear at that time. The British government, which had been threatening to sue the Stock Exchange over its restrictive practices, came to an agreement with the Exchange providing for liberalisation in the shape of negotiable commissions and the opening of the market to outside owners, a package which was quickly christened 'the Big Bang'. As events unfolded it became clear that these changes would be the catalyst for a sweeping reorganisation of the London market that would end in the disappearance of the Stock Exchange floor. The physical market-place was replaced in 1986 by an electronic one in which large commercial and investment banks traded freely with stock-brokers in a way which neither New York or Tokyo were prepared to allow.

THE FIRST GLOBAL ISSUES

London's Big Bang was only part of a rapidly accelerating 'globalisation' of securities markets, still led by the Eurobond market which continued to break new ground. In February 1984 Texaco came to market with a US$1 billion convertible issue. The issue was twice as large as any previous corporate Eurobond issue. It was the first to be marketed on a global basis, with the lead-manager Credit Suisse First Boston drawing up precise geographical distribution areas and delegating specific management groups to cover these areas.

Helped by the soaring US dollar, primary market activity in the Eurodollar and Eurobond markets rose sharply. New issue volume rose sharply to $108.4 billion equivalent. The rapid growth was also driven by increasing 'securitisation' (see Chapter 5) and by financial liberalisation in a number of countries. The USA abolished withholding tax on foreign purchases of US bonds, helping to break down the barriers between the domestic US market and the Euromarket. Japan liberalised the Euroyen market in December 1984, allowing foreign issuers to the market.

Perhaps the first true global equity issue was the 1984 British Telecom issue; in addition to being a huge domestic issue, a large tranche was placed internationally. The stock simultaneously opened to trading on three different stock exchanges in Britain, Canada and the USA. It marked a large milestone on the route to development of the Euroequity market.

Two other notable deals in the year were the issue by the Rockefeller Group of a five-year US$100 million Eurobond issue, which was backed by a surety bond provided by Aetna Casualty & Surety Company. The backing by the insurance company allowed the Rockefeller Group to borrow without financial disclosure, which, as a private entity, it was unwilling to do. The deal was done in May. An even more discreet deal was done in July by Anonymous, a borrower that would not even disclose its name. The seven-year, US$100 million deal was guaranteed by Aetna, allowing the borrower to come to market without disclosing its name.

During 1984 the liberalisation of the Japanese market was continued by allowing government agencies and private corporations to issue Euroyen bonds. Certain foreign banks were allowed entry into the syndicate which controlled distribution of Japanese government bonds. The Ministry of

	Eurobond market	Stock markets	Financial environment
1983	Sweden $1bn issue	UK/SE agreement on Big Bang	
1984	Texaco $1 bn convertible Euro-yen market liberalised $4 bn Sweden issue	British Telecom issue Barclays buys de Zoete, Wedd Others follow suit	US withholding tax abolished Continental Illinois in difficulty
1985	ECP market takes off $1.1 bn Daimler-Benz Euro-equity issue Euro-yen FRNs, zeros and dual-currency allowed	TSE sets up bond futures market	Bundesbank liberalises in Germany; Canada 'Little Bang' Plaza agreement
1986	Bull/bear bonds Heaven/Hell, ICONs Deferred coupon FRNs FR CMOs Crisis in perpetual FRN market	UK 'Big Bang' Foreign brokers allowed on TSE	US$ falls sharply Federal Reserve tightens policy
1987	Growth of asset swaps	October crash	
1988	AIBD becomes DIE under UK FSA	RJR buyout	

FIGURE 3.2 1983–1989

Finance relaxed restrictions (notably that requiring a second audit by a Japanese firm) which had discouraged foreign firms from listing their equities on the Tokyo Stock Exchange. In London, March 1984 saw the first fruits of Big Bang: purchases by Barclays Bank of a sizeable stake in de Zoete & Bevan and Wedd, Durlacher, Mordaunt, and on the same day Midland Bank's announcement of a stake in W. Greenwell & Co., a stockbroking firm specialising in the gilt-edged market. Other domestic and foreign banks swiftly followed suit in a frenzied round of mergers and acquisitions.

Part of this was driven by the banks' realisation that 'securitisation' – the process of substituting securities for bank borrowing – was eating into their basic business. For example, a notable feature of the Euromarkets in 1985 was the explosive growth of short-term issues in the form of Euronotes. A true Eurocommercial paper market began to emerge during this year. The Euronote market began to develop in 1978, with a facility for New Zealand, but it really only got underway in 1984–5. In September 1984 the Kingdom of Sweden announced a US$4 billion borrowing with three options: to borrow at ⅛th per cent over LIBOR, to invite banks to bid for short-term advances, or to issue Euronotes. Shortly thereafter came the first issue of true Eurocommercial paper: by ELF Aquitaine, for up to US$200 million.

BIRTH OF EUROEQUITY AND A PERPETUAL BLOODBATH

The years 1985–6 were the time when the Euroequity finally arrived. A $1.1 billion equivalent issue for Daimler/Benz in December 1985 was followed by a string of issues during 1986 for, amongst others, KLM, News Corporation, Electrolux, Peugeot, Hanson Trust, Credit Suisse, and in September, Fiat. This was an offering of $2.1 billion of equity being sold in to the secondary market by Libya, which had earlier invested in the company. The Fiat issue had major problems, but they did not impede the $7.6 billion issue for British Gas in December 1986.

This period was perhaps the peak of deregulation world-wide. Aside from London's Big Bang, the Bundesbank in Germany announced sweeping liberalisation of domestic markets in May 1985, permitting currency swaps, certificates of deposit, floating-rate notes, and zero coupon bonds for the first time. In Japan the Ministry of Finance permitted Euroyen floating-rate notes, dual-currency, zero-coupon and domestic warrant-linked bonds. In October 1985, the Tokyo Stock Exchange opened its government bond futures market (which was to become phenomenally successful: within 12 months the contract had become the most actively traded in the world, easily doubling the volume in US Treasury bond futures). Canada's 'Little Bang' allowed outsiders to buy into securities houses at this time. The French government moved to liberalise its financial system with the replacement of the syndicate system of government bond issue by an auction, the standardisation of government bond terms to enhance liquidity, the introduction of commercial paper and certificates of deposit, and in February 1986 the foundation of the MATIF (Marché à Terme des Instruments Financiers) – a very successful financial futures market.

The Eurobond market was naturally well designed to respond to the spirit of innovation which was in the air, and 1986 was a year in which numerous innovations were brought to market: bull/bear bonds, bull floating-rate notes, heaven and hell bonds, ICONs, deferred coupon and step-down bonds, and floating-rate Collateralised Mortgage Obligations (CMOs). (These are discussed in Chapters 5 and 6.) During this year the major Japanese firms began to make their mark. They owed this to the rapid growth of the Euroyen market following continued liberalisation in Tokyo, together with the very rapid growth of Japanese corporate bonds issued at low coupons in US dollars, coupled with equity warrants. Nomura, Daiwa, Nikko and Yamaichi all rose to places amongst the top fifteen. More ominously perhaps for the major US firms, Nomura and Daiwa took fourth and fifth places respectively for US corporate issues. Traffic in the reverse direction – of foreign houses into Tokyo – was much less successful. Although six foreign brokers were allowed to take their seats on the Tokyo Stock Exchange in 1986 (so that the nominal percentage of foreign brokers – 6 out of 93 – compared well with that in New York – 17 out of 1,366) the volume of business they were able to attract remains very small as of the time of writing.

The year 1986 in the Eurobond market also saw a major crisis in the market for perpetual, undated FRNs. Although there had perhaps been some signs of uneasiness beforehand, the crisis was mainly triggered by the arrival of floating-rate CMOs. These gave the investor a rich spread over LIBOR – 50 basis points or more – and at the same time, a final maturity. Investors were quick to ask themselves why they held perpetual FRNs giving them a spread of $^1/_{16}$ or $^1/_8$ per cent over LIBOR. However, when they came to sell, buyers were found to be few. Perpetual FRN prices crashed, to 85 or below in some instances – unheard of levels for an FRN which should in theory return to 100 each time the floating-rate coupon is fixed (see Chapter 4). New issues dried up, as did secondary market trading.

The débâcle in the perpetual FRN market severely damaged the FRN market in general during 1987, and conditions were difficult for most of the year. In conjunction with severe weakness in the US dollar, and a rising trend in interest rates after about April, investors began to become extremely cautious. Issuing houses responded to the trend by moving away from innovative new issue types, which might prove to have poor secondary market trading liquidity, and re-emphasising the traditional, classic issue techniques: a simple bond structure, fairly priced to attract investor demand. Instead of pricing bond issues aggressively, and taking the profit out through the interest rate or currency swap behind the bond, now the tendency was to squeeze the swap spread in order to provide an attractive yield to investors.

BIG BANG AND THE STRUCTURE OF THE MARKET

During this period, major structural changes were at work in international securities markets from another source: London's 'Big Bang'. US and Japanese banks, forbidden to trade corporate securities in their home country, eagerly seized the chance to do so, as did a number of French, German and other foreign banks, with the result that the trading structure in London was changed radically.

The Financial Services Act, which accompanied Big Bang, laid down a number of requirements for securities trading. Eurobond houses, unaccustomed to any form of supervision, suddenly found themselves confronted with elaborate regulatory procedures. London firms were forced to become members of a registered Securities Regulatory Organisation – in almost all cases the Securities Association, itself a product of the merger of the Stock Exchange and a grouping formed by the major international bond houses. Also as part of this process, for the first time, Eurobond houses operating in London found that they had to conform to certain minimum capital requirements in order to stay in business. Naturally, these stipulations provoked considerable protest from firms who had never had the slightest intention of dealing with the British retail market, but used London simply as a place in which to deal with, amongst others, Japanese insurance companies, German savings banks, French mutual funds and American investment houses.

The wider repercussions of Big Bang were mainly felt in an acceleration of the trend towards global securities trading, and the continuing process of liberalisation in other markets. In Switzerland, for example, the decision by Nestlé in November 1988 to open its share register to foreigners played a part in forcing a wider rethink. During 1989 the Swiss National Bank withdrew from the Admissions Board which approves foreign securities for listing on the Swiss stock exchange; this followed a recommendation from the Cartel Commission that the Board be dissolved, in view of its domination by the Big Three Swiss banks who were accused of using it as a vehicle for discriminating against foreigners. July 1989 saw radical moves by Spain to liberalise and modernise its stock market.

The bull markets of 1986–7 emphasised the trend towards global trading which was, however, brought to a halt by the Crash of October 1987.

Investors retreated to their home markets, and securities firms followed them. As mentioned in Chapter 1, the volume of true cross-border equity trading by that stage was not as yet large in comparison with the global bond markets, and the events of 1987 certainly checked the relative growth of international equity trading. As the market environment in 1987–8 turned more benign, however, investors began to venture back into global markets, attracted particularly by Japan, where the stock market after an initial shock rode out the crisis with relative ease and performed strongly during 1988. In retrospect one of the major structural effects of the Crash proved to have been a beneficial focusing on the need to make securities settlements systems safer and more efficient to reduce the risks of a chain default from another market break, as exemplified by the report from the Group of Thirty referred to in Chapter 1.

Looking back over the last decade of international securities trading, several themes stand out: the huge increase in interest rate instability, primarily due to October 1979 and its aftermath; as a result, the development of new hedging techniques by which bond issuing houses could hedge their positions in the futures markets or by shorting US Treasury bonds; the move in the Eurobond market away from the traditional syndicate structure, towards the bought deal; in those cases where the syndicate structure still continued to be used, the growing importance of the grey market and the brokers, with the corresponding decline in importance of true 'placing power' for many participants in the bond market; the impact of the swap market in driving new issue pricing during much of the period; and the frantic pace of innovation, with new instruments being spawned ever more frequently – even though they were sometimes of dubious liquidity in the secondary markets. All of these developments were linked with a parallel stream of changes in stock markets, ranging from the working out in the USA of the consequences of May Day to Big Bang in London and the growth of Euroequity trading and issuing techniques. In the rest of the book we explore these themes in more depth.

Part Two
Global Asset Choices

4 Table d'Hôte: The Basic International Menu

In this section of the book we take a look at the various classes of asset open to the global investor. We begin with what might be called the traditional instruments: bonds, floating-rate notes, equities, convertibles and warrants. The aim is to highlight the range of choices in the different markets for the international investor. Later in the book we shall take a look at some of the markets by country.

THE WORLD BOND MARKET

By way of a start, it may be helpful to give some overall figures. Table 4.1 compares some of the various markets. These figures exclude convertibles and FRNs. Of the $9,399 billion total at end-1988, direct central government debt comprised $4,023 billion. Government debt was most important to the US, Japanese and Italian bond markets. Total borrowings by these governments account between them for 75 per cent of world government

Table 4.1 Total debt of the 18 most actively traded debt markets, by currency (US$ bn equivalent)

	1981	*1982*	*1983*	*1984*	*1985*	*1986*	*1987*	*1988*
US$	1,489	1,759	2,074	2,370	2,830	3,309	3,717	4,085
Japanese yen	607	649	756	773	1,070	1,473	2,033	2,131
Deutschmark	305	320	312	293	417	588	783	730
Italian lira	143	152	175	186	278	423	554	543
UK sterling	181	171	174	153	207	227	310	274
French franc	100	106	104	110	174	252	334	371
Canadian dollar	129	136	149	161	171	194	228	281
Swedish krona	75	62	68	67	88	117	146	140
Danish krone	66	69	69	71	103	136	171	160
Swiss franc	55	60	59	55	77	107	142	144
Dutch guilder	40	46	47	48	70	96	130	134
Belgian franc	46	36	34	33	51	71	96	95
Australian dollar	51	50	52	59	60	70	91	121
Spanish peseta	23	22	21	24	34	61	76	79
Norwegian krone	17	15	17	16	22	28	36	37
ECU	0	1	3	5	10	20	37	41
Irish punt	7	8	7	8	11	16	22	19
New Zealand dollar	5	6	6	6	8	12	15	14
Total	3,342	3,668	4,129	4,439	5,681	7,202	8,920	9,399

Source: Merrill Lynch, *Size of the World Bond Markets, Year-End 1987*, and *Currency and Bond Market Trends*, 11 May 1989.

debt (35 per cent US, 30 per cent Japan and 10 per cent Italy). A more detailed survey of important national markets, with an outline of the major types of bond available, is set out in Appendix 1 at the end of the book. This survey will be supplemented in Chapters 9 to 12 on the Eurobond market and in Chapter 15 on national bond markets. See also Appendix 2 for some details on different interest bases in the different markets.

STRAIGHT BONDS

The global investor is usually interested in bonds for the same reason as the domestic investor – stability of principal and certainty of cash flow. The classical bond bears a fixed rate of interest, and matures on a date fixed at the time of issue. So, from the time of issue, all of the cash flows on the bond – except the reinvestment income – are known in advance. This relative certainty has made the bond an attractive investment instrument for those who need funds on hand at some future date, such as pension funds or life assurance companies. The mathematics of valuing such a bond are set out in Appendix 2.

Because bond investors are mostly interested in safety of principal, they are interested in the stability of their bonds' value – that is, in how volatile they are. This is affected by three main factors:

(a) the bond's coupon;
(b) the bond's yield;
(c) its maturity.

Mostly, volatility increases as the coupon and yield fall, and as time to maturity increases. But there are quirks. A short zero coupon bond may be more volatile than a long bond with a higher coupon, because the coupon effect outweighs the maturity effect. The measure of a bond's volatility is its duration, which is the weighted average of the bond's cash flows, weighted by the appropriate discount factors (see Appendix 2). A duration of 4.5 years would mean a 1% change in yield will change the bond's price by 4.5%.

For the global investor, duration/volatility comparisons are complicated by the fact that one is often comparing markets of very different yield structure. Duration (or, strictly, modified duration – see Appendix 2) is a good measure of a bond's riskiness in that it measures the price impact of a basis point change in yield. However, suppose you are holding $100 worth of UK gilts in your portfolio yielding 9 per cent with a duration of 6.5 and $100 worth of yen bonds yielding 4.5 per cent with a duration of 8.0. This does not mean your yen holdings are necessarily riskier than your gilts because a one basis point change is twice as likely in the gilts market, given that yields are twice as high. (So a one basis point change in gilts implies

Table 4.2

	Average yield	*Yield volatility*	*Price volatility*
4/12/80–5/3/81	8.7%	18.0%	15.1%
1/8/85–31/10/85	6.2%	31.4%	15.5%
19/2/87–21/5/87	4.3%	41.3%	15.7%

Source: Salomon Brothers, 'A Note on Duration and Volatility in International Fixed-Income Markets'.

half the yield volatility that a one basis point change in the yen market would imply.)

Putting that another way, comparing yield volatilities across markets will produce different price volatilities if the bonds in the two markets have different yield levels. A price change of 10 per cent can be produced, in bonds yielding 5 per cent, by a yield change of 25 per cent. To produce the same price volatility in bonds yielding 15 per cent needs only a yield change of 15 per cent. As an example, consider the price and yield volatilities in Japan at different periods given in Table 4.2.

When yields averaged around 4 per cent it took a 40 per cent swing in yields to produce the same volatility in prices as was caused by an 18 per cent yield change when the level of yields was over 8 per cent. Duration is defined as sensitivity to a basis point change in yield – a change of .01 per cent. But that basis point change comes to represent a bigger proportional change, as yields fall: a change of yield from 8 per cent to 8.01 per cent is a swing of $0.01/8 = 0.125$ per cent while a change from 4 per cent to 4.01 per cent is a swing of $0.01/4 = 0.25$ per cent. This is perhaps all a very roundabout way of saying that the riskiness of a bond is governed partly by its duration and partly by its yield level. Duration measures the bond's sensitivity to a basis point change, and the yield level affects the probability of such a change. A one basis point change is proportionately smaller for a high-yield bond and so will tend to occur more often.

The next important category for the global investor is the floating-rate note. Floaters have traditionally been in heavy demand among investors in times of volatile interest rates. Their principal value is stable compared to bonds.

The standard structure is a bond bearing a coupon which changes every six months, fixed at a margin, or spread, over LIBOR (London Inter-Bank Offered Rate – the interest rate charged by prime banks in London for lending to other prime banks). Clearly, under normal circumstances, on the day when the coupon is to be fixed, the instrument looks rather like a six-month bank deposit. The investor will earn a rate linked to the six-month inter-bank deposit rate.

Since a bank deposit always has a principal value of 100 per cent the FRN should normally have a value of 100 ('re-price to par') on the coupon-fixing day. That will not always be true, because if the margin over LIBOR is now seen as inappropriate (because the issuer's credit standing has improved/weakened) the FRN might stand at a premium/discount. But certainly the principal value of an FRN is normally insensitive to general interest rate changes, unlike that of a fixed-rate bond. (See the section on FRN valuation in Appendix 2.) A wide range of specialised FRNs have been issued, some of which are touched on in Chapter 6. (See also the author's *New Financial Instruments*, John Wiley, New York, 1988.) They include:

(a) Index variations:
  (i) one-, three- and six-month LIBOR,
  (ii) LIBID (London inter-bank bid rate),
  (iii) LIMEAN (average of LIBOR and LIBID),
  (iv) six month LIBOR reset monthly,
  (v) X per cent minus six-month LIBOR ('reverse' or 'bull' FRN),
  (vi) Lower of 103 per cent of one-month LIBOR or $^3/_{16}$ per cent over six-month LIBOR,
  (vii) $^3/_8$ per cent over three-month LIBID, maximum $12^3/_4$ per cent ('capped'),
  (viii) 91-day Treasury bill rate,
  (ix) Rate fixed every 49 days by Dutch auction;
(b) FRNS convertible into fixed-rate bonds at investor's option;
(c) FRNs convertible into fixed-rate bonds automatically at a set rate ('drop-lock');
(d) FRNs convertible into another currency;
(e) FRNs with warrants into fixed-rate bonds;
(f) FRNs with warrants into equity;
(g) FRNs with warrants into another currency.

The first FRN was issued, as we saw in Chapter 2, by ENEL in 1970, and the market grew rapidly. The most rapid growth took place in the late 1970s and early 1980s as the liquidity of the FRN market attracted banks to lend via FRNs rather than through syndicated credits. If they had to lend at unrealistic spreads, the reasoning was, it might as well be on a tradeable asset. A corollary point is that the FRN market has proved itself capable of handling huge issues. The UK issue of $4 billion, in 1986, which was easily absorbed despite the pricing, shows this. Such FRNs have great liquidity and the trading attractions of the instrument have compensated for its intrinsically low yield.

By the mid-1980s, though, the FRN market had come under pressure from two competing sources of funds. These were the Euronote market (discussed in Chapter 13) and swap-driven bond issuance (discussed in

Table 4.3 Issuance of FRNs 1983–8 ($m)

1983	20,123
1984	31,203
1985	56,439
1986	49,216
1987	12,253
1988	19,251

Source: Merrill Lynch, *1988 International Bond Issuance Activity*, February 1989. Figures excluded 'repackaged' FRNs.

Chapter 7), which often raised funds at 50–60 basis points below LIBOR, while the FRN market provided funds at a spread over LIBOR.

The logical response was for the FRN market to move away from LIBOR towards LIMEAN (average of LIBOR and the bid rate, LIBID) and even towards LIBID. By 1986 a prime sovereign credit such as the UK could offer its FRNS at LIBID − 10 basis points and still be eagerly sought after. However, other issues, which were never likely to be so tradable, were also brought to the market at low spreads, leading to considerable indigestion. The climax came with a bloodbath in the perpetuals market (see Chapter 3). The figures in Table 4.3 for the issuance of floating-rate notes in the Euromarket show that the market as a whole was severely damaged by these factors.

CONVERTIBLE BONDS

In Chapter 6 we will look at various hybrid securities. Convertibles and preferred stock are the oldest of these. Preferred is debt-like equity; a convertible is equity-like debt. The holder of a convertible bond can exchange the security, at his option, for the equity of the issuer in accordance with the terms of the bond indenture.

For example, a $1,000 bond might be convertible into common at $50 per share, i.e. it is worth 20 shares. If the price of the equity went to $75, the convertible would be worth $1,500. The actual fixing of the conversion price is set by the issuer, normally 15–20 per cent above the price of the outstanding shares.

Convertibles are a rather specialised market: first because they are relatively complex to value, at least compared with other traditional instruments; secondly, because they are generally used in only a few countries. In most domestic markets, convertibles are a relatively small and specialised sector. There are substantial markets in the USA and Japan and to a lesser extent in the UK, as Table 4.4 shows.

Table 4.4 The convertible universe: market size by country of borrower (as % of world total, 30 September 1988)

Japan	44.8
USA	29.5
UK	11.3
France	3.7
Australia	2.3
Italy	1.9
Switzerland	1.8
Other	2.8

Source: Capital International

There is a fair amount of Euroconvertible issuance, though in recent years this has been overtaken by the use of bonds with equity warrants (see Table 4.5).

The argument in favour of the convertible is that you are provided with equity upside coupled with the defensive nature of a bond. This is not necessarily so. For example, in the USA, in the early 1970s convertibles tended to be issued by low-quality, small-capitalisation companies, and tended to be relatively illiquid. The stock market collapse of 1973–4 left investors seriously under water on convertibles which proved to be difficult to sell. Over the ensuing decade the market began to recover and convertibles performed fairly well during the 1982–7 bull market, so much so that during 1987 at least sixteen convertible mutual funds were set up, attracting over $900 million in funds. As all this money flowed into a rather narrow market, new convertible issues were priced more and more aggressively. So when the market crashed in October 1987, convertibles fell by 16–18 per cent – hardly defensive.

There have been several variants on the concept. During the bull markets of 1987 a number of British firms (and others) issued Euro-convertibles with puts attached. An example was the £100 million 5¾ per cent convertible puttable Eurobond, lead managed for Next PLC by Credit Suisse First Boston, which promoted the concept with enthusiasm. The

Table 4.5 Euroissues of convertibles vs equity warrants ($m)

	Convertibles	*Equity warrants*
1985	4,637	2,743
1986	5,858	14,811
1987	13,093	23,535
1988	4,803	28,320

Source: Euromoney Bondware.

bonds carried an unusually high conversion premium of 152 per cent, but protected the investor with a put option. Under this he could put the bonds back to Next in 1992 at 129, for a yield to maturity of 11.74 per cent.

In the expectation that the puts would never be needed, Next did not provide in its accounts for the cost of the put option. Then came the Crash, and in the following year interest rates rose in the UK. By December 1988 Next's shares were trading at 136p against a conversion price on the bonds of 430p. Investors seemed highly likely to take up the put option, and Next had to take a substantial charge against profits for the cost of the put.

Another retailer, Burton, with a similar problem took a different route. The terms of the bond were revised to encourage investors to hold on for a further five years, thereby saving Burton from having to make a £40 million provision in its accounts. Another variant of this approach was the 'rolling put'. A typical example was the Slough Estates 6 per cent 2003 convertible. Here, holders are entitled to sell bonds back to the company on a series of dates between 1993 and 1998 at prices which will always guarantee a yield to maturity of 9.45 per cent from the issue date to the put date.

Japanese convertibles – like so many other Japanese markets – are a little different. Japanese companies issue convertibles with the hope – and to some extent the understanding – that the bondholders will convert during the life of the bonds and that it will thus not be necessary to repay the principal. The strength of the Japanese market has meant that most issues are converted before maturity; sometimes, however, things go adrift. An example was Iwatsu, who issued a SWfr50 million convertible in January 1984, when the stock was riding high, at a conversion price of ¥ 1,873. By the end of 1988, with only a month to go to maturity, the stock had sagged to 1,000. Mysteriously, the stock then proceeded to rise 60 per cent to 1,600 – a level sufficient (given movements in the Swiss franc versus the yen) to make conversion worthwhile – while comparable stocks drifted sideways.

WARRANTS

Bonds with equity warrants resemble convertibles except that the warrant can be traded separately. There is one other difference: when the warrants are exercised new money is normally used to subscribe for the shares, and the total capitalisation of the borrower increases. This is unlike the conversion of a convertible bond which merely shifts debt capital into equity capital. Until the warrant is exercised the holder has no rights to vote at shareholder meetings nor to participate in dividend distributions.

The price of a warrant depends on a number of factors. The main lure of a warrant is the leverage it offers. Consider a share with a price of $43.

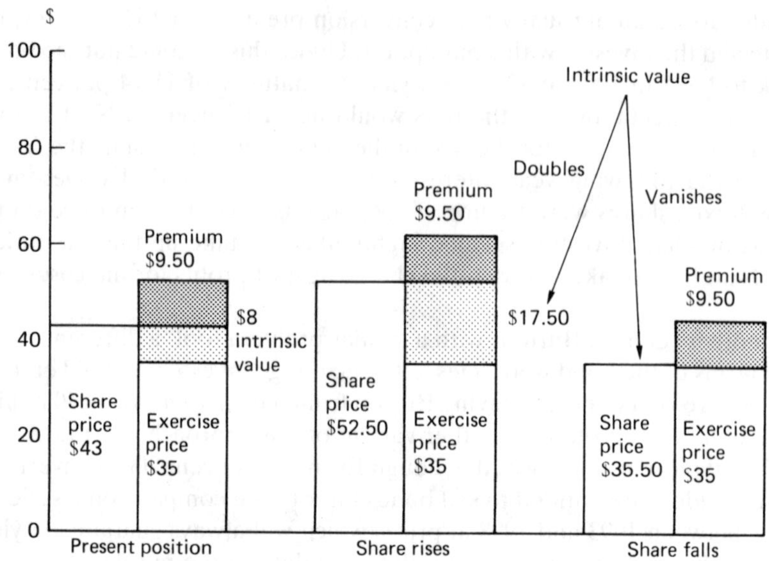

FIGURE 4.1 Warrant leverage
After D. O'Shea, *Investing for Beginners*

Suppose there is a warrant to subscribe at $35 for the shares in any year for the next six years, and the price of the warrant itself is $17.50.

Clearly, if the warrant could be bought for nothing, there would be a profit of $8 between the subscription price ($35) for the shares and the price for which they could be sold ($43). This immediate profit is the so-called 'intrinsic value' of the warrant. But in this case the market price of the warrant exceeds the intrinsic value by $9.50. This is called the 'premium'.

The premium exists because the warrant has a time value. During the time you own the warrant, there is a chance the share price will rise further. It might rise, say, to $52.50. Then the warrant would have an intrinsic value of $17.50 ($52.50 – $35). And you would gain all of that rise in the share price. But for that chance you pay only a fraction of the share's price. So it is worth paying a small premium to have that chance.

The premium implies a breakeven rate of rise of the equity. The break-even point is:

$$\frac{\text{Warrant premium}}{\text{Share price}} \times 100$$

So, in our example, over the six years of the warrant, the share's price must rise by at least $9.50/$43, or 22 per cent – an annual appreciation of 3.7 per cent. One should also allow for the dividends lost by buying the warrant rather than the equity (though against this should be set the lower interest costs of the lower capital outlay).

The interest to the speculator is that the premium tends to be set by these longer-term factors. So it tends to be stable in the short run. Hence the warrant's price tends to move one-for-one with the underlying share. Look again at our example. In this case the share price is about 2.5 times that of the warrant: this is known as the gearing or leverage of the warrant. The higher the leverage, the greater the profit/loss potential. Suppose that the premium remains stable. Then a rise of $9.50 in the share, or 22 per cent, would imply a rise of $9.50 in the price of the warrant, or 53 per cent ($9.50 on $17.50). The warrant's gain is the underlying gain multiplied by the leverage.

For the global investor, the main supply of warrants nowadays comes from the Eurobond market. As we saw in Chapter 2, the first warrant issue in the Eurobond markets was in 1964. Until 1981, this section of the Eurobond markets was relatively small and in fact no issues were made in 1980 or 1981. The 1979 issue total was $380 million. 1982 saw a marked increse in activity and in 1986 the market became very large (Table 4.6) with paticular activity by Japanese issuers.

Developments in this market are discussed in more detail in Chapter 12 on Euroequity and equity-linked Eurobonds.

Table 4.6 Issuance of equity warrant bonds, 1963–88 ($m)

1963–7	90	1978	–
1968	82	1979	380
1969	235	1980	–
1970	38	1981	–
1971	50	1982	658
1972	40	1983	1,944
1973	125	1984	1,630
1974	–	1985	2,743
1975	–	1986	14,811
1976	40	1987	23,535
1977	125	1988	28,320

Source: 1967–84: P. Aldred, *Convertibles and Warrants*, Euromoney Publications, 1987; 1985–8: *Euromoney Bondware*.

RECENT WARRANT DEVELOPMENTS

A more recent development has been the introduction of warrants on fixed interest instruments. Developments here have taken two main forms. First have been warrants attached to bonds which allow the investor to buy another bond at some pre-fixed level. These allow the investor to gamble on the possibility of a further decline in interest rates. Second, there have

Table 4.7 Issuance of fixed rate bonds with debt warrants attached 1980–8 ($m)

1980	250	1985	138
1981	831	1986	0
1982	2,390	1987	382
1983	3,160	1988	47
1984	5,435		

Source: 1967–84: P. Aldred, *Convertibles and Warrants*, Euromoney Publications, 1987; 1985–8: *Euromoney Bondware.*

been a number of 'naked' warrant issues – warrants unaccompanied by other funding. Mostly these have been issued by banks or investment banks, able to hedge the risks entailed.

The first warrant of the former kind was sold by the Kingdom of Sweden in a Yankee issue in December 1980. It sold a five-year note with a warrant attached that allowed the holder to buy another five-year note with an identical coupon at par. The warrant expired after six months (worthless, as it turned out). During 1981 more than a dozen issues were made in the Euro- and US markets. Table 4.7 shows the early development of the market and its later slowing down as the interest rate cycle bottomed out.

How often the technique is used will clearly be influenced by expectations about the immediate course of rates: if rates are expected to drop in the short term, investors are more likely to be attracted by the warrants.

Valuing such a warrant, like an equity warrant, falls into two parts: first, its intrinsic value. This is the difference between the price of the bond deliverable against the warrant, and the price that would be payable for such a bond in the market-place. Secondly, we must determine the premium – the excess of the warrant's price over the intrinsic value. The size of the premium determines the breakeven price, or yield, of the deliverable bond. We can compare this breakeven with our view of rates and decide whether or not the premium is worth paying. Or, again, we can take the scientific approach, applied in the options market, and run Black-Scholes or Cox-Ross-Rubinstein models through the computer to provide a valuation though this is less applicable for long-term options. (This topic is discussed in more detail in the author's book *New Financial Instruments*, John Wiley, New York, 1988.) Warrants have proved a very fertile source of innovation in the financial markets, and a number of warrant applications have been devised, which are discussed in Chapter 6.

EQUITIES

At the opposite end of the spectrum to the fixed-rate bonds with which we began lie the equity markets. The main equity markets, ranked according to market capitalisation at the end of 1988, are shown in Figure 4.2.

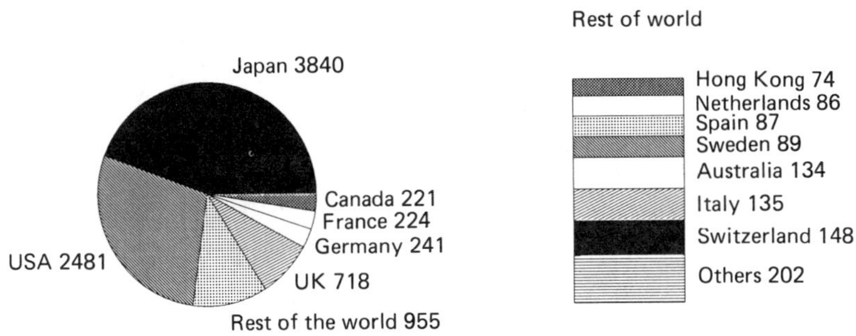

FIGURE 4.2 Major equity markets: market capitalisation end-1988
SOURCE: Morgan Stanley Capital International

Figure 1.7 in Chapter 1 shows the growth in turnover in the major markets, especially the explosive growth of Japan. We discuss the major markets individually in Chapter 16. In all these markets, the global investor is faced with a profusion of subtly different instruments, discussed in the next section. Table 4.8, while necessarily incomplete and abbreviated, may serve as a helpful introduction.

All countries have ordinary (common) shares and preferred shares. In certain countries – such as Switzerland – ordinary shares are divided into registered and bearer, with the former only available to nationals of the country.

TYPES OF EQUITY

In this section we consider the various types of equity that are traded internationally. The classical equity (*ordinary* or *common*) consists of a share in the ownership of a company. Ownership of the equity entitles the holder:

(a) to a vote at the company's annual general meeting on any resolutions that may be put by the board:
(b) a vote on the election of the board;
(c) voting rights on any proposed takeover of the company;
(d) a proportionate share of any dividend paid by the board of the company to its shareholders.

There have been numerous variations on this theme. *Deferred ordinary* have no right to a dividend until a future, specified date. These shares are often issued by, for example, mining companies where there must be a substantial investment before profits can flow in. *Non-voting* or *restricted voting* shares have often been used to keep control of a company while

Table 4.8

	Australia	*Canada*	*France*	*Germany*	*Italy*	*Japan*	*Switzerland*	*UK*	*USA*
Deferred	Yes					Yes		Yes	
Preferred:									
Cumulative	Yes	Yes						Yes	Yes
Participating	Yes	Yes						Yes	
Redeemable	Yes	Yes						Yes	Yes
Non-voting	Yes	Yes	Yes						
Floating rate		Yes							Yes
Contributing	Yes								
Warrants	Yes	Yes				Yes		Yes	Yes
Restricted:									
Non-voting		Yes	Yes[a]	Yes[b]		Yes	Yes[b]		
Subordinated		Yes							
Depositary receipts						Yes		Yes	Yes
Instalment receipts		Yes							
Participation bonds			Yes						
Savings					Yes				
Royalty trusts									Yes
Master limited partnerships									Yes
Shares retired with profits						Yes			

(a) Certificats d'investissement
(b) Participation certificates

raising capital. They have generally been frowned on by stock exchanges, since the shareholders are deprived of influence on the company. But in the USA recently a number of companies – including General Motors, with its E and H shares tied to its subsidiaries EDS and Hughes respectively – have used the technique. (See also below regarding participation certificates.)

The most common equity variant is probably the *preference share*. Here, the shareholder receives the right to be paid a dividend ahead of the ordinary shareholders. Often the tradeoff is that the preference shareholder has no voting rights, except on matters that affect the safety of the preferred dividend. In some cases preference shares are *redeemable*. In others they are *participating*, i.e. they receive a share of the profits over and above the preferred dividend, once ordinary shareholders have received a dividend. Preference shares are often *cumulative*, i.e. if a dividend is missed then the preference shares must also be paid the missing dividend before ordinary shareholders can receive one.

Floating-rate preferred are an important instrument in the United States. While the yields on these stocks are low, for tax reasons, and thus they are unattractive to the international investor, the concept is an interesting one which may migrate overseas (and has already been used in Canada). Rates on the stock were originally fixed by a formula in relation to Treasury bill rates. As rates rise, the rate on the stock is refixed on the next rate setting date, when the stock price should trade back to par. The attraction to the issuer, on the other hand, is that for tax reasons the issuer pays a lower rate.

Money market preferred (MMP) were introduced in August 1984 with the aim of ensuring that the stock really did trade to par on reset dates, which was not always true with earlier versions. This mechanism has proved the most successful of the various methods chosen to achieve the objective. The rate on the stock is fixed by means of a Dutch auction. The technique has been very successful, though some auctions have failed. For example, in the fourth quarter of 1988 Shearson Lehman took a $70 million loss as underwriter on some MMP issued by MCorp, when that bank's difficulties forced it to seek Federal assistance.

Another class of instruments is the *participation certificate* or *certificate of investment*. The participation certificate (Partizipationsschein/bon de participation) is widely used by Swiss firms: these are non-voting, bearer shares which entitle the holder to a share of the profits of the firm. For example, in the first six months of 1986 there were 57 issues of bearer participation certificates, or BPCs. These represented 42 per cent of the total Swiss market volume of equity issues in that period.

Traditionally the Swiss have restricted foreigners' direct ownership of registered voting shares in Swiss companies. This practice ran into severe criticism when Nestlé bought the British company Rowntree in 1988; the point was made that there was no reciprocity with Switzerland in takeovers. Nestlé responded eventually to the criticism by announcing that foreigners would be allowed to own its registered shares. It thereby provoked a collapse in the bearer shares (which foreigners owned) and a sharp rise in the registered (owned by the Swiss), thereby adding injury to insult.

The participation certificate technique has also been used in other markets: for example Germany (Genusschein). The market was dormant until 1984, with very few issues. An interesting exception was the 1969 issue by Audi-NSU: the certificates expired in 1983, but during their life investors had a claim on a share of the licence income from the production of Wankel engines. In 1984 an amendment to the Banking Act, allowing banks to count PCs as part of their capital under certain conditions, encouraged interest.

German participation certificates vary widely in structure because there is no law defining the instrument. Individual issues thus differ considerably in maturity, redemption and termination rights and income rights. From the investor's point of view the instrument provides upside while being defensive. The Schröder Münchmeyer Hengst index of participation certificates dipped during the October 1987 crisis but hardly at all in comparison with ordinary shares. On the other hand, the collapse of Kloeckner & Co. in 1988 highlighted the risks of the instrument. In this case, the company's majority shareholder agreed to write off its equity holdings in the company as part of a rescue deal with Deutsche Bank. Since the Genusschein holders were subordinated to the equity holders, they also were wiped out. A great deal depends on the details of each individual issue, as this case shows.

The attraction for the issuers is that the payments on the certificates are treated as interest, not dividends. An example is the issue in October 1986 by Allianz, the German insurance company, of 3.2 million profit participation certificates to raise around DM700 million. Of these, 1.9 million were for international issue. The choice of profit participation certificates, carrying no voting rights, was controversial. But in exchange, the investor is guaranteed a minimum yield of 5 per cent, with a put after 15 years, and he ranks ahead of ordinary shareholders. The annual dividend is 20 per cent above the dividend paid on ordinary shares, as compensation for the absence of tax credits on dividends, for Allianz's payments are tax-deductible.

French non-voting shares are called *certificats d'investissement* (CIs) and have been widely used to raise funds for nationalised industry. The certificate is divided into two parts: the first allows new investors to participate in the profits of the company but carries no voting rights. The second, held by the government, carries the voting rights. Important issuers included Credit Lyonnais, Banque Nationale de Paris, St Gobain and Paribas. By way of example, St Gobain issued investment certificates (CIs) in July 1986 and subsequently offered voting right certificates (VRCs), at the time of its privatisation, at a price of Frfr10 per VRC. At the time of privatisation, St Gobain CIs were quoted at Frfr307 and shares were offered at Frfr310.

Some privately controlled companies took advantage of the technique to raise funds without giving up control: Pechelbronn, L'Oréal and Groupe Victoire. CIs were not particularly popular with investors and often fell to sharp discounts against the ordinary shares. On denationalisation, Paribas, St Gobain and others allowed CI holders to convert into ordinary shares and in August 1988 the Paris Stock Exchange allowed a market in voting rights to be set up for CI holders to buy voting rights. Only the CI holders could buy, and the CI automatically converts to an ordinary share when the right is exercised to purchase voting rights.

Bearer shares (Inhaber/porteur) in Switzerland are shares which entitle the holder to a share of the profits and may be freely bought by foreigners, while *registered shares* (Namen) in Switzerland are generally open only to Swiss nationals. The recording of a shareholder's name in the register of shareholders is subject to approval by the board of directors. The decision by Nestlé in October 1988 to open its registered shares to foreigners triggered a drastic fall in the value of Swiss bearer shares and may have started a process of re-evaluation of these restrictions, in the light of Swiss companies' eagerness to buy into foreign corporations. The issue of foreign companies' reciprocal ability to buy into Swiss firms has been raised by a number of countries, such as the UK.

Participating bonds bonds where the investor receives a return linked to the profitability of the company – have been used in several countries such as France, Germany, the UK and Norway. In the latter country they have been used by the savings banks, which are mutual institutions, to raise quasi-capital through the issue of primary capital certificates (PCCs). An example is the issue in February 1989 by Sparebanken Moere of NKr100 million of PCCs which paid a yield linked to its profitability. In Germany, profit-sharing bonds confer on their holder, in addition to interest on the bond, a right to a bonus determined on the basis of the profits earned by the issuer. Profit-sharing bonds convertible into equity can also be issued. In Switzerland profit-sharing bonds (Genusschein) were introduced to facilitate corporate reconstructions, and the statute specifies that they may only be issued to shareholders or creditors of the company – they are an attempt to replace lost capital. The participation certificate (see above) is more normally used. Looked at more broadly, participating bonds could be considered to include a number of the newer types of bonds discussed in Chapter 6 on synthetics: bonds have been issued linked to stock exchange indexes, commodity prices and other items.

ROYALTY TRUSTS AND MASTER LIMITED PARTNERSHIPS

These instruments are at the moment mainly US instruments which may nevertheless in time become more important overseas. Royalty trusts emerged as the result of an attempt to unlock the value hidden in oil companies' equity. Stock markets were often undervaluing the implied stream of earnings from oil and gas production because of the companies' other activities. The solution was to spin off the ownership of, and earnings from, the oil and gas wells into a trust which earned royalties on production. An example is the San Juan Basin Royalty Trust, which in late 1980 was carved out of properties owned by Southland Royalty. Southland conveyed to the trust a 75 per cent net profits interest from its leasehold and royalty interest in the San Juan Basin in New Mexico. It is the largest trust in the industry, with reserves of 46.4 million barrels of oil equivalent, of which 95 per cent is natural gas.

Master limited partnerships (MLPs) emerged in the USA as a means of creating tradeable assets from partnerships. The first MLP was created in 1981 for Apache Petroleum, which converted interests in 33 oil and gas limited partnerships into one publicly traded vehicle. The technique was later used in US real estate financing as investors sought passive taxable income to offset passive losses, which ceased to be deductible under the 1986 tax reform. But further restrictions limited the applicability of this technique, and prices of MLPs collapsed. Energy MLPs were especially hard hit as oil prices fell. The Apache MLP, sold for $20 per unit in 1981, was liquidated at $2.50 per unit in 1988. However, the technique could be attractive in certain circumstances.

OTHER INNOVATIONS

Several other innovative types of equity have been introduced in the United States in recent years, some of which have been brought also to the Euromarket and may transfer to other equity markets. They include:

(a) equity commitment and contract notes;
(b) Puttable equity;
(c) convertible exchangeable preferred stock – convertible into equity, exchangeable into debt;
(d) increasing rate exchangeable preferred stock;
(e) equity whose dividend is linked to the performance of key subsidiaries.

One of the major developments has become the blurring of the line between debt and equity. One accountant has defined the difference between debt and equity as whether or not the issuer is obligated to expend resources to make the holder of the security whole. In theory, he must do so only for debt issues. But this does not cover the case of puttable equity, or indeed of equity contract notes or commitment notes. Similarly, perpetual debt has caused the same confusion. The issue is important not merely to investors trying to assess the shape of the company's balance sheet, but also to regulators – in the case of banks – and indeed the tax authorities, who are keen to cherish the distinction between interest payments, which can be deducted from tax, and dividend payments, which cannot.

Like floating-rate preferred, *equity commitment* and *contract notes* were the result of the strong demand by banks for capital raising in 1982–4. Both instruments are part of a category which might be called mandatory convertibles. After their initial issuance, mandatory convertibles rapidly became very popular. In 1984, 40 per cent of capital raised by the top 50 US bank holding companies was attributable to the issuance of mandatory convertibles. The concept also proved to be transferable to the Euromarket.

An equity contract note is a note exchangeable at maturity for primary equity securities having a market value equal to the principal amount of the notes. If the holder of the notes does not choose to receive equities at maturity, the issuer will undertake to sell the equity on behalf of the holder. If this sale cannot be made for any reason, the holder is required to accept equities.

After its successful use in the USA, the concept was applied in the Euromarkets in January 1986 with an issue by Thomson-Brandt International BV, guaranteed by Thomson SA. Thomson issued US$50 million of equity contract notes, at a coupon of 8 per cent and an issue price of 100, with redemption in ordinary shares of Thomson-CSF. Redemption is at the holder's option any time after September 1986 at a rate of 6.194 shares per $1,000 principal amount of notes.

The attraction to Thomson is that, while the structure has much of the appeal of a straightforward convertible, such as a lower coupon than on an ordinary fixed income bond, because it is redeemable only in equities it can be shown as capital on the company's balance sheet from the beginning.

Another class of mandatory convertible is the *equity commitment note*. J. P. Morgan issued the first equity commitment note in April 1982. Unlike the equity contract note, the note holders are not obliged to purchase equity with the notes. Instead, Morgan is committed to redeem the notes with the proceeds of an equity issue at some future date. This structure proved very popular, and a large number of later equity commitment note issues led to the Federal Reserve setting certain limits. Most notes have been issued with floating rates based on LIBOR. Issue sizes have ranged from $50 million to $250+ million.

DEPOSITARY RECEIPTS

As a by-product of the 'globalisation' of the securities markets, the market for American Depositary Receipts (ADRs) has grown sharply. An ADR is a receipt evidencing ownership of a foreign equity. A US bank will take custody, at its overseas branch, of a number of shares of a foreign company. It will then issue a receipt in the USA stating that X shares are held on its books overseas and will continue to be so held while the ADR exists. (In 1986 a tax of 5 per cent was introduced in the UK on conversions of equity into ADRs which has somewhat cut back UK ADR creation.)

ADRs were invented in the late 1920s by Morgan Guaranty. In 1983 the SEC issued a rule requiring all new ADR programmes to comply with US regulations for supplying corporate information. In 1985 the SEC permitted ADRs to be traded on the over-the-counter market, rather than requiring a full listing on one of the exchanges. There are about 180 Australian companies with ADR programmes, 150 Japanese and 150 from the UK; in all there are about 30 countries represented in the market.

With the globalisation of the world's equity markets, ADR trading grew to more than \$4 billion in 1987 compared with \$1.8 billion in 1983. Estimates of the total number of programmes outstanding are difficult – some of the South African programmes are not particularly well publicised, for example. But it is thought there are now more than 700 foreign companies whose shares trade in the USA as ADRs on the New York, American and NASDAQ exchanges. Prominent companies include Heineken, Sony, Imperial Chemical Industries, Reuters, Toyota, British Telecom and Fuji Photo.

Since 1983, all new-issue ADRs must be registered with the SEC. But those already trading were grandfathered, and also an exemption was given to firms with fewer than 300 US shareholders or less than 100,000 ADRs outstanding. Because of these provisions, of the total of 700 companies with ADR programmes, only 250 are registered with the SEC.

A recent innovation has been the introduction of ADRs on debt, in the form of an issue backed by French OATs (see Chapter 14). To date this has not been particularly well received, as the retail equity investors who are the typical user of ADRs are unfamiliar with the underlying instrument, while those who know that market are probably large enough investors to trade direct. However, the concept may well prove valuable in the long run.

There are many advantages to an ADR for the US investor. First, the process of buying stock overseas can be time-consuming and expensive, as the US broker will charge a commission and the broker overseas will charge a second commission. Then, it will be necessary to arrange safekeeping overseas, or to have the stock shipped to the US (which will require an insurance premium). Dividends will be paid in foreign currency, and it may cost more to convert them into US dollars than the value of the dividend unless the holding is very large.

By contrast, the dividend on an ADR is paid in US dollars, and they can be held at a US depositary bank, which will keep track of recapitalisation plans, rights issues, subscription rights, exchange offers, annual meetings and the like. The bank will receive dividends, pay any withholding tax, convert the proceeds into dollars, and pay the resulting dividend to the stockholder. There is a price for all this convenience: each institution involved in the chain – local custodian, US depositary bank – will take its cut from the dividends paid.

International depositary receipts (IDRs) are the non-US equivalent of ADRs; there are also other such programmes – continental depositary receipts in Holland and bearer depositary receipts in the UK, for example.

FUTURE DEVELOPMENTS

The spate of innovation and financial engineering which hit the fixed-rate debt markets in the early 1980s, triggered by the growth of the swap and option markets, seems to have slowed down. But its counterpart in the equity markets, driven by the increasing globalisation of the markets and the growing acceptance of other markets' instruments, will probably continue at a steady pace.

One development which may yet emerge is some variant of the unbundled unit concept. An attempt to create unbundled units by four companies (American Express, Dow Chemical, Pfizer and Sara Lee Corporation) was made in December 1988. In exchange for existing common stock, these companies offered investors three new component securities: a 30-year bond paying interest at the stock's current dividend rate; preferred stock that initially pays no dividend but matches any dividend increases on the common stock during the 30 years; and an equity appreciation certificate that entitles the investor to any increase in the stock's value beyond a certain point set for each company, after the bond matures. These met an initially cool reception, largely because they convert voting equity into non-voting debt certificates. The concept was finally killed by the SEC's insistence that for earnings-per-share purposes the unbundled units would continue to be considered as equity. But clearly the application of financial engineering to the equity markets has further to go. In the next two chapters we look at some of the developments that have already taken place in the fixed-income markets.

5 A la Carte 1: Asset-backed Securities and Zero Coupons

In recent years the inventiveness of investment bankers has multiplied the number and range of instruments open to the global investor. In this chapter and the next we look at some of the most important innovations. Two of the most important classes are asset-backed securities – those backed by mortgages or other assets, including those with 'credit enhancement' – and zero-coupon securities. Of the innovations in recent years, these two classes of securities have had the most widespread international adoption.

As investors have become more conscious of corporate 'event risk' – the impact on bondholders of leveraged takeovers such as those of RJ Reynolds or BAT – so the attractions of this specialised sector (sometimes referred to as 'structured finance') have grown. Moody's reported that in the USA in 1988 the structured finance sector's issuance grew to \$132 billion from \$91 billion in 1987. Notable developments included the securitisation of military receivables by the US government, as its budget pressures increased, and rapid growth in credit-card-backed transactions. The mortgage-backed market in the UK also grew rapidly, with £4 billion of issues. In Australia, since its emergence in 1985, the mortgage-backed market has grown steadily, with A\$1.6 billion outstanding at end-1988 and predictions of A\$3 billion by end-1990. In France, Law 88–1201 of December 1988 provided for the creation of *fonds communs de créances* or funds for investing in debt: the purpose is to encourage securitisation (*titrisation*).

SECURITISED LOANS

One of the major trends of the 1980s in several countries was the tendency to replace bank loans or mortgages by turning to the securities markets. Often these issues were backed by the underlying asset. The process was christened with the ugly name of 'securitisation'. A natural instrument for this purpose was the floating-rate note: an interesting example was the \$155 million FRN for Credit for Exports (CFX) in December 1984. CFX is a UK shell corporation whose specific function is to raise funds in the capital markets and on-lend them to Brazil. The loan repayment schedule exactly matches that on the notes. There is no guarantee on the FRN, but the loan payments due to be made by Brazil are guaranteed by ECGD, the UK government Export Credit Guarantee Department, so note holders are able to take the view that, indirectly, their risk is the UK government. The FRN had an eight-year maturity (average life 5.3 years) with a spread of ⅛ per cent over LIBOR. The net result is very cheap medium-term money for Brazil, while the benefit to ECGD is that the funding has no subsidy element: ECGD does not fund the borrower.

The securitisation process also encompasses the repackaging of receivables – car loan receivables, credit card receivables, lease receivables – into tradable securities, and credit enhancement. The latter technique is more familiar in the United States but has been used in the Eurobond market. In the US, there have been two suppliers of credit enhancement: the banks, which have provided letters of credit to support new issues, and the insurance industry. A number of special-purpose insurance companies such as the American Bond Assurance Corporation (AMBAC) and Mortgage Bond Insurance Association (MBIA) were established in the early 1970s. Financial Guaranty Insurance Company (FGIC) was founded in 1982 and Bond Investors Guaranty in 1983; Financial Security Assurance (FSA) was formed in 1985 with the specific objective of writing 'security insurance' on corporate financial instruments.

The major benefit of credit enhancement for the issuer is that it makes what is, perhaps, a complex transaction much simpler to sell. The investor has the comfort that if for some reason the transaction falls apart, he can still be paid out by the insurance. Clearly, the investor needs to be satisfied that the guarantor has the financial ability to protect him, and also that the guarantor's obligation in such an event is unconditional. If these conditions are satisfied, an unconditional surety bond from an unquestioned insurance company with tough underwriting standards, or a letter of credit from a top-class bank with a good reputation for credit analysis, creates an insured or guaranteed debt instrument which can be sold to other investors without their requiring updated financials or complex analysis of the underlying issue. This enhances liquidity of the issue and gives the investor comfort that he will be able to sell the paper if the need arises.

An example of the technique of credit enhancement in the fixed-rate market was the ten-year $120 million issue by De Bartolo Capital Corporation in July 1986, guaranteed by Financial Security Assurance. The lack of market familiarity with both the borrower and the guarantor left the issue relatively poorly received, despite the fact that the guarantor was of triple A standing. As yet, credit enhancement is not widely accepted in the Euromarkets, but this will change over time, particularly in view of its use in sterling mortgage-backed securities.

MORTGAGE-BACKED SECURITIES

The biggest single area for securitisation to date has been mortgages, particularly in the USA. Mortgage securitisation began to grow explosively in the USA in the 1970s. It was fuelled by two major developments: the growth of support for the market by GNMA, FNMA and FHLMC (respectively Government National Mortgage Association, Federal National Mortgage Association and Federal Home Loan Mortgage Corporation), and the interest rate instability of the period. This badly hurt many thrift institutions. It drove them to find new ways of managing the balance sheets.

This financing need spilled over to the Eurobond market in 1984, when thrift institutions began issuing floating rate notes backed by collateral in the form of mortgage-backed securities issued by FNMA and GNMA. The next stage was to bring to international markets the collateralised mortgage obligation (CMO), an instrument first developed in 1983. The idea behind the CMO is to repackage the underlying mortgage pool to reduce cash flow uncertainty. To take an example, consider a $400 million pool of mortgages. A typical CMO would take this $400 million pool and split it four ways. There would be three bond issues of $100 million each. The first would be the 'fast pay'. (Often referred to by market participants as the A bonds.) All principal repayments, up to the first $100 million, would be applied to this tranche. The second tranche (or B bonds) would be the 'medium pay': the second $100 million would be applied to this tranche. The third $100 million would be applied to the 'slow pay' tranche (the C bonds). Figure 5.1 shows an example.

The fourth class of bond is the Z bond. The Z bonds combine features of zero-coupon bonds and mortgage pass-throughs. They receive no coupon payments until all earlier classes have been paid off. The cash flow from the remaining collateral is then paid to the Z bond holders. While the earlier classes are being paid down, the interest earned by the Z bond is added to the principal balance. So during the accrual period, the cash that would be used to pay interest on the Z bonds is used to speed the pay-down of the shorter-maturity classes.

By virtue of their structure, most CMOs have been rated AAA. This is based not on the creditworthiness of the issuer, but on the collateral. The conservative structuring of CMO issues means that most are overcollateralised. This is not to say, however, that CMOs are riskless; during 1987 $13 billion of structured mortgage-backed financings were either put under credit review or downgraded by Moody's because the standing of the institutions providing credit enhancement came under question. Similarly, the bankruptcy of Residential Resources (see below) raised problems of timely payment in a CMO.

From the investor's viewpoint, the major concern in buying CMOs – apart from credit – is uncertainty of cash flow. The cash flows to the

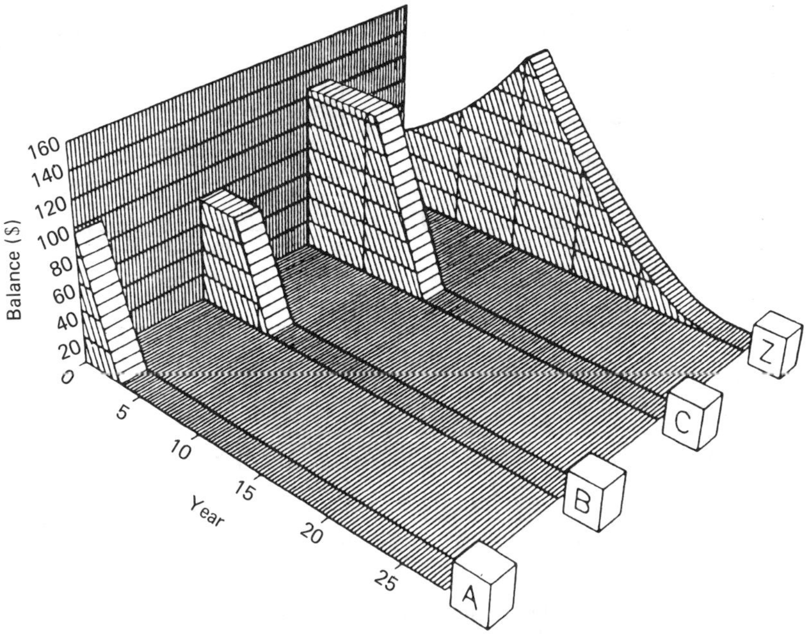

FIGURE 5.1 Outstanding balances of CMO classes (Salomon Brothers Mortgage Securities II Inc. CMO Series 1984–2; dollars, in millions)

SOURCE: Copyright © 1986 by Salomon Brothers Inc. J. S. Spratlin and P. Vianna, *An Investor's Guide to CMOs*. Salomon Brothers, New York, May 1986.

investor will vary with the prepayments of the underlying mortgages. The diagram shows the impact of different prepayment assumptions on the different tranches. Clearly, the investor must accept some uncertainty about cash flows – unless the issuer guarantees a repayment schedule. Of course, the introduction of such a guarantee means the investor must look not only at the collateral but also at the standing of the guarantor.

The main impact of CMOs on the Eurobond market has been through the issuance of floating-rate CMOs (FRCMOs). The first of these were brought to market in September 1986 by Shearson Lehman and Centex Acceptance Corporation. The issues were for $150 million and $120 million respectively, with floating-rate tranches of $43 million and $37 million respectively. Within three months, $6.5 billion of floating-rate CMOs were issued. The floating-rate CMO was immediately successful for two basic reasons. It inherited the existing fixed-rate CMO market, and it was integrated into the Eurodollar FRN market.

A key feature of the floating-rate CMO market is the use of the cap (a maximum rate of interest). While capped FRNs have been issued on the basis that it suited the issuer to include a cap, the cap is essential to the

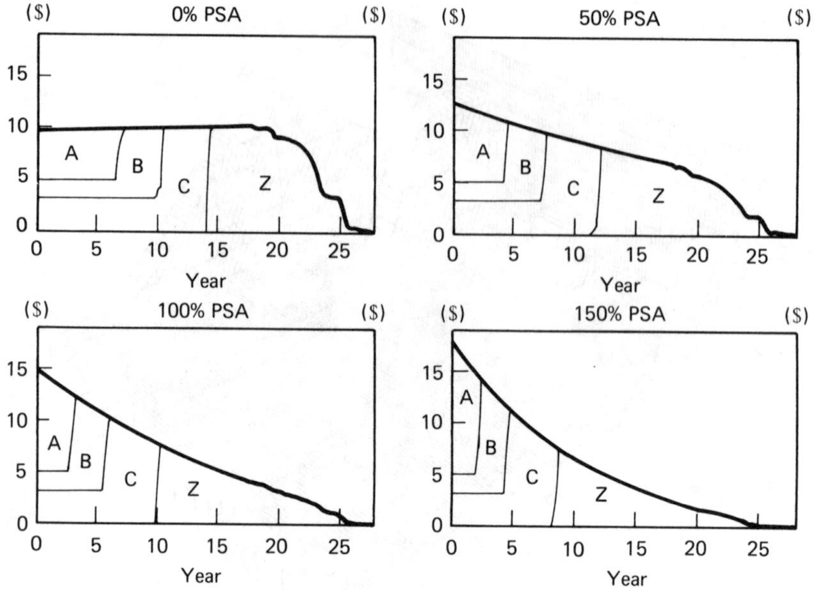

FIGURE 5.2 Collateralised mortgage obligations: CMO cash flows various prepayment rates (Salomon Brothers Mortgage Securities II Inc. CMO Series 1984–2; dollars, in millions)

SOURCE: As in Figure 5.1. Copyright © 1986 by Salomon Brothers Inc.

FRCMO issuer. The CMO uses a separate legal entity holding the pool of underlying mortgage loans to meet its interest payments. The CMO's legal independence gives important protection to the bondholder against entanglement in the potential bankruptcy of the CMO's sponsor, which may be a weaker credit. But because it is independent the CMO pool is inherently constrained on the interest rate it can pay on the floating tranche, given that most of the mortgages are fixed rate.

To handle this problem, seven of the early FRCMOs include reverse floater tranches. These 'Q' tranches have interest rates changing in the opposite direction to the LIBOR index. Some FRCMOs include accrual or zero-coupon tranches that do not pay interest until the retirement of all other tranches. The absence of payments on these tranches while the floating tranche is outstanding frees cash flows to support it in higher interest rate environments. But none of these techniques can protect the CMO against infinitely higher movements of LIBOR. So the cap is vital to ensuring the CMO's ability to meet its floating obligations.

Commercial mortgages as well as residential ones have been securitised in the Euromarket. In December 1984 Prudential Corporation of America came to the market with a $1,300 million deal secured on a portfolio of mortgages. In February 1985 New England Life Mortgage Funding

Corporation brought a deal for $298 miillion backed by mortgages on commercial property. Prepayments are not passed through but reinvested by the issuer in fresh mortgages that meet a cash-flow test, or they may be invested with New England Life, which guarantees a 9 per cent yield. This structure is much more acceptable to the Euromarket, which is used to fixed bullet maturities. The first single-building deal was by Fisher Brothers Realty in the same month, for $160 million secured by a mortgage on 605 Third Avenue, New York.

An example of the problems that can arise in trading the more specialised form of mortgage-backed derivatives came with the bankruptcy in January 1989 of Residential Resources Mortgage Investment Corporation (RRMIC) of Arizona; it had borrowed money to invest in CMO residuals (rights to the remaining cash flows after all other tranches of the CMO have been satisfied). Residuals are highly volatile and RRMIC was very exposed to rising interest rates. RRMIC had a subsidiary, Residential Resources Inc., which had issued CMOs. They had been rated AAA; Moody's immediately placed the issues on its Watch List, not because it felt the investor was unlikely to be repaid in full, but because of the danger of the CMOs becoming entangled in lawsuits from RRMIC's shareholders. Other problems that have arisen have been the EPIC affair (in which the servicer of the mortgages, contractually obliged to pass on the mortgage interest and principal repayments to bondholders, instead held on to them to cover cash flow problems) and the Glacier affair (in which the underlying mortgages were non-existent owing to fraud).

ASSET-BACKED ISSUES

The largest single corporate bond offering in history was an asset-backed issue: a $4 billion issue backed by car loans from General Motors Acceptance Corporation. This segment of the market has built on the technology learned by issuers and investment banks in the mortgage-backed industry and applied it to other markets. A recent successful application on a global basis was the $1 billion three-year issue by Citibank, backed by credit card receivables, in January 1989. The deal was registered with the US SEC, with an $850 million tranche lead-managed by First Boston and a $150 million Euromarket tranche led by Citicorp Investment Bank Ltd. The notes were issued through a special trust, National Credit Card Trust 1989–1. They were rated AAA, with the backing of a 12 per cent letter of credit from Union Bank of Switzerland (i.e. UBS guaranteed to cover defaults on the underlying assets up to 12 per cent of the total).

A key point in these complex, asset-backed issues is the efficiency of the processing of the underlying assets. This was vividly illustrated in the case of the California Student Loan Finance Corporation. In October 1987 the corporation, which had issued $1 billion of bonds to finance student loans, changed its computer software for keeping track of borrowers. The new system ran amok, losing track of many borrowers, and the default rate soared. Bank of America, the trustee on the bonds, took a $96 million charge in the fourth quarter of 1988 related to this and other loan loss problems.

An interesting application of the asset-backed market was the issue in December 1988 by Continental Bank of $140 million in floating-rate notes backed by senior debt from around twenty-five US leveraged buyout companies. The deal was overcollateralised and represented the first effort to securitise LBO debt. Asset-backing is also key to the repackaging of ex-warrant Japanese bonds (see Chapter 12 and Appendix 5) and to the repackaging of perpetual floating-rate notes, which emerged as a partial solution to the perpetual FRN crisis of 1986.

In fact, the 'instantaneously repackaged' perpetual FRN emerged as an instrument in its own right in 1988. The technique was used in a very clever application in France which exploited local tax laws. Rhône-Poulenc brought a $1.3 billion issue at LIBOR + 100. Rhône-Poulenc made a prepayment of the interest due after year 16, which amounted on a discounted basis to about 25 per cent of the issue. Merrill Lynch, the lead manager, took this repayment and invested it in US zero coupon bonds, which pay off the principal in fifteen years' time. Thus this is in fact a fifteen-year issue for the investor, and notionally a perpetual (thus equivalent to tax-deductible equity capital) for the issuer. A similar deal was done for Bull (Figure 5.3). Not unnaturally, the French tax authorities were not keen to see the concept developed further.

ZERO COUPONS

The second important new bond market sector to develop internationally during the 1980s was that for zero coupon bonds. One or two issues were made on a zero coupon basis in the 1960s in the US municipal bond market by Michigan, Minnesota and certain other states, and in the Euromarket by BP Tanker-Eriksberg in June of 1966. But for all practical purposes, the zero coupon market began in 1980 with some private placements, followed by the first public issue in April 1981, by J. C. Penney. (It had been preceded in March 1981 by Martin Marietta with the first deep discount bond.) Like interest rate swaps, zero coupon bonds were treated to begin with as a curiosity that would soon disappear. If not, why had they not been used before?

The answer as far as zero coupons is concerned probably lies in a combination of two factors. These were the historically high levels of

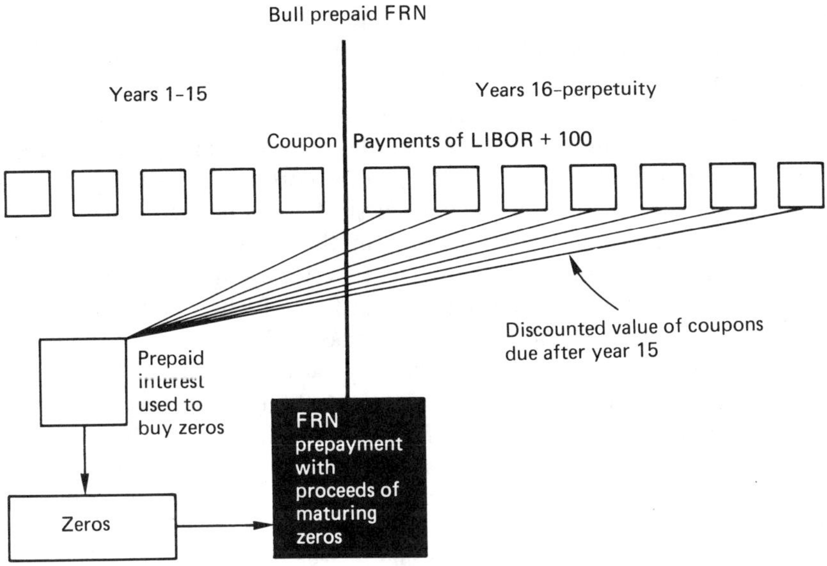

FIGURE 5.3 Bull prepaid FRN

interest rates in 1980–1, and the realisation of certain tax advantages for zero coupon issuers. The high rates of 1980–1 meant that zero coupon bonds were attractive to the investor. For the investor, the zero coupon has two key attractions. First, it locks in the reinvestment rate on his investment. The conventional yield to maturity measure on a bond is not strictly accurate. It assumes that interim coupon payments can be reinvested at the same yield to maturity. Since a zero coupon has only one cash flow, at maturity, reinvestment risk does not arise.

Secondly, since the zero coupon has only one cash flow, at maturity, its duration (see Appendix 2) is equal to its maturity. Its duration is always longer than that of a conventional bond of comparable maturity. Therefore, a zero coupon is much more volatile. When rates fall, this makes it a very attractive investment. Indeed in the first twelve months after the start of the zero coupon market, gains of up to 40 per cent were seen at the long end. An investor in long-term zeros would have earned a total compound rate of return in 1983–6 of nearly 200 per cent.

These factors made zero coupons attractive to investors. So issuers were able to make pre-tax savings ranging from 50 to 150 basis points. A second inducement to the growth of the zero coupon market was a temporary tax benefit. Until July 1982 the US tax authorities permitted straight-line amortisation of the original issue discounts. This had the effect of accelerating the tax deductions of the issuer. That made zero coupons attractive financing instruments.

The original reason for the development of the zero compound market lay, then, in high interest rates and special tax advantages. The latter still persist in a number of cases. But there is a more basic advantage to zero coupons. They add investment value. First, they cut out reinvestment risk. Second, they rectify a fault inherent in the basic concept of yield to maturity. This flaw arises out of the fact that it is a single rate. It is applied to all of the payments from a bond, regardless of when they happen.

Consider a ten-year and a twenty-year bond. Each has a coupon of 14 per cent but the twenty-year bond has a yield to maturity of 13 per cent. The ten-year has a yield of 14 per cent. Although both bonds have an identical first coupon amount of $70,000, due in six months' time, the present value of these two flows, discounted at the bond's yield to maturity, is different ($65,421 versus $65,574). Yet, in a truly efficient market, a buyer of a coupon due in six months should pay a consistent price regardless of the shape of the yield curve. What is needed is a yield curve where each individual payment is valued at its own separate yield to maturity. This is the so-called 'spot rate yield curve' or 'zero coupon curve' – the theoretical term structure. On this yield curve, every point represents the yield to maturity of a zero coupon bond to that maturity date. (See the author's book *New Financial Instruments*, John Wiley, New York, 1988, for the calculations.)

In general, when the yield curve slopes up, the zero coupon curve will lie above the yield curve. The nearer elements of a bond's cash flows are being discounted at a lower rate. Therefore, to achieve breakeven, the further elements must be discounted at a relatively higher rate. Conversely, a downward-sloping yield curve will imply a zero coupon curve below the yield curve.

The first zero coupon bonds were introduced in August 1982, consisting of receipts evidencing ownership of principal or interest due on Treasury bonds. Different investment banks introduced different 'brands' – TIGRs, CATS – whose names tended to have a feline connotation. They were followed by the US Treasury's introduction of Separate Trading of Registered Interest and Principal of Securities (STRIPS). STRIPS were introduced in February 1985. Under this system, selected Treasury securities are held in the book entry system operated by the Federal Reserve in a way that allows separate trading and ownership of the interest and principal payments. The first such bonds were the 11¼ percent of February 2015.

Despite some initial teething problems, the market for STRIPS by December 1986 had grown to $109 billion par amount, 47 per cent of the entire market for Treasury zeros. The stripping process is now continuous, and can significantly affect individual issues. For example, in March 1989 a total of $2.6 billion of Treasury notes and bonds was stripped; and at that date, of $18, 864 million of the 7.5 per cent of November 2016, a total of $9,503 million (55 per cent) had been stripped.

In addition to this continuous activity occasional surges take place for specific reasons. For example, the US body responsible for digging the thrift industry out of trouble (Financing Corporation or FICO) will buy STRIPS to guarantee the payment of principal on its debt. (That is, a $100 million 10 per cent FICO issue due in the year 2000 will be backed by $100 million of STRIPS maturing in 2000. You just have to hope the US thrift industry will stay alive long enough for FICO to find the 10 per cent interest.)

ZERO COUPON ISSUES IN OTHER MARKETS

It was inevitable that the zero coupon concept, once it had been proved viable in the US, would spread to other countries. But the extent to which the concept was able to travel was much affected by tax questions. Different countries treated the discount element of a zero coupon issue in different ways. Initially, the Japanese investor benefited from a very favourable treatment. Another aspect, perhaps not widely touched upon, is that the zero coupon bond presents certain advantages to those who do not wish to draw attention to their income. Unlike the normal bearer Eurobond, with its coupon-clipping, the investor makes a single payment and receives back a single payment, without having to handle intervening income.

In May 1985 the zero coupon technique was used ingeniously by BP which borrowed $160 million through a dual issue of zero coupon bonds and annuity notes, combining the cash flows to produce a synthetic normal coupon bond. The zero coupon component had an issue price of 38.55, which itself was partly paid – 12.05 per cent due in June and 26.50 per cent in December 1985. The maturity date was 20 June 1995 and the issue amount US$182.46 million. The annuity notes matured a year earlier, on 20 June 1994. The issue amount was $100 million, with a coupon of 10.5 per cent (compared with 10.75 per cent yield on the zero coupon portion). The annuity notes were also partly paid so that the total payment in the first year was slightly lower.

By combining the zero coupon – with its rising outstanding liability – with the declining liability created by the sinking fund on the annuity bond, BP achieved a combined structure equivalent to a current coupon bond, which it then swapped into a floating rate of interest. The attraction of structuring this deal in this way was to tap a perceived pool of demand at that time for zero coupon notes. The all-in cost to BP is estimated at 20 basis points below Treasuries on the fixed all-in coupon. A large part of this saving was from the part payment feature. BP did not have to pay interest to investors on the portion not initially paid. It could fund the first six months more cheaply through the short-term market than the bond coupons, thus saving around 20 basis points per annum.

In December 1985 a similar technique was used by the World Bank. This was a three-part deal. It consisted of a $200 million fifteen-year Eurobond maturing in 2000 together with a thirty-year serial zero coupon bond. The serial zero repays in annual tranches starting 2001. The third part is the purchase by the World Bank of stripped US Treasury bonds with a face value of $200 million which are used to repay the Eurobond at maturity. The arrangement results in a steady annual flow of payments to the investor, mimicking the interest payments on a conventional bond. After the Eurobond matures, the serial zero redemption amounts produce about $20 million per annum for the remaining fifteen years. The use of the $200 million stripped Treasuries eliminates the need for the World Bank to provide for a large interim redemption amount, and the combined structure produced a 40 basis point saving for the Bank.

Zero coupons have now been offered in a range of currencies: sterling, Deutschmarks, Australian dollars, Luxembourg francs, and Danish krona, amongst others. Like interest rate swaps, after an initial period of puzzlement, they have become widely accepted as financing tools.

6 A la Carte 2: Synthetics, Warrant-Linked and Other Exotica

A rich seam of innovation has been tapped in recent years by international financial markets – notably the US market and the Eurobond market – and this chapter touches on some of the items of interest. In this chapter we look at various kinds of bond created by marrying the bond to something else: either a different currency, in the form of a dual-currency bond; a warrant, to create an equity link, or a link to another bond; an option on currencies or interest rates; an index, such as the Nikkei or FAZ equity incides; or a commodity such as gold or oil. What follows is inevitably a very brief survey of a complex subject; those wishing more detail may want to look at the author's book *New Financial Instruments* (John Wiley, New York, 1988).

SYNTHETICS

Synthetic securities are those whose features mimic another asset, which an investor may not be able to buy directly, or as cheaply. The definition of what is or is not a synthetic security is not always clear-cut. Securities have been structured in many different ways for legal or tax reasons, but some of them may look like synthetics without necessarily having had that intention. Synthetics is a term also used to refer to securities created from asset swaps (see below).

In any event, what follows is an attempt to pick out some of the more prominent kinds of synthetic security. We also cover here index-linked bonds, because they could be seen as a form of synthetic. They give the investor access to a particular rate of return which could not be earned otherwise. For example, 'bull' or 'bear' bonds linked to stock indexes allow the investor to hedge the movement of an entire market without having to access the stock index futures markets (which in any case do not exist in some of the countries involved).

Dual-currency bonds have had perhaps the widest success, being launched in the Euromarkets in 1981. They are bonds whose issue price is fixed in one currency, and redemption value and coupon in another. The main attraction of the dual-currency bond is that it gives a hedge to the investor who is not quite certain which way exchange rates will move.

The first deals were in Swiss francs. Typically, a Swiss franc issue was launched on the public foreign market with an issue price set in Swiss francs, and a redemption value in dollars of a set amount per Swfr5,000 bond. More recently, yen-dollar dual-currency bonds became popular, and the technique has now been used in a wide range of currencies.

We will look at an issue for First City Financial in 1985. The issue price for each Swfr5,000 bond was par, and the redemption amount was fixed at $2,800. The bond had a ten-year maturity. The implied exchange rate between Swfr5,000 and $2,800 is Swfr1.79 to the dollar. That compares with the exchange rate at the date of issue of Swfr2.45; so the initial US dollar par value was $2,040.82.

Thus at the exchange rates at the time of issue, a Swiss investor could buy just over $2,000 for his Swfr5,000. But by having the dual-currency bond he was guaranteed a redemption of $2,800, whatever the exchange rate. Suppose at maturity the exchange rate is above Swfr1.79. He will have earned more than his initial outlay of Swfr5,000 when converting the principal back into Swiss currency. For example, if the exchange rate stayed the same (Swfr2.45), in ten years' time the investor would be able to convert back his $2,800 to give Swfr6,860. If the dollar rises, the investor benefits even more.

If the dollar falls to the Swfr1.79 level, the investor receives Swfr5,000 – the same as his initial investment. So the investor is protected against a dollar fall, down to the exchange rate implied by the set redemption amount. He takes the risk of a fall below that level, but gains from a rise.

The investor is protected further because the coupon he receives, in Swiss francs, is usually set at a higher level than it would be for a straightforward Swiss franc issue. By calculating the benefit of the extra coupon over the life of the issue, the investor can work out a breakeven exchange rate at which level he would have done as well by buying an ordinary Swiss franc issue from the same borrower. If the dollar falls below that level, then he is worse off buying the dual-currency issue.

We look at a comparison of the First City dual with a US dollar 10-year straight with an 8.75 per cent coupon and a Swiss franc straight with a 6 per cent coupon. As Table 6.1 and Figure 6.1 show, the investor in First City Financial's dual currency issue is better off as long as the Swiss franc remains above about 1.60 at maturity.

In 1981–3, a number of issuers came to the market, including GMAC, Sears, Shearson/American Express and Baxter Travenol. In the summer of 1984, the Swedish Export Credit agency (SEK) created a reverse dual-currency bond with interest payable in dollars and principal in Japanese yen. The first dual-currency bonds tended to have coupons payable in the high interest rate currency, i.e. dollars, and principal in a low rate currency, i.e. Swiss francs. The reverse transaction appealed to Japanese investors' eagerness to enjoy high currency yield at the price of expsoure to possible long-term devaluation of the dollar against the yen.

Table 6.1 First City Financial dual-currency issue

Exchange rate	*Cumulative return in US$*[1] *Dual currency*	*US$ straight*	*Swfr straight*
3.00	3,554.00	3,104.21	2,320.38
2.85	3,593.69	3,104.21	2,347.77
2.70	3,637.78	3,104.21	2,478.20
2.55	3,687.06	3,104.21	2,623.98
2.40	3,742.50	3,104.21	2,787.97
2.25	3,805.34	3,104.21	2,973.84
2.10	3,877.15	3,104.21	3,186.26
1.95	3,960.00	3,104.21	3,431.35
1.80	4,056.67	3,104.21	3,717.30
1.65	4,170.91	3,104.21	4,055.24
1.50	4,308.00	3,104.21	4,460.76
1.35	4,475.56	3,104.21	4,956.40

1. i.e. cumulative coupon payments + redemption value.

The so-called '*heaven and hell*' bond was a development of the dual-currency bond. This was introduced in November 1985 with an issue for IBM. In a dual-currency bond, the principal amount is fixed in terms of the implicit conversion rate. The interest flows depend on exchange rates over the bond's life. By contrast, the heaven and hell structure gives investors an upside and a downside risk on the principal amount. The two are mirror images as Figure 6.2 and Table 6.2 show.

The IBM issue was for $50 million of ten-year bonds, with a coupon of

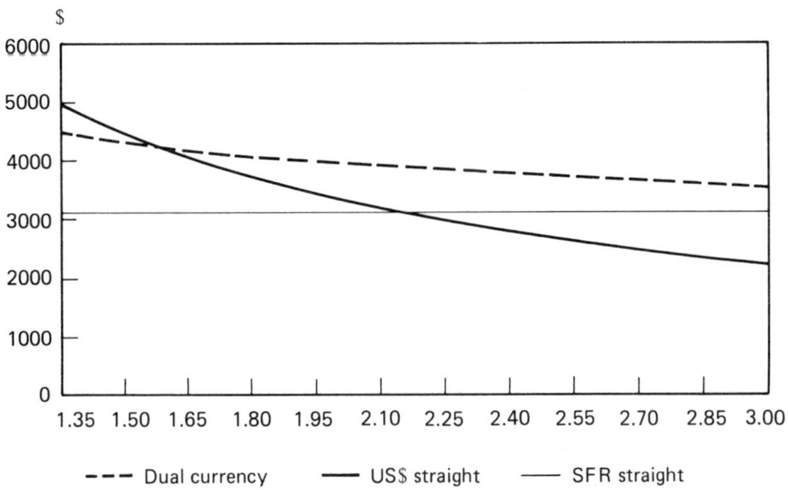

FIGURE 6.1 First City Financial dual-currency issue: final value at different exchange rates

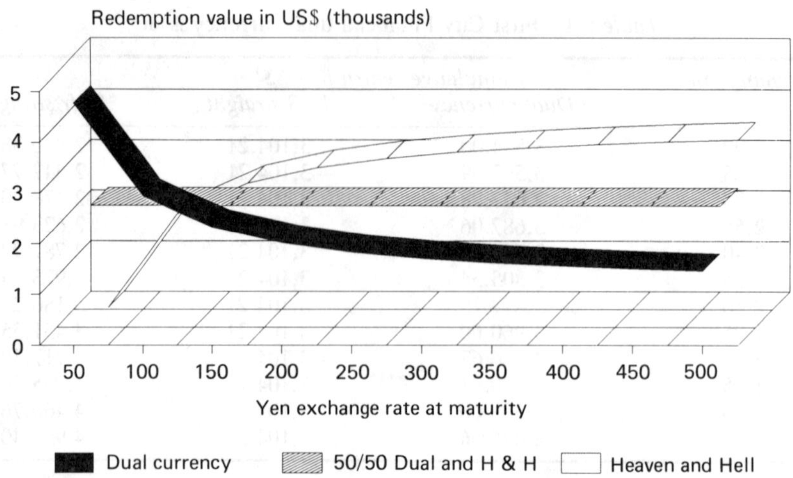

FIGURE 6.2 Dual currency vs Heaven and Hell: holding 50 per cent in each neutralises them

10¾ per cent, and a redemption amount at par if at maturity the yen/US dollar rate is ¥169. If the rate is higher than that, redemption is over par. If the rate is lower, redemption is below par. The precise formula is that the redemption amount is equal to $100 \times (1 + (z - 169)/z)$, where z = the spot rate at maturity. For example, if the yen/dollar rate stands at 170 at maturity, the repayment amount would be $100 \times (1 + (170 - 169)/170) = 100.59$.

Table 6.2 Dual currency vs heaven and hell

Exchange rate at maturity	*Cumulative return in US$*[1] *Dual currency*	*H&H*	*Average*[2]
50	4,774	34	2,404
100	2,930	1,874	2,402
150	2,316	2,487	2,402
200	2,009	2,794	2,401
250	1,824	2,978	2,401
300	1,701	3,101	2,401
350	1,614	3,188	2,401
400	1,548	3,254	2,401
450	1,497	3,305	2,401
500	1,456	3,346	2,401

1. i.e. cumulative coupon payments + redemption value.
2. e.g. (4,774 + 34)/2.

BULL/BEAR BONDS

Another important concept is the so-called 'bull and bear' bond. This was pioneered by SEK (Swedish Export Credit) in June 1986. The issue was for Y=20 billion, with a coupon of 8 per cent. The redemption price of the bonds is linked to the Nikkei average of 225 stocks on the Tokyo exchange. It came in two tranches: a bull tranche and a bear tranche.

The bull tranche has a 'strike' level of 26,067. That is to say, if the Nikkei index at redemption in July 1991 is at 26,067, redemption will be at 100 per cent. The redemption price is reduced by 0.4425 per cent for every 100 points the index falls below the strike level, and increased by a similar amount for any rise above it. There is a cap and a floor on the extent to which the investor can gain or lose: the maximum capital gain for the bull is at 28,461 for the Nikkei (at 110.59 per cent), while the maximum loss is when the level of the Nikkei falls to 16,979 (the bond falls to 60 per cent). Correspondingly, on the bear tranche, the strike level is set at 19,373, with the same floor and ceiling levels.

Figure 6.3 and Table 6.3 show the results for various levels of the Nikkei for a ¥1,000,000 investment. Clearly, the bull bond and the bear bond offset each other, so that an investor who held equal amounts of both would always receive the same amount at redemption, no matter what the level of the Nikkei. However, he would also always receive less than a comparable straight bond with a similar coupon: this is the saving to the issuer, and the amount that the investor gives up in paying for the ability to have options on the Nikkei.

In fact, of course, the bull bonds and bear bonds were sold to different

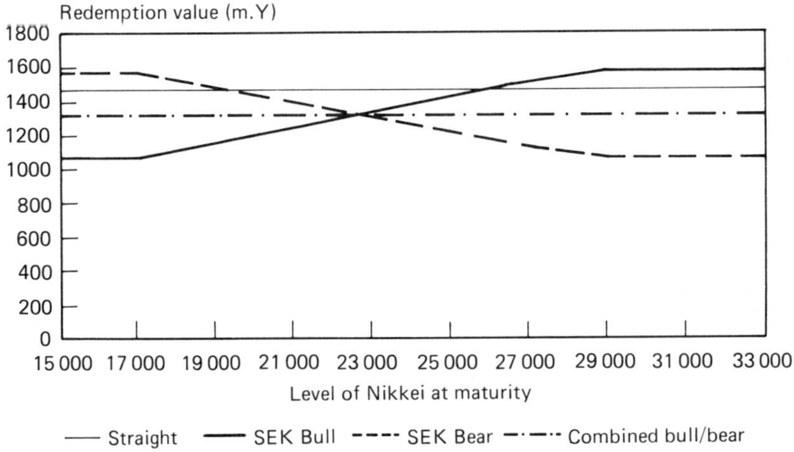

FIGURE 6.3 SEK bull/bear, linked to Nikkei-DJ

Table 6.3

Nikkei-DJ at maturity	*Straight*	*Cumulative final value* *Bull*	*Bear*
15,000	1,469,328	1,069,328	1,575,228
17,000	1,469,328	1,068,113	1,574,333
19,000	1,469,328	1,156,613	1,485,833
21,000	1,469,328	1,245,113	1,397,333
23,000	1,469,328	1,333,613	1,308,833
25,000	1,469,328	1,422,113	1,220,333
27,000	1,469,328	1,510,613	1,131,833
29,000	1,469,328	1,575,228	1,069,328
31,000	1,469,328	1,575,228	1,069,328
33,000	1,469,328	1,575,228	1,069,328

groups of investors. The bear bonds could be sold to Japanese institutional investors which had huge paper profits on their Japanese stocks. They were loath to sell the shares because of their long-term and mutual relationship with some of the companies in which they had shares. They feared that their hidden profits would be reduced significantly when share prices dropped. They could hedge their positions by investing in the bear bonds, as stock index futures were not available in Japan at that time.

Correspondingly, the bull bonds would be placed with investors who were optimistic for the stock exchange, but were attracted by a high current coupon. On the other hand, looked at overall, the terms are not unduly over-generous to the investor. Between 19,373 and 26,067, both bulls and bears lose out in that possible maximum losses for both bonds are 40 per cent, while maximum gains are only 10.5 per cent.

The bonds were designed to limit the exposure of the borrower. The redemption values balance each other out, so that whatever happens to the Tokyo stock market, the total repayment in 1991 is always 85.3 per cent of the principal amount. SEK was able to swap the proceeds of the bonds to gain funding at considerably less than LIBOR.

This kind of structure has been used in several subsequent issues: Deutsche Bank issued DM200 million with a redemption amount linked to the FAZ share index (although in this case investors in the bear tranche were better rewarded than their bull counterparts, as Deutsche judged there were more bulls than bears). The Kingdom of Denmark issued five-year bull/bear bonds in French francs in October 1986. The redemption amount was linked to the official Stock Exchange index (CAC) of the Paris stock exchange. Later the same month, the Kingdom of Denmark used the same technique again to raise $210 million via the first bull/bear gold linked Eurobond.

INDEXED BONDS

The first use of indexation was for government bonds, which were indexed to inflation or to some inflation hedge such as gold; the first use of Eurobond indexing was the use of currency-linked bonds such as the European Unit of Account bond for SACOR in 1961. But in this section we deal with bonds whose redemption value is linked to some other index such as a commodity price, stock exchange index or another bond.

The first indexations apart from currency tended to be gold, for example the issue by Refinemet, which in February 1981 issued fifteen-year 3 per cent bonds indexed to the market price of 100,000 ounces of gold. In April 1986 Mitsui & Co issued three-year bonds indexed to the US Treasury thirty-year bond: in fact, at least eight such issues were launched for various borrowers in the first half of 1986, most of them linked to the 9 per cent Treasury bond due in 2016.

A different technique was employed by Guinness Finance in July 1986 when it made its first Eurobond issue. It was a $100 million issue of Stock Performance Exchange Linked (SPEL) bonds with a redemption amount linked to the New York stock exchange composite index. The SPEL bonds are linked to the index via the formula:

$$\text{Variable index amount} = \$10{,}000 \times ((X - 166)/166)$$

The coupon on the three-year issue was set at 3 per cent. This was fixed at ½ per cent below the calculated average annual dividend yield of shares on the NYSE. Table 6.4 shows the redemption values on a principal amount of $10,000.

Investors thus have an equity surrogate. They receive about the same yield as they would get from the underlying shares but with protection against capital loss since the bonds redeem at a minimum of par. Since this issue was only a bull tranche, rather than the bull/bear structure, Guinness

Table 6.4

NYSE index at maturity	*Redemption value*
120	10,000
150	10,000
180	10,843
210	12,651
240	14,458
270	16,265
300	18,072
330	19,880
360	21,687
390	23,494

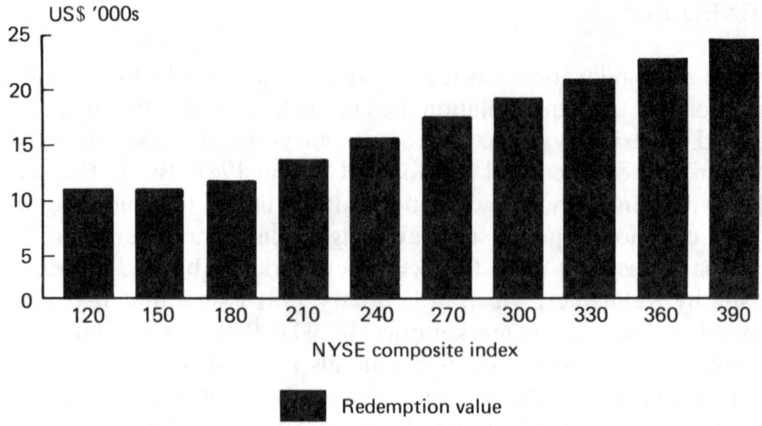

FIGURE 6.4 Guinness SPEL Bond: final value at different NYSE levels

was left with an exposure to the redemption amount depending on the NYSE index. It eliminated this through a swap in which it agreed to pay 7.55 per cent semi-annually in return for receiving 3 per cent together with the variable redemption amount, whatever that turned out to be. The bonds were placed primarily among retail investors in the Far East and to some extent in Europe.

OPTION-RELATED INSTRUMENTS

In recent years a number of issues have included currency options. One such issue was the *Indexed Currency Option Note (ICON)*. This concept was introduced in October 1985 with a $100 million issue for the Long-Term Credit Bank of Japan (LTCB). The LTCB paid 100 basis points over Treasury bonds for its ten-year issue, whereas normally it would have expected to pay 35 to 45 basis points. In exchange, the investor receives a reduced payment of the principal amount if the yen is stronger than 169 against the dollar at maturity in ten years' time. Effectively, the investor has sold the borrower a European-style ten-year yen/dollar call option with a strike price of 169.

The redemption formula is as follows:

$$\left\{ \frac{(169 - S)}{S} \right\} \times F$$

where S = rate at maturity;
F = face value of note.

Here are some examples for a thousand dollar note:

Yen/dollar rate 1995	*Redemption amount*
	$
179	1,000
169	1,000
159	937.11
149	865.77
84.5	0

With ICONs, while the coupon is fixed in dollar terms, the principal is variable in dollar terms. By contrast, with a dual currency issue, the dollar value of the coupon stream is variable, while the dollar value of the principal is fixed. A useful method of comparing the two is to construct a chart showing the future value in dollar terms of ICONs, dual currency, Eurodollar, and Euroyen bonds.

Figure 6.5 shows the effects of changes in the exchange rate on the future value in dollars of four different 10-year Eurobonds. These are:

(a) a US dollar straight yielding 10.65 per cent;
(b) a Euroyen straight yielding 6.5 per cent;
(c) a yen/dollar dual currency bond with a coupon of 7.6 per cent payable in yen, repaying in dollars at yen 1.84 = US$1; and
(d) an ICON with a dollar yield of 11.25 per cent and the principal reducing at below yen 169 = US dollars.

The analysis assumes a current rate of yen 215 = US$1. The bonds have been constructed to meet at a breakeven rate of yen 147 = US$1.

As the chart shows, the dual currency performs less well than the Eurodollar straight bond until the breakeven rate, after which it performs

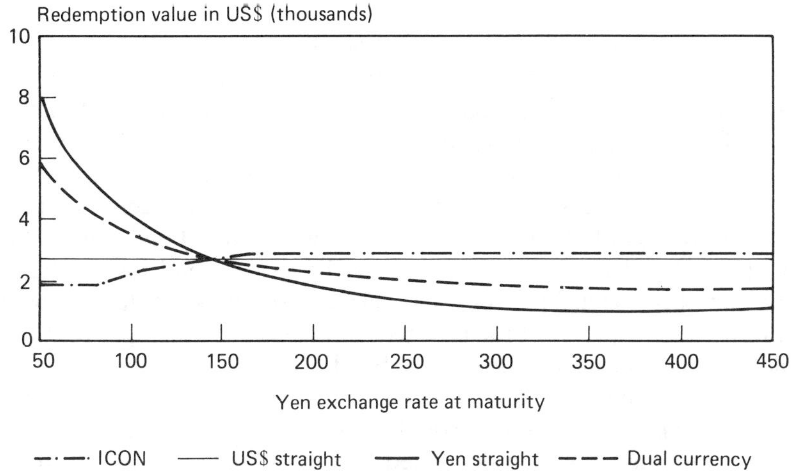

FIGURE 6.5 Index currency option note (ICON)

better; conversely, it performs better than the Euroyen straight bond until the breakeven point, after which the Euroyen straight performs better. In other words, it is always possible to replicate the dual currency bond with a portfolio of straight issues denominated in dollars and yen. Graphically, this is obvious, since the dual currency bond always lies between the two.

This is not the case for the ICON, which performs better than all the other issues until the breakeven point, after which it performs worse. In this sense, therefore, ICONs offer investors a unique package that cannot be duplicated in some other fashion.

WARRANT-LINKED BONDS

In one sense, warrants are nothing new to the market. As we saw in Chapter 2, the first Eurobond with warrants attached was issued in June 1964. But that applies really to warrants on equities – which are discussed later (Chapter 12 on Euro-equities and equity-linked bonds). Warrants on fixed income instruments, or currencies, are an outgrowth of the over-the-counter and traded options markets, which are more recent creations.

There have been a bewildering variety of warrant-linked instruments since 1980, when the Kingdom of Sweden introduced the first bond with a warrant attached to buy another bond. On the whole, however, they fall into five types:

(a) 'harmless' warrants, 'wedding' warrants and variants;
(b) 'naked' warrants;
(c) 'money back' warrants;
(d) 'income warrants';
(e) currency and gold warrants.

Harmless, or refunding, warrants were first introduced in 1985. The original concept was as follows. A $100 million bond would be issued, say at 10 per cent, for redemption in five years' time, and a call after three years. (This 10 per cent bond is often referred to as the 'front' bond or the 'host' bond – it 'hosts' the warrants.) A 3-year warrant was also issued, with expiry date at the time of the first call on the 10 per cent bond.

The warrant could be exercised into a new five-year bond, say at 9 per cent. (This bond is often referred to as the 'back' bond, or the 'virgin' bond.) So, if rates fell 1 per cent, the warrants would have value and would be exercised at expiry, but the proceeds of issuing the new 9 per cent bond could be used to call the 10 per cent bond.

This concept had a potential problem: if the warrants were exercised before the call date, the issuer could be forced to increase the amount of debt outstanding. The idea depended heavily on investors not exercising the warrants until the end of their lives. Experience shows that this tends to be the case, but in a longer-term warrant there can still be substantial early exercise. So there is still a risk from the issuer's viewpoint, particularly if the original issue had been swapped into floating-rate funds as the purpose of the exercise. To be left with unexpected fixed-rate debt was unattractive. In some cases issuers solved this problem by agreeing with their swap counterparties that a contingent swap would take place, i.e. swaps would be written to match any warrants exercised.

Another solution was introduced in October 1985: the 'wedding warrant'. Here the warrant is 'wedded' to the host bond, in the sense that until the call date on the host bond, the warrant can only be exercised by surrendering an equal amount of the host bond. That is, if I wanted to exercise into $1 million of the back bond, I must surrender $1 million of the host bond with the warrant for the exercise to be effective. After the call date on the host bond, exercise of the warrant is for cash.

NAKED WARRANTS

The next step in this concept was to use 'naked' warrants. Naked warrants had already been used for other purposes – see below – but in this context, naked warrants were applied to the problem of reducing borrowing costs on previously outstanding issues. In this sense, they 'securitise' the call feature on the bonds.

An example is the issue by Dutch State Mines in January 1986 of 150,000 warrants at $35 each. The warrants carry the right to buy, after two years, a three-year 10¾ per cent bond maturing in 1991. Not by coincidence, DSM had an outstanding issue of $150 million 11⅜ per cent bonds, callable from March 1988 and maturing in 1991. In effect, by issuing the warrants, DSM cashed in today the value of the call option two years hence. If rates did not fall, it would effectively reduce its all-in borrowing cost by $5.25 million – the warrant proceeds. But, in exchange, it committed itself to issue at 10¾ per cent if rates fell to the point that warrantholders exercised. It would be indifferent on that point only if the original borrowing had been swapped to final maturity – rather than call date.

The technique has been quite widely used by other financial institutions able to manage the risk inherent in such commitments. In October 1983 Phibro-Salomon issued 100,000 call warrants on sterling, and 100,000 put warrants, exercisable at $1.52 and $1.46 respectively, with a one-year exercise period. The same issuer later made issues of DM and ECU warrants. And in November 1985 Phibro-Salomon issued 150,000 warrants exerciseable into the 9⅝ per cent Treasury notes due November 1990; in this issue the warrant exercise period ran for two years, but was deferred for three years – until November 1988.

In February 1987 there was a rash of naked currency warrant issues by

Citibank, DG Bank, Swiss Bank Corp., Merrill Lynch and others. As an example, the Citibank issue was of up to 100,000 warrants, each entitling holders to buy $500 at an exchange rate of US$ = DM1.82. The exercise period for the warrants was two years, with exercise in minimum lots of 200. The primary rationale for these issues was seen as providing tradable currency options with a long exercise priod, in contrast to the Philadelphia or other exchange-traded options, where liquid markets exist mainly for nearby options, giving a practical maximum period of perhaps six months.

SYNTHETIC ASSETS FROM SWAPS

Another category of synthetic assets is the creation of synthetic floating-rate notes from fixed rate bonds coupled with an interest rate swap. There is also a similar, though rather smaller, market for creating fixed-rate bonds from floating-rate notes plus a swap.

Asset swaps are a way to shift paper from one market to another. Bonds have been issued consisting of floating rate notes swapped into fixed rates. An example would be the BECS issue in 1985, in which $100 million of UK government US dollar floating rate notes were swapped into fixed rate dollar bonds, producing 'synthetic US dollar gilt-edged bonds'. More often, a fixed-rate bond is coupled with an interest rate (and perhaps a currency) swap, to produce a synthetic floating rate note (see Chapter 7).

It was not long before investment banks realised the value of the asset swap technique. Put bluntly, a failed fixed-rate bond could be transformed into a floating-rate note and placed with banks, who are well accustomed to buying floating-rate instruments. A particularly widespread use of the technique has been in the Japanese equity warrant bond market.

At its height, bonds in this market were being issued with coupons as low as 1 or 2 per cent. This was because the attractions of the warrant (see Chapter 4) were so great, that the bond to which the warrant was attached could be relatively lowly valued. Thus, immediately after the bond was issued, and the warrants were stripped away from it, the straight bond would fall to a sharp discount: a price of $70 or even $60 per $100 nominal. Traditionally, many investors are not interested in buying deep-discount, low-coupon bonds for accounting and other reasons. Thus, while the warrant was a roaring success, the bonds would languish.

It was not long before the asset swappers perceived the opportunity. They would move in to buy the unwanted bonds, couple them with an interest rate swap, and sell them to the banks. These bonds, however, were operationally a great deal more complex to swap, because of the deep-discount nature of the cash flows. A simplified example is laid out in Appendix 5.

Asset swap activity has had both positive and negative effects. On the positive side, for every new issue, there is now generally a floor point below which the bond cannot fall. At some point it becomes 'swappable': the bond's spread over Treasuries is above the spread which the swap market requires to swap into floating rate. At that point, the bond can be redistributed into the floating-rate market. This provides a natural floor price for the bond in the fixed-rate market.

On the negative side is the liquidity effect. Bonds are asset swapped and sold into the banking market. There they are mostly held to maturity, because of the accounting and other complexities of reversing the swaps before maturity. This means that liquidity in the secondary market for these bonds has been severely impaired. In the case, for example, of some of the Japanese ex-warrant bonds, as much as 90 per cent of the issue may have been asset swapped. The remaining 10 per cent is not worth a market-maker's time or effort to trade, and so liquidity in the bond dries up.

There has also been a decline in the liquidity of the asset swap market itself. In the early days, a number of firms were active in the secondary market looking for paper to asset swap. Nowadays, with every lead manager well aware of what can be done in this regard, the tendency is for the lead manager to asset swap whatever cannot be placed directly as fixed-rate paper, thus limiting the amount of secondary market asset swap activity.

COUPON VARIANTS

This segment of the bond and FRN markets provides one of the richest and most exotic menus in the market. A number of the coupon structures that have been evolved in the market recently appear at first blush to bear no relation whatsoever to reality. In point of fact, of course, they represent careful engineering of coupon structures to meet highly specific investor requirements – usually Japanese.

In January 1986, for example, the European Investment Bank issued US$200 million of ten-year bi-annual interest payment bonds. The coupon on the bonds was 19 per cent, but it was paid only every two years. The annualised yield of 9.19 per cent was 10 basis points over the Treasuries at the time of launch, but the high bi-annual coupon was designed to attract investors with tax considerations in mind, particularly in Japan. A related deal was the US$100 million 7-year bond issued in April 1986 by the Banque Nationale de Paris, with an 8½ per cent coupon. The first interest payment was due in April 1991, in respect of the period from 8 April 1986 to that date.

In the FRN market one of the earliest of these structures was the YCAN or yield curve anticipation note, which later became known as the 'bull' or 'reverse' floater. The first issue was in February 1986, by the Student Loan

Marketing Association ('Sallie Mae'). The issue was priced at 17.2 per cent *minus* LIBOR. Thus as LIBOR fell, the coupon on the issue rose. The bull floater concept is attractive to investors when rates are falling, and so reverses the traditional appeal of FRNs as a safe haven for investors when rates rise.

The concept was followed quickly by other issuers including Christiania Bank and Citicorp. It quickly became very popular in the Japanese market with its strong emphasis on high coupons rather than capital gain. A large number of reverse floaters were issued in Japanese yen during the summer of 1986, for example Kansallis Osake Pankki, the Finnish bank, did several issues. One was issued in late July for ¥10 billion for five years, with coupon fixed as 14.7 per cent – (1.5 × six-month yen LIBOR). A second, in August, paid 15.125 per cent – (1.6 × six-month yen LIBOR).

The combination of a bull floater and a conventional FRN add up to a classic fixed rate bond. The Hong Kong Mass Transit Railway Corporation's FIRST (Fixed Interest Rate Substitute Transaction) consisted of HK$600 million of a conventional FRN at HIBOR (Hong Kong Inter-Bank Rate) + ⅛ per cent, and a bull floater paying 17 per cent HIBOR. Combining the two produces an all-in fixed rate cost of 17.125 per cent/2, i.e. $8\frac{9}{16}$ per cent.

PERPETUALS

One final category of exotica is the perpetual bond. Perpetuals, i.e. bonds having no pre-fixed redemption date, have a long history. Sir Henry Pelham arranged the first consolidation of British government debt into irredeemable bonds ('consols') in 1749. The subscribers to the foundation of the Bank of England in 1694 contributed £1.2 million of capital in exchange for a payment of £100,000 in perpetuity.

But the use of undated debt, i.e. debt having no final maturity, in private finance is much more recent. The first true perpetual was introduced by National Westminster Bank with a $300 million FRN issue in April 1984. The notes are not redeemable by the noteholders, but bear an attractive ⅜ per cent margin over LIBOR. The notes are junior subordinated debt, rated after outstanding debt but before common or preferred stock. Because of Bank of England requirements, subsequent issues of perpetuals by UK clearing banks had to be convertible into equity under certain circumstances in order to qualify for primary capital. But they represented an attractive method of raising primary capital without diluting the banks' equity base, and so all the major UK banks made one or more issues of perpetual FRNs.

However, in late 1986 the appearance of some richly-priced collateralised FRNs (see below) yielding LIBOR + 50 basis points or more led investors to question why they were holding perpetuals at LIBOR + ⅛ per cent. The resulting panic saw several clearing bank FRNs drop below 85, an enormous fall for an FRN. There was of course no question regarding the quality of the issuers, but trading in the whole perpetual market effectively closed down for a period.

During 1988 the market recovered gradually, and this emboldened investment banks to reintroduce the concept in a slightly different guise, the variable rate note. The VRN borrowed a feature from the US domestic preferred share market of the remarketed reset note. Under this system the interest rate on the security is reset from time to time; if the investor does not like the new pricing the investment bank will remarket it. This was the method adopted for the November 1988 issue by National Westminster Bank of $350 million: the investor can put the security back to Merrill Lynch if the new spread is not acceptable. If National Westminster and Merrill cannot agree what the new spread should be, the spread is automatically fixed at 70 basis points over LIBOR. The major flaw in the VRN concept is at this point, because when this happens – which is likely to be when the issuer is in trouble – the investor's right to put the security is suspended. That is, when the going gets rough, the exit is locked.

In the fixed-rate market, the first undated bond issue by a non-government non-bank entity was in January 1985 for KLM, the Dutch airline (majority owned by the Dutch government). The issue, in Switzerland, was for Swfr200 million ($75 million equivalent). It was subordinated, repriced every ten years, and redeemable at KLM's option at any repricing date. The coupon is readjusted after every ten years on the basis of the arithmetical mean of Swiss Bank Corporation's index of the overall yield to maturity of foreign bonds on the Swiss Stock Exchange, and the new issue foreign bond index (excluding States and Provinces) of Pictet & Cie, plus a margin of ⅛ per cent, rounded if necessary to the nearest ⅛ per cent. The rate for the first ten years was 6 per cent representing a premium of perhaps ¾ per cent over the rate KLM might have paid for ten-year subordinated debt. The issue was oversubscribed and quickly traded up to a price of 102, largely because of KLM's excellent reputation in the Swiss market.

7 Derivatives: Futures, Options and Swaps

This chapter considers three other key markets for the global investor: those for financial futures, options, and interest rate and currency swaps. They are becoming of increasing importance for the investor. October 1987 vividly demonstrated the impact of stock index futures; options are important investment tools, and swaps play a key role in the structuring and pricing of new bond issues, as well as having investment applications in their own right. The discussion in this chapter is necessarily short; a fuller treatment may be found in the author's book *New Financial Instruments* (John Wiley, New York, 1988).

THE GLOBAL FUTURES MARKET

In brief, futures contracts are standardised agreements to buy or sell a specific commodity at a specific time and place in the future, at a price established through open outcry in a central, regulated market-place. The two key components of the futures contract are that the agreement is standardised and the price is the only variable.

Let us take a simple example. I want to invest $100,000 in a US Treasury bond for delivery in June. I can wait until June – taking the risk that the price might move against me – or I can buy a futures contract. I go to the futures market and see that the price for 15 June delivery is 92; if I were to settle today, I would have to pay $92,000. I buy one contract. I do not pay for the bonds today. Instead, I put up a margin deposit.

The amount of this margin is fixed by the exchange at $4,500 per contract. So I put up $4,500 on deposit with my futures broker. The deposit is evidence of my good faith that I will fulfil my obligation to take delivery of the bonds in June. As bond prices vary, the value of my futures contract varies. I have a profit or loss on my purchase. If losses erode the value of my margin, my broker will call on me to put up extra margin. Conversely, if I earn profits, I will get back some margin. The aim is to keep the margin stable in line with the value of my obligation.

When the contract comes to settlement, suppose I decide to take delivery of the bonds. A settlement price for the bonds is fixed. Say that price is 105. Then I must pay $105,000 for my bonds; but on that settlement day, my futures contract is also worth $105,000. So I have a $13,000 profit on the futures contract which offsets the rise in price of the bonds. The futures contract has served to fix my bond purchase price.

Table 7.1 Top 10 contracts traded (000s) 1988

CBOT		*CME*	
Treasury bond futures	70,307	Eurodollar futures	21,705
Treasury bond options	19,509	S&P 500 futures	11,353
Soyabean futures	12,497	Yen futures	6,433
Corn futures	11,105	DMark futures	5,662
Soyabean meal futures	5,313	Live cattle futures	5,477
Ten-year Treasury note futures	5,200	Swiss franc futures	5,283
Soyabean oil futures	4,896	Yen options	2,944
Wheat futures	3,377	DMark options	2,734
Soyabean options	3,245	Sterling futures	2,616
Corn options	1,591	Eurodollar options	2,599

Source: Financial Times, 10 April 1989.

The market began in 1972, when the International Monetary Market (part of the Chicago Mercantile Exchange) opened futures trading in seven foreign currencies. The first interest rate futures contract was introduced in October 1975. But the first really successful interest rates futures contract was the 91-day Treasury Bill Contract introduced by the IMM in January 1976, followed in August 1977 by the Chicago Board of Trade (CBOT) futures contracts on US Treasury bonds. As Table 7.1 shows, the CBOT is less dependent than the CME on financial futures.

In September 1982, the London International Financial Futures Exchange (LIFFE) opened for business. It started with two contracts, for Eurodollars and the pound sterling. But by early December the initial complement of seven contracts had all been introduced: short sterling interest rates; long gilt-edged government securities; Swiss franc, Japanese yen and Deutschmark futures. More recently LIFFE has introduced a successful futures contract based on German government bonds (Bunds), following this up in April 1989 with a future based on DM LIBOR and an option on the Bund future. By June 1989 DM-denominated contracts accounted for 21 per cent of LIFFE's volume, with almost 490,000 contracts changing hands during the month. Indeed, in the first half of 1989, over 40 per cent of LIFFE's volume was non-sterling based, emphasising the international nature of the London futures market. In July 1989 LIFFE underwent a reorganisation whereby a holding company – LIFFE (Holdings) PLC – was set up to take on functions which are not part of LIFFE's statutory activity as a recognised exchange. Seats on the Exchange were traded for shares in the new holding company, to which are attached trading permits in the exchange.

The Tokyo futures market is much more recently established – October 1985. But in an astonishing explosion of trading, volume in the Japanese

Table 7.2 LIFFE trading volumes

	Futures	*Options*
1982	240,150	–
1983	1,365,630	–
1984	2,581,579	–
1985	3,372,915	169,950
1986	6,426,718	479,789
1987	12,426,718	1,174,031

Source: LIFFE.

government bond futures contract on the Tokyo futures exchange after only ten months exceeded that in the US Treasury bond contract. Daily trading in the Japanese contract reached an average of $32.8 billion in August 1986, compared with $19.7 billion in US bond contracts. In September 1988, the Tokyo Stock Exchange introduced futures based on its TOPIX equity index, and its Osaka counterpart introduced a contract on the Nikkei 225 equity index. In June 1989, the Tokyo International Financial Futures Exchange (TIFFE) opened for business, trading Euroyen and Eurodollar deposit contracts as well as a yen/dollar contract. There were one or two hiccups, with just 16 of 130 foreign banks and securities companies in Tokyo applying for initial membership, disappointing the Ministry of Finance (MoF) who had hoped for sixty to eighty foreign members. This seems to have been mainly due to cost considerations and also the rather rushed implementation schedule, and it seems likely that TIFFE (if the Tokyo Stock Exchange government bond and stock index futures are anything to go by) will be a very important futures centre.

The next important financial futures exchange to open after LIFFE was in France, where in February 1986 the Marché à terme des instruments financiers (MATIF) was opened. Initially an average of 350, perhaps 400 contracts per day was expected for its inaugural contract, a ten-year government long bond. But within the first week, the daily trading average was 3,400 contracts. The MATIF has gone on to establish itself as a serious challenger to LIFFE as a centre for derivatives trading in Europe, though it has suffered the odd problem, such as the Frfr250 million lost by the state-owned nuclear fuels company, Cogema, on the MATIF and in related options trading. A contract on French Treasury bills was introduced in 1986, which developed poorly, owing to the lack of liquidity in the secondary cash market, but in September 1988 the MATIF successfully introduced a contract on PIBOR (Paris Inter-Bank Offered Rate) and in the spring of 1989 a Deutschmark deposit contract to compete with LIFFE.

Other important financial futures exchanges operate in Toronto, Montreal, Singapore, Hong Kong and Sydney. A futures and options exchange in Denmark opened in September 1988. Work has been proceeding on a German futures exchange (DTB – Deutsche Termin Borse). This will trade futures on the DAX equity index (see Chapter 16) and options on fourteen equities, although it has been delayed by the need to reform the country's restrictive legal framework and by the conservatism of the German market. The DTB also plans to launch a Bund future to rival that on LIFFE.

Global expansion of the futures and options markets continues apace. A key issue is the battle between the new technology and traditional 'open outcry' (whereby prices are set by an auction in a 'pit' where traders shout bids and offers). The former is represented by Globex, a joint venture between Reuters and the Chicago Mercantile Exchange. This will allow traders to deal in CME contracts around the world while the CME is closed. The latter has until recently been insisted on by the CBOT, which went the route of setting up an evening session from 6 to 9 p.m. This session, by the spring of 1989, was trading 200,000 contracts a month, mostly in Treasury bonds with Japanese counterparties. Now, however, the CBOT has announced plans for its own computer-driven system, Aurora. Attempts are being made to combine the two. Globex seems to have succeeded in attracting substantial backing: the French financial futures exchange, MATIF, has linked up with it along with the New York Mercantile Exchange and the Sydney Futures Exchange.

LIFFE is in the process of developing a third alternative to Globex and Aurora: its Automated Pit Trading System (APT), which aims to emulate the features of 'open outcry' pit trading, for use outside the Exchange's normal working hours. LIFFE, the CBOT and the CME are exploring links between the three electronic systems. An alternative approach has been adopted by the Chicago Mercantile Exchange in setting up a mutual offset link with the Singapore Monetary Exchange (SIMEX) for three-month Eurodollar and US Treasury bond futures. This allows contracts opened on one exchange to be closed on the other. The link has helped SIMEX overtake LIFFE for Eurodollar trading, with 1.18 million contracts traded in Singapore during the first eight months of 1988 against 1.14 million on LIFFE.

Another interesting development is presented by Optionsmaklarna, the Swedish options exchange. It is the first exchange to go international: OM has set up operations in Helsinki and Paris as well as Stockholm and awaits legislative approval for an operation in Oslo.

EQUITY INDEX FUTURES AND THE INVESTOR

At its most sensational, the importance of futures markets to investors can be highlighted by a few quotations from the Brady report on the crash of October 1987:

the selling pressure in futures led to discounts of historic size... Enormous discounts of futures relative to stocks were free to develop as the futures market plummeted, disconnected from the stock market. The rest of Monday afternoon was disastrous. Heavy futures selling continued ...

All told, Monday, October 19 was perhaps the worst day in the history of US equity markets. By the close of trading, the Dow index had fallen 508 points, almost 23%, on volume of 604 million shares worth just under $21 billion. Even worse, the S&P 500 futures contract had fallen 29% on total volume of 162,000 contracts, valued at almost $20 billion.

(Report of the Presidential Task Force on Market Mechanisms, January 1988, pp. 34–6.)

The Brady report included a schematic of what happened on that day (see Figure 7.1). Since that day a number of steps have been taken which, it is hoped, will cut the risk of a repetition of Black Monday. They range from alterations in margin requirements to the imposition of 'circuit-breakers' – for example, the Chicago Mercantile Exchange agreed with the New York Stock Exchange to halt trading in S&P 500 futures if the contract moves more than 12 points (equivalent to a 100-point move in the Dow Jones Industrial Average) in a falling market.

Equity index futures were criticised in the aftermath of the October 1987 Crash, on the grounds that they triggered the crisis. My own view is that this was not the case. The crisis was caused by more basic problems. The

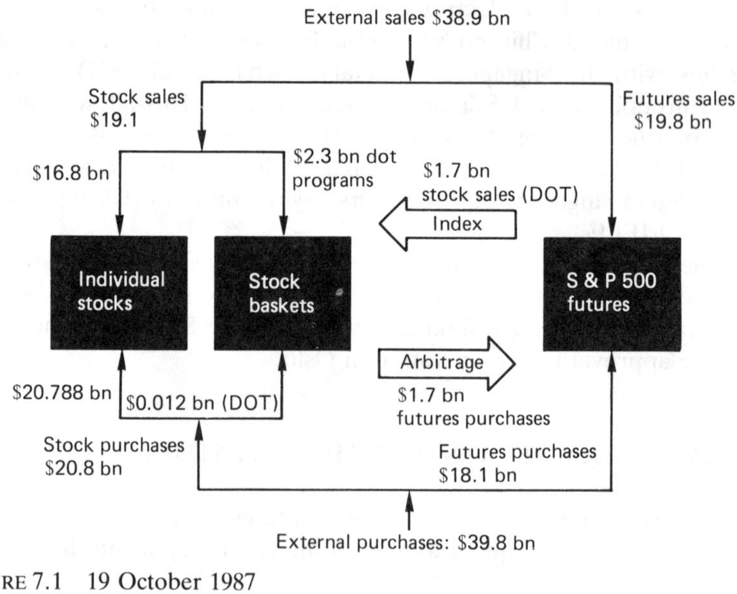

FIGURE 7.1 19 October 1987

futures markets were simply a more visible signal. But there is no doubt that the futures markets are volatile and have made equity markets more so.

An interesting study by the Federal Reserve Bank of New York[1] argued that:

> The futures markets are geared to facilitate and even favor rapid trading over more orderly trading. Equity markets emphasize smooth price movements by requiring the specialist to make a market in the security for which he is responsible. Linking these two markets via arbitrage forces the slower moving equity markets to acquire the rapid price fluctuations characteristic of the futures markets which are *designed* to handle them.

The study points out a second consequence of the existence of futures markets: since investors can hold equities through the futures markets, and since at expiry of the futures contract there is no delivery of the underlying shares, then:

> The total dollar value of a corporation's 'securities' (broadly defined to include the relevant stock equivalent of index futures contracts as well as stocks) is far larger than the actual market capitalization of that corporation . . . In other words, stockholder value will be affected by traders who may not have any interest in enhancing the fundamental economic value of the stock.[2]

Despite these problems, equity index futures will not disappear. They play a valuable role. For example, an important use for the equity index futures contract is in the construction of a 'passive' index fund. A portfolio consisting of Treasury bills and a long position in stock index futures will in theory produce the same return as that of a portfolio of common stock constructed to reproduce the underlying index. In addition, it will generally be much cheaper simply to buy the index futures contract than to buy the numerous individual shares, in the correct proportions, needed to replicate the underlying index. The transaction costs of the futures index approach will be much lower.

In the international arena, with all its settlement complexities, and the high commissions charged in certain markets, this aspect of equity index futures is even more attractive. The author recently had occasion to arrange the switch of an actively managed equity portfolio into a global index portfolio. The move required well over 1,000 stock transactions. From the date of the initial trade to the final settlement of the last equity bargain (in Italy) was a period of just over two months. Also, the exercise was not cheap.

It is expensive and laborious to trade into and out of national stock markets, in comparison with futures markets. The ability to switch country allocations on a 'top-down' basis by going into and out of equity index futures will probably, in the long run, become a very important part of global investing.

However, the futures alternative is not yet there. These are only fledgling markets: many countries do not yet have a futures contract on the local equity index. If adequate contracts can be set up, the lot of the global passive portfolio manager will be hugely simplified.

EQUITY INDEX FUTURES MARKETS

The first equity index futures contract was introduced in the United States by the Kansas City Board of Trade. It introduced an equity index futures contract based on the Value Line Average in February 1982. In April, the Chicago Mercantile Exchange began trading futures contracts based on the S&P 500 equity index. In May 1982 the New York Futures Exchange started trading futures contracts based on the New York Stock Exchange Composite Index.

The markets grew fast. During June 1983, futures trading in these three equity index futures contracts, expressed on a share equivalent basis, surpassed the volume of trading on the New York Stock Exchange by more than 11 per cent. On a typical day during the month, 58,432 contracts were traded, averaging around 103.1 million shares. This compared with a daily average volume on the NYSE of 93.3 million shares. Ever since March 1983, equity index futures trading has exceeded NYSE volume on a fairly regular basis.

The mechanics of these equity index contracts are as follows. Each of the contracts is an agreement to pay or receive $500 times the difference between the initial futures price and (a) the offsetting futures price, (b) the daily futures settlement price, or (c) the final settlement price of the underlying index on the day the contract expires. Positive differences are paid by sellers and received by buyers.

For our purposes the most important US futures contract is probably the S&P 500, since this has emerged as the dominant one in terms of trading volume. The Chicago Mercantile Exchange S&P 500 equity index futures contract is based on the S&P 500 composite index, which is made up of 400 industrial and 40 public utilities, and 20 transportation and 40 financial companies. Stocks in the index are weighted according to their aggregate market value. The value of a contract is $500 times the quoted futures price – at a price of 200, that would be $100,000.

The pricing of equity index futures contracts reflects, in its fundamentals, the pricing of other futures contracts. In theory, if the actual futures price is lower than the theoretical price implied by the cost of buying, and financing, an equivalent portfolio to the period concerned, then investors should sell their portfolios and replace them with a combination of Treasury bills and futures contracts.

In fact, of course, the situation is more complex. Because of the large number of securities involved, it is difficult to go long or short of an exact duplicate of the index. Also, changes in the index to reflect stock splits, stock dividends and the like comprise further complications in the matching process. In addition, there is the unknown degree of risk implied by the element of variation margin.

EQUITY FUTURES MARKETS OUTSIDE THE USA

In the UK, a contract on the Financial Times Stock Exchange index (FTSE or 'Footsie') was set up in 1984, and has successfully traded since, though not in huge volume, as tax considerations and investor conservatism slowed its growth. On an average day in early 1989 the FTSE traded 3,500 contracts worth £175 million. The chart in Figure 7.2 shows contracts traded in Japan together with the FTSE against volume on the S&P 500 (note that the FTSE volume is much smaller, being measured on the right-hand scale).

In Japan, equity futures trading was introduced by the Osaka Stock Exchange; in September 1988 came contracts on the Osaka exchange on the Nikkei 225 (supplementing a NK225 which had been traded, not outstandingly successfully, on the Singapore futures exchange, SIMEX)

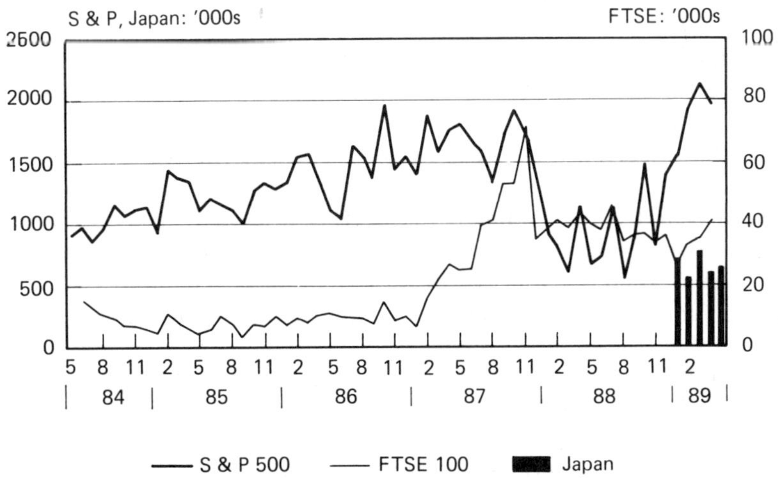

FIGURE 7.2 Equity futures contracts: monthly trading volume
SOURCE: Nikkei & Topix

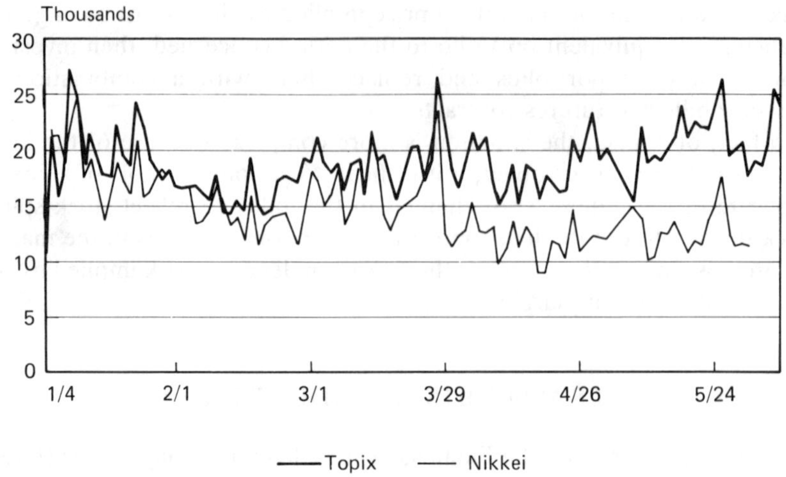

FIGURE 7.3 Japanese equity futures, daily volume, 1989

and on the Tokyo Stock Exchange on its First Section (TOPIX). Average daily volume during the first three months on the Nikkei 225 was 13,000 contracts, or $3.2 billion equivalent, while TOPIX volume averaged 12,000 contracts or $2.3 billion. In the first quarter of 1990 the Tokyo futures market became an important factor in the decline of the Japanese stock market.

FUTURES AND THE FIXED INCOME MARKETS

Financial futures began in the fixed income arena, and the futures markets here are far better established than in equities. The futures markets are critical to a number of bond markets. For example, the sterling bond market is often led these days by the gilt-edged futures contract, rather than the cash gilt market. This is because the cash market is tending to dry up relative to trading volume in futures (because the British government is paying down its debt, unlike the USA for example). Thus, those trading the market keep a close eye on how the gilt-edged futures contract is trading (and also the shorter, three-months sterling deposit futures contract).

Secondly, the futures contracts are important to investors hedging their positions in the bond markets. It often happens that an underwriter bringing, for example, a DMark Eurobond to the market will be nervous about the course of German interest rates, and so will hedge his risk in the Bund futures market. Interest risk hedging is a very important application for fixed income futures.

Table 7.3 Major fixed-income futures contracts (December 1988)

	Open interest[1]	*Trading volume*[2]
Treasury bills	27,204	6,323
Eurodollars	577,568	123,254
Treasury notes	78,925	30,860
Treasury bonds	439,595	338,302
Japanese government bonds	134,995	77,931
French government bonds	113,576	41,889
UK government bonds	34,551	21,343

Figures for each contract include all traded months. Treasury bills and Eurodollars: IMM. Treasury notes and bonds: CBOT.
1. 20-day average open interest.
2. 20-day average trading volume.

Source: Salomon Brothers, *Monthly Review of Futures and Options*, December 1988.

USE OF THE MARKET FOR HEDGING

Consider an institutional investor in US Treasury bonds (see Figure 7.4). On 1 April 1989 the investor expects in three months to receive US$1 million. She plans to invest in Treasury bonds. The investor suspects that rates are at or near their peak. She wants to lock in today's yield in case it falls before she receives the funds.

The first step is to buy ten futures contracts for September delivery. (This is the date nearest after her proposed investment date futures contracts are available for delivery in March, June, September and December.) Each contract for US Treasury bonds has a face value of US$100,000. So if she buys ten contracts, the total equals what she plans to invest in July. She buys them at the current price of 91.9375.

By 2 July, suppose that interest rates have dropped as expected. Accordingly, the price of bonds has risen. She sells the ten futures contracts at the new price of 107.125. This gives a profit of $15,187 per contract. Her total profit is $151,875.

She has now received her US$1 million. She invests it in Treasury bonds. The price of the cash Treasury bonds, as distinct from futures, has risen from 93.09375 to 107.625. Suppose she had been able to invest in April. She would have made a profit of $145,312. This is, in effect, an opportunity lost for the portfolio. But it is offset by a gain in the futures market of $151,875. (The two are not exactly equal because the hedge was not perfect: cash prices and futures prices moved slightly differently. This is called a change in the basis – basis being the difference between cash and futures prices.)

In fact, while the investor pays $1,076,250 for bonds with a face value of

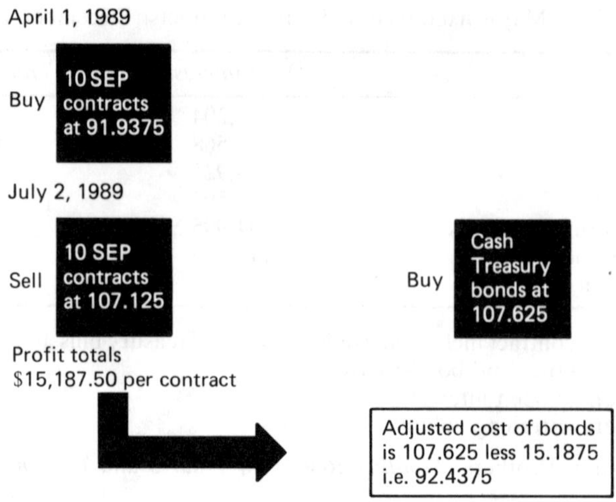

FIGURE 7.4 Hedging with futures

$1 million, the net cost is only $924,375 after we allow for the futures profit of $151,875. In effect, by dealing in April in the futures market, the investor has protected the July investment, and established, in advance, a yield higher than that available at the time the funds arrived.

SYNTHETIC BONDS FROM FUTURES

A more recent application of the futures markets is the creation of synthetic bonds. This is of particular interest to holders of overseas government bonds, such as the Japanese government bond, where investors are liable to withholding tax. By creating a synthetic bond through the futures market it is possible to circumvent withholding tax. A second reason to do this would be if the futures were cheap compared with cash.

An example is the Bund futures on LIFFE. At the end of September 1988 the London International Financial Futures Exchange (LIFFE) began trading futures contracts based on the German government bond (Bundesanleihe or Bund) market. Because it is not possible to sell Bunds short in the cash market, the contract was very attractive to firms wishing to hedge their cash Bund positions by selling futures. Within three months the contract was averaging ten to twelve thousand trades daily, competitive with the long-established gilt futures contract.

The Bund contract is based on a deliverable ten-year notional bond with a 6 per cent coupon. The contract size is DM250,000 nominal with maturities in March, June, September and December. There is only one delivery date for each contract, i.e. the tenth day of the delivery month (or if a holiday, the next Frankfurt working day) – in contrast to the US delivery procedure where bonds can be delivered at any time during the contract month.

Because the Bund is used by hedgers selling against their long positions in the bond market, the futures have tended to be oversold – they 'traded cheap to cash'. A synthetic Bund position can be created by investing in a money-market security and buying Bund futures. The futures position can be weighted so that the modified duration of the synthetic position matches that of a benchmark, such as a cash Bund or Treasury note. Suppose the investor is US dollar-based and wants a hedged synthetic Bund, and it is February 1989. He might invest $25.252 million in a four-month Eurodollar deposit yielding 9.375 per cent, and buy 206 June 1989 Bund futures contracts. This particular weighting results in a synthetic Bund with a modified duration equal to the 6 per cent Bund due 20 January 1999. Where the futures are oversold, such a position creates an attractive return compared with the cash Bund.

A further attraction to the offshore investor is that there is no withholding tax payable. The German government retreated from its attempt to impose withholding tax, but might change its mind again. Similarly, in the case of Japanese government bonds, where withholding tax is charged, synthetic Japanese government bonds created from the futures market can be attractive.

THE OPTIONS MARKET

Options applications for the global investor are chiefly an extension into other markets of the techniques applicable in sophisticated domestic markets such as the USA or UK. (These are discussed in more depth in the author's book *New Financial Instruments* and in, for example, L. G. McMillan, *Options as a Strategic Investment*, 2nd edn, New York Institute of Finance, 1986.) The major extension internationally is currency options, discussed separately in Chapter 8.

Exchange-traded options were introduced in 1973 by the Chicago Board Options Exchange (CBOE). The single most important CBOE innovation was to set up standard option prices and expiry dates. This allowed development of the secondary market which brought liquidity into options trading. As a measure of the success of the CBOE, by 1984 it was the second largest securities market in the world, in terms of the dollar value of underlying securities traded. By 1989 it was trading options on 178 listed and OTC stocks, Treasury bonds and notes, as well as the S&P 100 and S&P 500 indices. The effects of the Crash of 1987 hit the CBOE hard, and volume dropped to 400,000 contracts a day before picking up to 550,000 contracts in early 1989.

In 1978 the CBOE's example was followed by the European Options Exchange in Amsterdam; the EOE now offers options on a range of stocks, including five-year options on Akzo, Royal Dutch Shell and Unilever. In the UK options are traded both on LIFFE and the London Traded Options Market (LTOM), an offshoot of the Stock Exchange, set up in 1978. Options are available on about sixty companies, together with options on gilt-edged bonds and various currencies. In September 1988 the LTOM set a post-Crash record with almost 62,000 contracts trading in one day, almost 75 per cent of underlying equity turnover. In Canada, options are available on about forty stocks as well as on the Toronto 35 index and Canadian government bonds. Australia has options on bank bill futures, All Ordinary Share Index futures, and on a range of equities.

An options exchange in France, called the Monep, was launched at the end of 1987, and got off to a good start despite the inauspicious timing: by June 1988 trading had hit 26,000 contracts daily, though the more normal average is around 10–15,000. By early 1989 Monep was trading an option on the French CAC 40 index, as well as 11 individual stocks. In May 1988 the conservative Swiss opened the Swiss Options and Financial Futures Exchange (SOFFEX) and during its first trading year a daily average of 10,000 contracts was achieved in the 11 equity options (futures are not yet in place). However, liquidity remains a problem and more recently volumes have fallen back. There is an active exchange in Sweden (Optionsmaklarna) and in November 1989 an options market opened in Norway.

There is also an international over-the-counter market provided by a range of commercial and investment banks who will write options contracts on currencies, interest rates, stock indexes and certain futures contracts.

Options have many investment applications. They can be used for their leverage (see the section on warrants in Chapter 4) or for hedging uncertain risks. Investors can earn income from writing options. They do, however, complicate performance measurement (see Appendix 6).

OPTIONS CONTRACTS

An option is an agreement between two parties. One party sells the other the right to buy or sell an instrument under certain conditions. The instrument may be an equity, bond, futures contract, interest rate or foreign currency. The counter-party pays a premium for the privilege of buying or selling the instrument at a pre-fixed price, without committing to do so.

There are two basic types of options: puts and calls. A call option gives the buyer the right to buy or 'call away' a specified amount of the underlying instrument at the specified price during a specified period. A put gives the right to sell. The price at which the instrument may be bought is the 'exercise price' or the 'strike price'. The last date on which the option may be exercised is called the expiration date or the maturity date. The price paid for the option contract is called the premium.

A call option on the CBOE is best described by a simple example. An XYZ July 50 call is an option to buy shares on the underlying equity for $50 per share. The option expires in July. Market convention is that the option price is quoted per share, regardless of how many shares of stock can be bought with the option. The number of shares is normally 100. Thus, if the price of the XYZ July 50 call is quoted at $5, buying the option would ordinarily cost $500 ($5 × 100 shares) plus commissions.

The price of an option is determined by six factors:

(a) the price of the underlying instrument;
(b) the striking price of the option;
(c) the time remaining to expiry of the option;
(d) the volatility of the underlying instrument;
(e) the current, risk-free interest rate;
(f) the dividend rate or the interest rate on the underlying security.

At any given time, the only one of these variables which is not known is the volatility of the underlying instrument.

No-one can tell in advance what the volatility of the instrument will be during the life of the option. So traders have to make estimates based on past volatility and their judgement for the future. Hence, option pricing remains an art, not a science. Sophisticated formulas have been developed (the Black-Scholes model, the Cox-Ross-Rubinstein model, the Garman-Kohlhagen model and others). But the fact remains that these models simply produce theoretical calculations of the fair value of the options. At the end of the day, the value of the option is what the market-place will bid for it.

An important measure of the sensitivity of an option to the underlying asset is call delta. Delta is defined as the ratio of a change in the option premium to a change in the value of the underlying asset. Suppose we have a call option on IBM with a strike price of $120. IBM stock is trading at $130 and the option premium is $11.50. (Of that, $10 is the difference between the exercise price of $120 and the stock price of $130, and is called *intrinsic value*. The remaining $1.50 is called *time value*.) Now suppose IBM goes to $131 and the option goes to $12.25. A $1 rise in the stock has produced a $0.75 rise in the value of the option. Delta is $0.75/$1 = 0.75. Another way of looking at delta is to think of it as the probability that the option will be exercised. (See the author's *New Financial Instruments* for more discussion on delta, and its associated measures of gamma, kappa and theta. See also Appendix 6 of this book for a discussion of the special problems that options raise in performance measurement.)

CALL AND PUT OPTIONS ON BONDS

A call option on a bond is the right to buy a bond at a specified price; such an option is often embedded in a corporate bond. The terms of the issue often give the issuer the right to call the bond for redemption before maturity. That is, if rates are in the issuer's favour, he can exercise his right to the call option.

A callable bond can be thought of as a combination of a long position in a non-callable bond and a short position in a call option which the investor has written to the issuer. Analysing a callable bond, therefore, boils down to analysing the value of the call option.

The converse situation is a bond incorporating a put: the investor is able to sell the bond back to the issuer at a time and price specified in advance. A common structure might be a ten-year bond, puttable after five years. The existence of a put means the investor can treat the bond as if it were a five-year bond, while the issuer hopes that he has raised ten-year money.

Obviously, from the issuer's point of view, there is a risk that this will prove not to be the case. A particular complication occurred in the UK in 1987, when a number of convertible issues were made, perhaps with fifteen-year maturities, but with a put after five years. The issuers expected that during the fifteen-year life of the bond, its equities would rise to the point where investors would wish to convert into equity, rather than hold bonds to maturity.

However, the sudden arrival in October 1987 of the Crash meant that the equity prices at which conversion was to take place suddenly became extremely distant from current levels. In a number of cases, the auditors of the issuing firms insisted that provision must be made for the extra interest cost that would accrue on the bonds, given that it was unlikely that equity prices would rise to the conversion level within the five-year life of the bond. This meant that the financing was suddenly much less attractive.

THE SWAP MARKET

The international bond markets, and indeed major domestic bond markets, are closely linked with the international market for interest rate and currency swaps. While currency swaps developed gradually during the 1960s and 1970s, the currency swap market was not particularly closely linked to the bond market at this stage. The technique was used mostly by companies wanting to hedge longer-term foreign exchange exposures associated with the structure of their balance sheets or particular project financings.

The emergence of the interest rate swap, in 1980–1, together with the decision by the World Bank to embark on an ambitious currency swap programme, transformed the situation. Earlier issuers of new Eurobonds were relatively tied down. If they issued a Deutschmark bond, the extent to which they would hedge the long-term exchange risk of the bond was rather limited.

The growth of the currency swap market meant that for the first time, issuers would tap the currency market where they could raise the cheapest funds. They could then use the swap market to hedge their long-term exchange risk. Equally, the growth of the interest rate swap market meant a similar liberation in the choice between fixed and floating rate bonds.

It may be helpful to start with a brief outline of how a currency swap works. Suppose that ICI needs US dollars for its operations in the USA, and Du Pont needs sterling for its UK operations. A solution to their need is for ICI to sell its sterling to Du Pont for dollars. To cut out the risk of exchange rate movements, they contract to reverse the deal in, say, five years' time. Say ICI sells £10 million to Du Pont in exchange for $18 million. (Figure 7.5.)

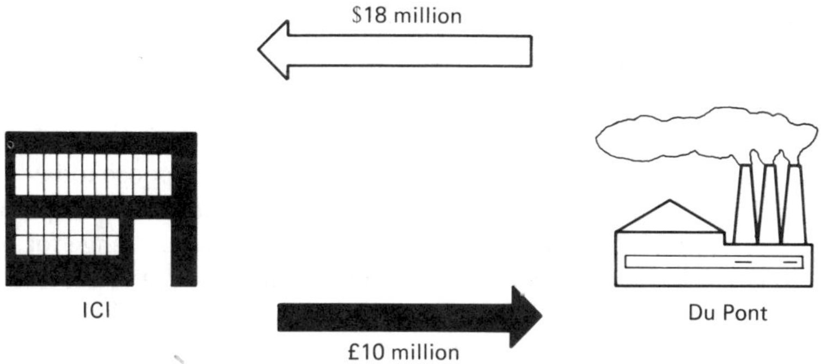

FIGURE 7.5 ICI sells £10 million for Du Pont's $18 million

Effectively, ICI is lending sterling to Du Pont, who are lending dollars to ICI. So during the life of the deal, ICI pay the rate for five-year dollar loans – say 10 per cent – and Du Pont pay the rate for five-year sterling loans – say 12 per cent. At the end of the deal, ICI and Du Pont re-exchange. (Figure 7.6.)

The cash flows are set out in Table 7.4 from ICI's point of view, assuming that ICI borrowed the £10 million to lend to du Pont, also at 12 per cent. At the start of the deal there is an inflow of £10 million from the original funding. This is paid across to du Pont at the start of the swap. In exchange, there is an inflow of $18 million from Du Pont. The net effect is an inflow of $18 million.

For each of the next five years, ICI pays its lending bankers £1.2 million in interest on the original funding, and receives a corresponding payment from Du Pont of £1.2 million, while paying out $1.8 million to Du Pont.

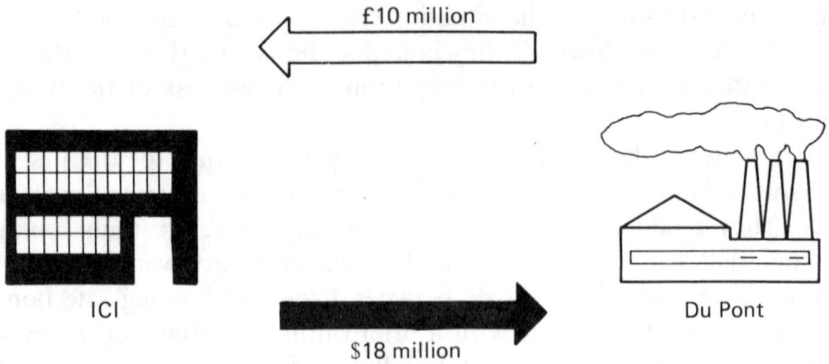

FIGURE 7.6 Unwinding the swap at maturity

(Normally these payments are netted off.) The last payment includes redemption of the principal amounts. The net result is that a sterling stream of cashflows is transformed into a dollar stream.

So now, let us look at an issuer who wants to raise five-year money in US dollars. Suppose his advisers tell him that the cheapest course would be to raise five-year Deutschmarks, and swap them into US dollars. How will this work?

Suppose the rate (ignoring fees) for five-year DM Eurobonds is 7 per cent and the bond is issued at par for DM200 million. Suppose today's spot US$/DM rate is $1 = DM2.00. Suppose that an American corporation wants five-year DM financing at a rate of 8 per cent, in exchange for being paid 10 per cent on the US dollar equivalent financing it will provide. We assume that the deal can be structured so that all interim flows, and the principal being re-exchanged at maturity, can be exchanged at a rate of $1 = DM2.00.

Here the issuer's bond cost is 7 per cent but he earns 8 per cent on the swap, so there is a net additional 1 per cent saving, making a total US dollar cost of 9 per cent per annum. What has happened is that the issuer, perhaps because it is a better known credit in the Euromarket, is able to raise five-year money cheaper than its swap counterpart: in exchange for

Table 7.4

	Swap Cashflows		*Original Funding*	*Net*
	(US$ million)	*(£ million)*	*(£ million)*	*(US$ million)*
Day 1	18	(10)	10	18
Year 1	(1.8)	1.2	(1.2)	(1.8)
Year 2	(1.8)	1.2	(1.2)	(1.8)
Year 3	(1.8)	1.2	(1.2)	(1.8)
Year 4	(1.8)	1.2	(1.2)	(1.8)
Year 5	(19.8)	11.2	(11.2)	(19.8)

Table 7.5

	Swap Cashflows (*US$ million*)	(*DM million*)	*Original Funding* (*DM million*)	*Net* *US$ million*)
Day 1	100	(200)	200	100
Year 1	(10)	16	(14)	(9)
Year 2	(10)	16	(14)	(9)
Year 3	(10)	16	(14)	(9)
Year 4	(10)	16	(14)	(9)
Year 5	(110)	216	(214)	(109)

passing on the cheap Deutschmarks, it is able to borrow cheap dollars. A more detailed example, working through the famous World Bank/IBM swap of 1981, is included in Appendix 5.

INTEREST RATE SWAPS

The interest rate swap market has also had a powerful influence on bond market developments in recent years. An interest rate swap lets an institution manage its liabilities, whether they be fixed rate or floating rate. Many people find the concept confusing. In the investment context, it may help to think of a fixed–floating interest rate swap as issuing a fixed rate bond to refinance a floating rate note, or vice versa.

The only difference is that in the swap there is no actual borrowing or lending. (This is where the market differs from that for currency swaps, where the principal amounts of the swap are actually exchanged under normal circumstances, at least at maturity.) Another analogy is with the foreign exchange market: an interest rate swap is a forward contract to exchange interest payments. An example may help.

Suppose it is 1 December 1988; you are the corporate treasurer of XYZ Ltd. You have borrowed floating-rate money from a syndicate of banks, for five years at six-month US$ LIBOR + ½ per cent, in an amount of $10 million. Your corporation does not have the financial strength to access the public bond markets. So it is hard for you to raise five-year money at a fixed rate. However, you fear that interest rates will rise. You decide to enter into a swap with a bank to fix for five years the cost of your interest rate liabilities, which would otherwise rise as LIBOR rises.

Suppose the bank quotes you a fixed rate of 9.5 per cent, payable semi-annually on a 30/360 basis (see Appendix 1) against six-month LIBOR. Payment on both sides is in arrears. Then you are committed to the cash flows given in Table 7.6.

On the other side will be the floating-rate income. The bank pays you six-month LIBOR. Consider two possibilities: LIBOR rises by ¼ per cent

Table 7.6

1 Jun. 1989	$475,000
1 Dec.	$475,000
1 Jun. 1990	$475,000
1 Dec.	$475,000
1 Jun. 1991	$475,000
1 Dec.	$475,000
1 Jun. 1992	$475,000
1 Dec.	$475,000
1 Jun. 1993	$475,000
1 Dec	$475,000

every six months over the period from a starting level of 8 per cent, and LIBOR falls by ¼ per cent. Then we will have (assuming for simplicity the LIBOR is paid also on a 30/360 basis – normally it is on actual/360 for US dollar swaps) the figures in Table 7.7.

The payments by the bank to you will exactly match your LIBOR payments to your banking syndicate, except for the latter's margin. So the LIBOR payments always net to zero, and your cost is fixed at the 9 per cent swap rate plus the ½ per cent syndicate margin, for an all-in cost of 10 per cent.

The origins of the interest rate swap technique were in the Eurobond market where fixed-rate issuers wished to raise floating-rate money. A typical example in the early days would be a Japanese bank. Because most banks typically lend money on a floating-rate basis, Japanese banks were not in the habit of issuing fixed-rate Eurobonds. They did not need fixed-rate funds. Therefore, their paper was relatively scarce in the fixed-rate bond market, and commanded attractive premiums. Thus, they were able to issue cheaply and then to swap into floating-rate funds.

Table 7.7

		Case I LIBOR rises	*Case II LIBOR falls*
1 Jun. 1989	$475,000	$400,000	$400,000
1 Dec.	$475,000	$412,500	$387,500
1 Jun. 1990	$475,000	$425,000	$375,000
1 Dec.	$475,000	$437,500	$362,500
1 Jun. 1991	$475,000	$450,000	$350,000
1 Dec.	$475,000	$462,500	$337,500
1 Jun. 1992	$475,000	$475,000	$325,000
1 Dec.	$475,000	$487,500	$312,500
1 Jun. 1993	$475,000	$500,000	$300,000
1 Dec.	$475,000	$512,500	$287,500

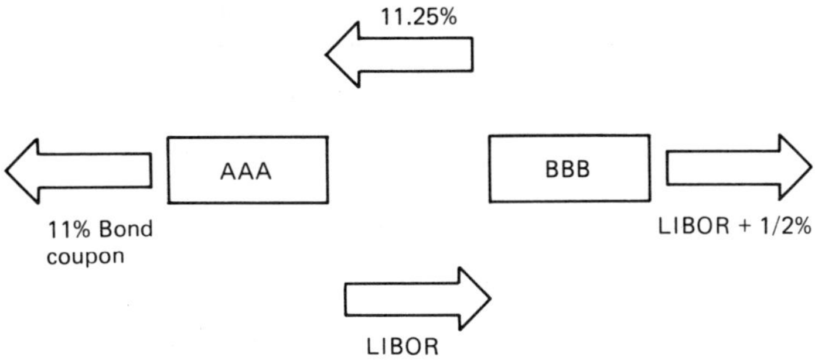

Net cost for AAA = 11 – 11.25 + LIBOR
= LIBOR – 0.25%
Net cost for BBB = 11.25 – LIBOR + LIBOR + 1/2%
= 11.75%
Saving for AAA = 3/8% Saving for BBB = 1/4%

FIGURE 7.7 Classical interest rate swap

An example would be as follows: a strong borrower, AAA, would pay LIBOR +⅛ per cent for a seven-year revolving credit from its banks, if it chose to arrange one. For a seven-year bond issue, it would pay 11 per cent. Conversely, a weaker borrower, BBB, must pay 12 per cent for a seven-year bond issue or LIBOR +½ per cent for seven-year money from his bank.

The difference between the two borrowers in the bank credit market is only ⅜ per cent; in the bond market it is 1 per cent – a 'credit differential' of ⅝ per cent. The first swaps used this differential to arbitrage. AAA issued a bond and entered into a swap with BBB. Both borrowers were able to save money; here, the ⅝ per cent is split into ⅜ per cent for AAA and ¼ per cent for BBB.

Once the swap technique had been invented, of course, people found many other ways of using it. The market has even been used by governments: the governments of France and Canada have both done swaps. In the longer run it is conceivable that the market may be used by central banks for yield curve management, just as in the past they have sometimes used forward exchange markets.

Interest rate swaps have been used to switch from floating-rate to fixed, from fixed to floating, from fixed-rate to zero coupon, from zero coupon to floating, from zero coupon to semi-annual fixed, and so on. Essentially, the combination of interest rate and currency swaps now means that any stream of cash flows can be transformed into virtually any other stream: annual AIBD basis Japanese yen payments can be transformed into quarterly US dollar, amortising lease type payments, if desired, at a price.

Table 7.8 Interest rate swap volume ($bn equivalent)

	1987		*1988*
	Jan.–Jun.	*Jul.–Dec.*	*Jan.–Jun.*
US$	139	148	156
Aus$	4	6	11
Can$	2	3	5
DM	10	12	20
ECU	1	1	3
Frfr	1	4	8
Sterling	9	11	22
Swfr	2	3	6
Yen	14	18	19
Total	182	206	250

Source: International Swap Dealers' Association (ISDA).

This immense flexibility has allowed issuers and their investment banking advisers to structure a huge range of new instruments (see Chapters 5 and 6). It has also led to rapid growth. Estimated volume in 1982 was around $1 billion, and when the author became involved in the market in 1983 it could take several days to find a counterparty for a fixed–floating swap in reasonable size. The market grew explosively to reach $300 billion by 1986; Table 7.8 shows subsequent growth.

The figures in Table 7.8 are by no means complete; they represent results of a survey of ninety members. Many banks and institutions active in the swap market are not ISDA members. Still on a statistical note, it is worth mention that, despite early worries about the credit risk implied in swaps, the same ISDA survey showed total write-offs of US$33 million on portfolios aggregating over $250 billion, a default rate of 0.01 per cent – considerably better than traditional banking default rates. (Although it should be said that a flurry in the London market was caused in February 1989 by a government veto on swap payments due from the London borough of Hammersmith and Fulham; partly for political reasons the municipality had used swaps and options to generate revenue from speculative transactions. As at the time of writing the matter is unresolved.)

For the investment manager, one interesting application of swaps is beginning to develop: swaps against an index. For example, in October 1988 it was reported that the pension fund for Ameritech undertook a $100 million swap under which it paid LIBOR less a spread, in exchange for receiving the total return on the Salomon Brothers Broad Investment Grade (BIG) bond index. This is an extremely attractive proposition form Ameritech's point of view. Suppose they invest in an asset yielding

LIBOR, e.g. an FRN. They enter into a swap paying LIBOR less a spread in return for the BIG total return. Their return looks like this:

FRN LIBOR + BIG total return − (LIBOR less spread) =
BIG total return + Spread

The swap guarantees them outperformance of their chosen index – in effect, it makes the profession of fixed interest management potentially obsolete.

ASSET SWAPS

The mechanics of a typical asset swap are as follows. In January 1987 an investing institution is offered US$5 million of Occidental Petroleum Corporation notes. They are senior unsecured obligations of Occidental, which at the time is rated BBB by Standard & Poors. Maturity of the notes is 15 March 1991 and they pay a coupon of 10 per cent semi-annually in arrears; the bond is a domestic US bond. They are redeemable on or after 15 March 1990 at the option of Occidental at 100 per cent of the principal amount plus accrued interest.

But the investor is a bank; it has no interest in a fixed-rate instrument, since this will expose it to interest rate mismatch. It funds at floating rates. Accordingly, the institution selling it the bond arranges an interest rate swap. The amount of the swap is US$5 million, the same notional principal as the amount of the notes purchased. It matures on 15 March 1991 to coincide with the notes' maturity date.

Under the swap, the investor effectively hands the coupon over to the seller. That is, it makes fixed payments semi-annually in arrears of 10 per cent of the principal amount on 15 March and 15 September to the selling institution. The fixed rate payments are calculated on a 30/360 day basis. The first fixed rate payment is for the full half year's coupon from 15 September 1986 to 15 March 1987 – i.e. US$250,000. (Because the bonds are sold to the investor flat, i.e. excluding accrued interest, the investor hands the accrued interest over to the selling institution.) In exchange for receiving the fixed-rate coupon, the seller makes floating-rate payments to the investor semi-annually in arrears at a rate of six-month dollar LIBOR plus 112.5 basis points (say) on the principal amount of $5 million. In the event that Occidental calls the bonds early, the seller grants the investor the right to terminate the swap early, without penalty.

So, from the investor's point of view, he has bought senior unsecured notes of Occidental, yielding LIBOR + 1⅛ per cent. The cash flows are as in Figure 7.8.

The transaction is not quite so straightforward from the point of view of

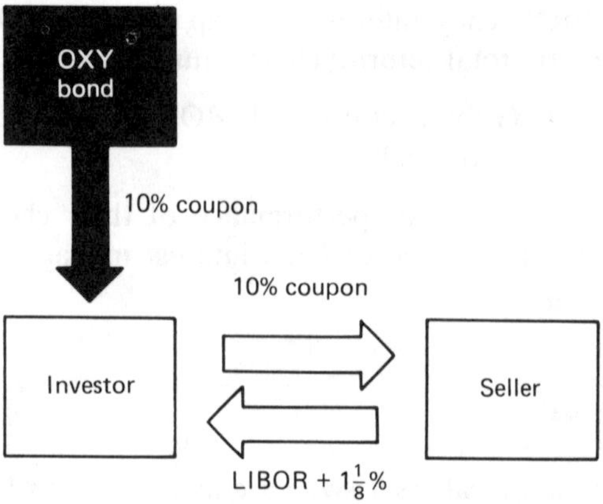

FIGURE 7.8

the seller. Two main issues arise: the handling of the premium or discount on the bond, and the swap termination. Given that market rates at the time of doing the deal were well below 10 per cent for the period to maturity on the bond, the bond itself traded at a premium. Thus the seller paid a premium for the bond, which it did not receive from the investor. This loss has to be funded, and factored into the price of the swap it gives to the investor. Also, the cost of funding the accrued interest has to be factored in. The second complication is the swap termination in the event that the bond is called early: the selling institution has effectively written an interest rate option to the buyer, which has to be properly priced (see Chapter 7 on options).

From early 1987 a stream of issues came to market consisting of swap-driven repackagings of earlier issues. An example was the series of issues called TOPS (Trust Obligation Participating Securities) – TOPS, TOPS2, TOPS3, etc. For example, TOPS2 consisted of $100 million of FRNs, collateralised by a portfolio of Japanese bank-guaranteed ex-warrant bonds (i.e. bonds originally issued with equity warrants, from which the warrants were stripped for separate sale). The underlying pool of 64 bonds were guaranteed by 18 different Japanese banks. This was the first synthetic FRN backed by a pool of issues rather than one. It has a sinking fund, reflecting the varying maturity of the underlying bonds. It was quickly followed by a large number of similar deals, until this type of repackaging became a standard part of Eurobond activity, particularly the repackaging of Japanese low-coupon ex-warrant bonds. The mechanics are set out in detail in Appendix 5.

Asset swaps of this type tend to work off mispriced bonds. Japanese equity warrant bonds often offered juicy terms on the warrants. Once the warrants were stripped from the bonds, they languished, to the point where they could be asset-swapped. One of the problems with this type of activity is that the bonds tend to disappear from the market, to be held in firm hands till maturity. This destroys all liquidity in the issue, so that any bonds that were not swapped but are left to be traded as deep-discount straights become extremely illiquid.

NOTES

1. S. Bhatt, *The Role of Stock Index Derivative Products in Equity Market Volatility*, Federal Reserve Bank of New York Research Paper No. 8709, December 1987.
2. S. Bhatt, *The Role of Stock Index Derivative Products in Equity Market Volatility*, Federal Reserve Bank of New York Research Paper No. 8709, December 1987, p. 4.

8 Foreign Exchange and the Global Investor

While the equity markets go back to the Muscovy Company of 1553 and the bond markets at least to the Grand Parti of Francis I in 1555, the foreign exchange markets go back to the mists of time: after all, in the New Testament, the money changers were chased out of the Temple. These markets are the oldest established and the most liquid of all. Estimates of daily trading volume in the markets vary, but according to the most recent joint survey by the Bank of England, the Federal Reserve and the Bank of Japan in the spring of 1989, the combined daily turnover of the three centres – London, New York and Tokyo – was almost $350 billion. By comparison, the 1988 average daily volume on the New York Stock Exchange was $6 billion and in Tokyo was $9 billion.

Foreign exchange markets are important to international investors in several ways. First, as a straight investment tool. One application is the use of international currency funds. The investor buys into, say, a yen fund, which is normally invested in short-term yen money market instruments; he has the ability to switch cheaply and quickly into parallel funds in other currencies as his currency view changes. Likewise, some funds have been launched as vehicles for active currency trading. Here, in a sense, the investor is buying into a currency trading operation. Depending on the skills of the traders, the fund will perform well or badly. Certain investing institutions have put funds into currency funds or currency trading funds on the basis that the risks in these funds are not well correlated with, for example, the US stock market, and so help diversification.

Second, and more important, any international investor, no matter where he or she invests, faces one basic risk: that of changes in exchange rates. The US investor who moved funds into, say, Germany in 1985 benefited over the next three years from a currency gain of around 100 per cent – $100 invested at DM3.46 could be sold back for $200 at DM1.73 three years later. Often, this is one of the main reasons for investing overseas – the hope of gaining from exchange rate movements. Clearly, in that case, the critical question is how best to manage the foreign exchange bet, if one is prepared to actively trade foreign exchange positions.

This is a large subject, the scope of which is outside this book. (See the author's *Foreign Exchange Handbook*, John Wiley, 1983, for a general discussion of the foreign exchange markets and exchange rate forecasting.) Clearly the investor needs to assess the relative trends in inflation, money supply growth (in so far as this is seen as a predictor of inflation), external financial surplus/deficit, domestic government deficits in relation to GDP, relative interest rates, and a host of other factors. The rewards of successfully predicting currency movements can swamp the pure investment returns from the underlying assets. Correspondingly, the penalty of error can wipe out a successful investment decision.

In other cases, the exchange risk is incidental to the primary investment purpose. Then the question is whether or not to hedge the risk away. Often this question is looked at differently by bond and by equity investors. For equity investors – who invest, at least in theory, for the long-run growth to be gained from equity exposure, and are often less used to assessing the macroeconomic ebbs and flows that drive exchange rates – the exchange rate factor has usually been secondary. But it can have a significant impact on performance. In either case, investors need to consider to what extent their currency exposures add (or reduce) the riskiness of their portfolio, and what, if any, actions should be taken to manage it.

FOREIGN EXCHANGE RISK MANAGEMENT – ACTIVE OR PASSIVE?

On the assumption that the investor is concerned to take steps to manage the foreign exchange risk – perhaps because he or she believes the argument that currency increases the volatility of the assets without adding return – the question is then what to do about it. The approach can be either passive or active.

For an active manager, there are two main ways of handling the currency diversification issue. The first, the more traditional approach, is simply to buy and sell securities denominated in the appropriate currencies. If you like the Deutschmark, you buy Bunds. If you like sterling, you buy gilts. There are some problems with this approach. There is a relatively narrower choice of credits in small markets, such as the New Zealand dollar, so that if one is backing a currency view one may not have an optimal choice of security. Similarly, there will be a variation in liquidity. The domestic government bond markets will generally be the most liquid, but these may not always be open to the international investor because of withholding tax or other considerations.

An alternative approach to the currency question is not to buy or sell securities denominated in the chosen currency, but rather to tactically hedge the existing portfolio. Thus, you might hold Japanese Euroyen bonds because you are bullish on Japanese interest rates. But for the same reason you might be bearish on the short-term outlook for the yen. So you would sell forward yen as a hedge on the currency, while holding on to the bonds.

Passive management implies the view that over the long term foreign exchange exposures wash out – *and* that the investor is not sufficiently confident of his ability to time market swings. The strategy can be executed either by never hedging – in which case the investor seeks to gain from a given pattern of currency diversification – or always hedging. In the latter case the hope would be that returns would be enhanced by widening the range of issues held, or that for the same return, a lower volatility – i.e. risk – can be achieved.

THE CASE FOR PASSIVE MANAGEMENT

For many investors a good case can be made for passive management of the foreign exchange risk. The most basic argument is 'it'll all come out in the wash'. That is, over a long period of time, currencies tend to swing back and forth and there is no a priori reason for knowing where in the cycle we are at any given time. The US dollar swung from DM1.67 in 1978 to DM3.46 in 1985 and to DM1.80 in 1989. If the investor is investing in a spread of international assets for the purpose of diversifying his risks, and has a long-term time horizon, then the impact of foreign exchange is itself a diversifying influence.

This argument assumes two things. First, that in the long run you cannot time the market consistently so as to make profits from foreign exchange. There are good reasons to believe this. Much analysis has been devoted to investors' ability to beat the stock market – and the bond markets – by market timing. In almost all cases it has been shown that they fail to do so in the long run. Why should the foreign exchange markets be different?

Of course, it is possible to do so for a year or two, but over ten or fifteen years is another matter. Banks can make money consistently in foreign exchange trading, but this is largely – in the very long run – because of the bid/offer spread. Position-taking in the market allows them to handle order flow, but there are very few banks indeed able to point to consistent profitability from position-taking over ten or fifteen years – over and above the profit that might have been earned by taking the capital employed and investing it in the equity market. There is no reason to believe that the return on capital employed in foreign exchange market timing is any higher than that on equity or bond market timing. Why should foreign exchange be different from any other market?

There is a second major set of arguments in favour of passive management of foreign exchange risk. This is that in the long run hedged and unhedged international investments should offer the same returns. Suppose they did not. That would imply that foreign exchange markets continuously over- or under-priced the cost of hedging a given currency. The cost was always above or below the actual change in value that took place. For any given period that might be true, since the hedging cost is technically driven by interest differentials. But in the very long run there is no reason to believe this would happen. If it did, it would imply that an investor in one country would be consistently rewarded for taking foreign exchange risk and an investor in another would be consistently penalised. That seems contradictory.

If we accept the argument for passive management – the opposing case is discussed below – then the next question is how to implement it, specifically the choice of neutral position. There are two possibilities: always hedged or never hedged. The bench-mark in the former case would be an unhedged index, and a hedged one in the latter instance.

The choice between the two depends on the investor's philosophy, of course. One possible approach, used by many investors in managing their domestic portfolios, is that suggested by modern portfolio theory, i.e. we opt for the choice that offers us least risk for the same return. Putting it another way, we look to choose a position on the efficient frontier. (Those familiar with this concept may choose to skip the next two sections.)

Efficient frontiers

Suppose you think that neither you nor anyone else has the gift of permanently timing the market right over the long haul. Then the modern portfolio theorist argues that you should focus on setting up an 'efficient' portfolio. You start by deciding how much risk you want to take. Risk is defined as variability of return. It is measured by the standard deviation of returns from an asset over time.

Suppose you are a US investor considering whether to invest overseas. Well, the Salomon Brothers High Grade Corporate Bond Index returned an annual 10.53 per cent in the ten years to 1988. Its annualised standard deviation was 15.4 per cent. Over the same period the Salomon Brothers Non-US Bond Index returned 12.29 per cent in US dollar terms. Its annualised standard deviation was 16.34 per cent. The non-US bond index gave higher returns, at the price of higher risk.

The point of modern portfolio theory is that risk falls as you include different types of asset, as long as their returns are not perfectly correlated. Diversification pays. Say you hold both equities and bonds. They won't normally both perform badly in the same year. So the weak performance of one will be offset by the other. The portfolio as a whole will be more stable than either asset individually. Diversifying reduces your risk.

Let's look at a practical example. Suppose you think, after studying history and making your forecasts, that the following asset classes will produce a certain pattern of risks and returns. Let's say, over the next five years, you expect:

	US bonds	*Non-US bonds*
Return	8%	9.5%
Risk	9%	12.0%

And let's suppose you think the returns will have a correlation of 0.4, i.e. US bond returns will vary in line with non-US returns 40 per cent of the time.

To work out the risk of the combined portfolio we need the covariance between the two assets, that is the standard deviation of each asset (or pair of assets, if there were more than two) multiplied together and weighted by the correlation between the assets. So the covariance is 0.09 × 0.12 × 0.4 = 0.00432. We'll also need the variances of the two assets, which is the square of the standard deviation (0.0081 and 0.0144 respectively).

Constructing a frontier

Now we can find the risk and return of a portfolio combining these elements. Suppose we start by holding everything in US bonds. Then we gradually push up the share of non-US bonds to 100 per cent. Finding the return is an easy calculation: a weighted average. The risk is a little more tricky.

Let's take the risk when we have 30 per cent in non-US bonds. The calculation is 0.0081 × 0.49 + 0.0144 × 0.09 + 2 × 0.7 × 0.3 × 0.00432 = 0.0070794. In words: (US bonds variance × square of 70 per cent weight) + (non-US bonds' variance × square of 30 per cent weight) + 2 × (70 per cent US weight × 30 per cent non-US weight × convariance).

That is the variance of the combined portfolio. To find the standard deviation we take the square root, which comes out at 0.084139 or 8.41 per cent. So now we do the sums for all the different weights and we get the results given in Table 8.1.

As you push up the share of non-US bonds, the risk of the combined portfolio falls from 9.00 per cent to 8.41 per cent when you have 30 per cent in non-US bonds. While the risk is falling, though, the return is rising. You can get 30 basis points more return for less risk, if you push the share of non-US bonds from 0 per cent to 30 per cent. The chart in Figure 8.1 shows the same thing visually. Obviously, if you're happy to take more risk

Table 8.1

		Combined portfolio	
US fixed	*Non-US*	*Risk*	*Return*
100%	0%	9.00	8.0
90	10	8.65	8.1
80	20	8.45	8.2
70	30	8.41	8.3
60	40	8.54	8.4
50	50	8.82	8.5
etc.			

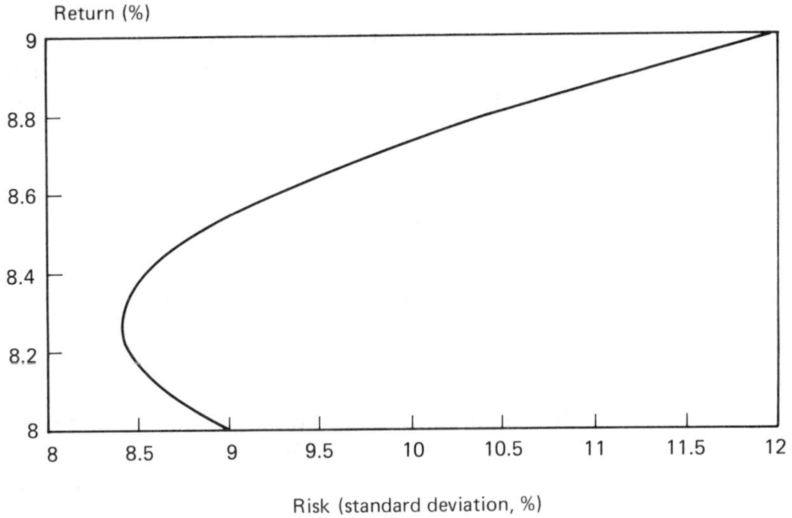

FIGURE 8.1 Risk and return: effect of higher share of non-dollar bonds

in exchange for more return, you can push the non-US bonds up to 50 per cent or even beyond.

CURRENCY-HEDGED BONDS AS AN ASSET CLASS

Applying this technique to the international investor's portfolio, we can consider whether or not the bond component of the portfolio should be hedged or unhedged. Putting it another way, the question is whether or not we should add another asset class to the two (US bonds and non-US bonds) that we have looked at here. The new asset class consists of non-US bonds hedged passively back into US dollars (i.e. always hedged, no matter what your market view). The impact of a new asset class depends on three things: (a) returns, (b) risk, (c) correlation of its returns to returns on other asset classes.

Proponents of the separate asset class argue that (in the long run) returns on non-US bonds will tend to equal those on US bonds of equal credit quality. High interest rates in high-inflation countries will tend to be offset by currency depreciation, and vice versa. Similarly, in the very long run, there should be no long-term gain from currency hedging. The forward discount or premium on the currency hedge should tend to equal the actual out-turn. Therefore, item (a), returns, should tend over time to be the same.

But (b), risk, is less. The volatility of hedged Japanese government bonds 1977–87 in US dollar terms was 6.4 per cent compared with the

11.5 per cent volatility of US Treasuries. German Bunds' volatility was 5.9 per cent. In contrast, both types of bond were more closely correlated with US returns on a hedged basis (at 0.42 and 0.54 respectively) than unhedged (0.32 and 0.38). But the risk reduction from hedging outweighs the higher correlation.

THE CASE FOR ACTIVE MANAGEMENT

Opponents criticise the preceding argument on several grounds. For one thing, it covers a particular period in time. Others produce different results: it was very foolish to hedge overseas assets when the dollar was collapsing in 1977–9 and 1985–7. Another argument is that if the proponents' case is true it should apply to all investors. But it can be shown that for a Japanese investor over this period it was a big mistake to move into hedged foreign bonds because he moved from a low-volatility market to a high-volatility one.

Also it may be that, as we said earlier, theory tells us currency should not provide a return to the investor. Theory says that would imply a contradition whereby an investor in country A is consistently penalised in relation to country B. But practice can differ. A UK investor in 1945, selling sterling to buy a dollar asset at $4.80 = £1, could have run that short position for forty years down to $1.03 in 1985. Currencies do have secular trends, because countries do. (Whether the active manager can consistently spot the trends is another matter.)

Again, the separate asset-class/passive hedging thesis assumes the relative volatilities of US and overseas bond markets in 1977–87 will continue. There is a good case to be made that the US bond market will not be as volatile as it was. Also, now that the German, Japanese and UK bond markets have created futures contracts, they may well become more volatile. In that case the US investor would be unwise to move from a lower-volatility market to what turns out to be a more volatile one.

The active hedger rejects the passive approach because it only works if observed volatilities and correlations from the past can be carried forward, albeit in adjusted form, to the future. The problem switches from being one of forecasting the direction of currency movements to forecasting relative volatilities and correlations. It is not necessarily clear that this forecasting problem is any easier to solve.

That is not an argument against international diversification, though. What is certainly clear is that an international portfolio will always be more diversified than a domestic one. If the returns on international and domestic bonds are equal – and in the long run, for credits of equal standing, this should be the case – then an internationally diversified bond portfolio should always be less risky than a purely domestic one.

EFFECTS OF INCLUDING EQUITIES

So far we have looked at the effects of including hedged international bonds in the portfolio. Many studies in a modern portfolio theory framework have argued that in fact international bonds have little place in an international portfolio because they are highly correlated with international equities.

This is true, on an unhedged basis, because in most cases the effects of currency swings – which of course affect both equities and bonds – have dominated other effects. On a hedged basis, however, the currency effect is stripped out and the correlation between international equities and bonds is reduced.

The chart in Figure 8.2 (JP Morgan Investment Management, *Benefits of Currency Hedging*, Exhibit 5, p. 5) plots the risk and returns over the following six asset categories, for a US investor, using the historical results for 1978–87. The underlying correlations for these periods were as follows:

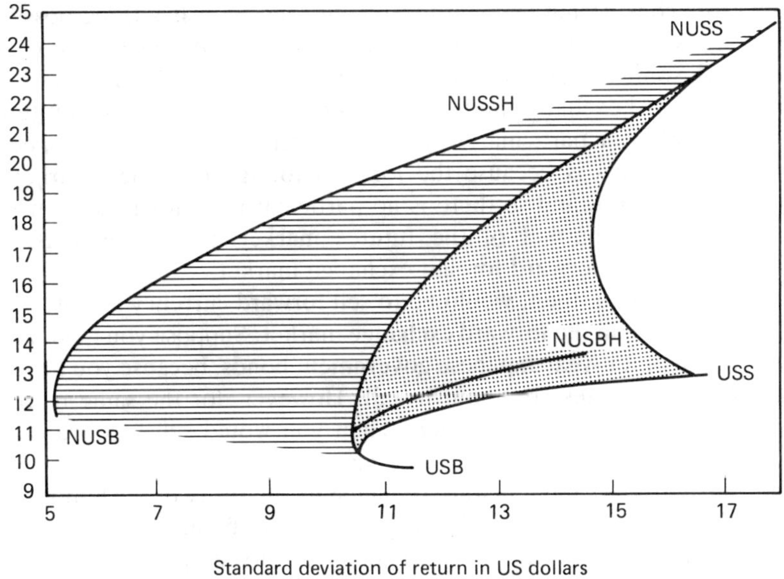

FIGURE 8.2 International equity and bond markets 1978–1987
SOURCE: J. P. Morgan Investment Management

US stocks (USS)	1					
US bonds (USB)	0.28	1				
Non-US stocks (NUSS)	0.39	0.25	1			
Non-US bonds (NUSB)	0.02	0.41	0.66	1		
Non-US stocks hedged (NUSSH)	0.54	0.11	0.77	0.08	1	
Non-US bonds hedged (NUSHBH)	0.12	0.54	0.39	0.68	0.20	1

That is, for example, over the period, non-US bonds were almost independent of US stocks (2 per cent correlation) while hedged non-US bonds were more closely linked (12 per cent correlation). Hedged non-US bonds were 54 per cent correlated with US bonds, while unhedged non-US bonds were 41 per cent correlated. Conversely, while non-US bonds were 66 per cent correlated with non-US stocks, the equivalent figure for hedged non-US bonds and stocks was only 20 per cent. Thus, in general, hedging increased the correlation between non-US assets and US assets, but it reduced the correlation of non-US assets amongst themselves.

MANAGING THE HEDGING OPERATION

An investor considering hedging foreign currency risk has three possible choices: forward foreign exchange, financial futures, or currency options (or, indeed, some of the so-called third generation hedging products which combine forward exchange and options). Of these three, financial futures are generally not a particularly practical choice unless there are special circumstances. This is because the forward foreign exchange market is outstandingly liquid, and so there is no particular need for futures, while the daily mark-to-market of the futures market is very cumbersome compared with the forward foreign exchange market.

The normal route, then, would be to sell forward currency against your equities or bonds, in the forward exchange market. Suppose you hold ¥150 million worth of ten-year Japanese government bonds, because you believe Japanese interest rates are about to fall. However, for the same reason, you expect a weakening in the yen. Then you would sell forward ¥150 million yen, for delivery in, say, three months' time.

The alternative is to sell forward to match the maturity of the bond – but this is much less attractive. Hedging a ten-year bond with a ten-year forward would be difficult, because the ten-year forward market is thin and illiquid. You would be conceding a substantial liquidity premium to the foreign exchange market for the privilege of executing the hedge. By the same token, unless you were willing to concede a second premium, you would be committed to holding the bond and its hedge to maturity.

If the forward sale is in US dollars, then you are in effect holding synthetic US dollar Japanese bonds. Depending on the relative slope of the yield curves (which will affect the forward exchange premium or discount) this manoeuvre can produce attractive results. Of course, there is an implied exposure to the shape of the yield curve, but this is generally of much lesser impact than the effect of currency movements.

However, the costs of this operation need to be properly measured. Suppose you are running the position for a year, with three-month forward contracts. You will roll the hedges four times. Suppose you are hedging yen assets and today's spot is $1 = ¥150. On the Reuters screen today is a three-month forward price of 129/125 meaning a seller of yen forward would sell at 150 − 1.25 = 148.75. Suppose rates do not change at all in the next three months. At maturity of the forward you buy back at 150 the yen you sold at 148.75 and you extend the contract at the same rate. You crystallise a cash flow difference (in this case a profit) and you pay the forward market spread each time you roll the contract.

By the latter is meant the spread, or mark-up, that the bank will charge over the inter-bank rate. Suppose the true inter-bank rate is 128/126: you are being charged a point each time you roll, say 4 points per annum. That costs 0.04/150 = 0.03 per cent per annum, or three basis points. (For other, less liquid currencies, or for amounts smaller than standard inter-bank size, the cost would be higher; for a diversified portfolio perhaps 6 or 7 basis points would be a sensible average figure.) More significant would be the cost of the odd cash flows thrown up by the rolling of forward contracts, particularly if losses require a sale of securities from elsewhere in the portfolio. Estimates of these costs vary but anywhere from 15–50 basis points, depending on size and frequency of cash flows, would be appropriate. In addition would be the costs of someone's time to handle the hedging programme, or an outside manager's fees. Total costs would probably be a minimum of ¼ per cent and could range up to ¾ per cent per annum. Consideration might also have to be given, in some cases, to the fact that the forward exchange gains or losses would be realised, while the gains or losses on the assets being hedged would generally be unrealised, with possible reporting/accounting implications.

CURRENCY OPTIONS

Another choice for the investor would be to use currency options. The over-the-counter market in currency options probably began to develop in the early 1980s, but the first listed currency options were those on the Philadelphia Stock Exchange, which were introduced in December 1982. Options are also traded on the IMM, which introduced an option on the Deutschmark in 1983, and the Chicago Board Options Exchange, which has options on Deutschmarks, Swiss francs, French francs, Canadian dollars, sterling and Japanese yen. Options have also been introduced on the London Stock Exchange on sterling and Deutschmarks and on the London International Financial Futures Exchange (LIFFE). Exchange traded options volume figures have grown strongly as shown in Table 8.2.

The Bank of England comments that 'Definitive data on the size of the OTC [i.e. off-exchange] market are not available .... There seems little doubt that the OTC market ... has grown at least as rapidly as the exchange-traded markets.'

Table 8.2

	$bn
1982	0.1
1983	7.4
1984	74.1
1985	185.5
1986	522.5
1987	892.5
1988	1,019.1

Source: *Bank of England Quarterly Bulletin*, May 1989, p. 237. Figure includes Philadelphia, Chicago (CME + CBOE), London (LIFFE + LTOM), Amsterdam, New York, Singapore and Sydney.

In general, exchange traded options extend up to nine months only, though the over-the-counter market offers longer-term options. It is also possible indirectly to buy long-term currency options by buying securities with imbedded currency options (see Chapter 6).

Options pricing for currency options follows the same basic principle as for other options pricing. But in the foreign exchange market, unlike most other markets on which options are available, there is a widely traded and liquid forward market. This means that the buyer or seller of an option has always the choice of comparing the option with the price available in the forward market: it also allows for the possibility of combining the two.

Because a currency option entails the transition from a currency with one set of interest rates to another currency with a separate set of interest rates, the time value of the option needs to be carefully considered. To be precise, the true determinant of intrinsic value is found by comparing the forward price rather than the spot price to the strike price.

This is because of the well-known fact that different interest rates in two currencies will produce a premium or discount on the forward exchange. Take a forward purchase of Deutschmarks with US dollars. If US rates are at 10 per cent compared with 5 per cent for Deutschmarks, the forward price will always be at a premium of 5 per cent per annum. This will imply that the calls on Deutschmarks will be expensive, relative to DM puts.

Suppose that the price of the currency expressed in US terms is $0.3500 per DM in the spot market, and $0.3600 in the forward market. Suppose one could buy a call option on the currency with a strike price of $0.3500, for, say, $0.0175 per DM. Then the intrinsic value would be $0.0100 (the difference between the rate available in the forward market and the strike price). The remainder of $0.0075 would be time value. The implied price of the put, therefore, would be $0.0075 (zero intrinsic value plus $0.0075 time value). Thus, the call would cost 5 per cent of the option contract value, while the put would cost about 2 per cent (\$0.0175/\$0.3500, compared with \$0.0075/\$0.3500).

Again, dealing costs would have to be looked at. Although the problem of crystallising cash flow losses as forward contracts are rolled would disappear, the up-front premiums would have to be funded. Also, the options market is less liquid and more expensive to deal in than the forward market.

Part Three
Eurobonds and Related Markets

9 The Eurobond Primary Market

The role of the Eurobond market is to provide capital for borrowers from all parts of the world in a wide range of currencies and instruments. The primary market is where the capital is actually provided, i.e. where Eurobonds are first sold to investors, as distinct from the secondary market, which is where the bonds are traded later.

Neither the primary nor the secondary market have a physical location: they are not confined to a stock exchange building, for example. They are telephone and telex markets. It is possible to participate in them from anywhere in the world. A glance at the AIBD Members' Handbook shows members from 37 countries. The names range from the Bank of China in Peking, through Kansallis-Osake Pankki in Helsinki, the United Bank of Kuwait and the Bank of Bermuda to Goldman Sachs and its peers in New York. As the next chapter explains, London plays an important role in the secondary market, while clearing and settlement arrangements are based in Brussels and Luxembourg, and the Association of International Bond Dealers is headquartered in Zurich.

So the primary market is not a place: it is a process. It is the market in which the bonds are first sold to investors. Second and subsequent sales form part of the secondary market.

It is hard to draw a clear dividing line. For any given bond, the primary market period runs from the launch of the issue until all the bonds are sold. That definition is not entirely clear-cut. The 'grey market' (discussed later) means that 'secondary market' trading of some of the bonds can be taking place even before all the bonds are sold.

Another definition relies on the AIBD Rule 227 which says that the value date for secondary market transactions is the next business day after the closing of the issue, or the seventh calendar day following the trade date, whichever is the later. Thus one could say that all trades done after seven calendar days before the bond payment date are secondary trades. The primary market exists while the bonds trade for settlement on the date of issue, without accrued interest.

In any event, what we mean is the process of first distribution to investors. As Figure 9.1 shows, the trading volume in the primary market is inevitably smaller than in the secondary market, but it is still substantial.

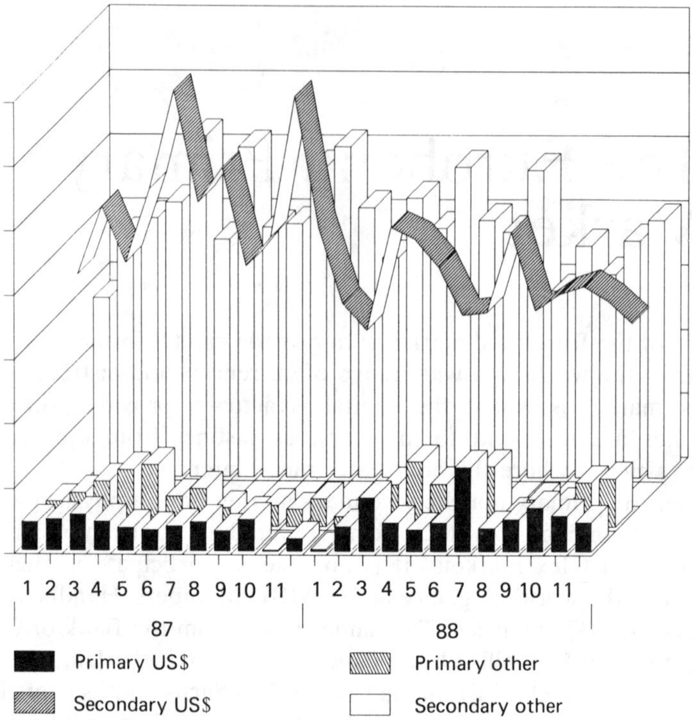

FIGURE 9.1 Straight Eurobonds, turnover $billion
SOURCE: AIBD

USERS OF THE PRIMARY MARKET: MAJOR ISSUERS

The Eurobond market serves the entire globe. So the issuers who use it vary widely. They vary over time, also, depending on who needs the funds from year to year. But generally, the issuers in the Eurobond market are of very high credit standing. This is because the market custom is to rely on 'name recognition' rather than US-style credit ratings. So someone wanting to raise money through a Eurobond issue must be well known and regarded as a high-quality credit. This has the paradoxical result that a well-known US firm such as IBM has in the past been able to raise funds more cheaply than the US government.

A good idea of the major issuers can be gleaned from Table 9.1 showing the top twenty issuers of 1980–8. As Table 9.1 shows, the market is dominated by large internationally known borrowers, consisting of sovereign, banking and corporate entities. Over and above these issuers, though, there are often different kinds of issuers who emerge in waves according to trends in the market or in response to a changing economic environment.

Table 9.1

Issuer	*$bn*
World Bank	22.4
European Investment Bank	17.5
Kingdom of Sweden	16.0
Kingdom of Denmark	15.6
General Motors	10.5
EEC	10.1
Citicorp	9.9
Republic of Italy	9.6
Republic of Austria	9.4
Canada	8.9
Kingdom of Belgium	8.7
Deutsche Bank	7.8
Swedish Export Credit	7.6
Banque Nationale de Paris	7.1
General Electric	6.9
Ford Motor Company	6.7
United Kingdom	6.5
Banque Française du Commerce Extérieur	5.7
New Zealand	5.6
Ireland	5.6

Source: *Euromoney Bondware.*

The years 1986–7, for example, saw very heavy issuance by Japanese corporations of Eurobonds with equity warrants attached. The strength of the Japanese stock market meant that coupons on these US dollar bonds could be pushed at one point below 1 per cent, where normal coupons on 'straight' bonds without warrants were of the order of 9 per cent. After swapping the proceeds back into Japanese yen they were able to borrow at negative rates of interest in yen terms. At other times, Australian dollars have been a fashionable currency for borrowers which naturally encouraged Australian entities to issue (see Chapter 11).

INVESTMENT BANKS AND THE SYNDICATION PROCESS

The way in which a Eurobond is brought to market has changed over time. Most of the changes have been in timing and technique rather than legal status. The legal mechanics are that the issuer sells securities to a group, or syndicate, of investment and commercial banks who then distribute them to investors. But within that framework there have been a number of changes, and to understand today's market it is useful to look at its origins.

In the halcyon days before 1979–80 the process was relatively leisurely. A bank or securities firm courted the borrower over a period and would then be given a mandate to arrange an issue. By virtue of receiving the mandate the firm assumed the leadership role in managing the issue and would be called the lead manager.

The lead manager sought banks or securities firms to join it in the syndicate at three levels: co-manager, underwriter and selling group. Depending on the size of the issue, there would be from two to ten co-managers who took substantial blocks of bonds and collectively formed, with the lead manager, the 'management group'. The co-managers were chosen on the basis that they had a special relationship with the borrower, or the lead manager, or were specially able to place bonds with investors.

Underwriters generally formed a rather larger group, each taking a smaller allotment of bonds than the co-managers. Again, they were chosen for relationship reasons or placement skills. Selling group members formed a still larger group taking a still smaller allotment of bonds. Often the selling group would include banks trying to break into the Eurobond market or into a relationship with the issuer or lead manager.

Once the syndicate was formed, its members sought to sell the bonds to their retail or institutional customer base. During this period the syndicate bought back any bonds sold off by customers whose market view was negative. This process of stabilising the price of the bonds helped to give other investors the confidence to buy the new issue. Once the lead manager judged that all the securities had been distributed into firm hands, the 'syndicate bid' for the bonds was ended and the issue was freed to trade normally.

A sample timetable would have been something like this:

Week of D − 14	Mandate awarded Issue strategy agreed with borrower Documentation begun
Week of D − 7	Co-managers invited Documentation finalised
D-day	Announcement of issue Lead manager sends invitation telex to underwriters and selling group members
D + 1	Documentation sent to underwriters and selling group members
D + 4	Deadline for underwriters' acceptance
D + 8	Preliminary allotments set internally by lead manager
D + 9	Pricing day: issue terms finally fixed Deadline for final indications of subscriptions from selling group
D + 10	Offering day Allotment telexes sent to underwriters and selling group members

D + 11–23	Syndicate stablisation period: the issue is supported by syndicate bid until distribution is judged to be complete
D + 24	Payment day Syndicate members pay for securities acquired and funds paid over to borrower

By comparison, the issue process today tends to be much more compressed. The main reason for this was the arrival in 1979–80 of the so-called 'bought deal'. In the process outlined above, the borrower awards the mandate on D − 14 and the terms of the issue are fixed on D + 9. So the borrower is on risk for over three weeks: it is not certain what the issue will cost until D + 9. In the highly volatile rate environment of 1979–80 (during which Federal funds moved 12 per cent in six weeks at one point) this was a large risk. Hence investment banks offered to buy the issue from the borrower at a certain rate: they then assembled a syndicate as quickly as possible to reduce their risk.

MARKET PRACTICE TODAY

Current practice is best perhaps shown by some examples. As far as the market is concerned, the launching of an issue will normally be announced through specialist screen-based services on the Reuters Monitor system or Telerate which will carry announcements like this:

> 1216 SCREEN INSIDER IIID
>
> – EUROFIMA IS TAPPING THE AUSSIE DOLLAR MARKET WITH AN AUS DLR 75M 7-YEAR STRAIGHT ISSUE. THE NON-CALLABLE DEAL HAS A COUPON OF 13PC AND AN ISSUE PRICE OF 101 1/4. LEAD MANAGER JP MORGAN IS SEEKING CO-MANAGERS. FM NP, X-DFLT. FEES ARE 1 1/4PC FOR SELLING AND 3/4PC FOR MAN AND UND COMBINED. DUE DATE IS FEB 3, 1995. DENOMS ARE 1000 AND 10,000. LISTING LUX. PAY FEB 3. EARLY QUOTES ARE LESS 1.90–1.80.

This translates as follows. At 12.16 p.m. the Screen Insider service put an announcement on Reuters page IIID that Eurofima (a multinational consortium of European railways for purchasing rolling stock) was raising seventy-five million Australian dollars. The bond is a seven-year straight, i.e. without equity features or other unusual features, and cannot be 'called' for early redemption before its maturity. It bears an interest rate of 13 per cent but is being issued at a premium of 1¼ per cent above par. The lead manager is JP Morgan & Co. and they are looking for co-managers.

The documentation of the bond will contain certain standard clauses: FM is *force majeure* (i.e. the managers and underwriters can be discharged from their obligations in the event of certain specified disasters). NP means negative pledge: the issuer has pledged that other creditors will not obtain a better claim on its assets than the bondholders. X-DFLT means cross-default: if the issuer defaults on other obligations the bond will come due for early repayment.

Selling fees are 1¼ per cent and management and underwriting fees combined are ¾ per cent. The maturity date of the bond is 3 February 1995, and the bond is issued in denominations of A$1,000 and A$10,000. The bonds will be listed in Luxembourg. The issue date is 3 February 1988. Early indications of the grey market price are 'less 1.90 bid, less 1.80 offered'. That is, dealers in the grey market are bidding for the bonds at the issue price (101¼) less 1.90: a price of 99.35. They will sell at 99.45.

The relationship of the grey market price to the total of fees is important. Here, the total fees are 2 per cent and so the bonds are said to be trading 'within fees': a bank in the deal would earn 2 per cent (less any praecipium) and could sell, if it chose, at a discount of 1.9 per cent earning 10 basis points overall (assuming the stabilisation account doesn't erode the underwriting fees). So overall the syndicate would not be losing money at this stage. A weak issue would trade 'outside fees' and the syndicate would lose money. (The praecipium and the stabilisation account are explained below.)

After looking at the issue process in broad terms, it may be useful to look at another deal in some detail. On 29 April 1986 Morgan Grenfell launched an issue for American Cyanamid: a 9 per cent, £30 million five-year Eurosterling bond. A telex was sent to co-managers requiring their response by 5 p.m. the next day. The issue was fully underwritten by the co-managers; there were no separate underwriters. The timetable went like this:

7 May	Indications of selling group interest to be given to Morgan Grenfell
9 May	Signing of agreement among managers and subscription agreement
	Final allotments fixed and allotment telexes despatched
20 May	Payment by subscribers and closing of the issue.

Thus the co-managers were committed from 5 p.m. on April 30, and the borrower knew the terms on which it was raising funds. The co-managers faced the market risk, and also did not know for certain the amount of bonds they would be allotted until 9 May.

Clearly, the market risks have been shifted from the borrower to the co-managers. Undoubtedly there have been sustained periods when the business of underwriting new issues has been unprofitable as a result of this shift in market balance; equally, it is inevitable in the long run that the pendulum will swing back to a point nearer balance. The first attempts in this direction have been made by certain firms' introduction of US-style syndication techniques – the so-called 'fixed-price reoffering'. This is in fact a return to traditional Euromarket methods prevailing before the arrival of the bought deal, albeit at a less leisurely pace. The technique is that the issuing price for the bonds is agreed by consensus between the issuer, the lead manager and the syndicate. It is fixed at a price which all concerned believe is sustainable in the market. Syndicate members commit to re-sell the bonds at a price agreed with the lead manager until the deal 'breaks syndicate'. This shifts the market timing risk back to the issuer. Also the length of time needed to negotiate the price usually means that it is difficult to tie the issue in with a swap. Hence, the technique has definite limitations and is unlikely to oust the bought deal completely. However, the benefit to the borrower is that it makes an issue which trades well at launch time, and thus hopefully makes the market more receptive to any future issues. From the point of view of the underwriters of the issue the technique has the merit of restoring some balance to the risk/reward ratio. The ratio of risk to reward, of course, is influenced by the availability of fee income as well as market risk.

FEES AND EXPENSES

In the early periods of the market, the levels of fees on bond issues were relatively fixed and secure. The growth of competition has eroded this stability. As an example, the Cyanamid issue discussed earlier carried fees of 1⅞ per cent. These were broken down into selling group commission of 1¼ per cent and management and underwriting commissions (combined) of ⅝ per cent.

However, the invitation telex stated that 'The balance of the combined management and underwriting commission after deduction of unreimbursed expenses and adjustment for stabilisation costs (if any), will be divided among the managers, including the lead manager, pro-rata to their underwriting commitments.'

The terms of the issue included a 'cap' on the issuer's legal and related expenses of £35,000. Thus, any cost over-run on expenses would be deducted from the management and underwriting commission.

Similarly, any losses incurred by the syndicate in supporting the issue before trading restrictions were lifted – 'stabilisation costs' – would also be deducted. In addition, a 'praecipium' of ⅛ per cent was deducted from the management and underwriting commission by the lead manager.

In making the appropriate calculations, the lead manager would bear in mind the recommendations of the International Primary Market Association (discussed later) regarding fees. The IPMA's Recommendation II states that:

1. All management fees should be paid pro rata within four weeks from the closing date after deduction of praecipium only. Where management and underwriting fees are combined, 40 per cent should be deemed to be the management fee. Underwriting fees should be paid pro rata within 90 days of the closing date after deducting or adding the items listed below.
2. Direct out of pocket expenses of the bookrunning lead manager which exceed the expense reimbursement by the issuer should be charged against the underwriting fees only to the extent of 10% of such fees.

Stabilisation costs have for some time been a bone of contention between lead managers and syndicate members, with the latter contending that there were abuses. Supposing that an allotment of £1.5 million were made on the American Cyanamid issue. Then the selling group commission would be deducted from the bond's price (of 100 in this case). So selling group members and managers and underwriters, would buy the bonds at 98.75 (100 − 1.25).

The management fee would be 40 per cent of the ⅝ per cent combined management and underwriting fee, or ¼ per cent. From this would be deducted the praecipium of ⅛ per cent, leaving a net management fee of ⅛ per cent or £1,875.

The remaining 60 per cent of the fees, or ⅜ per cent, would in the past have been subject to deduction of unreimbursed expenses and stabilisation costs, with a possible minimum payout of 0 per cent. Thus, a co-manager in the issue might earn in the worst case £1,875. These problems, together with continuing cut-throat competition for new issues which meant that stabilisation was often needed, led the IPMA, in April 1989, to lay down that lead managers of new pre-priced deals could no longer deduct stabilisation costs from syndicate members' fees. It remains to be seen whether this will remedy the situation.

Against the fees, of course, would need to be set the profit or loss on the underwriting position. If the bond were to move by, say, three points during the period before distribution was complete, which would be by no means uncommon, there would be a profit or loss of £45,000. Clearly, the essence of successful underwriting is skill in reading the market rather than living off the fees.

A final point on fees is the question of *listing*. The bond, once issued, will normally be listed for quotation in Luxembourg or London. Traditionally Luxembourg was the cheaper option but in January 1989 the International Stock Exchange reduced its fees to make London more competitive. Maximum listing charges were reduced from £10,000 to £4,000 for applicants already listed and from £13,500 for new applicants. The 6p per £1,000

Table 9.2 Top ten Eurobond lead managers

1963–7	1968–73	1974–8	1979–83	1988
Deutsche Bank	Deutsche Bank	Deutsche Bank	CSFB[3]	Nomura Securities
Kuhn Loeb & Co.	Morgan & Cie	CSFB[3]	Deutsche Bank	CSFB[3]
S. G. Warburg & Co.	S. G. Warburg & Co.	WestLB[6]	Morgan Stanley	Deutsche Bank
Hambros Bank	CSWW[4]	S. G. Warburg & Co.	S. G. Warburg	Daiwa Securities
Morgan & Cie	Dresdner Bank	Dresdner Bank	Merrill Lynch	Yamaichi Securities
First Boston Corp.	WestLB[6]	UBS[5]	Salomon	Nikko Securities
N. M. Rothschild & Sons	Commerzbank	Commerzbank	Morgan Guaranty	Merrill Lynch
White Weld & Co.	Lehman Brothers	Morgan Stanley & Co.[8]	Soc. Gen.[7]	Bankers Trust
BCI[2]	Kuhn Loeb & Co.	Banque Paribas	Goldman Sachs	Paribas
Dillon Read & Co.	AmRo[1]	Orion Bank	Dresdner Bank	J. P. Morgan[9]

1. AmRo: Amsterdam-Rotterdam Bank
2. BCI: Banca Commerciale Italiana
3. CSFB: Crédit Suisse First Boston, formerly CSWW
4. CSWW: Crédit Suisse White Weld
5. UBS: Union Bank of Switzerland
6. West LB: Westdeutsche Landesbank
7. Soc. Gen.: Société Générale de Banque
8. Previously Morgan & Cie
9. Previously Morgan Guaranty

Sources: F. G. Fisher, *The Eurodollar Bond Market*, Euromoney Publications 1979; I. M. Kerr, *A History of the Eurobond Market*, Euromoney Publications, 1984; *Euromoney Bondware*.

charge will be uniform for all issuers (previously new issuers had to pay 8p per £1,000). The traditional requirement that two market-makers on the exchange had to be offered a participation has been lifted. (It had been an annoyance to Eurobond houses who argued that the market-makers would only come in if the deal was bound to be a roaring success and made no effort to place the paper.) Issuers will also be allowed to produce listing particulars in the printed form they choose: particulars need no longer be circulated in the Extel Financial statistical service.

By way of historical perspective, Table 9.2 may help to show how it has always been tough to stay at the top of the primary market – apart from a few illustrious names, market leaders have come and gone.

IMPACT OF FOREIGN EXCHANGE AND ECONOMIC FACTORS

One of the key factors influencing the standing of many houses in the market might be called the economic hinterland. That is, a firm which is strong in a market which is supplying funds to the Euromarket will do well. So, Japanese firms have benefited from the strength of Japan's economy: as Japanese investors have poured funds into the Eurobond market, Japanese issuing houses have benefited. Another important factor is the related movements in foreign exchange rates.

For Eurobond investors the impact of foreign exchange has always been key. Investors' views of the prospects for different currencies drive their demand for issues in those currencies. First, by holding an asset denominated in an appreciating currency, they expect to have a capital gain. Secondly, the strength of the currency generally pushes down interest rates in that country's money and bond markets as funds flow into the country.

So, as interest rates in the currency fall, investors in newly issued bonds in a strong currency may well expect to see capital gains on the bonds themselves, as well as currency gains on the bond. Thus, if investors believe that the Japanese yen is likely to strengthen, their demand for Eurobonds denominated in Japanese yen will be strong. Syndicate departments of investment banks are well aware of this, and seek to sell new issues in those areas of the market where there is currently demand.

Hence, for example, the weakness of the US dollar during 1985–8 meant a sharp fall in the volume of new issues denominated in US dollars (see Table 9.3). International investors were unwilling to buy bonds denominated in the currency they did not like. Accordingly, other currencies took up the slack – notable the yen, sterling and to some extent ECU.

These effects, in turn, have an impact on the relative standing of leading

Table 9.3 Eurobond issuance by currency ($ bn equivalent)

	1982	*1983*	*1984*	*1985*	*1986*	*1987*	*1988*
US$	46	42	71	102	122	62	87
Swfr	11	14	13	15	23	25	26
Yen	1	1	2	7	18	22	17
DM	6	6	7	12	16	13	24
ECU	2	2	3	8	7	7	12
Sterling	1	2	4	7	10	14	23
Can$	1	1	2	3	6	6	13
Aus$	0	0	0	3	3	9	8
Dfl	2	2	2	2	2	1	3
Frfr	0	0	0	1	3	2	2
Other	0	0	0	2	4	5	6
Total	70	70	104	162	214	166	217

Source: Merrill Lynch, *International Bond Issuance Activity*, February 1989.

securities houses. There are very few firms which can be said to be truly independent of their currency base. Thus, when the US dollar is strong, US investment banks can be expected to perform well in the so-called 'league tables' showing which firms have lead managed the largest number of bonds. Conversely, the strength of the Japanese yen can be expected to benefit Japanese houses, sterling strength will help the relative standing of British firms, and so on. There are a number of firms, of course, whose strength is such that they are successful across all markets: the Japanese firms have succeeded in muscling their way into the US dollar market (see Table 9.4), and Deutsche Bank has traditionally been strong in a range of markets, so that despite ranking thirteenth in the dollar table it ranked third over all in 1988.

Table 9.4 US$ Eurobonds: top 10 lead managers (1988)

Manager	*Amount (Sbn)*
Nomura Securities	13.8
CSFB/Crédit Suisse	8.0
Daiwa Securities	6.8
Yamaichi Securities	6.1
Nikko Securities	5.5
Merrill Lynch	4.2
Goldman Sachs	2.9
Industrial Bank of Japan	2.5
J. P. Morgan	2.5
Bankers Trust	2.2

Source: Annual Financing Report, *Euromoney*, March 1989.

THE GREY MARKET

At one or two points we have referred to the grey market. This term refers to a market which developed, as we saw in Chapter 3, in 1979. In it, dealings take place in bonds before they have been formally issued. (The equivalent in the US Treasury bond market is called 'when-issued' trading.)

When the grey market began, syndicate managers objected to it because they felt that it undercut the stabilisation process. If a bond's price was seen to be falling in the grey market that in itself could bring out more sellers and made the stabilisation process more expensive. It was also extremely embarrassing for the lead manager of a mispriced issue to see the bonds trading at a substantial discount in the secondary market before placing was complete.

Another objection to the grey market was that the bonds did not actually exist and might not exist in the event of a drastic change in circumstances (i.e. cancellation of the issue under a *force majeure* clause). This has not generally been a problem but a classic instance was the issue by Bell Resources of a package of A$1 billion equivalent of Euroconvertibles. This was announced in early October 1987; after the stock market crash of October 19 the lead manager, Merrill Lynch, pulled the deal. A number of firms had traded in the paper on the grey market and found all deals summarily cancelled.

One of the running problems in this market has been the practice of short selling of an apparently mispriced issue by market-makers. They generally rely on the lead manager to 'stabilise' the issue by buying back bonds in the market. As we saw earlier, stabilisation costs tended to be deducted from management fees, so that in effect the short sellers are profiting at the expense of the syndicate members – rather than, necessarily, the lead manager who bears responsibility for mispricing the deal.

A deal which rekindled the controversy over this issue was an issue for ECU100 million by Toyota, launched in January 1989. Shortly after the launch, CSFB, the lead manager, found it controlled 120 per cent of the issue. It moved to penalise the short sellers by indicating it would only sell bonds to them so that they could cover their positions, at a penal price of 105 (which was regarded in the market as a relatively moderate squeeze compared with those seen in other deals 'ramped' in the secondary market – see Chapter 10). Shortly thereafter CSFB announced it would no longer make prices to brokers (see Chapter 10 on the role of the brokers).

One solution to the problem of stabilisation has been adopted by certain houses, called 'take-and-pay' trading. Under this approach the lead manager guarantees to make available a set amount of bonds at a set price to syndicate members, without deduction of stabilisation costs. Under this arrangement syndicate members should – in theory – only bid for paper they know they can place, and can be sure of receiving it.

THE INTERNATIONAL PRIMARY MARKET ASSOCIATION

It was to grapple with these and related issues that the International Primary Market Association was founded in December 1984. Previous to this, there had existed a subcommittee of the Association of International Bond Dealers (discussed in the next chapter) concerned with the primary market. However, it was felt that there was a need for a body independent of the AIBD to regulate practice in the primary market.

After its formation the IPMA worked out a number of recommendations to cut out problem areas in the new issue process. A glance at these shows where some of the market's problems have been over the years:

Rule I: Lead managers to provide documentation at least one full business day before deal signing.
Rule II: Standardises commission arrangements.
Rule III: Sets out limits in deductions on stabilisation account.
Rule IV: Lays down minimum information on new issues to be set out in invitation telexes.
Rule V: Bans sham co-managements.
Rule VI: Limits the gap between indicated minimum and maximum underwriting commitments.
Rule VII: Requires £ and $ FRN allotments in multiples of 1 million.
Rule VIII: Requires final allotments within three days of the first invitation on pre-priced (bought) deals.
Rule IX: Requires minimum 50 per cent protection in bought deals syndicated amongst managers only.
Rule X: Penalises late payment of fees.
Rule XI: Governs arrangements for delivery of certificates.

Some of these (Rules II and III) have been discussed earlier; some are self-explanatory. Rule V relates to the practice which had developed where lead managers invited co-managers to participate on the basis that they would not actually have to buy any bonds: the co-manager simply allowed its name to appear in the list of syndicate members. The aim was to create the appearance that a bond was being widely placed, so enhancing secondary market liquidity by encouraging trading. Disguising the probable illiquidity of the bonds in this way meant that investors were being misled.

Rule VI aimed to combat the situation where an underwriter might be told that its commitment would be, say, '$1m to $5m', by laying down that the minimum must be at least 75 per cent of the maximum. Rule IX is concerned with 'protection'. If a co-manager sells some bonds to an investor and then finds that because the deal is going well, allotments are reduced, it might have a problem. Protection means that the lead manager guarantees to make available a certain amount of the bonds. Thus a co-manager might ask for, and be given, protection on $1 million of bonds; it could then be sure of being able to buy that amount from the lead manager.

REGULATORY CONSTRAINTS

Normally, at this stage, the bonds constituting the new issue are collectively represented by a single global certificate. This is to contribute to the so-called 'lock-up' process, under which physical delivery of new issues is delayed for 90 days, in order to meet with the United States' SEC 'seasoning' requirements, which lay down that an issue which is not registered with the SEC must not be distributed in the United States. Distribution is an elastic term, and has generally been held to mean that the securities must first of all 'come to rest' outside the United States as a result of the distribution, before being sold to US residents.

Thus all Eurobond issues will normally carry a clause stating that the offer and sale of the bonds have not been and will not be registered with the SEC under the 1933 Securities Act, and that the bonds will not be offered and sold in the USA or to US nationals wherever located until at least 90 days after the final distribution by the underwriters has been completed. (Recently the SEC has been considering loosening its private placement controls – by a proposed amendment to its Rule 144a – and there has also been consideration of Regulation S defining what is an offshore transaction, with a possible 'lock-up' period of 40 days. At the time of writing these proposals had not yet been finalised.)

To prevent individual bonds being sold into the United States before this seasoning period was completed, the practice grew up of arranging for a 'global certificate' for the bond. Under this system, when the bond issue is launched, a global certificate is deposited with the clearing system, say Euroclear, to represent the bond. Trading in the bonds does not result in physical delivery of the bonds until the global certificate is split up into definitive certificates, which is not allowed to happen until Euroclear is informed by the lead manager that 'all bonds have been distributed', a telex which is customarily not sent to Euroclear until at least 90 days or possibly more after the date of issue.

These elaborate precautions serve to cut down on the risk that the SEC might consider that the bonds were being distributed in the United States without being registered – a criminal offence in the USA. In 1982, the SEC adopted a system of 'shelf registration' under its rule 415, which allowed for a much more rapid registration process. This meant that US firms, who were prepared anyway to file financial data with the SEC, could for the first time contemplate a so-called 'universal' bond issue: an issue launched in the United States, coupled with distribution also in the Eurobond market.

However, most Eurobond issues remain normally unregistered with the SEC, with selling restrictions in force. Similarly, selling restrictions for the UK or Japan may also be observed from time to time, for similar reasons.

IMPORTANT CURRENCY SECTORS IN THE EUROBOND MARKET

The Dollar Eurobond Market

The US dollar segment of the market remains the most important, though its pre-eminence is increasingly being challenged by the Japanese yen. The weakness of the dollar from 1985–7 discouraged new issues in that currency. But the importance of the dollar sector is still unquestionable: there is the widest variety of issues, the deepest and most liquid markets, and the widest variety of hedging instruments.

The dollar Eurobond market has traditionally served as an important source of funds for US corporations, though these borrowers have come and gone with the strength of the currency. When the dollar is strong, and dollar bonds attractive to international investors, US corporations have aggressively tapped the market. Conversely, dollar weakness tends to lead to a withdrawal. (Although this phenomenon is less marked than it was, with the emergence of the swap market, yet, on the other hand, growing international concerns about the leverage and 'event risk' of US companies has partly offset this.) Thus, in 1985 when the dollar was at its peak, US corporations borrowed $39.6 billion overseas compared with $80.2 billion domestically. The yield differential between ten-year US corporate Eurodollar bonds and US domestic yields was roughly 75 basis points: Eurobonds were cheaper.

Similarly, the weakness of the dollar (and, perhaps, the growth of the currency swap market) has contributed to a cutting-back by US corporations of dollar issues in the Euromarkets relative to their issuance in other currencies.

Table 9.5 US corporate borrowing in the domestic market and overseas ($ bn)

	1983	*1984*	*1985*	*1986*	*1987*	*1988*[1]
Overseas	7.9	23.0	39.6	43.1	22.1	12.9
Domestic	38.5	52.0	80.2	159.1	126.6	82.0
Total	46.4	75.0	119.8	202.2	148.7	94.9
Overseas %	17	31	33	21	15	14

1. Jan.–Aug.

Source: Merrill Lynch, *Global Liability Management*, September 1988.

Table 9.6 US corporate borrowing in the Eurobond market

	1983	*1984*	*1985*	*1986*	*1987*	*1988*[1]
US$	6,002	19,391	29,904	30,333	14,128	7,036
Total	7,904	23,038	39,632	43,103	22,112	12,923
US$ %	76	84	75	70	64	54

1. Jan.–Aug.

Source: Merrill Lynch, *Global Liability Management*, September 1988.

The Yen Eurobond Market

The second most important sector in the market is now the Euroyen market. The first Euroyen issue was in 1977, but liberalisation did not get fully underway until December 1984 when Euroyen issues were permitted to government agencies and private companies (having been previously limited to supranationals). During 1985, the range of instruments that could be offered was widened. Table 9.7 shows the effects on the growth of the Euroyen market.

Table 9.7 Issue amount of Euroyen and Samurai bonds ($ bn)

	1981	*1982*	*1983*	*1984*	*1985*	*1986*	*1987*
Euroyen	1	1	2	2	10	30	62
Samurai	11	12	15	17	26	24	41

Source: Merrill Lynch.

Table 9.7 also shows the effects on the Samurai market of Euroyen liberalisation. The Samurai market is the Japanese equivalent of the US Yankee or the UK bulldog market: the domestic market for foreign bonds. There are several reasons for the relative loss of competitiveness of the Samurai market. They include higher commissions (the domestic market is dominated by the Big Four securities houses, while in the Euroyen market, banks are free to compete).

A second problem for the Samurai market has been the more cumbersome registration procedures. Given that 70–80 per cent of most new yen issues are swapped nowadays into other currencies (see Chapter 7) the difficulty of putting together swaps against Samurai issues – because the swap rates moved more quickly than the registration procedures – meant that the Euroyen market has been the cheaper source.

An interesting attempt to boost the appeal of the Samurai market was made by the World Bank in June 1986. It launched a ¥30 billion fifteen-

Table 9.8 Development of the Euroyen market

1970	First issue of yen-denominated foreign bonds (Samurai bonds) by the Asian Development Bank.
1973	Japan Securities Dealers Association founded.
1975	Resumption of Samurai bonds permitted. Formation of Mikuni & Co. (bond rating agency).
1976	Japan Over-the-Counter Trading Co. set up to stimulate OTC trading.
1977	First Euroyen bond issue by European Investment Bank.
1979	First yen CD issue permitted. First gen-saki (bond sale/repurchase) with foreigners allowed. First corporate Samurai issue by Sears Roebuck. (Also the first unsecured bond issue by a corporation; prime Japanese issuers were later allowed to issue unsecured bonds.) Japan Bond Research Institute (rating agency) founded by Nikkei.
1980	Exchange control liberalised. Previously, what was not permitted was forbidden; now, what is not forbidden is permitted.
1984	Government agencies and private corporations permitted to issue Euroyen bonds. Certain foreign banks permitted to join the government bond underwriting syndicate. Euroyen CDs permitted.
1985	Euroyen FRNs, zero coupons, dual currency and warrant bonds permitted. Trading in government bond futures permitted. Moody's Investors Services Japanese subsidiary opened.
1986	Any borrower rated A or better permitted to tap Euroyen market. Foreign commercial banks permitted to make Euroyen issues. Tokyo Offshore Banking Facility opened. First foreign members of Tokyo Stock Exchange allowed entry. Lock-up period on Euroyen bonds reduced from 180 to 90 days.

year issue, known as Series 34. It may be merged with any subsequent bonds carrying the same coupon and maturity date to create a large block of fungible World Bank paper in the Samurai market, so enhancing liquidity. It is the first time that the Japanese authorities have permitted the issue of bonds in fungible series form for any issuer other than the Japanese government itself.

Another attempt by the World Bank to boost the appeal of the Samurai market came in the form of the so-called Daimyo bond. In April 1987 the World Bank launched a ¥40 billion bond, listed in Luxembourg and cleared through Euroclear/Cedel but exempt – like a Samurai – from the customary 90-day seasoning period and thus allowed to be traded immediately in Japan.

A notable feature of the yen market has been the proliferation of strange and exotic coupon and redemption structures (see Chapters 5 and 6). Mostly these have been designed to achieve a high current coupon at the expense of capital gain. This is to attract investment from Japanese insurance companies, who can only pay dividends on their endowment insurance policies from interest income. However, more recently, with encouragement from the Ministry of Finance, there are signs that the insurance companies have begun to focus more on the concept of total return.

The ECU Eurobond Market

The ECU bond market is a pure creation of the Eurobond market. There is no domestic market, since there is no country whose currency is the ECU. There are two distinct ECUs, the private ECU and the official ECU. Their composition is identical, but private ECUs can be created by bundling together the appropriate amounts of currencies into a basket. Official ECUs can only be held by official institutions and are created as a result of swap arrangements between the European Monetary Cooperation Fund and members of the European Monetary System. Private and official ECUs are not exchangeable, or fungible to use the technical term.

The ECU as an official currency was born on 18 December 1978, as part of the setting up of the European Monetary System (EMS) of linked exchange rates by members of the European Community (EC). The EC regulation which created it defines the ECU as a 'basket of members' currencies', that is the sum of fixed amounts of each of the members' currency. The first definition of the amounts fixed the makeup of the ECU from its beginnings to the first revision, which took place on 17 September 1984, when the Greek drachma was included, Greece having joined the EC in the interim. In September 1989 the basket was revised again to accommodate two new members, Spain and Portugal. Table 9.9 shows the effect of the changes.

Revision of the amounts of currency in the basket usually takes place every five years, so the next revision will be due in September 1994.

Table 9.9 ECU composition

	1979–84	*1984–9*	*1989–*
Deutschmark	0.82800	0.71900	0.6242
£ sterling	0.08850	0.08780	0.08784
French franc	1.15000	1.31000	1.332
Italian lira	109.00000	140.00000	151.8
Dutch guilder	0.28600	0.25600	0.2198
Belgian franc	3.66000	3.71000	3.431 (Belgian and Luxembourg franc combined)
Luxembourg franc	0.14000	0.14000	
Danish krone	0.27700	0.21900	0.1976
Irish punt	0.00759	0.00871	0.00855
Greek drachma	0	1.15000	1.44
Spanish peseta	0	0	6.885
Portuguese escudo	0	0	1.393

Between revision dates, changes can be made if the weight of one of the currencies has changed by more than 25 per cent. In fact during the last period the weight of the drachma fell by 47 per cent without provoking a revision, since it was felt the weight of the drachma was too small to worry about.

The value of the ECU in US dollars is found by taking the dollar value of 0.6242 Deutschmarks, adding to it the value of 0.08784 pounds sterling, etc. The EC provides an official value each day using central-bank-provided exchange rates at 2.30 p.m.; the result is quoted on Reuters Monitor page FXEZ. As well as being the official unit of account for all EC transactions, the ECU also plays a key role in the EMS, since EMS members' exchange rates are defined in terms of a 'central rate' fixing their currency in terms of ECU.

Official ECUs can only be held by the central banks of the EC and other central banks who have been given permission. Private ECUs are traded like any other currency. In the Bank of England's 1986 foreign exchange survey, ECU trading was reported at around $900 million daily. Major commercial banks provide continuous quotes for the ECU (normally they have computer systems for calculating the ECU value from the currency rates held in their systems) and these can be seen on the appropriate Reuters/Telerate screens. ECU lending by banks in the BIS reporting area grew from ECU14 billion in 1983 to ECU90 billion in 1988.

An ECU clearing system is operated by the Bank for International Settlements in conjunction with the ECU banking association which has about 85 members world-wide; all ECU transactions are cleared daily through this system. A number of banks will make foreign exchange prices spot and forward for the ECU; they will also take ECU deposits. ECU certificates of deposit have also been issued.

Until recently, one problem with trading private ECUs was that the Deutsche Bundesbank defined the ECU as an index-linked unit of account. The use of these is banned in Germany (because of past inflationary excesses in the 1930s). The restrictions were revoked only in June 1987.

The EC Commission is keen to develop the role of the ECU as a step towards creating a single monetary area in Europe. The first steps, therefore, have been for an exchange market, a clearing system and bank deposits in the currency to develop. The next step has been to encourage the development of other financial markets. The first moves here were in the bond market: in April 1981 the Société Financière pour les Télécommunications et l'Electronique (SFTE) issued the first ECU bond. Table 9.10 shows the development of the market.

Most of the issues were straight bonds (sometimes with equity warrants attached) but a few floating-rate notes have been brought to the market. In a number of cases the FRNs were convertible into a fixed rate and have mostly been converted. The top three borrowers in the market have been

Table 9.10

	Issue volume (million ECU)	*Issue number*	*Average size*
1981	202	6	33.7
1982	800	19	42.8
1983	1,915	44	43.5
1984	3,500	64	54.7
1985	9,000	127	70.9
1986	7,136	83	86.0
1987	6,607	71	93.1
1988	9,420	90	104.7

the European Investment Bank, the EC and the World Bank. According to BIS figures, the ECU accounted for 3.9 per cent of the total stock outstanding of international bonds, compared with 6.2 per cent for sterling and 9.5 per cent for Deutschmarks.

The Deutschmark Eurobond Market

The Deutschmark market is one of the more peculiar Eurosectors, since in effect there is no clear distinction between Euro-DM bonds and foreign DM bonds, unlike the distinction, say, between Eurodollar and Yankee bonds, or Euroyen and Samurai bonds. All German bond issues must be lead managed either by a German institution or by the German subsidiary of a foreign institution.

Major changes in the German domestic market, which have had Euromarket repercussions, were introduced by the Bundesbank on 1 May 1985. In the past, the Bundesbank banned currency swaps out of new issues in the Deutschmark market; these were now permitted. The Bundesbank also announced that foreign banks incorporated in Germany would be permitted to lead-manage Deutschmark issues. For the first time it also permitted such novelties as certificates of deposit, floating-rate notes and zero coupon securities to be denominated in Deutschmarks. However, the turnover tax stifled the CD market at birth.

Some of these markets had mixed success. Zero coupon securities, after an initial flurry, seem to have faded. The dual currency sector suffered from the disastrous launch of the first issue by Export Development Corporation of Canada; to date, that has been the only issue – compared with the large number in Japanese yen.

The FRN market suffered also from an initial indigestion, complicated by the fact that fifteen of the first 27 issues were capped (i.e. had an upper limit for the floating rate – which reduced the protection for the investor if rates rose sharply). After the initial activity, the capped Deutschmark FRN market became very illiquid. Another innovation – Deutsche Bank's bull/bear bond (see Chapter 6) which was followed by a similar issue for Eurofima – has been hindered by another regulatory body. After advice from German bank regulators that institutions should not use such bonds as stock market hedging instruments, demand fell.

The next step in the liberalisation of the markets was the introduction of a quota for foreign banks in the Federal bond consortium. German government and agency bonds were placed through a consortium of 73 banks. In 1986, nineteen foreign banks were allowed to join the consortium, with a 20 per cent share of the total volume of business. The benefits of this liberalisation are a two-edged sword, however, since consortium members are obligated to take paper regardless of market conditions.

The development of the German market was hurt by the reimposition of withholding tax and the subsequent volte-face when it was quickly removed. International investors switched from German government bonds to, amongst others, Dutch government bonds (see Chapter 15) and secondly from Eurobonds issued by borrowers domiciled in Germany (caught by the tax) to non-German Euromark issuers. However, the situation now seems to have stabilised.

The Sterling Eurobond Market

The United Kingdom has sophisticated capital markets, but over the years until 1979 they were stifled into a domestic role by exchange controls. The abolition of exchange controls in 1979 allowed the sterling markets to integrate truly into the international scene, and also allowed the market to develop a fuller range of activity. In 1980, the first full year after exchange controls were lifted, total sterling new issues (excluding UK public sector issues) were just over £750 million. By 1982 the new issue flow had risen to £2 billion and by 1988 it had risen to £16.5 billion. The major domestic market is for gilt-edged (see Chapter 15) or government bonds, while there are smaller markets in corporate bonds, Bulldogs (foreign bonds issued in sterling) and mortgage-backed issues.

As in a number of other countries during the 1980s, the London market has been shaken up by deregulation. In 1986 a series of changes were made which collectively were nicknamed 'Big Bang'. Before 'Big Bang', the UK markets for gilt-edged and equities were both controlled by the Stock Exchange. They worked on 'single capacity'. That is, there was a division between stockbrokers and stock-jobbers. Jobbers were market-makers. They could not deal with the public. Brokers dealt with the public but acted as agents rather than market-makers.

This system was swept away to be replaced by US-style 'dual capacity' whereby market-makers could also deal with the public and with investing institutions. At the same time, outside shareholders were allowed to assume full ownership of stockbroking and stock-jobbing member firms on or after 31 March 1986. The other crucial change at this time was the introduction of the Financial Services Act of 1986 (see Chapter 18) which for the first time introduced some regulation of the secondary Eurobond market in London by the British authorities. (Although of course the 'Governor's eyebrows' have always been a potent control in the hands of the Bank of England: disapproval by the Governor had a way of becoming painful if the offender did not fall in line). The primary market has always been steered by the Bank of England, which prefers to see issues led by either a British firm or else a foreign firm with similar capacities from a country offering reciprocal opportunities for British owned banks to lead issues in that country. If this reciprocity is not granted then foreign firms are restricted to co-management positions only.

Although the first Eurosterling issue was made in 1972, the second, for the European Coal and Steel Community, did not appear until 1977, when the market began in earnest. The major issuers in this market in recent years have been the UK building societies (savings and loan institutions) seeking long-term funding for their mortgage portfolios, and a number of banks. There have also been a number of issues by retail names – a rash of convertibles before the October 1987 Crash (see above).

More recently straights have come back into favour. An example would be the issue on 30 January 1988 of a £100 million bond by John Lewis PLC: a fifteen-year bond with a coupon of 10½ per cent priced at 100.233. Because UK rates were high at the time and expected to fall, the bond was issued as a partly-paid, with £31.875 per cent payable on 6 February and £68.358 per cent payable on 3 August. The effect of this was to allow the investor to profit on the capital gain on £100 of bond by paying only £31.875 – provided rates fell. Naturally, if they rose, there would be equally large proportionate loss.

The Budget of 1989 swept aside the last remaining restrictions on the UK markets when the old rules placing restrictions on public sterling issues of less than five years' maturity by corporate borrowers were relaxed. The first issue after the relaxation, for Abbey National Building Society, was for eighteen-month floating-rate notes yielding LIBOR flat. Attached to them were debt warrants exercisable at par into a new issue of fixed-rate ten-year bonds carrying an 11 per cent coupon. The life of the warrants was twelve months. The market priced the warrants at about 1.5 per cent. Thus if rates rose during the life of the warrants, investors will not exercise their call on the 11 per cent bonds, and Abbey National earns a £3 million profit which subsidises the cost of the bond. If rates fall, investors exercise the warrants and the Abbey National raises £200 million of fixed-rate funds which can be swapped into floating-rate money.

The Canadian Dollar Eurobond Market

The Canadian dollar and the US dollar are closely linked, as are the financial markets of the two countries. As in so many other countries, deregulation of the financial markets in Canada took place during 1985–8. In December 1985 the province of Ontario raised the 10 per cent ownership limit on the purchase of security houses by financial institutions to 100 per cent. After twelve months, the decision was ratified by the Federal Government. Canadian banks, trusts and insurance companies were given a headstart by limiting foreign ownership to 50 per cent until June 1988. Wood Gundy was bought by Canadian Imperial Bank of Commerce and Dominion Securities by the Royal Bank of Canada, in both cases after a number of abortive merger attempts.

Foreign investment in the domestic market is concentrated on government bonds which are not subject to withholding tax. Withholding tax is charged on interest paid to non-Canadian investors for issues in the domestic market with less than five years to maturity. Thus Canadian issuers raising short-term funds tend to issue domestically, seeking longer-term funds from the Eurobond market. The first Canadian dollar Eurobond issue was made in 1974 by the British Columbia Municipal Finance Authority, and the market has grown slowly and steadily since then. It is often coupled with the Australian market (see below) as a higher-yielding market linked to the US dollar. As such, a number of German banks and industrials have actively issued in Canadian dollars as they have in Australian dollars, trading on Continental investors' liking for familiar names paying a high yield, regardless of currency risk.

The Australian Dollar Eurobond Market

Like the Canadian dollar, the Australian dollar bond market is usually seen as a high-yielding alternative to the US dollar. As such, it has been an attractive home for a number of German issuers such as BMW and the German banks, trading on Continental investors' name and yield preferences.

The first Australian dollar Eurobond was issued in 1976, but the market remained small for many years, only really taking off in 1985. The market remains a small one, opening up in waves as currency swap opportunities materialise (since issuers typically swap the currency proceeds back into another currency). Issues are normally limited to a size of about A$75 million; maturities are fairly short, concentrated in the one-to-five year range.

During 1988 the domestic Australian bond market began to expand rapidly. In the first few months of the year A$2.7 billion (US$2.21 billion) of fixed-rate medium-term corporate paper was issued. This was partly thanks to the reduction in government borrowing as the budget moved into surplus and partly to the imposition on the banks by the Reserve Bank of Australia of risk asset weightings requiring increased capital. This encouraged a switch from borrowing to bond issuance.

The Swiss Franc Market

Finally, although it is not technically part of the Eurobond market, we should look at the Swiss franc market. It is a parallel market to the Eurobond market, a traditional foreign bond market: the Swiss National Bank has always forbidden Eurobonds in Swiss francs. There has been a slow, progressive easing of the old constraints on the market, notably in 1985 when the ceiling on the size of a public bond issue was removed, and in May 1986 when it abolished the distinction between public issues and private placements. The significance of this lay in the fact that traditionally Swiss public issues had been rigidly controlled by the Big Three Swiss commercial banks, each of which led a syndicate which always consisted of the same members. Issues were lead managed in rotation by one of the Big Three. Private placements, however, were less formal. They were confined to the shorter term – eighteen months to eight years. Public issues had a minimum maturity of eight years. This system is now breaking down: in August 1987, for the first time, the Big Three participated in syndicates led by foreign banks.

A number of foreign institutions have moved into the Swiss market in recent years with a view to extending their global presence. Yet their impact has not been as large as in, say, Frankfurt, and certainly not as large as in London. One notable features has been the strong Japanese involvement, because the Swiss market is an attractive source of funds for Japanese companies. They have issued large amounts of equity warrant bonds (see Chapter 12). These are attractive because of the low coupon, relatively small currency risk and attractive implicit pricing on the equity.

Other Eurobond Markets

The markets discussed above are the main sectors of the Eurobond market. The French franc has been important from time to time, and as the country's domestic financial reforms (see Chapter 15) become more firmly established, the market is likely to increase in importance. Others, like the Kuwaiti dinar, the Finnmark, even (in the 'good old days') the Venezuelan bolivar, have come and gone; but interest in these markets is generally fitful at best. The main currency markets provide – fairly – continuously active primary and secondary markets; the minor currencies only become active when special circumstances trigger investor interest.

10 The Secondary Market

No matter how wonderful a bond he holds, the investor will always want to be able to sell it, if he should unexpectedly need cash. To do this, there has to be an active and liquid secondary market. The secondary market is where bonds are traded, after the new issue period is over, for the remainder of their life. Liquidity – the ability to deal in reasonable size at the current market price – is the key problem in any secondary market. It must be said that in the Eurobond market it is very variable. Some issues which are large and widely held, such as the Canada 9 per cents of 1996, are actively traded. This encourages investors to buy them, and so the process becomes self-feeding. Conversely, a number of issues, such as the spate of equity warrant-linked Japanese bonds of 1986–7, and some of the more specialised bonds discussed in Chapters 5 and 6, are notoriously illiquid. In general, the more recent the issue, the more liquid it is. After a certain period, the bonds tend to settle into the hands of investors planning to hold them to maturity, and they disappear from sight.

As Table 10.1 shows, the fixed-rate Eurobond market's overall trading turnover has historically compared well with major government markets (compare also Figure 9.1), but the wider spreads show relatively less liquidity in individual issues. Whereas a large slice of US Treasury bond trading, for example, is concentrated on just eight issues (the on-the-run 2, 3, 4, 5, 7, 10, 20 and 30 year bonds – on-the-run meaning the most recently auctioned) the Eurobond trading is spread over several thousand issues, with over 500 traded regularly and perhaps 2,000 traded from time to time. Thus some issues are quite illiquid. The author has painful memories of

Table 10.1 Liquidity measures

Market	*1986 outstanding ($bn)*	*Turnover (times p.a.)*	*Trading turnover ($bn)*	*Average bid/offer spread (%)*
Government bonds:				
USA	2,000	12×	24,000	0.06
Japan	900	5×	4,500	0.14
Germany	130	7×	910	0.20
UK	200	9×	1,800	0.06
France	60	5×	300	0.15
Eurobonds:				
Fixed	350	8×	2,800	0.30
Floating	150	6×	900	0.10

Source: County NatWest, quoted in P. Gallant, *The Eurobond Market*, Woodhead-Faulkner, 1988.

being short on one occasion of $7.5 million of Japanese equity warrant bonds: it took four days to find the paper, at any price.

The main components of any market are its participants, the rules of the market and a settlement system. Participants in the secondary market consist of investors, market-makers and other securities firms, and brokers who intermediate between market-makers. The rules of the system are mainly set by the Association of International Bond Dealers (AIBD). The settlement systems are provided by Euroclear and Cedel. We will now discuss each of these three components in more detail.

MARKET PARTICIPANTS

In the early days of the Eurobond market, the volume of secondary market trading was very small. During the 1960s, the London stock market was not very interested in Eurobond secondary trading. It was left to other firms such as White Weld and Strauss Turnbull, together with Samuel Montagu and Dominion Securities, amongst others.

Difficulties included the fact that the international telephone network was still rudimentary, and there was no proper clearing system. During 1968, the primary market experienced record volume, but the secondary market experienced enormous problems from the sudden growth in trading. This led to the involvement of the AIBD and the formation of Euroclear (see Chapter 17).

At this stage, bonds were sold to clients on the basis that they were effectively private placements: that is, the client could not necessarily expect to be able to re-sell before maturity. Secondary market trading amounts were very small, usually between US$10,000 and US$25,000 and trades of US$100,000 were rare. In the primary market, tickets might be written for US$1 million to US$2 million, but these blocks would normally be held to maturity.

By comparison, today, the secondary market works smoothly, at least in terms of the mechanical process of bond settlement and delivery, and standardised trading rules. There will usually be at least one market-maker for each Eurobond issue listed by the AIBD in its weekly listing of outstanding issues (though it has to be said that in fact many of those listed as market-makers in the book turn out to be rather less than that in reality). The number of market-makers listed against a particular issue is a starting point for assessing its liquidity.

Most trading operations divide the market into sectors (see Chapter 9 for more discussion of market sectors) such as Deutschmark bonds, dollar bonds, supranationals and so on, with the fineness of the gradations depending on the size of the operation and number of traders. Each type of bond will need a different trading style. Equity warrant bonds, for example, force the trader to be in constant touch with the Japanese stock market, given the number of Japanese equity warrant bonds outstanding, and thus with the Big Four Japanese security firms amongst others. Zero coupons are another very specialised market, requiring careful contact with the key specialist players. Straight dollar supranational or major sovereign bonds, by contrast, are more widely traded and liquid.

To see how the process works, let us consider a trader who is overbought – 'long' – $2 million of Canada 9 per cent bonds maturing 1996. This is a large issue – $1 billion outstanding – and is quite actively traded at the time of writing. He or she wants to sell the bonds. At this stage, there are three possible choices. The first, and ideal, route would be to sell them to a client. Suppose that none want to buy them. Then the trader can sell either to another trader, or through a broker. Selling to a trader is simply a matter of ringing round a number of possible counterparties to see if they have any interest and, if so, selling the bonds to them.

ROLE OF THE BROKER

The problem with this method is that a number of counterparties may become aware that we want to sell. An alternative is to talk to a broker. The broker's role is to go to possible counterparties and, without revealing the name of the seller, indicate that he has a client wanting to sell $2 million of the Canada 9s. If he finds a buyer at a price acceptable to the seller, he tells the buyer 'You own them', 'Done', or words to that effect. Likewise, he tells the seller that the trade is done. He then sends a telex confirmation to both parties. The trade is then settled seven days later through Euroclear or Cedel, as explained in Chapter 17. For his work in finding a counterparty he is paid a small fee, called 'brokerage'. This is negotiable between brokers and their customers but would usually be around 0.05 per cent.

The benefit that the broker provides to his customers is total anonymity; the buyer will never know the identity of the seller. This is possible because the securities are cleared through one of two international clearance systems, Euroclear or Cedel. They effectively insulate buyers from sellers. This insulation meant that when the firm of Purcell Graham set up as brokers in 1978 it was now possible for professional market-makers to deal freely amongst themselves without ever knowing who their counterparts were. In turn, this allowed them to sell short a new issue without the knowledge of the syndicate manager, which led to a good deal of controversy. Many new issue managers resented the emergence of the brokers and tried to combat their influence, but the passage of time seems to have entrenched them in the system.

The broker's risk is that in the interval between telling the buyer the bonds are sold and telling the seller that the deal is done, the seller has changed his mind, or there may have been a misunderstanding between the two parties. In this case the broker's risk is that the firm may have to 'substantiate its price', i.e. to fulfil the original trade agreed regardless of the fact that one side is disputing its terms. Thus the broker may lose money even though in theory it is not acting as a principal to the trade.

A well-known example of this type of problem occurred in April 1987 during the course of a trade between Wood Gundy and Burns Fry, on the one hand, and Merrill Lynch on the other, handled by Gintel. A new Can$50 million issue for British Columbia Telephone was launched by Merrill at a price deemed aggressive by the market. After 48 hours, Merrill owned 120 per cent of the issue. It decided to move up its offer price to 120 to punish the short sellers. Buy-in notices were issued in June, for settlement early July. Wood Gundy and Burns Fry took strong exception to the buy-in terms, claiming they were punitive, and refused to pay Gintel, filing a lawsuit instead against Merrill Lynch; the matter was later settled out of court.

As this incident shows, disputes can happen between highly professional firms, and this is where the Association of International Bond Dealers can be of great value to the market.

MARKET RULES: THE ROLE OF THE AIBD

The Association of International Bond Dealers held its first meeting at the Great Eastern Hotel near Liverpool Street in London on 18 April 1969. At the time, its significance seemed little more than social. Its aims, detailed in the press announcement inviting membership applications, were:

(a) To promote friendly relations between member firms and between representatives.
(b) To provide a basis for joint examination, discussion and elimination of mutual technical problems.
(c) To maintain a close liaison with the international bond issuing houses.

The original aim was to make the AIBD an offshore entity while still incorporated within the UK. This proved to be technically difficult, and as a result in 1970 the legal headquarters of the AIBD was transfered to Zurich.

It is probably fair to say that one of the main early intentions was to provide a convivial framework for a social club for the fledgling Eurobond market. But by 1969 the growth in secondary market trading had started to cause serious settlement problems, and the AIBD became involved.

By today's standards delivery procedures in 1969 were antiquated. Bonds were traded for physical delivery in either New York or Luxembourg with two separate settlement methods. Trade confirmations were often sent by post. They did not arrive in time to be checked before the issue of delivery instructions. It is said that at one point by April 1969 about 20 per cent of Eurobond deliveries were failing. The difficulties of this period led to a number of firms, including First Boston, Weeden & Co. and Dominick & Dominick, pulling out of Eurobond market-making. According to H. C. Donnerstag, by this time the Eurobond market-making community was down to six or eight members.

To help meet the problems, the AIBD set up a Committee for New York and European Settlements, This undertook a key role in sorting out the settlements problems, in conjunction with the foundation of Euroclear, formed in December 1968 under the sponsorship of Morgan Guaranty Trust Company of New York (see Chapter 17).

The other key committee set up by the AIBD in its first phase was the Standard Market Practices Committee. This framed the first actual trading regulations, and produced the first AIBD yield tables.

Most AIBD members' day-to-day contact with the AIBD probably comes from its annual meetings (usually in some attractive location where pleasure can be combined with business), its semi-annual members' register listing all its members and where they work, and its weekly listing of bonds in issue together with those firms which make markets in these bonds. But there are a number of other functions.

One of the important roles of the AIBD has been the development of training programmes for entrants to the market. The AIBD Education Committee organises an annual seminar in Montreux in Switzerland. Attendants are given a course of lectures on the market before taking an examination which results in a Diploma. A related role is setting industry standards, such as the AIBD yield tables and calculators, and the settling of technical issues such as bond printing standards.

The AIBD has also laid down, over the years, a series of rules governing trading practices. Of these the most important in practical terms are probably those governing buy-ins and arbitration. The buy-in occurs when a trader, having sold short a bond he does not own, cannot cover his position. If by twenty-one days after the value date of his sale the bonds have not been delivered, then the buyer issues a buy-in notice. This gives the seller a further fourteen days in which to complete. If the seller still has not completed then the buyer contacts a firm nominated by the AIBD and this firm is instructed to buy the securities at the best rate available in the open market. The problem arises that if the only seller is intent on punishing the short sellers, the price can in principle bear no relation to reality. The Wood Gundy/Burns Fry affair or the case in September 1987 when Dean Witter subjected short sellers of the Farm Credit 11⅝ per cent of 1993 to a buy-in at a price of 112, raising the price to 121 the next day, is an example of the problem.

This type of situation makes the AIBD's role in the settlement of market disputes, such as that between Dean Witter and Wood Gundy and others, of great importance. Its role is not confined to such well-publicised cases: inevitably, dealings between a large and polyglot community from diverse backgrounds can give rise to misunderstandings and errors. Article 22 of the AIBD's statutes lays down that the AIBD:

> . . . shall maintain and make available to interested parties, in particular its members,
> (1) institutions and proceedings for conciliation
> (2) institutions and proceedings for arbitration.

The AIBD fulfils this requirement by running a panel of conciliators and arbitrators who are assigned by the AIBD to settle disputes. Conciliation is the first stage, and is kept deliberately low-cost: parties may not be represented by professional counsel. If conciliation breaks down, one or other party may take the dispute to arbitration. A court of arbitration, based in Switzerland but able to move elsewhere, will consist of two or four arbitrators and an umpire. Its decisions are binding.

The AIBD's expenses in both types of dispute are paid by the parties according to the AIBD's decisions in each case; an advance payment on account of costs must be made. For conciliation, each party bears its own costs; after arbitration, the AIBD may award costs to one side or the other.

Recent developments in the UK under the 1986 Financial Services Act have meant an enhanced role for the AIBD. This is discussed in more depth in Chapter 18.

HEDGING

A trader running a position in Eurobonds faces several risks: liquidity risk, credit risk, interest rate risk, and possibly currency risk. Liquidity risk – the risk that when the time comes to sell, or buy, there are no buyers/sellers – is a fact of life that has to be lived with, as is credit risk. Interest rate and currency risk, though, can be hedged.

Currency risk is fairly straightforward: for most currencies there is a liquid forward exchange market. There is one point of detail: the trader would not normally hedge to maturity. That is, if he owns a five-year bond, he would not sell five years forward. This is because the long-term forward exchange market is much less liquid and by the same token more expensive to deal in. Normally he would take out a one-month or three-month forward contract. Because the forward exchange rates are determined by interest differentials (see the author's *Foreign Exchange Handbook*, John Wiley, New York, 1983) he is in fact taking an implied position on the relative shape of the two currencies' yield curves. But compared with the gyrations of spot foreign exchange markets, this risk is for practical purposes generally very small. (See Chapter 8 on foreign exchange risks.)

Interest rate risk is a much trickier proposition. Take the case of a five-year straight dollar Eurobond, a classic example of the kind of bond a trader might hold in inventory. There are two ways to hedge the interest risk implied in this: by shorting US Treasury bonds or by selling futures.

It is fairly straightforward to sell US Treasury bonds short, because one can borrow the bonds one does not have, in order to make delivery on the short sale, through the 'reverse repo' market.

The 'repo' market is a huge market in the United States for the overnight sale and repurchase of Treasury bonds. A 'reverse repo' is a borrowing of Treasury bonds through the medium of a purchase and overnight sale. Effectively it is a borrowing secured by cash. (Repo's can be done for longer periods, and also against other instruments such as bonds issued by US government agencies, but the central market is for overnight repo of Treasury bonds.) The mechanics work like this:

Day 1

Sell short $5 million 8⅞ per cent Treasuries due 15 February 1994 for value Day 2.

Buy $5 million 8⅞ per cent 15/2/94 against placement of $5 million cash security, for value Day 2, with resale fixed for Day 3. (Effectively this is an overnight borrowing of the bonds against cash security.)

Day 2

The transactions take place:

	Assets		Liabilities
Short sale: Cash received	$5m.	8⅞% 15/2/94 delivered	$5m.
Reverse repo: 8⅞% 15/2/94	$5m.	Cash payable	$5m.

Assuming that we want to roll the position for another day, we would then enter into another overnight repo from Day 2 to Day 3. So on Day 3 we would have the Day 2 repo unwinding, to be offset with the new Day 3 repo, and thus the position is rolled over from day to day. The cost of the operation is the coupon on the Treasury, 8⅞ per cent (since we buy back the bond tomorrow with another day's accrued interest) less the interest paid to us (the reverse repo rate) on our cash deposit.

There are refinements to this process, ignored for simplicity; the most important concerns allowance for accrued interest, which was an important element in the bankruptcy of Drysdale Securities in 1982 and triggered fresh arrangements in the repo market whereby the value of accrued interest is allowed for in collateral calculation. Another important point is that we need to borrow one specific bond. Having contracted to deliver the 8⅞ per cent of 15/2/94, eyebrows will be raised (and more than that) if we deliver 7 per cent of 15/1/94. So we are vulnerable to a squeeze in that specific issue, which can drive down the interest rate paid to us on the cash deposit. The bonds are said to 'go on special', and the reverse rate might fall to as low a 1 per cent per annum.

SPREAD SHIFTS

On balance, though, it is fairly straightforward to use the Treasury market to hedge a dollar Eurobond position. But there is an important risk, because the Treasury market and the Eurobond market do not move in exact tandem. Consider the case of an underwriting house which brings, say, an IBM Eurobond to market at five-year Treasuries plus 25 basis points. It owns perhaps half the issue, say $100 million worth, at that spread. Thus, it is very vulnerable if the five-year Treasury rates were to rise sharply, and thus the price on five-year Treasury bonds to fall.

To hedge its risk, it will sell short $100 million of five-year Treasuries (approximately – depending on whether or not it seeks a more precise hedge by the use of 'duration' – see Appendix 2). Suppose now that a crisis occurs, and the five-year US Treasury yield jumps from say, 10 per cent to 11 per cent. The theory is that the fall in the value of the firm's holdings of IBM Eurobonds will have been more or less offset by the rise in the value of its short position in five-year Treasuries.

But traditionally, the Eurobond market responds more sluggishly than the domestic US market. As US Treasury bond prices fall, Eurobond prices fall less; as Treasury bond prices rise, Eurobond prices rise more slowly. This means that the Treasury bond is at best an imperfect hedge. This was a lesson learned expensively by many firms in April–May 1986 when the US bond market weakened sharply. The Eurobond market did not.

The reasons for the relative sluggishness of the Eurobond market *vis-à-vis* the domestic Treasury market are twofold. First, still, it is the case that there are significant numbers of Eurobonds which are locked away by retail or other investors for the longer term. These bonds do not trade actively, and therefore there is less liquidity in many issues. This may at times tend to dampen price movements. Secondly, and more importantly, while the US treasury bond market is influenced only by US interest rate expectations, the Eurobond market is also powerfully influenced by views on the currency. As US Treasury bond prices fall, because US interest rates are rising, so generally the prospects for the US dollar will improve. There is thus a somewhat offsetting effect for the Eurobond investor. He may be losing in the principal value of his bonds, but the currency equivalent in his domestic currency will be deteriorating less because of the currency benefit.

FUTURES HEDGING

The alternative way to hedge is through the futures market. There are in theory various choices available to the futures hedger: the five-year Treasury note contract on the New York Futures Exchange, the ten-year Treasury note contract on the Chicago Board of Trade, or the twenty-year Treasury bond contract also on the CBOT. But in practice the only one of these which has meaningful liquidity is the last. (An example of how futures hedging works is set out in Chapter 7 on derivatives.)

The futures hedge can never be perfect, though. The hedger faces a yield curve risk, hedging a five-year instrument with one priced off a twenty-year instrument. More importantly, there is a substantial 'basis risk' between the futures market and the cash Eurobond market because, as we have just seen, Eurobonds trade in a different way than Treasuries. So the futures, driven by the cash Treasury market, will not necessarily move to offset the Eurobond market.

Efforts have been repeatedly made to devise a Eurobond futures contract to meet this market need. But they have always been defeated by the difficulty of devising a technically satisfactory 'basket' of Eurobonds to represent the market as a whole. Whereas there are relatively few twenty-year US Treasury bond issues outstanding at any one time, so the futures contract is linked to a fairly homogeneous pool, this is not the case in the Eurobond market. A reasonably successful municipal bond future has been devised in the USA in the face of similar problems, however, and it is hoped that the introduction of the TRAX system (see Chapter 18) will help overcome a related problem, of obtaining adequate price information on the underlying bonds. So it is possible that in time a Eurobond future could be developed. If so, it would greatly enhance the hedging process.

11 Issuers, Intermediaries and Investors

After all is said and done, issues must be placed with investors. We have looked at the issue process, and how the bonds are traded. Why do investors buy, or not buy? How do issuers and intermediaries tailor their product to demand? What are their risks and problems?

WHY INVEST IN EUROBONDS?

For the institutional investor, there are generally two reasons for investing in the Eurobond markets. Tax, and choice. The fact that interest on Eurobonds is paid gross, without any deduction of withholding tax, is a major attraction for those international investors exempt from taxation, such as supranational bodies or investment corporations located in low-tax areas. The process of reclaiming withholding tax, even if you are exempt from it, is laborious and time-consuming.

But a more important factor is the freedom of choice afforded to the international investor. Take the case of an American pension fund which wants to invest internationally. If the Eurobond market did not exist, it would be faced with making investments in relatively limited domestic markets. For example, the UK industrial bond market was moribund for many years. The German bond market has traditionally been dominated by mortgage banks and related entities with low issuance by industrial corporations.

But in the Euromarket, it has become possible for this American pension fund to invest in bonds issued by companies such as IBM, Kodak, Sony, ICI and Mercedes. These credits are familiar to it, yet it can buy their bonds in Deutschmarks, Swiss francs, Japanese yen or sterling. Thus, the Eurobond market has made international diversification much easier for bond investors. Also, in a number of countries, the major corporations have chosen to tap the Euromarket rather than their own, more restricted, domestic markets. The UK is a case in point. Bonds in 1987 were issued in the Euromarket by ICI, Grand Metropolitan and others rather than in the domestic sterling market, because of the greater flexibility of the Euromarket.

Another more mundane point should not be overlooked. The existence of Cedel and Euroclear (see Chapter 17) means there are efficient international depositories for Eurobonds. The administrative aspects of investing internationally are thus greatly simplified, compared with having

Table 11.1 Some defaulted Eurobonds

Issuer	*Lead manager*
Famous Schools	S. G. Warburg
Farrington Overseas	Drexel
Equity Funding	Paribas
Four Seasons	Kredietbank
US Financial Overseas	Goldman Sachs
Maritimecor	Bankers Trust
Daylin Int.	S. G. Warburg
Eidai	Nikko Securities
United Merchant Overseas	Lehman Brothers
Itel finance	Kidder Peabody
Saxon Industries	Bear Sterns
Grupo Alfa	CSFB
Blocker Energy	CSFB
Pengo Finance	Kleinwort Benson
Turbo Resources	Orion Royal Bank
Grupo Pliana	Merrill Lynch

Source: I. M. Kerr, *A History of the Eurobond Market*, Euromoney Publications, London, 1984.

to set up safekeeping arrangements in a dozen or more countries if the investor were confined to domestic markets. For those running large portfolios, administrative simplicity has much to commend it.

Finally, there is one other benefit from the Eurobond market to the investor. To a degree, the Eurobond and Euroequity markets bring the assurance – normally – that a security brought to the market by one of the major international Euro houses will generally be reasonably respectable. There will have been a 'due diligence' process of some sort, carried out by people whom the investor can normally respect. Thus the Eurobond and Euroequity markets do add a kind of 'seal of approval' to a particular stock or bond. Generally issues brought by the top firms can be assumed to be fairly respectable, though the guarantee is by no means absolute (as Table 11.1 shows).

LIQUIDITY

A key point for the investor is liquidity. It is vital to the investor to know that if he buys a bond he can sell it without difficulty if his cash flow needs change. Liquidity is the ability to sell a reasonable amount of a security without much affecting its price. There are shades of grey: 'reasonable' and 'much' beg questions. They vary over time in line with market conditions. Certainly a minimum 'reasonable' quote for a straight fixed bond would be

$250,000. If there were any difficulty in trading this amount one would not hesitate to class the bond as illiquid.

This means investors tend to prefer large issues. More people trade large issues; there are more bonds available to trade. So they tend to be more liquid. A large 'bench-mark' issue, such as (at the time of writing) the Canada 9 per cent 1996 bonds, would normally allow a block of $2 million or $3 million to be traded at the going market price without moving the market. In the floating-rate note market, the criterion would be rather different; in its heyday a market-maker would expect to trade blocks of $5 million or even $10 million in the larger issues as a normal market amount. The perpetuals crisis cut back liquidity in the FRN market generally, but block sizes are still larger than in the fixed-rate market.

The AIBD has never had the equivalent of the London Stock Exchange's Quality of Markets Committee. Hence it is not possible to track the liquidity of the market in any systematic way. All one can say is that there was clearly a period during 1986–7 when liquidity was deteriorating under the pressure of a number of influences. The tendency to asset-swap dubious issues, the growth of highly specialised pre-placed issues such as ICON bonds (see Chapter 6) and the general upward trend in interest rates, which was inflicting losses on market-makers who held inventory, all contributed. But during 1988 there was something of a recovery in liquidity, as issuers were persuaded to bring classic, straight issues in a larger size, thus enhancing their tradability.

Bound up with the question of liquidity is that of transparency. There is no good way to gather price information in the Eurobond market, except by calling a market-maker. The AIBD has introduced a reporting tape but even this is of little help when it comes to trying to establish the price of a bond during trading hours. Unlike the New York Stock Exchange tape, or the London market's SEAQ system, there is no continuous price display mechanism for the Eurobond market. A number of houses put prices up on Reuters Monitor screens, but these are updated once a day, if at all. In this respect, the Eurobond market is gravely deficient compared with major equity markets, where prices are adequately updated. In its defence, though, should be added that the corporate bond market in both the USA and the UK is little better. The coming of the TRAX system (see Chapter 17) should help improve matters.

RELATIVE SPREAD

Another point of interest to the investor is the question of relative spread. That is, the bond's yield relative to other comparable bonds. This is bound up with liquidity, but spreads are also affected by credit risk, swap factors and relative supply. As a bond becomes less liquid, so its spread will tend to widen against those on other bonds. The most usual way of measuring a dollar bond would be the spread against US Treasuries. Computerised systems (such as that provided by The Bloomberg) allow investors and traders to monitor the spread of one bond against another over time.

As a bond ages, it tends to lose liquidity. Illiquid bonds tend to have wider spreads against Treasuries. Thus, over time, the bond's spread will tend to drift upwards, all other things being equal. Other liquidity-related factors that affect the spread of the bond against Treasuries will be the number of declared (and actual) market-makers in the bond, and the presence or otherwise of active 'anomaly' switchers who tend to trade in and out of bonds after looking at their historic yield spreads on a system such as The Bloomberg. Classical straight bonds tend to be more liquid than other types; some highly specialised bonds – such as the heaven and hell bonds (see Chapter 6) – are notoriously illiquid and for practical purposes never trade.

Another important set of factors driving spreads are perceived credit risk factors. For example, in times of recession, the spreads on corporate bonds will tend to widen out against those on Treasury bonds. The reverse tends to apply in times of boom. An international banking crisis tends to push the spreads on bank bonds out relative to those on other bonds. Similarly, if a particular country is in economic difficulties, the bonds issued by borrowers from that country will tend to weaken relative to other bonds. Correspondingly, bonds issued in an attractive currency will display relatively lower spreads. Credit and other considerations will tend to be overriden by the desire of investors to own instruments in that currency.

Another factor will be relative supply. Heavy issuance by a particular borrower will cause a widening of the spread required on that borrower's issues. For example, during 1986–7 Denmark, with a large current account deficit to finance, issued aggressively in a large number of bond markets. When the country came back to the same market for the third or fourth time, there was a definite tendency for investors, who were already 'full up' with Danish paper, to require higher spreads before they would take on more of the paper. (See Table 11.2.) Conversely, a shortage of a particular kind of stock will cause a tightening in spreads. For example, when an issuer calls an outstanding issue for redemption, without replacing it with a new issue, spreads on other outstanding bonds by that issuer, and perhaps by related borrowers, will tend to narrow.

SWAP-DRIVEN ISSUANCE

Spreads at the time of issue will generally be set by the lead manager in line with existing spreads as determined in the secondary market (see Chapters 9 and 10). However, there have been notable – and notorious – exceptions, particularly during 1985–6. This period was one of heavy international use of the swap technique (see Chapter 7) while the swap market was still relatively young. Thus lead managers who secured the swap mandate could make large profits on the swaps. So they had an incentive to bring the issue to market, almost regardless of price. This meant that a number of issues were brought to market at spreads to Treasuries which made the combined issue/swap package work, rather than the spread that was right for that issuer at that time. The inevitable result was that most of these issues rapidly fell in price in the secondary market. Investors lost large sums.

Normally, issuers are reluctant to sell a mispriced bond, since investors tend to be 'once bitten twice shy'. They will be less interested in buying the next bond from that issuer, if the last one flopped badly. But a number of issuers took an aggressive view of the matter – notably Denmark, and General Electric Credit Corporation (GECC). They argued that if the lead manager chose to bring a bought deal at a price which was unrealistic, thereby inflicting losses on those who bought the paper at the time of issue, this was the misfortune of those concerned, and should not be of serious concern to the issuer. Also, during 1985–6, when interest rates were still falling, a number of these mispriced deals were rescued by the bull market. In the more difficult conditions of 1987–8, this was no longer possible, and there was a swing back towards a more conservative pricing of issues. A contributory factor here was that the fat spreads on swaps had almost all disappeared as the latter market became more efficient.

TAX AND JURISDICTION RISK

Finally, an important consideration from the investor's viewpoint is the issue of withholding tax, for two reasons. First, the existence or otherwise of withholding tax determines whether or not a bond is attractive. The investor will generally prefer to buy a Eurobond rather than a domestic bond issued by the same corporation at the same yield if there is a withholding tax applicable to the domestic bond. But secondly, the investor will be sensitive to related risks. A classic example of this was the bungling decision by the United States in 1986 unilaterally to abrogate its tax treaty with the Netherlands Antilles.

Many American firms had used the Netherlands Antilles as a route to issue Eurobonds. By issuing through this jurisdiction they were able to pay interest to investors gross, rather than having to deduct withholding tax. However, the American announcement meant that a number of issues could now in theory qualify as callable. The indentures of the bonds stated that the issuing corporation had the option of calling the bond for immediate payment if withholding tax became payable. A number of zero coupon bonds, for example, were callable at prices substantially below those prevailing in the market at the time. In the fullness of time, the US Administration grasped its error and made concessions. But the net effect was to make investors particularly sensitive to the question of jurisdiction under which the bond was issued. Many of them were unwilling to invest in bonds issued through the Netherlands Antilles unless there was a premium payable relative to other jurisdictions.

THE ISSUER'S VIEWPOINT

It is obviously useless to create an issue that investors will buy unless it interests an issuer. What, then, do issuers need? First, financing appropriate to their structural needs. That is, an issuer will consider the structure of his present balance sheet, and the nature of the requirement for which the funds are being raised. Funding for a specific project in a specific country will be approached differently from financing for a country borrowing to finance a short-fall in its balance of payments.

Therefore, the first question will always be: for what purpose are the funds being raised? If it is a corporate borrower raising funds to strengthen its balance sheet, then equity would be a prime candidate. On the other hand, issuing new equity dilutes the control of existing shareholders. If this is undesirable, but equity is still wanted, the company can issue preferred stock. A problem with both equity and preferred stock is that the dividends must be paid after tax. Interest payments are more tax-effective than dividends and generally equity issues are more expensive, take longer to arrange and are smaller than most debt issues.

These considerations will make many companies reluctant to issue equity or preferred stock, and they will want instead to issue debt. However, it may be that they would like in due course to issue equity to strengthen the balance sheet. In this case, the company might consider issuing a convertible bond. The interest payments on the bond will be deductible for tax purposes. But when the time comes to allow conversion of the bonds into equity, the company will be able to issue equity at what is probably a favourable rate.

Typically, convertible bond issues allow for the conversion of bonds into equity at a premium price, often 20–25 per cent. That is, the issuer is able to sell the equity at a 20 per cent better price through the convertible, while at the same time being able to deduct interest payments on the bond until conversion. When the conversion takes place, of course, the tax factor works the other way, and dilution is also an issue.

If the company sees no need to issue further equity, or is already perhaps very low-geared, a straight debt issue may be preferable. The company will decide between long-term debt, or short-term debt. The former tends to be more applicable in cases where the company is seeking to finance, say, a major investment such as the construction of a new factory, or perhaps the financing of an acquisition of another company.

Conversely, if the finance is needed, perhaps, to support an expansion of sales by providing sales finance, then shorter-term, revolving facilities might be more appropriate, either by means of bank credit, or perhaps the issuance of commercial paper or, say, medium-term notes with maturity of up to three or four years. For example, GMAC, the financing arm of General Motors, is a heavy issuer of medium-term notes which are geared to match the maturity of its loans to the purchasers of its cars.

Then, too, the issuer will consider the currency of financing. General Motors, financing US dollar loans to US purchasers of cars, will normally prefer to raise its finance in US dollars. But, as mentioned earlier, if it finds that financing is available in, say, New Zealand dollars at attractive rates, it would be prepared to consider a New Zealand dollar bond issue, swapped into US dollars to eliminate the exchange risk.

Alternatively, a company may wish to issue in another currency to match the assets that it has in that currency. For example, Shell might issue an Australian dollar bond with a view to investing the proceeds in the activities of its Australian subsidiaries. Or, alternatively, the issuer may decide to finance opportunistically in a given currency because it believes that that currency will weaken. This, of course, is a risky move; a number of companies have been brought almost to their knees by borrowing in what looked like cheap currency which subsequently strengthened. Classic examples include J. Lyons, who issued bonds in 'low-interest' Swiss francs during the 1960s, only to find that the depreciation of sterling cost many times more in principal repayment than the savings in interest.

As mentioned earlier, investors are sensitive to the location of the issuer because of the question of withholding tax. Also, questions of country risk arise. Investors will in future be reluctant to buy bonds issued through financing vehicles located, for example, in Panama in view of that country's recent political difficulties. Thus, the issuer will wish to finance through a subsidiary located in a country which is politically stable, and has a favourable tax regime.

Other considerations which might affect the issuer's choice of financing structure might be particular to its own business. Thus, for example, a number of mining corporations have issued bonds whose repayment value is linked to the metals which the company mines. Barrick Resources, for example, has issued bonds where the repayment value is linked to a given amount of gold, which the company mines. Similarly, Standard Oil of Ohio has issued bonds linked to the price of oil. Here, the issuer is able to feel sure that it can finance the repayment because if the price of the repayment value of the bond goes up in line with the price of the commodity, the issuer believes that it will be experiencing extra profits as a result of the rising value of its sales.

TYPES OF ISSUER

Sovereign States

Sovereign borrowers tend to approach markets in a different fashion. They borrow normally for three reasons. First, for specific projects, such as a hydroelectric facility, which would normally (but not always) be handled through the syndicated credit/project finance market. Second, major infrastructure (roads, railways) which needs long-term finance, suitable for the bond market, and where often the sovereign entity acts as guarantor (such as the Italian state railways, Ferrovie dello Stato which borrowed

Table 11.2 Denmark's 1986 borrowings

Issue date	*Amount ($m)*	*Currency*	*Swap into*	*Maturity*	*Lead manager*
February	27	NZ$	US$	1989	Paribas
	38	A$	US$	1989	BofA
March	54	¥	US$	1996	Daiwa
April	59	¥	US$	1991	Yamaichi
	252	ECU	—	1996	Kredietbank
	250	US$	—	1993	UBS
May	106	US$	SFR	1991	Morgan Guaranty
	100	US$	DMK	1993	UBS
June	32	¥	US$	1993	Nippon Credit
July	300	US$	—	1991	Goldman Sachs
	105	Dfl	—	1996	ABN
	63	Dkr		1991	Privatbanken
	97	¥	DMK	1993	Mitsubishi
	98	¥	US$	1991	Dai-Ichi Kangyo
August	65	¥	US$	1993	IBJ
	500	US$	—	1989	CSFB
	1,000	US$	—	1996	Morgan Guaranty
	65	¥	US$	1991	Morgan Stanley
September	128	¥	US$	1992	Paribas
	120	US$	—	1996	Goldman Sachs
	64	Dkr	—	1991	Privatbanken
	117	FFR	—	1991	Société Générale
October	367	DMK	—	1991	WestLB
	122	DMK	—	1993	WestLB
	120	US$	—	1993	Société Générale
	300	US$	—	1991	Morgan Stanley
	50	US$	—	1989	Merrill Lynch
	37	C$	US$	1991	Morgan Stanley
November	1,000	US$	—	1998	Shearson Lehman
	81	¥	US$	1996	Nikko Securities
December	153	FFR	—	1991	Crédit Lyonnais
	300	US$	—	1996	Salomon Brothers

Source: P. Gallant, *The Eurobond Market*, Woodhead-Faulkner, 1988.

DM500 million in December 1987 under state guarantee). Third, to finance balance of payments shortfalls: an example would be the Kingdom of Denmark, which aggressively tapped the Eurobond market during 1986 on no less than 33 occasions. (Table 11.2.)

Overall, in the Eurobond market, sovereign borrowers rank as one of the most important – often the most important – category. As Table 9.1 showed, eight of the top ten borrowers during the 1980s have been sovereign or supranational borrowers. An important mechanism for borrowing on a large scale has been the sovereign floating-rate note market. The era of the 'jumbo' FRN was inaugurated by the Kingdom of Sweden, which issued a $1 billion FRN, to be followed in 1986 by a $4 billion FRN. Naturally, with issues of this size, trading liquidity was extremely good, and given the triple A standing of the issuers, a wide range of market participants were prepared to hold the securities. They rapidly became important bench-marks.

Although the FRN market remains unique in its ability to handle a huge issue size, sovereign borrowers requiring smaller amounts tended to find that as the swap market became more efficient it was often cheaper to issue a fixed-rate bond and swap it into a floating rate, the combined package being generally at sub-LIBOR levels – usually LIBOR minus 30 to LIBOR minus 50 basis points – compared with the sovereign FRN market, where rates were generally at LIBID or possibly just below. Competition from the swapped bond market, therefore, resulted in a drying up of the flow of FRN issues in 1986–7, which was complicated by the crisis in the perpetuals market.

Corporations

From its earliest beginnings, the Eurobond market has been an important source of funding for corporations which are internationally known. For such an issuer, the alternative is naturally to issue in its own domestic market. There are at least three considerations in making the choice between the two:

(a) the relative spread between the two markets, in terms of interest rate cost (including fees);
(b) speed and flexibility of issue, and registration requirements;
(c) access to new pools of investors.

As explained in Chapter 2, the primary factor driving US corporations to issue originally in the Eurobond market was none of the above; it was the imposition of, in effect, exchange controls by the US administration at the time of the Vietnam War. After their removal, however, US corporations and others generally would weigh up the three factors mentioned above as primary determinants of where to issue.

Very often, speed and flexibility were dominant factors. Until the introduction of Rule 415 (see below) registration procedures in the United States required registering with the SEC for each issue, a cumbersome process which could take up to a month. In fast-moving markets, such a delay was unacceptable. An issuer who wanted to move quickly was effectively forced into the Eurobond market.

A Eurobond issue in the early years of the market took at most, say, three to four weeks, so that a delay of as long again to handle the SEC registration procedures would be out of proportion. In addition, many borrowers were unwilling – particularly sovereign borrowers – to submit to the detailed financial scrutiny required by SEC procedures.

Since the bonds were not registered with the SEC, there were selling restrictions in force. Eurobonds could not be offered to US nationals at the time of issue. It was possible for US investors to buy 'seasoned' bond issues in the secondary market, however. The custom grew up – although without legal force – that a bond which had been in existence for more than 90 days would be considered to have 'settled in firm hands' and thus be seasoned (see Chapter 9).

Secondly, for a certain category of issuers, the Eurobond market consistently provided cheap funding. This category consisted of those corporations who were effectively household names in Europe. Thus, an IBM, for example, could raise funds in the Eurobond market more cheaply not only than in its own name in the United States, but also more cheaply than the US Treasury could borrow in the US domestic market. Its international standing was such that Eurobond investors were prepared to buy its paper at extremely low rates.

Thirdly, and a related point, by issuing in the Eurobond market, a corporation could tap a new pool of investors who, for various reasons, might not purchase a domestically issued corporate bond (the main reason normally being either withholding tax considerations, or the anonymity of the bearer Eurobond, compared with the registered US corporate bond). By accessing a broader pool of investors, a corporation could hope to reduce its overall cost of funding.

TERMS AND CONDITIONS

A final consideration for the issuer in deciding whether to go to the Eurobond market rather than the domestic market will be the terms and conditions applicable in the two markets. Traditionally, the Eurobond market has been restricted to issuers of the very highest quality. Issuers of this standing normally are able to issue bonds which are unsecured.

By contrast, in the domestic market, there may be traditional or customary restrictions preventing this. For example, in the UK a corporation issuing a domestic long-term bond would normally have been expected to comply with certain covenants and other restrictions. Likewise, there are a number of restrictions in the domestic Japanese market on issuers. Traditionally, the Japanese Ministry of Finance imposed restrictions on the type of bond which was acceptable in the domestic Japanese corporate bond market. Security had to be provided, or else the guarantee of a Japanese bank. Such restrictions did not apply in the Euromarket, hence a number of top quality Japanese firms were keen to issue unsecured bonds in the Euromarket, rather than pay the cost of a bank guarantee or having to put up security in the domestic Japanese market.

THE INTERMEDIARY'S VIEWPOINT

There is a very wide range of firms involved as intermediaries in the capital markets. For the majority of large firms, there is broadly speaking a three-way split in their activities: between origination, distribution and trading.

The origination (often known as the 'buy side') is the process by which mandates for new issues are won. That is it encompasses the research and development of new financial concepts, their presentation to potential issuers, and the negotiations of the terms and conditions of any new issue. Once the mandate has been secured, the next stage in the origination process is for the syndicate desk to put together a syndicate who will buy the issue from the issuer.

At this point, once the investment bank owns the issue, the distribution process (the 'sell' side) comes into play. Here, the firm's sales staff will present the issue to potential investors, seeking to place them in firm hands, i.e. investors who will hold the bonds for at least a reasonable period, if not to maturity. Placement into the hands of those who plan immediately to trade the paper again for a small profit is known as 'loose' or 'weak' placement.

Once the distribution process is complete, the paper has settled in the hands of longer-term holders. At this point, responsibility for the issue will generally pass to the trading team, who will be responsible for making a continuous market in the paper over time, so that existing holders can be assured of a liquid secondary market in which they can dispose of their paper.

For many firms, a basic question is whether they act in the role of principal, or as agent for other parties. In the Euromarkets, many firms act as principals, but are in practice dealing purely on behalf of clients. That is, they are not 'market-makers', who stand ready on a continuous basis to make prices in bonds to other firms 'on the street'.

This distinction has been recognised by the Association of International Bond Dealers (AIBD) (see Chapter 10) when it set up its Council of

Reporting Dealers. The membership of this Council consists of firms who have made a commitment to the market-makers in a number of bonds.

If a firm is acting merely as an agent, then of course its risks are very much reduced. In fact, such a firm's only risk will normally be that it enters into a transaction on behalf of a client, only to find that the client reneges on the deal, or there has been some misunderstanding, leaving the firm to reverse the deal and take any possible loss. For firms that act as principal, however, the risk are clearly much greater.

First, there are the normal trading risks. A firm might enter into, say, a $5 million position in a bond, only to find that due to changing market circumstances, or an unfavourable event impacting the firm which has issued the bond, its price might fall as much as by, say, 10 per cent leaving the firm to face a $500,000 loss. Alternatively, as happened in the floating-rate note market, it could be that the damage might be even more severe: firms which held positions of $20 million or $30 million in bank floating-rate notes, which were expected to trade like money-market instruments with matching liquidity, found themselves unable to shift the paper at almost any price. FRNs which were priced at an issue price of 100 were dealt in the market-place at prices of 75 or 80, a 20 or 25 per cent loss of principal on perpetual floating-rate notes. The trading risks, therefore, include both market risk and liquidity risk.

A second set of risks is undertaken by those firms who underwrite new bond issues. It has been said that 'a lead manager can expect to have to buy back as much as 20 per cent of a new bond issue'. Thus, a firm which is the lead manager of a new issue might find itself owning say $20 million to $30 million of a new issue, 20 per cent of the total issue, with little immediate chance of trading out of the position. The firm then faces both market risk and liquidity risk again. Offsetting this would be the fees earned on the underwriting, together with the 'prestige' of being a lead manager.

However, intense competition in the underwriting business over the years has very often meant that for periods of a year at a time, the risk/reward ratio was heavily weighted against the underwriter. Intense competition to secure mandates from leading borrowers meant that issues were being brought to market on unrealistic terms. The lead managers would get left with large chunks of the issue which would then fall in price until a realistic market price had been established. As many firms came to realise that the glory of being on the 'tombstone' was being paid for in very hard cash, and the risk/reward ratio was severely imbalanced, so many firms began to decline to come lead managers in issues which were seen as unrealistically priced.

Faced with the prospect of holding a substantial block, say $20 million, of a new issue, with little ability to trade out of the position in the short run, underwriters evolved hedging techniques to try and reduce their risk. The two most favoured techniques would be either to enter into offsetting financial futures contracts, or else into an offsetting short sale of Treasury bonds. (See Chapter 10.)

Thus, suppose that the EEC comes to market with a five-year bond issue which is priced to yield 35 basis points over the five-year US Treasury bond. An underwriter holding $20 million of the bond might sell short $20 million of US Treasury bonds to try and reduce the market risk. If rates rise, the value of the EEC bonds will fall, but the short position in Treasuries will show a profit.

The difficulty here for the underwriter is that the Eurobond market and the Treasury bond market do not move in parallel. Typically, Eurobonds respond less quickly to adverse interest rate movements than do Treasury bonds, but more quickly to weakness in the dollar. Thus the hedge is by no means perfect, and indeed in April–May of 1986 a number of firms endured large losses on their underwriting positions because the hedges did not work. The spreads between Treasury bonds and Eurobonds moved sharply.

Likewise, hedging with financial futures is by no means perfect, because of the existence of so-called 'basis risk': the risk of a change in the relationship between the financial futures markets and the underlying bond or 'cash' markets.

The existence of these problems has led firms to establish a complex hierarchy of risk position limits and controls, in addition to those imposed by the regulatory bodies (see Chapter 18). Thus, a firm might lay down limits of the following type:

> Maximum underwriting position in any one issue, $10 million or 5 per cent of the issue, whichever is less. Maximum exposure to issuers from any one country, $15 million for OECD members, $5 million for other countries. Maximum exposure in paper up to three years, $25 million; three to five years, $15 million; over five years, $10 million. Maximum unhedged exposure to be 25 per cent of these limits. Total FRN positions permitted: perpetuals, $5 million; dated, sovereign issues $10 million; dated, corporate issues of A or better $10 million. Investments in bond of grades triple B or below to be subject to individual approval. No investment in private placements, or unquoted instruments, without reference to management.

12 Equity-Linked Bonds and the Euroequity Market

Discussion of the Eurobond market would not be complete without looking at how it has developed towards including equities. This is of course part of the process of 'globalisation' of equity trading referred to in Chapter 1 but it also reflects the realisation by specific Eurohouses that their client base could be deepened by developing equity capabilities. As international equity issuance developed, the traditional Eurobond syndication techniques were applied and adapted to create a Euroequity market.

EQUITY WARRANT BONDS

The first steps, of course, came with equity-linked bonds. As we saw in Chapter 2, before the Eurobond market was a year old it handled the issue of an equity-warrant-linked bond. Until 1981, this section of the Eurobond markets was relatively samll and in fact no issues were made in 1980 or 1981. During 1981 the Japanese Ministry of Finance (MoF) eased restrictions by Japanese issuers of warrant-linked bonds, and 1982 saw a marked increase in activity. In the following four years the total rose from $3.2 billion in 1983 to $19.3 billion in 1986, with particular activity by Japanese issucrs, who pushed the 1988 total up to $28 billion (see Table 4.5). The continuing strength of the Japanese stock market during the first half of 1989 meant that no less than 34 per cent of new Eurobond issuance during the period consisted of equity warrant bonds, compared with 16 per cent for the similar period of 1988. These issues dominated the US dollar sector, with $40 billion of warrant bonds issued as against $27 billion of straight dollar-denominated bonds in the first half of 1989.

In June 1988 the excessive flow of new issues led (as so often in other Eurobond market sectors) to a temporary collapse. Nine professional market-makers met in London and agreed to make a secondary market in issues of US$150 million or more. The crisis induced the lead managers – dominated by the Big Four Japanese firms, Nomura, Daiwa, Nikko and Yamaichi – to cooperate more closely in ensuring smooth marketing.

The Japanese Ministry of Finance imposes a queuing system on would-be issuers, the lead managers meet on a regular basis to monitor coupon and price levels, and the secondary market-makers also meet monthly. In January 1989, following encouragement from the MoF, the Big Four Japanese securities houses agreed informally to make markets to selected non-Japanese houses in Tokyo in a range of issues. In the difficult first quarter of 1990, when the warrant market collapsed in line with the falling Tokyo market, a temporary moratorium on new issues was imposed.

Because the Japanese Stock Market was seen as very attractive during this period, it was possible for Japanese corporations to issue warrant linked bonds with very low coupons, falling at one point to 1 per cent per annum. Investors buying the bond with warrants attached expected to make so much profit from the warrants that they were prepared to accept the low coupons. Since most of these issues were in US dollars, the Japanese corporation would then typically enter into a currency swap against the bond. As a result its all-in financing cost in Japanese yen was generally negative – that is, the market was paying it to borrow. Naturally, an explosion of issuing activity took place, since these terms were of course extremely attractive to corporations needing long-term funds.

For the investor, these bonds have two attractions. First, the warrant was seen as a geared play on the Japanese Stock Market. The primary attraction of a warrant is the gearing, or leverage, that it offers – see Chapter 4 – and on a leveraged basis, while the Japanese Stock Market was ever-rising, warrants on Japanese equities were very attractive. If, to acquire the warrant, one had also to buy a bond with a low coupon, this was seen as worthwhile by many investors. A second attraction of the warrants, though probably less important, was that they avoided withholding tax. Had the investor owned the underlying equity, withholding tax would be payable on the dividend; this does not apply to the warrant.

STRUCTURE OF A TYPICAL WARRANT ISSUE

A typical Japanese equity warrant bond would be that issued in April 1986 by Best Denki Co. The bond is a five-year one (as required by the MoF) maturing 14 April 1991. The issue size was $45 million (rather small) and the coupon 3 per cent. The bond is guaranteed by Sanwa Bank and listed in London. The warrants, which were immediately detachable from the bond, expire 22 March 1991. They allow the purchase of 636 shares, at an exercise price of ¥1,423.3 and a fixed exchange rate of ¥181.05. The exercise price is governed by MoF guidelines, being 2 per cent over the then share price. The 'warrantability' – the amount of stock that can be bought using the warrants – is limited to the amount of the bond issue to which the warrants are attached. Issue price on the bonds is always par (though in good market conditions they immediately trade to a premium of course).

Because the coupon on the bonds is very low, when the warrants are stripped out they immediately become deep-discount bonds. They have only a very limited attraction to investors on this basis, a problem compounded by the small sizes of many issues. In these circumstances the normal procedure is to 'asset-swap' the ex-warrant or 'rump' bonds (see Appendix 5).

The value of a bond with equity warrants attached consists of two parts: the value of the bond as a fixed-rate debt instrument, and the value of the warrant. The minimum theoretical value of the warrant is the number of shares which could be bought with one warrant, multiplied by the market price of the shares less the option exercise price. Valuation is complicated by cross-currency considerations; a detailed analysis can be found in the author's book *New Financial Instruments* (John Wiley, New York, 1988).

One of the problems for lead managers is that coupon levels tended to be standard for all issuers, no matter what their quality. Some differentiation here has now emerged, but because the coupon had a very important element of 'face' or prestige the differentiation is still very limited. The low coupons on the issues – because of the attractiveness of the warrant – meant that after swapping back into yen the issuers were borrowing at a negative interest rate. However, the accounting implications of the delayed potential equity issuance were not really showing up properly in balance sheets, and it is thought that moves will be made to tighten up in this area, which may slow the new issue volume in future.

Large deals are possible in this market. For example, on 20 January 1988 Canon Inc. announced that it would issue $1 billion in four-year warrant bonds, with $600 million being launched in Europe through Yamaichi International and $400 million in Asia via Nomura in Singapore, with the European bonds being listed in Luxembourg and the Asian tranche in Singapore. In a deal of this size it is not uncommon to see this use of an Asian and a European tranche.

CONVERTIBLES

Another important link between the Eurobond market and equity markets is the convertible sector. Table 12.1 shows 1987–8 Euroconvertible issuance by country of issuer.

The three main centres for such issuance are the US, Japan and the UK, as would be expected from countries with relatively large and internationally important stock markets. Because these markets are substantial, there is a wide range of market-makers in them, thus investors are generally able to trade in them on a continuous basis. The sophistication of the underlying stock markets means that it is generally possible for a market-maker to protect his holding of convertibles effectively at times when prices are falling by a short sale of the equity in the domestic stock markets. In the case of other stock exchanges, the discontinuities between the behaviour of the convertible bonds and their underlying common stocks are too great for hedging of this nature to prove satisfactory.

Table 12.1

	US$m equivalent	
	1988	*1987*
Australia	926	1,789
Canada	186	348
France	790	0
Japan	691	2,976
Netherlands	113	0
Spain	200	0
UK	1,503	3,164
USA	819	4,570

Source: International Financing Review, 7 January 1989 and 2 January 1988.

ISSUES CONVERTIBLE INTO SHARES OF ANOTHER COMPANY

Several companies have used their large holdings of equity of another company in order to back an issue. Typically, the instrument has been used in situations where companies have failed in a takeover bid and hold a large block of stock. There have been at least fifteen issues in the USA arising from such situations. In the Euromarket, a parallel technique was used in 1986 by News Corporation. It offered two hundred thousand preference shares exchangeable into 'B' ordinary shares of Reuters Holdings. The $200 million proceeds of the issue strenthened the equity base of News Corporation, and at the same time allowed it to dispose at a high profit of much of its holding in Reuters. The proceeds were almost three times the $68 million valuation of the Group's 9.5 per cent holding of Reuters' shares when the news agency went public in June 1984.

EUROEQUITY

Companies have become accustomed to satisfying their debt financing requirements all over the world, becoming totally indifferent as to whether they borrow in dollars, Swiss francs, Japanese yen or Australian dollars, as long as the swap mechanism provides them with the currency they ultimately need at a price which is economic. The next logical step was to seek equity capital from international investors.

The Euromarkets, with well-developed international distribution channels, have naturally become involved in this process. The breakthrough probably came in 1985 with the various issues by Nestlé, Esselte and British Telecom. Nestlé, for example, was able to tap the international equity market three times in the space of less than five months for over US$400 million, each time at a higher share price.

Table 12.2 Issuance of Euroequity ($bn)

	1985	*1986*	*1987*	*1988*[1]
UK	0.1	1.6	5.9	–
USA	0.2	1.7	2.6	0.8
France	–	1.4	2.4	–
Canada	–	0.4	0.9	0.1
Germany	–	0.4	0.9	0.2
Switzerland	1.1	0.9	0.8	0.2
Netherlands	0.4	0.2	0.4	–
Australia	0.1	0.2	0.2	0.4
Spain	–	–	0.2	0.4
Other	0.4	1.2	1.2	0.8
Total of which	2.3	8.0	15.5	2.8
Privatisation	0.1	1.8	7.5	0.3

1. Jan.–Sept.

Source: Euromoney, March 1989.

Issue volume in 1984 was approximately $1.2 billion. As Table 12.2 shows, volume expanded sharply thereafter until the Crash of October 1987, which effectively stopped the fledgling market in its tracks.

Two major routes have been followed in distributing new international equity issues: the Euroequity syndicate (akin to a Eurobond syndicate) and the 'geographically targeted' syndicate. Examples of the first are the issues by Nestlé and Hanson Trust, and of the second British Telecom, Electrolux and Swiss Bank Corporation.

A list of significant early international issues would include in August 1986 $200 million for Hanson Trust, $1.1 billion for Daimler-Benz AG in December 1985, and several others. In 1987 the most spectacular, and the most painful, was the issue for BP, which opened before and closed after the Crash, causing large losses for underwriters.

Prior to that issue, the largest international stock offering had been the secondary market placement of $2.1 billion of Fiat shares in September 1986. The shares came on to the market in unusual circumstances – being the disposal by the Libyan government, in conditions of great secrecy, of its large holdings in Fiat – and the offering met with severe problems. Partly this was due to the pricing, at only a 4 per cent discount from the previous day's closing price, but it was also largely caused by the antiquated settlements procedures prevailing in Milan.

The Fiat deal highlighted the critical importance of the settlements issue in the further development of the Euroequity market. The growth in international clearance and settlement systems has been crucial to the Euromarkets. This is discussed in the equity context in Chapter 16 and in Chapter 17 on settlement systems.

Perhaps as a result of its Fiat experience, Deutsche Bank's position in

Table 12.3 Top ten lead managers, international equities ($ million)

1987	*Amount*	*1988*	*Amount*
Goldman Sachs Int'l	3,763	Goldman Sachs Int'l	1,926
CSFB	1,268	Nomura Securities	1,306
Merrill Lynch	1,055	Morgan Stanley	616
S. G. Warburg	1,010	SBC	556
SBC	998	Shearson Lehman	541
Paribas	983	Merrill Lynch	416
Daiwa Securities	977	Yamaichi Securities	395
Wood Gundy	746	Mediobanca	362
Salomon Brothers	666	Salomon Brothers	349
Deutsche Bank	618	Deutsche Bank	320

Source: Euromoney.

the ranking of international equity lead managers fell from first in 1986 to tenth in 1987 as Table 12.3 shows.

Trading in the Euroequity market is hard to measure; perhaps the best indication is the turnover figures from the International Stock Exchange in London on its SEAQ International (the screen-based system which quotes firm prices on selected non-UK equities). Average monthly turnover in 1988 was around 165 million shares; the average for the first quarter of 1989 was 250 million, suggesting some recovery after the Crash of 1987.

MULTI-CURRENCY EQUITY

A development took place in the UK market in 1986 which will in the long run have importance for the Euroequity market: multi-currency equity. Most countries do not allow companies incorporated locally to denominate their capital in other currencies. Exceptions include Singapore and Luxembourg, which permit capital – at least of local subsidiaries of foreign companies – to be in ECU (European Currency Units). During 1986, the United Kingdom gave permission to several US banks to switch the capital of their UK subsidiaries from sterling to dollars. Permission was also given to Scandinavian Bank to switch its capital from sterling into a basket of four currencies, including sterling.

The rationale for the Scandinavian Bank group was that its balance sheet was largely in non-sterling loans, and the requirement to keep capital in sterling meant that as sterling fell, the shareholders had to put up fresh capital to maintain existing levels of business. Scandinavian Bank's new capital structure consists of 50 per cent dollars, 20 per cent sterling and 15 per cent each for Deutschmarks and Swiss francs. There were four classes of share, one for each currency. One share from each class has been combined into a 'capital currency unit'. The constituent shares can only be bought or sold together; no share can be transferred unless an equal number of shares of the other classes is also transferred at the same time. Accounts will be published, and dividends declared, in sterling. Reserves will be allocated to each currency class in proportion to the sterling value of the shareholders' capital contributions. Further issues of shares will be conditional on shareholders accepting shares in all classes, so that each class contains the same number.

13 The Eurocurrency Market

The Eurobond market could not exist in isolation. It has links with many other markets. Of these, perhaps the most intimate connection is with the Eurocurrency market. A crude definition of the Eurocurrency market would be that it is the market-place in which bank deposits are traded, outside their country of origin. Thus, the market for dollar deposits between banks in London is referred to as part of the Eurodollar market. Dollar deposits traded in the United States are part of the domestic dollar markets. (There is an exception to this: the so-called International Banking Facilities – see below.)

The origins of the market can be traced back to the latter part of the 1950s. Market legend – which bears a considerable grain of truth – is that the creators of the market were the Russians. (A case has been made for an even earlier starting date for the market – Chinese deposits at the time of the Korean War.[1]) The Soviet Union was concerned that the accumulation of dollars which it was earning by selling oil and other goods to the West might be subject to politically determined actions, such as a freeze, if they were deposited in the United States. Yet the dollar was an attractive currency in which to invest. Accordingly, they began placing their deposits with banks in Paris (through, amongst others, the Banque de l'Union Européenne, whose telex answerback 'Eurobank' is said to have been responsible for the name of the market).

The deposits built up in Paris and London; then, in 1958, a sterling crisis brought on by the return to convertibility led the Bank of England to ban the use of sterling for financing third-party trade. Now there was an active source of demand for these surplus dollars: Russian supply met London merchant bank demand, and the market began to grow. During the 1960s growth was further assisted by various American restrictions, notably restrictions on foreign loans by banks in the USA, and the Federal Reserve's Regulation Q, which limited the rates banks in the USA could pay for funds.

In its early days, the market was regarded as arcane and mysterious. Nobody could quite understand how it worked, where it came from, or why it was growing so fast. There was considerable academic controversy as to how far, if at all, the growth of the market was related to the size of the US balance of payments deficit. At one time, it was held that the market was entirely due to the fact that the USA was then running a current account deficit. It would disappear when the deficit disappeared. This proved not to be the case. The real reason for the success and growth of the Euromarkets is that they are not subject to reserve requirements or domestic banking controls. This makes the market inherently more efficient than its domestic counterparts.

An example may show the effects. Consider a bank with the alternative of taking a deposit in the United States or of booking the deposit through its London branch in the form of a Eurodollar deposit. Suppose that the domestic deposit attracts a 3 per cent reserve requirement; suppose that the reserves must be held in the form of non-interest-bearing deposits at the Federal Reserve. Assume the deposit is for \$100. Then if the deposit is taken in the USA, only \$97 is available for on-lending; the other \$3 must be placed with the Federal Reserve, earning no interest. Suppose the bank pays 10 per cent on the deposit. Then the \$97 must be lent out at 10/0.97 = 10.31 per cent to cover the extra costs of the sterilised reserve balance of \$3 – that is, if rates are at 10 per cent, the reserves cost 0.31 per cent. Clearly, a bank which does not have to hold reserves can afford to bid, say, ⅛ per cent better and lend ⅛ per cent cheaper, beating the US bank by 0.25 per cent and still have a profit margin of 0.06 per cent. (See Figure 13.1.)

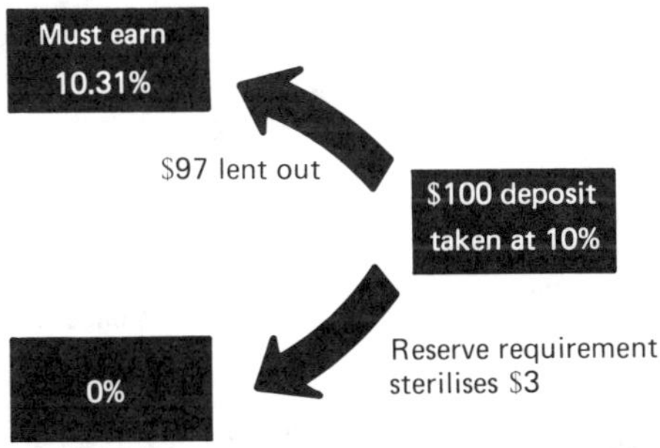

FIGURE 13.1 Impact of Reserve requirements

Encouraged by the liberal and sophisticated control of the Bank of England, the market in London grew rapidly, while that in Paris was held back by the more rigid attitude of the Banque de France, and by the fact that France in the 1960s was not yet seen as being politically entirely stable. However, after an initial period in which London dominated the market, it began to spread on a world-wide basis. The so-called 'Asian dollar market' began to develop, encouraged by the authorities both in Singapore and in Hong Kong. US banks, in some cases reluctant to incur the expense of operating out of London, began to book Eurodollar deposits through the Bahamas, which also operated a liberal regime as far as external currency deposits were concerned. Finally, in 1981, the US authorities decided 'if you can't beat 'em, join 'em' and moved to create 'International Banking Facilities'. These allowed banks to run Eurodollar deposit operations onshore in the USA, provided that certain restrictions were met. Basically these meant that IBF funds cannot finance domestic business. More recently, the Japanese authorities have followed suit, permitting the creation of the Japan Offshore Market.

STRUCTURE OF THE MARKET

The Eurodollar market is now a global one, operating by telephone, telex and Reuters Dealing System around the globe. The major players in the market are commercial banks, investment banks, international corporations, central banks, supranational bodies and sovereign governments. Figure 13.2 shows the structure of the Euromarket's sources and uses of funds by country, both gross (i.e. before netting of assets and liabilities) and net. Thus, the largest net borrower from the market is Japan, and the largest net lender is Switzerland.

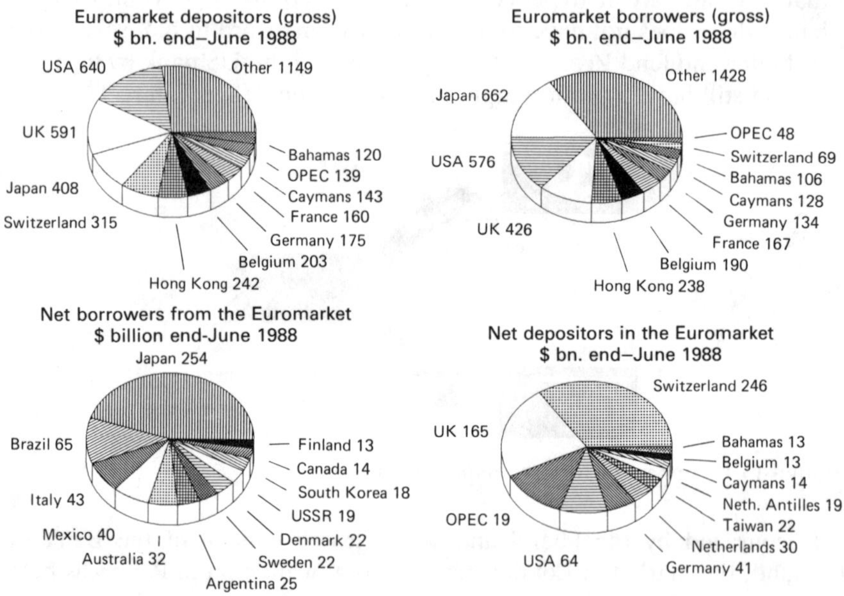

FIGURE 13.2 Euromarket depositors and borrowers, gross and net, end-June 1988

SOURCE: *Bank of England Quarterly*, February 1989

To see the workings of the market, let us take an example. Consider a firm such as Exxon. Exxon has a placement of $10 million in funds to make for three months. Exxon calls various banks, and on the basis of the rates quoted decides to place the deposit with Barclays Bank. An interest rate of 10 per cent is agreed on for the three-month deal (which actually runs for 91 days). Since the Eurodollar market uses a 360-day year, the interest due is calculated at US$252,777.78:

$$10/100 \times 91/360 \times \$10,000,000 = 252,777.78$$

On the start date of the deposit a CHIPS (Clearing House Interbank Payment System in New York) payment is made by Exxon out of its account at, say, Citibank in New York to Barclays Bank's New York branch for account of Barclays' branch in Nassau, in the Bahamas. The funds never actually leave New York; they are simply credited to Barclays' Nassau branch on a memorandum account at Barclays in New York. At maturity, Exxon decides that it wishes to roll over the deposit for a further three months; on checking the rates, it finds that Mitsubishi Bank's branch in Singapore now bids a better rate, and accordingly it instructs Barclays in New York to pay Mitsubishi Bank in New York for account Mitsubishi Singapore. Again, the funds do not leave New York.

The existence of a wide range of players in the market-place naturally means that the Eurodollar market has a yield curve, just as its domestic counterparts do. As an example, consider Table 13.1.

Table 13.1

Eurodollars		*Treasuries*
1 month	$9\frac{1}{8}$–$\frac{1}{4}$	
2 months	$9\frac{3}{16}$–$\frac{5}{16}$	
3 months	$9\frac{1}{4}$–$\frac{3}{8}$	8.59
6 months	$9\frac{3}{8}$–$\frac{1}{2}$	8.83
12 months	$9\frac{9}{16}$–$\frac{11}{16}$	8.97
2 years	$9\frac{9}{16}$–$\frac{11}{16}$	9.07
3 years	$9\frac{9}{16}$–$\frac{13}{16}$	8.93
4 years	$9\frac{9}{16}$–$\frac{13}{16}$	9.02
5 years	$9\frac{9}{16}$–$\frac{13}{16}$	8.99

Source: Reuters Monitor pages EDDD and WGVS on 30/1/89.

INTERNATIONAL INTEREST RATE LINKAGES

Inevitably the yield curve in a Eurocurrency will generally resemble that of its domestic counterpart. For example, the above Eurodollar yield curve could be compared with the US domestic yield curve. (The curve shown is for the US Treasury bond market, because the interbank term deposit market in the United States is relatively undeveloped: there is only a market for term CDs, and to a much lesser extent, Federal funds.) Obviously, if depositors have the freedom to switch from the domestic market to the Eurocurrency market and back again, arbitrage will ensure that interest rates in the two markets are rarely out of line. This does not apply, though, when exchange controls inhibit transfers out of one market into the other.

The existence of exchange controls can mean that the two yield curves have radically different shapes. For example, during 1981 the French franc was under severe pressure in the European monetary system. Speculators would borrow Euro French francs, and use them to buy dollars. They hoped that the franc would devalue, so that when they came to repay the French francs, their worth in dollars would have fallen and the speculator would make a profit. To prevent this, the Banque de France undertook technical operations to defend the franc by driving up short-term Eurofranc rates. Domestic French franc rates were left untouched, at around 8 per cent.

Short-term Euro French franc rates, however, showed a very different pattern: overnight French francs were traded at one stage at rates varying between 3,000 and 5,000 per cent, while the one-month rate was in the region of 300 per cent. This, of course, made it prohibitively expensive for speculators to borrow Eurofrancs, and discouraged their short selling of the currency. Inevitably, these pressures were felt in the Eurobond market: those who were funding their holdings of Euro French franc bonds by borrowing short-term francs found that the 'cost of carry' became prohibitive. The bond might be yielding 10 per cent; paying 3,000 per cent to fund your holding started to become uneconomic!

These tactics by the French authorities could only work because they had been at great pains to build a 'ring fence' round the Euro franc market. Leakages from the domestic market into the Euromarket were effectively prevented by a detailed, complex barrier of exchange controls. Otherwise, clearly, Frenchmen would borrow domestic money at 8 per cent and lend at 3,000 per cent. This issue highlights the importance of the link between Euromoney markets and their domestic counterparts.

If the authorities of the country concerned wish to manipulate their currency by administrative controls, they must prevent leakages between the domestic market and the international market, otherwise their administrative controls would be overwhelmed. If, on the other hand, like the US authorities, the central bank concerned is relaxed about flows between the two markets, the interest rates in the two markets will be closely parallel: though not normally identical, since rates in the domestic market will be affected by internal controls such as reserve requirements.

A related issue for central bankers is how effective their control of domestic monetary policy can be, if there is a substantial Eurocurrency market in their currency. The most obvious example is the US dollar. When the US is tightening its domestic monetary policy, there will be a tendency for funds to flow from the Euromarket into the United States. As an example, in 1978, when the Federal Reserve was trying to tighten domestic monetary conditions, it was felt necessary to impose reserve requirements on funds borrowed by American banks from the Eurodollar market, in order to stop liquidity pouring into the United States from overseas.

THE ROLE OF THE AUTHORITIES

The key fact about the Eurocurrency market and the reason why it has been a freewheeling, fast developing source of international financial innovation is that it is entirely exempt from direct regulation by central banks. The traditional liberal attitude of the Bank of England, under which it regulated only the sterling deposit activities of banks based in London, and placed no controls on the Eurodollar business, meant that banks could operate in the Eurodollar market entirely free from central bank restrictions.

This did not, of course, mean that they escaped prudential supervision; each central bank has always retained the authority to instruct a bank operating under its jurisdiction not to act imprudently. The Bank of England, in London, for example has always kept an eye on the Eurodollar activities of banks based in London. However, it did not impose any reserve requirements or other restrictions on a formal basis.

As the market grew larger, however, the central banks of the countries most concerned – broadly speaking, those countries comprising the so-called Group of Ten (the USA, Canada, Japan, Sweden, the UK, Germany, France, Italy, Belgium and the Netherlands, with Switzerland as an associate) began to become more involved in tracking the activities of the market. Their involvement grew after the 1973–4 international financial crisis when the Eurocurrency market became an important turntable for recycling international balance of payments flows. The coordinating activities involved in tracking the market were undertaken by the Bank for International Settlements, the 'central banker's central bank'.

LINKS BETWEEN EUROCURRENCY, EUROCREDIT AND EUROBOND MARKETS

The basic link between the Eurocurrency market and the Eurobond market, slightly overstated, is this: no Eurocurrency, no Eurobonds. That is, the Eurobond market depends on the existence of a pool of internationally mobile funds which can switch from currency to currency, country to country, and instrument to instrument. The point was made – more sedately – a long time ago by the Bank for International Settlements: 'That the Eurodollar market and the Eurobond market should grow together is no coincidence. . . . The . . . banks that underwrite these bond issues need to maintain a pool of dollars. . . .' (See Chapter 2.)

If the cash market were taken away, the investor who sold out of Eurobonds would have to switch back into a domestic currency. Provided there were no risk of exchange controls, this would not of itself cause enormous problems, but withholding tax issues would then arise, as would the question of applicable reserve requirements (for banks). The integrity and efficiency of the Eurobond market would be greatly hindered by abolishing the free flow of funds at the shorter end of the cash market. For the Eurobond market was itself invented in order to tap this pool of money.

On a more day-to-day level, the connections between the markets lie in the yield curve. The investor has the choice between non-tradable bank deposits (if available in the maturity required) and tradable Eurobonds. The Eurobond market, also, extends the yield curve beyond the bank deposit market: the latter extends (in certain major currencies – dollars, sterling, Deutschmarks and Japanese yen) out to five years, or in some cases even seven years, but no further. Eurobonds (at least, floating-rate notes) have been issued as far as forty years, and in some cases without maturity date (perpetuals).

From the investor's viewpoint, there is a yield curve for bank deposits, and a yield curve for paper. Eurocommercial paper stretches from today to, say, six months hence; bank certificates of deposit stretch from today out to five or perhaps seven years; floating-rate notes can be looked at as six-month paper (or to the next coupon reset date), but have been issued for twelve and longer years; Eurobonds have been issued for maturities as short as one year, and as long as forty.

The investor, therefore, has a choice of instrument and maturity; so, too, does the borrower. The borrower can issue a bond, or alternatively can go to the syndicated credit market. The classical syndicated credit works like this. A borrower determines that it requires funds, say $100 million. It approaches a bank, usually one with which it has a fairly long-standing relationship, and asks it to arrange the financing. This bank will be the lead bank for the transaction. Usually, this bank will commit to provide the finance (it will 'underwrite' the facility) if the syndication is not as successful as hoped (see Figure 13.3).

The lead bank will negotiate the broad terms and conditions with the borrower, and once these are determined, it will approach a group of other banks. Three might agree to take $15 million each; they will become the 'co-leads'. Assuming the lead bank also takes $15 million, this leaves $40 million to be syndicated out into the market in pieces of $5 million or $10 million. Often those banks taking the larger amount, of $10 million in this example, will be called co-managers; those taking $5 million only will be called participants. Increasingly, as deals grow larger and are syndicated more quickly, banks taking participations in the credits will seek to sell them down to other banks, simply 'skimming' all or part of the associated management fees to try and enhance profitability. As this process develops, the syndicated credit is becoming more akin to a security, traded in a secondary market (see below).

The borrower might want something more complex. Let us suppose that he is seeking finance for the construction of a power plant. The construction will take, say, seven years from beginning to end, since it is a green field site in the middle of a totally undeveloped country. His options, assuming he wishes to finance the project on a stand-alone basis, might be to issue a seven-year bond, or to take a seven-year syndicated credit. The

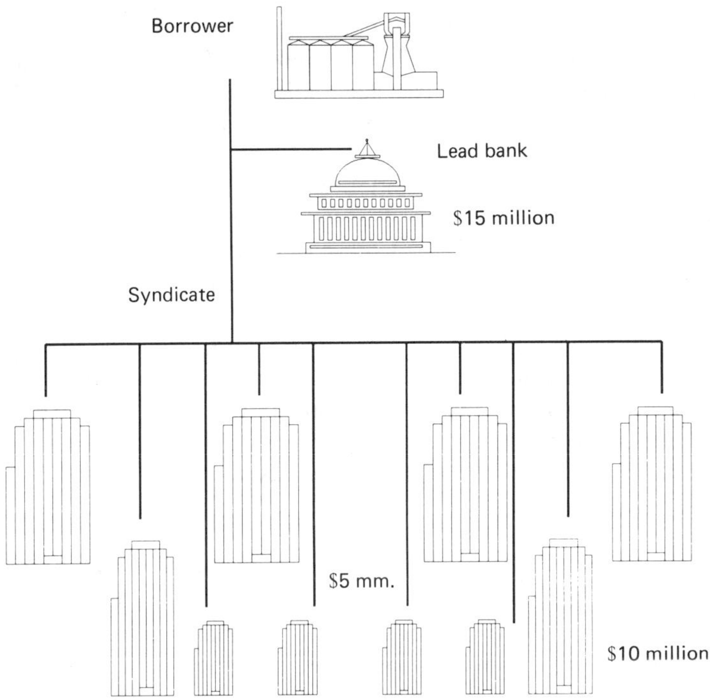

FIGURE 13.3 Syndicated credit

syndicated credit market, unlike the Eurobond market, offers a number of quite sophisticated alternatives, notably project finance. Assuming that the project can be made to look sufficiently attractive, it may well be possible for the borrower to finance on a project finance basis and obtain 'non-recourse' funds; that is, the banking lenders take the risk that the project fails, and if it does fail, do not come to the borrower for repayment of the money. This is more attractive than the Eurobond market, which would normally expect the borrower to repay the funds regardless.

SECURITISATION

In recent years, as we have mentioned, the Eurobond market and the syndicated credit market have begun to blur together. Traditionally, the syndicated credit was not a tradable instrument. The Eurobond was. Thus, for the lender or investor, the Eurobond had the advantage of liquidity; its owner could sell out, and receive cash. Not so the syndicated lender who was locked into maturity. Recently, however, there has begun to develop a market for loan sales. For decades, banks have sold, participated, placed or syndicated their loans – usually only with other banks. The 'new' loan selling started to develop in 1983. Estimates of the early US loan sale market were that the volume was negligible in 1982, $5 billion in 1983, $15 billion in 1984, and $40 billion in 1985. In this context, loan sales are defined as sub-participation of loans, that is where loans on one bank's books are sold to maturity, and on a non-recourse basis to another investor, not necessarily a bank. The common methods of selling loans are (a) assignment, (b) novation, (c) sub-participation.

Assignment, completed by notice to the borrower, is the basic conventional manner of selling a loan. It removes the participation from the seller and invests it in the buyer, giving the buyer a direct claim on the borrower. Novation involves amending the loan documentation so that the seller is replaced by the buyer as to rights and obligations. This is more expensive, since the other parties to the documentation will be involved. But it is desirable in cases where the loan perhaps has not been fully drawn, so that the seller would otherwise be obligated to put up funds for any further draw down.

Sub-participations can be either funded or by way of 'risk'. The latter is more common in Europe than in the United States because of legal problems, except in the banker's acceptance market. In broad terms, a funded sub-participation is an agreement whereby the buyer (or sub-participant) will put the seller in funds for an agreed participation in a loan. In return the seller pays to the buyer a pro rata share of the payments of principal and interest received from the borrower. A risk sub-participation would provide that, instead of the buyer funding the seller, the buyer guarantees in return for a fee a proportion of any failure of the borrower to pay.

The Euromarket has developed, in addition to the above, specific techniques for loan transferability. In 1984 the concept of saleable loans was developed into the transferable loan structure. Two separate transferable loan structures have been developed, based on different legal routes: one on assignment and the other on novation.

The transferable loan instrument (TLI) mechanism uses the concept of assignment. It gives each member the right, once the loan is fully drawn, to convert its portion of any instalment into one or more TLIs. The transferable loan certificate (TLC) uses the concept of novation. It provides for each member to receive one or more TLCs having an aggregate face value equal to its commitment and/or its participation in the loan. Legally, the TLC is an agreement to effect future novation. The TLC is not a debt instrument or security, but a consequence; the holder cannot sue the borrower on the TLC alone, whereas the TLI is itself a debt instrument giving rise to a right to sue.

EURONOTES

The Euronote market is an important alternative to the syndicated credit market. It allows for the issue of short-term securities which can then be traded. It, and its longer-maturity sibling, the medium-term note, is discussed in the next chapter.

NOTE

1. Jacques Attali states that in June 1950 the advent of the Korean War meant that:

> The Bank of China . . . feared that its dollar reserves . . . would be seized. In order to forearm herself better against any possible American enquiry, the funds were deposited with the Banque Commerciale pour l'Europe du Nord and registered in a special account opened in the name of the National Bank of Hungary. The Chinese began by placing $5 million there for six months. Then . . . the bank, burning to get rid of these dollars so as to protect them better, redeposited them with the BNCI, Banque de l'Union Parisienne and the Bank of America.
>
> (In *A Man of Influence: Sir Siegmund Warburg 1902–82*, pp. 193–4.)

Part Four
Major National Markets

14 Money Market Paper

In the previous chapter we looked at the Eurodeposit market in relation to the Eurobond market. Another important set of markets is the range of short-term securities markets, both in the Euromarkets and in domestic markets.

The rapid pace of globalisation of the world's bond and equity markets during the 1980s was not really matched in international money markets – partly because international links were relatively well developed already via foreign exchange market activity, but also because central banks were less keen to encourage shorter-term money flows. We look briefly in this chapter at some of the major instruments, including medium-term notes (MTNs) which in some ways resemble medium-term certificates of deposit in being a longer-term extension of a money market instrument: MTNs are in essence an extension of commercial paper.

Global money markets remain dominated by US dollar instruments. A recent survey estimated that 75 per cent of total global money market paper of $1.9 trillion was US$-denominated. Estimated outstandings as of the second-half of 1988, in US dollars, are given in Table 14.1.

Of these instruments, floating rate notes are covered in Chapter 4, and domestic certificates of deposit are generally unattractive relative to their Euro equivalents either because of lower rates caused by domestic reserve requirements (e.g. US CDs) or the possibility of withholding tax (Japan). A full survey of global money markets would be beyond the scope of this book but the Tables 14.2 to 14.4 give some details on six important markets.

ECU TREASURY BILLS

A new international money market which may grow in importance is that for ECU Treasury bills. The announcement in August 1988 that the British government would issue Treasury bills denominated in European Currency Units (ECU) was a major surprise to the market. Treasury bills are such a core source of finance to a government that the notion of their being issued in foreign currency was itself a shock. Others, however, hailed the move as a masterstroke: a typically pragmatic move by the Bank of England to promote the use of the ECU while its Continental counterparts took the less productive route of pressing for the introduction of a single European central bank which would manage the ECU and the European Monetary System (EMS).

There has been a fairly active ECU Eurobond market (see Chapter 9);

Table 14.1 Global money market size: ranking by instrument (US$ bn equivalent outstanding)

US$	Domestic commercial paper	420
US$	Treasury bills	397
US$	Euro FRNs	130
¥	Domestic CDs	114
US$	Euro CDs	100
Can$	Treasury bills	68
US$	Agency discount notes	65
US$	Domestic CDs	60
US$	Eurocommercial paper	60
¥	Gen-saki	60
£	Certificates of deposit	59
Aus$	Bank bills of exchange	46
US$	Yankee bankers' acceptances	40
US$	Yankee commercial paper	35
Can$	Bankers' acceptances	29
Pta	Letras del Tesoro	28
Frfr	Bons à Taux Fixe (BTF)	25
US$	Domestic bankers' acceptances	25
£	Euro FRNs	17
Can$	Commercial paper	16
Can$	Provincial Treasury bills	16
£	Eligible bank bills	16
US$	Yankee CDs	10
Aus$	Trading Bank CDs	8
Aus$	Treasury notes	8
Dm	Euro FRNs	7
£	Eurocommercial paper	6
£	Treasury bills	5
	Other[1]	26

1. Includes ¥ Euro CDs and Euro FRNs, ECU FRNs, Aus$ promissory notes, NZ$ bank-accepted bills and Treasury bills, ECU UK Treasury bills, Aus$ non-bank certificates of deposit, NZ$ Trading Bank certificates of deposit, Irish Treasury bills, Aus$ Yankee FRNs and commercial paper, NZ$ Yankee FRNs and commercial paper, and ECU Yankee commercial paper.

Source: Merrill Lynch Guide to Global Money Market Instruments, Merrill Lynch Capital Markets, New York, 1988.

what has been lacking up to now has been a good, liquid short instrument to attract investors even when rates seem likely to rise. The first steps here were taken by the Italian government in October 1987, when it began issuing interest-bearing Treasury certificates of just over one year in maturity. But because they are subject to 12.5 per cent withholding tax, and because the first auctions only allowed bids from certain Italian institutions, the programme remained largely domestic to Italy.

The announcement by the British government of its plans to issue up to ECU500 million of one-, three-and six-months discount Treasury bills was

Table 14.2

	US Commercial paper	*US Treasury bills*
Definition	Negotiable short debt of companies, finance companies and banks issued in the domestic US money market	US government short-term obligations issued in the domestic US money market
Market size	US$420 bn (Sept. 88)	US$397 bn (Sept. 88)
Issue size	US$15 m +	US$6–9 bn
Issue frequency	Continuous	3,6-month: weekly 1 year: 4-weekly
Maturity at issue	1–270 days (mostly 30–60 days)	91,182,364 days
Round lot	US$1 m	US$5 m
Average trade	US$5 m	US$25 m
Minimum trade	US$100,000	US$10,000
Form of quote	Discount yield	Discount yield
Bid/offered spread	5–10 basis points	1–4 basis points
Yield spread to bench-mark	Flat to Federal Reserve Composite	Nil (they are the bench-mark)
Liquidity	Very good	Excellent
Form of certificate	Bearer	Book-entry
Form of instrument	Usually discount	Discount
Coupon frequency	None	None
Day count	Actual/360	Actual/360
Regular settlement period	Same or next day	Primary: Thursday after auction Secondary: same/next day
Custody	Physical in US	Book-entry at the Federal Reserve
Withholding tax	None	None

aimed at filling the international market's needs. From the government's viewpoint, it was felt that it did not actually need the funds (the ECU announcement was coupled with the calling in of a $2.5 billion FRN for early repayment) but that the Bank of England would be able to invest in higher-yielding ECU instruments and earn a running arbitrage, as well as gaining kudos for helping the development of the ECU.

On 14 September the Bank of England announced the details of the terms of the ECU Treasury bills as well as a list of 29 institutions which had undertaken to make a secondary market in the paper and to participate in the first series of monthly tenders for new issues of ECU bills. The Bank also announced it would be prepared to make prices to buy back the bills from the market, at least until the secondary market was adequately established.

The bills are for one, three and six months; they are issued at a discount; they are not subject to withholding tax. The main method of payment for and delivery of the bills is through the Euroclear and Cedel clearance

Table 14.3

	US$ Euro CDs	*US$ Eurocommercial paper*
Definition	Negotiable receipt for US$ deposited in a bank outside the US for a set time at a set rate of interest.	Negotiable short-term promissory notes issued by companies, banks, finance companies, and governments in the Euromarket.
Market size	US$100 bn (Jun. 88)	US$60 bn (Jul. 88)
Issue size	US$1–100 m	Up to US$500 m
Issue frequency	Continuous	Continuous
Maturity at issue	30 days–5 years	7–365 days (average 85 days)
Round lot	US$5 m	US$5 m
Average trade	US$5 m	US$2 m
Minimum trade	US$1 m	US$0.5 m
Form of quote	Yield to maturity	Yield to maturity
Bid/offered spread	5–15 basis points	5 basis points
Yield spread to bench-mark	Flat to LIBID	LIBID − 20/LIBOR + 20
Liquidity	Excellent	Very good
Form of certificate	Bearer	Bearer
Form of instrument	Coupon	Discount or coupon
Coupon frequency	<1 year: at maturity >1 year: annually	If interest bearing, at maturity
Day count	Actual/360	Actual/360
Regular settlement period	Two business days	Two business days
Custody	Physical in London; usually cleared through First Chicago Clearing Centre, Euroclear or Cedel.	As for Euro$ CDs
Withholding tax	None	None
Purchase restrictions	None	Cannot be sold to US investors

systems, though the ECU Banking Association is studying the feasibility of a London-based clearing system.

The first issue was made on 11 October 1988, of ECU900 million (split into ECU200 million of one-month, ECU500 million of three-month and ECU200 million of six-month paper). The tender was oversubscribed in all three maturities, by multiples between 3.5 and 4.6; bills were allotted at between $\frac{3}{16}$ per cent and ¼ per cent below ECU LIBID, allowing for immediate arbitrage by the Bank of England back into the banking system, had it felt so inclined. The most recent tender, on 13 December 1988, was for ECU650 million (ECU200 million one-month, ECU 250 million three-months and ECU200 million six-months). Tenders were required on a bid yield basis (actual/360 days calculation) for a minimum of ECU500,000; issue and settlement were for value 15 December. The programme seems

Table 14.4

	¥gen-saki	*£ CDs*
Definition	Repurchase agreement involving a ¥ CD or bond. Not a security. Not negotiable.	Negotiable receipt for sterling funds deposited in a bank or building society in the UK for a set period at a set rate of interest.
Market size	$60 bn (Jun. 88)	$59 bn (Mar. 88)
Issue size	N/A	£5 m
Issue frequency	As required	As required
Maturity at issue	CDs: 2 days to 1 month Bonds: up to 1 year (usually 2 months)	Usually 30–365 days
Round lot	¥–10 bn	£1 m
Average trade	CDs: ¥1–10 bn Bonds: ¥100 m–¥10 bn	£5 m
Minimum trade	¥100 m	£500,000
Form of quote	Yield to maturity	Yield to maturity
Bid/offered spread	N/A (not negotiable)	$^1/_{16}$–$^1/_8$%
Yield spread to bench-mark	Below comparable bill and CD rates	Clearers: LIBID – Others: LIBID
Liquidity	Poor	Clearers: very good Others: good
Form of certificate	Can use bearer/ registered bonds/CDs	Bearer
Form of instrument	Can use coupon/ discount bonds/CDs	Coupon
Coupon frequency	N/A	At maturity
Day count	Actual/365	Actual/365
Regular settlement period	Flexible	Same day
Custody	Bonds and CDs usually remain with seller in separate a/c	Physical in London
Withholding tax	Payable if a coupon is received	None
Purchase restrictions	May apply to US investors	None

to be running successfully and provides a valuable addition to the range of ECU instruments.

EURONOTES

Because of their short maturity, Euronotes are often traded in banks' Treasury departments along with other money market instruments and Eurodollar deposits. Contrariwise, because they are debt instruments, other firms trade them alongside Eurobonds and other securities.

The Euronote market can be classified into two broad areas: *underwritten* facilities, and *non-underwritten* facilities. There are many names for the various facilities, as individual commercial or investment banks have tried to differentiate their products. In this context, we will refer simply to underwritten note facilities, on the one hand, and Eurocommercial paper on the other.

Despite the bewildering variety of products, it is probably fair to say that the market has now settled down to the point that one can say: (a) underwritten note facilities are generally for those who want a medium-term back-up line on which they do not intend to draw – typically, to back up a US commercial paper facility; (b) Eurocommercial paper, like US commercial paper, is for actually raising funds and is, generally, going to be quicker and more flexible than the underwritten facilities – at the price of not being certain of raising the funds.

Eurocommercial paper (ECP) existed in its own right before the arrival of underwritten facilities. Attempts were made in the early 1970s to develop a Eurocommercial paper market, which reached a peak of $2 billion in outstandings. But in 1974 the lifting of US balance of payments controls cut back the market, as US corporations found it cheaper to fund domestically. The growth of today's market began with underwritten facilities.

Underwritten note facilities began in 1978, with an issue by the New Zealand Shipping Corporation. But the instrument attracted little attention. None were issued in 1979, and the 1978 to 1983 period saw only a total of 86 facilities representing US$9 billion. In 1984, approximately $18 billion were issued, and in the first nine months of 1985 a total of $32 billion.

The revolving underwriting facility (RUF) and its siblings, the note issuance facility (NIF), SNIF (short-term NIF) and the like, typically consist of a medium-term commitment by the underwriting banks to buy notes issued by the borrower. The mechanism by which the paper is sold is typically the tender panel under which a group of underwriting banks agree to bid for the paper, or the sole placing agent under which the borrower employs the services of a single bank or investment bank to place paper at a certain price.

More recently, there has been a tendency to develop facilities that give the borrower several options in raising funds. These facilities have become known as MOFFs (multiple option funding facilities) or GNFs (global note facilities).

Typically, they will allow the borrower to access either the Euronote market, US commercial paper or bank lines, including a swing line. This is required by the US rating agencies for any facility being used as a standby for US commercial paper; part of the line must be available in the form of same-day funds. Borrowers using a global note issue can at any time switch out of commercial paper and into Euronotes. They may then use the swing line as a bridging loan for a few days, while the rather more cumbersome Euronote mechanisms is activated.

During the early development of the market, the emphasis was mainly on underwritten facilities. More recently, however, the emphasis has tended to shift towards issues which are not underwritten – true Eurocommercial paper. The reasons for this are partly the emphasis of central banks on capital weightings, and partly structural. Early underwritten facilities used the rather cumbersome device of the tender panel. (This was in part because a number of the issues were for Australian entities, and for Australian tax reasons a tender panel was desirable.) However, many tender panel banks were not specialists in the placement of short-term securities and the paper traded weakly as a result.

Many borrowers deserted the tender panel system for direct dealer relationships. In December 1985, for example, Nestlé cancelled a $1 billion Euronote facility in favour of a Eurocommercial paper programme, for an unlimited amount, with a single dealer. Another major example would be Export Development Corporation of Canada, which has a Eurocommercial paper programme of unlimited size, which is also denominated in Canadian as well as US dollars. The ECP market is clearly maturing into an important short-term source of funds for global borrowers. Figure 14.1 shows how paper is increasingly being placed into firmer hands: primary turnover is now dominating the secondary market.

A novel development in the ECP market was the introduction by Swedish Export Credit (SEK) of dual-currency commercial paper. The rationale for this was SEK's finding that some 25 per cent of ECP is sold hedged through the spot and forward foreign exchange markets. The aim of the concept was to allow non-dollar based investors wishing to sell the paper before maturity without having to unwind the foreign exchange transaction. The investor still receives a dollar note hedged into his preferred currency, but at liquidation sells the package back rather than unwinding it.

SEK was involved in another innovative ECP programme, nicknamed 'Miracle': ECP linked to Japanese government bond futures. On purchase an investor is offered a choice of bull, bear or neutral paper. On redemption, the holder of bull paper will receive a return directly linked to the Japanese government bond futures contract which reflects any price rise. An investor opting for bear paper is guaranteed a minimum interest rate, while an investor opting for neutral paper gains if there is little movement in the futures.

An extension of the ECP market into Switzerland was complicated by the existence of Swiss stamp tax. A way round this was found by Unilever NV through the issue of 'Swiss payment rights'. As there is no physical security – the issue is in book-entry form only – the stamp tax does not apply. The concept is designed to tap retail Swiss investors interested in a high-quality corporate name with a short maturity. Other issuers using the concept include the World Bank (issuing continuously offered payment rights or COPs) and Canada's Export Development Corporation.

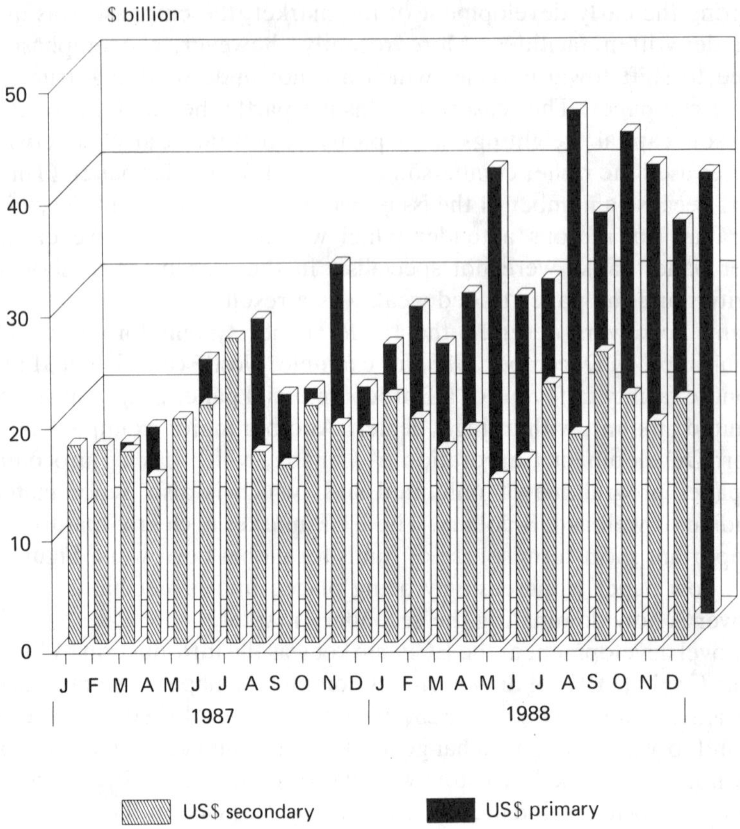

FIGURE 14.1 ECP turnover: primary vs secondary market
SOURCE: AIBD

A number of ECP programmes have employed asset-backed structures; one of the most adventurous was that by Hifin Ltd, a Cayman Islands charitable trust. Hifin buys trade receivables originated by Union Carbide in the UK, Germany and Switzerland, funding these purchases by the issuance of ECP.

MEDIUM-TERM NOTES

The medium-term note is in effect an extension of the commercial paper (CP) market's issuing technique, of issuing paper on demand by the investor against a set of posted interest rates, beyond the 270 day limit (in the US market) or the ECP limit of 365 days. Medium-term notes, in themselves, are not particularly different. They are perfectly ordinary, classical fixed-rate corporate bonds. The major innovation lies in their relatively short maturity, and, more importantly, in the fact that they are generally offered on a continuous basis. Using a continuously offered medium-term note programme, a corporation can sell individual notes on a continuous basis in relatively small amounts, typically \$2–5 million. In effect, MTN programmes resemble commercial paper programmes. They extend commercial paper issuing techniques from the maximum CP maturity of 270 days: they run from nine months to ten years. In addition, MTN issuers do not usually have lines of credit or other outside backing for their issues – a common occurrence in the commercial paper market.

Issue mechanics are that MTNs are generally sold on a best-efforts basis through dealers acting as agents on the issuer's behalf. Issuers usually post rates and offer notes over a range of established maturities: typically nine months to one year, one year to eighteen months, eighteen months to two years, and so on. Within any maturity range, however, the investor has the option of choosing the final maturity of each note. The rate scale is set at a spread over comparable-maturity Treasuries, and is adjusted in response to the issuer's needs and general market conditions. While corporate bonds are frequently issued for more or less than par value, MTNs are always offered at par. Later, of course, they can trade at a premium or discount in the secondary market. MTNs may carry either a fixed or floating-rate coupon and are generally non-callable for the life of the issue. Common indexes for the floating-rate notes are A1 rated commercial paper, and LIBOR.

As with other Eurobonds, interest accrues on MTNs on a thirty-day month, 360-day year basis. While other corporates pay interest semi annually from the issue date to maturity, MTNs pay interest on a fixed schedule, regardless of issue and maturity dates. GMAC MTNs, for example, pay interest every 1 April and 1 October, regardless of when they were issued. (See Appendix 2.)

The MTN market began in the United States and developed there for a decade and a half before spilling over into the Euromarket. The market was effectively created by GMAC in 1972. In the early years a major problem was the insistence of the SEC that it approve any amendment to all corporate bond registration statements. This resulted in GMAC having to 'put someone on a plane every time we changed our rates'. As Table 14.5 shows, however, the arrival of Rule 415 in 1982 provided a substantial help to the market. A second major catalyst was the appointment of Merrill Lynch and Salomon Brothers as agents for GMAC's MTN programme in 1983. Their commitment to developing secondary market liquidity encouraged investors, which in turn encouraged new issuers.

A sign of the maturity of the market can be seen perhaps in two key signals: firstly, 1985 saw two huge deals for GMAC, one for \$3 billion in April, and one for \$5 billion in December. A second sign of the growing

Table 14.5 MTN programmes publicly registered (1980–5)

Year	*No. of filings*	*Volume ($m)*
1980	3	175
1981	4	795
1982	16	2,783
1983	14	2,559
1984	38	10,621
1985	51	19,818
Total	126	36,751

Source: N. J. Kimelman and G. A. Brown, *Continuously Offered Medium-Term Note Programmes*, Salomon Brothers, New York, February 1986.

importance of the market was the entry of the World Bank, with a $500 million programme in April 1986 of continuously offered longer-term securities (COLTS), being made available in maturities of three to thirty years or longer.

In the same month, the Euro MTN market opened, with an issue by First Interstate of $150 million, and a programme of $200 million for the Nordic Investment Bank. In August, Pepsi announced that it would establish an MTN programme, and is believed to have issued between $75 million and $100 million during the first three months or so of the programme.

The chief concern of investors in the Euromarkets has been liquidity. One approach to this problem has been taken by Merrill Lynch in respect of a programme for Electrolux. This structure, called multi-tranche tap notes, demands that for any one tranche the borrower must issue at least $50 million of paper, after which a tap is operated up to a set amount. This means that there is always a core of paper to provide liquidity.

The announcement by GMAC of a $1 billion MTN programme in the Euromarkets was another large step forward, as was the announcement in November 1988 by the Federal National Mortgage Association (Fannie Mae) that it was increasing its global MTN programme from $1 billion to $2 billion; of its outstandings, about 25 per cent were placed in the Euromarket. By the end of 1988 the Euro MTN market had grown to around $4.4 billion from $350 million in 1986. Issuers included AT&T Credit Corporation, the Australian Wheat Board, the Kingdom of Belgium, Hong Kong's Mass Transit Corporation, the Kingdom of Spain and Petrofina.

15 Major Bond Markets

In the past it was possible to look at, say, the German government bond market purely in the context of the German government's financing plans, the German inflation outlook, the prospects for the exchange rate, and so on. This is no longer possible in the same way: one must also consider the market's links with that for US Treasury bonds, UK gilts, Japanese government bonds, as well as the DM Eurobond market. The free flow of capital between these markets has meant they can no longer be looked at in isolation. For the global investor, it is a matter of weighing one up against the other. His choices are wide.

In most countries, the government bond market is the largest and most liquid: the securities are of the highest credit quality, most investors are permitted to trade in them, and the financial authorities actively encourage liquidity so as to enhance the government's ability to sell its debt. This means that the logical alternative for a Eurobond investor is very often the government bond of the currency in which he wishes to invest.

Thus government bond markets compete with the Eurobond market. The lack of liquidity in the Eurobond market in 1986–7 encouraged a number of major international investors to switch their global investing more in the direction of domestic government bond markets. In these markets, liquidity was ample, trades of a decent size could be handled quickly without moving the market, and it was possible to move in and out freely according to one's view of the market.

Depending on the investor's country of origin, this may or may not involve him in withholding tax considerations. Even then, however, judicious switching between bonds prior to coupon dates can generally alleviate the problem.

The growth of international government bond trading has been greatly encouraged by the development of government bond futures markets in several countries. The US, Canada, Japan, Germany, the UK and France all have active financial futures contracts based on domestic government bonds. This is of great help to the investor who wants to change his market view quickly without necessarily trading the underlying security.

Here the government bond markets have an advantage over the Eurobond market. It has never, to date, been feasible to develop a Eurobond futures contract. It would have to be based upon a basket of bonds, and this has posed serious technical difficulties. (However, the US markets have developed a viable futures contract on municiple bonds, having overcome a parallel difficulty.) The use of the futures market to create a synthetic government bond to overcome the withholding tax aspects of buying the bonds directly also makes these markets potential substitutes for Eurobonds (see Chapter 7).

Government bonds are of course also available in the Euromarket. Canada, Denmark, Italy, Sweden and the United Kingdom have all actively tapped different segments of the market. The UK government floating-rate note of 1986, at $4 billion, was the largest single issue in the Euromarkets of the time, and provided a bell-wether FRN with substantial liquidity for traders.

More recently, the British government has announced its intention to start issuing Treasury bills denominated in ECUs. It thereby aims to enhance the development of a shorter-term market in ECUs, and provide a liquid investment alternative for ECU investors. (See Chapter 14.)

THE US GOVERNMENT BOND MARKET

The US Treasury bond market may be taken as the most important international market, despite the growing importance of Japan's financial markets. The transparency and liquidity of the market make it very attractive. Also, the issuers' habit of comparing the cost of funds with that of the US Treasury, whether they issue in New Zealand dollars or Deutschmarks, by analysing the all-in swapped cost, means that one of the most frequently posed questions regarding a new issue, or an existing secondary market issue, is: 'What is the spread against US Treasuries?' That is, for a non-dollar issue, given the existing swap rates between the currency concerned and the US dollar, if the security were to be swapped into dollars, what spread would it yield over the comparable-maturity US Treasury bond?

Investors and issuing houses have in their minds some 'traditional' spread for each issuing entity at which it 'should' be issuing, in comparison with US Treasuries. Thus, a top quality sovereign credit might be expected to come at say 15 basis points over Treasuries in the five-year maturity. These spreads vary according to the pressures of supply and demand (see Chapter 9).

Another reason for the importance of the spread against Treasuries is the enormous growth in the US Treasury bond market, which has meant that it is now by far the most liquid and active internationally traded bond market. This, in turn, has made it a useful market in which to undertake hedging against dollar Eurobonds. The process by which this is done – and the risks – are discussed in Chapter 10.

In general, compared to other markets, there has been little innovation in the US Treasury bond market (as distinct from related markets such as Treasury bond futures). The Treasury has taken the view that investors want a steady flow of standardised issues which give predictability and thus enhance liquidity. The main exception to this statement is the introduction of STRIPs (see below).

The US Treasury currently auctions six different Treasury notes, with original maturities of two, three, four, five, seven and ten years. Treasury bonds with thirty years maturity are also auctioned regularly. Lack of market interest caused the Treasury to stop auctioning a fifteen-year bond in October 1980 and a twenty-year bond was auctioned regularly between 1981–6 and then dropped. There is a regular auction cycle under which, for example, the February auction consists of the three-, ten- and thirty-year bond. Two-year notes are sold each month, three-year notes in each quarterly funding operation (which takes place in February, May, August and November). Five-, seven- and ten-year bonds are sold in the in-between months.

A major technical problem is the regular farce caused by the fact that under US law there is a statutory limit on the amount of debt the government may issue. As the debt grows, the limit has to be regularly lifted. Political posturing in Congress has often meant that the limit is not raised in time, forcing the Treasury to hold back from issuing. On at least one occasion the Federal government had to be shut down and employees sent home because there was no money to pay them.

There is a regular market in the trading of bonds before they exist. This is called the 'when-issued' or 'wi' market and transactions are carried out 'as, when and if' the bonds are issued. This market comes into existence when the date of an auction is announced. Another market, called the 'wiwi' market exists for the trading of issues where an auction date is expected to be announced but has not yet been; for obvious reasons this is a less widely traded market.

Secondary market trading is almost entirely over the counter. A few issues are listed on the New York Stock Exchange but the amount traded there is immaterial. The OTC market normally trades in minimum blocks of $1 million but trades of $100 million or more are by no means uncommon.

There is a wide range of participants. In addition to normal investors and market-makers, many people use the Treasury market for hedging; interest rate swap houses, for example, routinely use Treasuries for hedging US dollar swaps, often in large size; Eurobond trading houses likewise (see Chapter 10); and there is activity related to the futures and options markets. Thus liquidity in the market is first-class for those issues 'on the run', i.e. the most recently auctioned two-, three-, four-, five-, seven-, ten-and thirty-year issues. Older issues are relatively less liquid but it is still generally possible to trade in them without difficulty.

An important feature of trading is the 'repo' market. This is a market for the overnight sale and repurchase of Treasury bonds. It is used by the major dealers to finance their inventories. A dealer owning $5 million of

Treasury bonds will sell them to an investor with a commitment to repurchase them the next business day. Thus effectively the bonds are financed overnight. (See Chapter 10 for the applications to Eurobond hedging.)

In 1984 the US Treasury took several steps to encourage new sources of funding: the abolition of withholding tax, to encourage foreign purchases of Treasury bonds; the first issue of a specially-targeted Treasury bond issue for overseas investors; a new twenty-year bond with a five-year call provision; and its first concession to the zero-coupon market, the STRIPs (Separate Trading of Registered Interest and Principal) programme.

The latter has had a fairly radical impact on the zero-coupon market (see Chapter 10). The market for Treasury zero-coupon securities can be divided into two parts: receipt products and STRIPs. Receipt products were developed in August 1982 in the form of TIGRs (Treasury Investment Growth Receipts) and CATS (Certificates of Accrual on Treasury Securities) and their subsequent 'feline' competitors. Investment banks issued receipts certifying ownership of either the interest coupon due on the Treasury bonds, or of the principal amount. They have effectively been overtaken by the STRIPs market. By the start of 1989 the total volume of STRIPs had grown to \$77.7 billion, out of a total of \$1,167 billion Treasury coupon bonds outstanding. The distribution of the market is shown in Table 15.1. As can be seen, coupon strips tend to be concentrated in the shorter and intermediate issues, while the preponderance of thirty-year bond stripping has meant that the weight of principal strips is at the longer end.

Table 15.1

Maturity	*Coupon STRIPS*	*Principal STRIPS*	*Total*
1989–98	68	26	62
1999–08	25	23	25
2009–18	7	51	13
Total	100	100	100

Source: Merrill Lynch. *Fixed Income Weekly*. January 20, 1989

The mechanics of the STRIPs programme are that Treasury bonds are held in the book-entry system operated by the Federal Reserve banks in a manner that permits separate trading and ownership of the interest and principal payment. The Treasury does not directly sell zero-coupon securities; Treasury auctions continue to take place in the traditional manner. The separation of Treasury bonds into individual interest and principal components is done at the discretion of a bond-holder with access to a book-entry account at a Federal Reserve bank.

THE JAPANESE GOVERNMENT BOND MARKET

For many years after the Second World War the Japanese government obeyed the so-called 'Dodge line' named after the American banker involved in the country's financial restructuring. This in effect forbade government borrowing except for investment purposes. As time went by the definition of investment became rather elastic until the oil crisis of 1973 forced full-scale government borrowing. Thus the government bond market in Japan is younger than many others. However, the size of the Japanese economy means that even though the government's fiscal policy is conservative, there is a sizeable market in Japanese government bonds (JGBs).

Issues in the JGB market restarted in 1966 with seven-year coupon bonds. An underwriting syndicate for the government bonds was formed to handle the issue. In 1972 the maturity of new issues was lengthened to ten years, and this has been the commonest initial maturity since.

The impact of the 1973 oil crisis was to force the government into deficit in a large way. The JGB market had to expand sharply. As a result, the volume of trading in the bond market multiplied twelve-fold, from ¥17 trillion ($47 billion) in 1972 to ¥203 trillion in 1978 ($676 billion at ¥300 = $1).

In 1977 the first major moves were made towards financial liberalisation. The first discount, or zero coupon, bonds were issued, with maturities of five years. However, as the yen came under upward pressure, foreigners were temporarily forbidden to buy these bonds. In 1979 the first medium-term coupon bonds were issued, with initial maturities of two, three and four years. These bonds were placed, for the first time, by an auction system similar to that used in the USA. This has since been extended to all medium-term issues.

In 1982 the government issued fifteen-year floating rate notes directly to trust banks and other financial institutions. There has so far been no public issuance of government floating-rate debt. In the same year the first twenty-year fixed rate bonds were issued directly to life insurance companies. In October 1986 such bonds were issued publicly for the first time.

The government still needs large amounts of funding, to roll over the greatly expanded issuance of the mid-1970s which is now falling due, although the overall financing requirement of the government is growing more slowly, thanks to strong economic growth and also to large-scale sales of assets (Nippon Telephone and Telegraph, Japan Airlines and Japan Tobacco).

In the interest of lowering its funding costs and modernising the markets it has encouraged liberalisation of the markets. Rigid underwriting rules, which would have imposed an intolerable burden on the banks, had to be

Table 15.2 Japanese national bonds outstanding (¥trillion)

Fiscal year	*Outstandings*
1970	3.7
1975	15.8
1980	71.9
1985	136.6
1986	147.3
1987	154.1
1988	158.0

Source: Merrill Lynch, *Currency and Bond Market Trends*, 27 January 1989.

relaxed. The development of secondary market trading had to be encouraged to convince the investors of the liquidity of the market.

JGB turnover growth had slowed somewhat in 1978–84, though the increases were large in absolute terms: by 1984 volume had reached ¥600 trillion ($3 trillion at ¥200=$1). The pace of growth in 1985–6, however, was truly astonishing: the annualised total for the first four months of fiscal year 1986 soared to ¥2,500 trillion ($15.6 trillion at ¥160 = $1). This surge was largely due to the government permitting banks as dealers in the over-the-counter market in 1984. The measure was but one in a long series of liberalisation measures which, as we saw in Chapter 9, began by proceeding at a slow – almost glacial – pace. They have now resulted in – compared with earlier years – an almost fully liberalised financial market in Tokyo.

The most recent move (April 1989) was to expand auction bidding from 20 to 40 per cent of new government bond issuance. This has allowed foreign firms to compete more aggressively with Japanese firms to secure access to newly-issued bonds. For example, in the August 1989 auction, of Y=236 billion of bonds auctioned, Salomon Brothers acquired ¥72 billion, Shearson Lehman ¥19 billion and CSFB (Japan) ¥16 billion, while Nomura Securities took ¥50 billion. As the Ministry is in the process of choosing 'primary' dealers for the market these bids have doubtless been designed in part to impress, and it is not clear that the firms concerned have been making money on the trades.

Around 95 per cent of the turnover in the JGB market is in large-lot over-the-counter trading between banks and securities houses. Only 5 per cent goes through one of the Tokyo, Osaka or Nagoya Stock Exchanges. However, the Tokyo Stock Exchange has been the home of a wildly successful futures contract. Within ten months of its introduction in October 1985 its trading volume had exceeded that of US Treasury bond futures.

In July 1987 a yen bond futures contract was introduced on the London International Financial Futures Exchange; this has not been particularly successful: first because there is a marked tendency round the world for the first exchange to introduce a futures contract to hold on to its lead – business goes where the liquidity is; secondly, there were problems arising out of the fact that physical delivery of JGBs outside Japan is not permitted, so the LIFFE contract did not exactly match the Tokyo contract.

An unusual feature of JGB trading is the 'bench-mark' concept. Up to 90 per cent of cash trading in the JGB market is usually concentrated in one issue, called the bench-mark issue. Unlike the US system whereby there is a 'run' of most traded issues which are those most recently auctioned, the bench-mark can continue in being even after other issues have been auctioned. In fact, there is general reluctance to make the most recent issue the bench-mark. If it then trades to a lower yield than other issues, this puts pressure on the issuing syndicate to accept a low coupon on the next issue.

What happens is that the bench-mark is chosen as the result of cooperation and competition between the Big Four. For example, in 1986 the bench-mark to begin with was No. 78. (In the JGB market successive issues are given a number.) There was then a long struggle between No. 78 and No. 89 for dominance. No. 89 had four major disadvantages: first, it had a coupon of 5.1 per cent, much lower than the 6.2 per cent coupon of No. 78. The security houses prefer to trade high coupon issues because of the inventory costs. Second, there were then three separate tranches of No. 89, not fungible until December of that year. Third, No. 89 was not supported by Nomura, the largest securities house, which preferred to maintain No. 78. But when dominance finally passed to No. 89, the yield on No. 78 jumped by 60 basis points relative to the market within seven days. So for the outside investor it is crucial to be in close contact with the major firms involved in determining the bench-mark – being left behind when the smart money is moving out of an ex-bench-mark is an expensive exercise.

Another unusual feature of JGB trading is the small number of settlement days. Before August 1987 there were only three settlement days per month. This allowed free speculation for each intervening ten-day period, one of the reasons allowing for manipulation of the market by the Big Four securities houses. Overheating in the market in May 1987 caused concern at the Bank of Japan, which insisted more settlement days be introduced. When this was suggested, yields rose 70 basis points in five days. From August 1987 the number of settlement days rose to six per month.

The settlement system will probably move towards continuous settlement as in the US market. But this would then cut back liquidity in the market unless adequate mechanisms are introduced for short selling. There is no 'buy-in' procedure as there is in the Eurobond market (see Chapter 10). A repo market equivalent to that in the US for the borrowing of bonds has only just been set up (April 1989).

There is a form of repo market in the shape of the 'gen-saki' market. But this does not at present adequately provide bond borrowing facilities. 70 per cent of gen-saki trades are between industrial corporations and securities houses whereby the latter finance their bond inventory using the bonds as collateral, and most gen-saki trades are for three months.

Yet failure to deliver would constitute serious loss of face and lead to sanctions from the rest of the financial community. It remains to be seen whether the new repo market will succeed in filling the gap.

Another distinctive feature of the Japanese government bond market, as in other Japanese bond markets, is the so-called reverse coupon effect. Unlike most other countries, where investors typically prefer low coupons so that the bulk of their earnings come in the form of capital gains, the major Japanese insurance companies in the past (though this may now become less of a factor, following MoF pressure) have preferred high coupons. This allows them to pay higher dividends on endowment policies (which cannot be paid out of capital gains).

City banks, which hold large blocks of strategic equity stakes with low yields, also like high coupon government bonds as an offset. Thus a rise in rates tends to be led by low coupon bonds; a fall in rates by high coupon bonds. However, during 1989 the Federation of Bankers Associations of Japan has introduced a change in the accounting rules for securities assets held by banks, to include capital gains. Thus banks also will be placing less weight on high coupon bonds.

THE GERMAN GOVERNMENT BOND MARKET

The German government bond market has often been popular with foreign investors on currency grounds, when the Deutschmark has been strengthening. (However, in the past, many investors were deterred by exchange controls – in 1972–4 the market was effectively closed to foreign investors, to discourage excessive upward pressure on the DMark – and by a 25 per cent withholding tax, which was abolished in 1985. It was reimposed at a rate of 10 per cent in 1988, and then removed in 1989.)

German bond and financial markets have traditionally been strictly controlled by the Bundesbank, which has resulted in great conservatism and resistance to innovation. As we saw in Chapter 9, however, the years 1984–6 saw considerable liberalisation and the markets have become much more flexible, although the government's tax policy continues to keep much activity offshore.

The Bundesbank keeps a close eye on trading; it operates a control-number system which allows it to track trading. Suppose in the course of its market operations, the Bundesbank finds it is buying government bonds that have been outstanding for less than a year. It retraces the control number and claims back issuing commission from the appropriate member of the government's issuing syndicate – on the grounds that the dealer has reneged on its obligation to ensure the debt is placed in firm hands.

The German government issues three main types of bond. Bundeskassenobligationen and Bundesschatzanweisungen are short-term (up to six years). They are not normally listed on a stock exchange, and are issued in blocks of DM100 million to DM2.5 billion. Larger issues in this market are almost as liquid as Bunds. Bundespostanleihen and Bundesbahnanleihen are issued by the Post Office and the Railways under government guarantee; the issue size is typically DM1–2 billion. These are generally less liquid than Bunds and trade at a slight yield premium.

The third type of bonds are Bundesrepublikanleihe or Bunds. They generally have maturities up to ten years. There has been a long-term trend in Germany towards shorter maturities (as in the USA) which has been reversed in the last two or three years. The government issued two thirty-year bonds in 1986 for the first time since the Second World War. Trading in these is rather illiquid, though, and for practical purposes, the market has a maximum maturity range of ten years. The average maturity for government paper is 6.5 years compared to 8.5 years for US Treasuries and ten years for gilts.

The normal issue size is DM4–6 billion and the normal trading block in the cash market is DM5–10 million, with a bid/spread of 0.15–25 – depending on market conditions of course. The total size of the Bund market at end-1987 was $140 billion compared with $990 billion of US Treasuries, $590 billion of Japanese government bonds and $210 billion of UK gilts. The relatively low size of the public German government bond market is largely due to the historical pattern whereby the public authorities issued Schuldscheindarlehen (certificates of indebtedness) to the banks who then refinanced them by issuing bank bonds. With the growth of foreign interest in the government bond market – foreigners have relatively little interest in Schuldschein – Bund issuance is likely to grow at the expense of the Schuldschein market.

Bunds are traded over-the-counter and on the German stock exchanges. The latter trades 11.30 a.m. to 1.30 p.m. while the OTC usually trades from 9 till 5 p.m.; there is also an active London cash market (helped by London's exemption from the German government's securities turnover tax) which trades the same hours (i.e. 8 a.m. to 4 p.m. London time). In the London market bid/offer spreads tend to be 0.20 (i.e. 20 pfennigs) with prices good for DM5 million, again depending on market conditions. One recent estimate of global daily turnover in the OTC market was DM46 billion.

The international market has grown strongly, centred in London (compare Figure 1.10), as foreign investors have been attracted by the strength of the currency. From 1.5 per cent in 1982 the share of foreign buyers grew to 58.3 per cent in 1986. German banks have been lobbying for the abolition of the Borsenumsatzsteuer – the tax on stock market turnover, which has meant that trading in, for example, Deutschmark FRNs is handled out of London rather than Germany. (To dramatise the point, Dresdner Bank launched its first DMark FRN on 1 May 1985 – even though that was a holiday in Germany.) However, they have so far had little success.

No withholding tax is currently payable, but the authorities imposed a 10 per cent tax in 1988, payable on coupon payments but not on accrued interest. Vigorous protests from several quarters led to its abolition during 1989.

THE BRITISH GOVERNMENT BOND MARKET

The United Kingdom government debt market – commonly called the gilt-edged or gilt market – is unique among major government bond markets at the moment in that it is shrinking. The British government is paying down debt because it is running a budget surplus. For historical reasons, however, there is a large outstanding stock of debt. For the same reasons, gilts bear names like Treasury, Exchequer, Funding, Conversion, Transport, Electricity, Gas, Redemption and so forth. The names have no meaning except for identification: all the bonds are direct obligations of Her Majesty's Government.

Over the years, the Bank of England's pressing need to sell bonds led it to devise a number of strategies for tapping pools of demand. Thus, for example, it is possible to buy very low coupon gilts, bearing coupons of 2½ or 3 per cent, which were designed to appeal to high taxpayers who preferred to earn their return in the form of capital gain. Another subset of bonds is those which are 'tax-free to non-residents'. On application to the Inland Revenue, interest is payable on these bonds without deduction of income tax at source (which is otherwise standard practice). Another subset of bonds is the irredeemables: bonds without maturity date which will pay interest for ever (or rather until the UK government ceases to exist or repays the bonds). These include War Loan and Consols: such stocks are the most volatile of all because of the fact that the longer the maturity of a bond, the more volatile it is (see Appendix 2).

Another group of stocks is called Convertibles. Unlike the convertibles discussed in Chapter 8, these are not convertible into equities, but into a different gilt at some time in the future. The government has thus written an option to the investor. The first of these was issued in 1973, the Treasury 9 per cent Convertible 1980; each £100 nominal was convertible into £110 nominal of Treasury 9 per cent 2000 as an alternative to redemption in 1980.

A special category of government bonds unique to the UK (of the markets we are considering in this book) is that of Index-Linked. These were introduced in 1981. The first issue, Treasury 2 per cent Index-Linked 1996 was restricted to pension funds, but in 1982 all investors were allowed access to the market. The bonds pay interest and principal linked to the retail price index in the UK. Because there is an eight-month lag in the payments they do not provide 100 per cent protection against inflation, but they do give broadly satisfactory protection. For the international investor, however, these stocks are of fairly limited interest because of their specialised nature.

Liquidity in the gilts market is generally excellent, helped at the moment by the fact of excess capacity arising from 'Big Bang' (see Chapter 3). The impact of Big Bang was particularly strong in the gilt-edged market. The total value of gilts outstanding at the time of the change was £110 billion, with an average daily turnover of £1.25 billion. Into this market erupted 29 primary market-makers, of whom eleven were US firms.

By comparison, there were at that time 37 primary dealers in the US, with a value of outstanding Treasury debt of $1,000 billion, with an average daily turnover of $55 billion. The number of market-makers is gradually being whittled down by attrition – Citibank, Merrill Lynch, Security Pacific Hoare Govett and Morgan Grenfell being notable departures, but on the other hand two of the Japanese Big Four have now moved in. Average daily turnover had risen to about £4.25 billion by the end of 1988, of which around half was business between market-makers. The Bank of England estimated that by that period the costs of dealing in the market had fallen by about 60 per cent from its pre-Big Bang level. Partly as a result, market-makers were collectively losing £2 million a week by the end of 1988 – down from £4 million the year before but still unsustainable in the long run.

One major difference from the US system is that the Bank has said firmly that it 'is not prepared at this stage – essentially for prudential reasons – to envisage the development of an unregulated market in repurchase agreements in government securities such as exists in the United States.' This means that only primary dealers can short gilt-edged stock, for they are allowed to borrow bonds through the inter-dealer broker mechanism. Thus funding of positions is expensive, which reduces liquidity.

In the primary market, the Bank now uses two main issuing methods. The first is offers for sale by tender. New stock, or large new tranches of existing stock, are issued to firms tendering for the stock. All successful bidders pay the same price. It is the lowest price at which tenders are accepted. But higher bidders receive priority in allocations. (To spread the impact on cash flow, the stock is often issued on a partly-paid basis.)

The second method is 'tranchettes' of existing stock. These are small tranches sold by the government to the Bank of England which then sells them into the market when it chooses. However, as mentioned earlier, the main problem currently in the gilts market is that far from issuing large new quantities of new stock the Bank's main occupation currently is buying it back from the market.

THE FRENCH GOVERNMENT BOND MARKET

During the 1960s and 1970s French financial markets were tightly controlled with the twin aims of serving domestic planning goals and of defending the franc against foreign speculators. But all the tight controls failed to defend the franc from being driven under by the speculators in 1981–3, when the Socialist government's 'dash for growth' led to the franc losing 20 per cent of its value against the Deutschmark in eighteen months.

In early 1983 the French government recognised the logic of its failure and moved drastically towards financial stringency and also financial deregulation. The policy of deregulation was carried on under the next, conservative, government, so it has become bipartisan. Moreover, the

Table 15.3 French financial market reforms: a chronology

1983	Issue of renewable, single-coupon bonds (Obligations Renouvables du Trésor – ORTs). Issue of exchangeable Treasury bonds
1984	Abolition of compulsory deduction at source on interest payments to non-residents.
1985	Introduction of certificates of deposit (CDs). Resumption of French franc Eurobond issues (discontinued since 1981). Non-bank investors allowed to buy Treasury bills. Government bond auctions replace traditional syndicate. Commercial paper introduced.
1986	Foundation of financial futures market (Marché à Terme des Instruments Financiers – MATIF). First floating-rate Euro French franc issue.
1987	Thirteen primary dealers in government bonds appointed. Treasury bond maturities and issuing calendar standardised. Credit controls abolished.

advent of 1992 (the EEC's 'one market') seems likely to make French deregulation irreversible. All of which means that the French government bond market is of more interest to the foreigner, particularly since the market itself has been drastically reformed.

The French Treasury yield curve now consists of the following: discount bills, with maturities up to one year; coupon-bearing notes (Bons du Trésor à Taux Fixe et Intérêt Annuel – BTANs) out to five years and bonds (Obligations Assimilables du Trésor – OATs) out to 25 years. There are also some floating-rate OATs, discussed in more detail below. This range of instruments has been designed as a coherent group with an issuing system that makes them liquid by any standard. Existing issues are regularly reopened; the coupon is set at the beginning of the year, and new tranches are sold at a discount or premium as yields fluctuate.

The government has thus moved greatly to simplify the structure of the market. Until 1985 government bonds had no standard form. Thus there were various types of straight bond (bullet, sinking fund or convertible into floating rate) and floating-rate notes (with some convertible into straights) and indexed bonds and zero-coupon bonds: Fonds d'Etat Libérés d'Intérêt Nominal or FELINs (a term copied from the US where the private zero coupon market bonds backed by Treasuries had names like CATs and TIGRs).

The issuing process was also radically reformed. In 1986 the 'grey market' was institutionalised; it exists between the OAT auction day (the first Thursday of every month) and payment day for newly-issued stock. There is also a 'when-issued' market between the announcement of the auction and the auction itself. Thirteen primary dealers (Spécialistes en Valeurs du Trésor – SVTs) make continuous secondary markets. In exchange they are compensated by being allowed to submit non-competitive bids at auctions – they may receive collectively 20 per cent of the amount for which they bid at the average price of the auction.

Investors in French bonds can hedge through the futures market, MATIF. Founded in February 1986, the MATIF grew successfully to a high volume of trading – typically 40,000–70,000 contracts per day. Its future is a ten-year government bond future based on a theoretical ten-year 10 per cent coupon government bond; each contract is for Frfr500,000 of the bond. Deliverable issues must be between seven and ten years maturity and must have a coupon date at least fifteen days after the futures contract expiry date.

The MATIF OAT contract provides a good means of hedging the OAT, which in itself is for trading purposes a very attractive instrument. The OAT and the BTAN between them cover the bond yield spectrum. The major difference between them is – apart from the BTAN's being up to five years and the OAT over five – that the legal status of the BTAN is a negotiable instrument, while the OAT is a security. Thus the latter comes technically under the legal monopoly of the Compagnie Française des Agents de Change and the bonds are listed on the Stock Exchange. BTANs are not listed and thus trade freely over-the-counter; OATs on the other hand benefit from the continuous market-making of the SVTs.

The OAT is generally speaking the most liquid and actively traded instrument in the French bond market; in addition, the major London-based securities firms make active markets in OATs. Since August 1987, repurchase agreements between residents and non-residents have been permitted – based on domestic interest rates. Interest calculation conventions differ slightly from US or Euromarket norms. For domestic trades on

OATs, the standard value date is two business days after the trade date. Accrued is calculated using actual/actual up to the calendar day after the trade date. For international trades on OATs, the value date is seven calendar days after the trade date. Accrued is calculated using actual/actual up to the calendar date after the value date. So far as concerns tax considerations: there is no withholding tax on non-residents for government bonds issued after 1 October 1984, and there are no restrictions on foreign investment in OATs.

An interesting and innovative move recently by the French government was to arrange the issue of American Depositary Receipts (ADRs – see Chapter 4) backed by OATs. This is the first time that debt-backed ADRs have been issued. Although the initial reception was poor, because of unfamiliarity, one may expect that in time volume will improve.

THE DUTCH GOVERNMENT BOND MARKET

Although the Dutch market is a secondary one, it is important to foreign investors as a substitute for German bonds (a) because there is no withholding tax, and (b) there is a stable exchange rate against the Deutschmark, thanks to the guilder's membership of the European Monetary System which implies fixed limits on the currency's movements against the Deutschmark.

In January 1986 the Dutch capital market was deregulated. The most important changes were:

(a) The introduction of bullet issues (i.e. redeemable in a simple payment at maturity). Prior to 1986 bonds had to have sinking fund redemptions with at least four partial redemptions drawn by lot and seven years minimum maturity (equivalent to an original average life of 5.5 years).
(b) Euroguilder notes were allowed to be listed on the Amsterdam Stock Exchange. The previous ceiling of Dfl150 million per issue was removed.
(c) Short-term guilder bearer securities, i.e. CDs and commercial paper, were allowed. Floating rate notes were also allowed.
(d) Branches or subsidiaries of foreign banks were allowed to lead-manage guilder-denominated securities under certain circumstances; foreign co-managers were allowed to take up to 33 per cent (formerly 20 per cent) of an issue.
(e) The new-issue calendar, which controlled the timing of issues, was abolished. However, issues of Dfl50 million or more, or of an original maturity of less than two years, have to be reported to the Dutch central bank at least three days before issue. For other issues the date of announcement and the closing date of subscription are fixed by the Central Bank in compliance with the wishes of the issuer as much as possible.

Table 15.4 Demand for state public bond issues (per cent of total)

	1984	*1985*	*1986*	*1987*
Dutch institutions	49	57	44	35
Foreign investors	15	24	33	42
Dutch individuals	16	12	13	15
Banks	20	7	10	8

Source: Dutch Ministry of Finance, quoted in 'The Dutch Bond Market', *Banque Paribas Capital Markets*, London, May 1988.

In January 1988 a further round of liberalisation permitted zero coupon bonds, original issue discount bonds and medium-term notes (two to five years). Indexed issues are still prohibited. The effect of this liberalisation has been to increase sharply the level of foreign interest in the Dutch market because of the arrival of bullet issues, which makes the market comparable to other markets, and also because of the new flexibility of the system. Table 15.4 shows that even before the latest round of liberalisation foreigners had become the largest single group of investors.

The government is by far the biggest issuer on the domestic market, accounting for 65 per cent of total volume. Outstandings have doubled in the last five years, due to persistent high budget deficits. Individual issues are large. Although the Dutch market is about half the size of the German Bund market, the five largest issues (as of May 1988) were all larger than the largest German issue. Sizes ranged from $2.79 billion equivalent to $4.51 billion compared with $2.38 billion for the largest Bund.

In May 1988 the Nederlandsche Bank (the central bank) created a bond market intervention fund. Its purpose is to function as an open market intervention account for stabilising bond yields; the fund was used for the first time in April 1989, by which time the fund had been built up to Dfl1,750 million ($825 million) by using the fund to underwrite state loans.

Trading in the bonds is active in London, amongst other centres, as well as in the Netherlands, where trading takes place through the Stock Exchange or the Amsterdam Interprofessional Market (AIM). The AIM was set up in May 1986 to try to bring business back from London by lowering transactions costs for large investors. For amounts of over Dfl2.5 million Dutch banks and brokers may trade on a net basis with Dutch investors. The price includes commission, handling fee and stamp duty. These transactions do not pass through the jobbers, but have to be notified to the AIM desk at the Stock Exchange within fifteen minutes. When the AIM was introduced about 20–25 per cent of the market is thought to have been traded abroad. The Dutch Central Bank believes this figure has not fallen much: both the AIM and overseas trading have grown. Although the

AIM has stopped more trading going offshore, transactions costs in the Netherlands remain above those in London.

OTHER BOND MARKETS

For the international investor it is mainly the Eurobond markets and the government bond markets which are of interest, hence we have devoted most of the space in this chapter to the government bond markets. Their liquidity and size makes them attractive to mobile money. In other sectors of domestic bond markets one has the same problem as the Eurobond market, namely a wide range of non-homogeneous issues leading to relatively poor liquidity. For the sake of completeness, however, we outline briefly some of the other important bond markets in the various countries covered.

The first group of markets is the traditional foreign bond markets. These are bonds issued domestically in a number of countries for foreign issuers. Internationally the most important of these has traditionally been the Swiss market, which is currently undergoing drastic changes and difficult times. Under pressure from the Cartel Office to allow greater competition, the Big Three Swiss banks currently are thought to control over 90 per cent of the public market, up from around 70 per cent in 1987; foreign firms have been under pressure. However, the prospect of the abolition of fixed commissions and restrictive practices, while beneficial to issuers, might cause further problems to market participants.

In the USA there is the so-called 'Yankee' bond market in which governments like Canada, the UK and others have issued from time to time, together with other top-quality borrowers. Here too activity has not been as dynamic as in the Euromarkets, while its UK counterpart, called the 'bulldog' market, has been dying on its feet – hampered by restrictive requirements on covenants and limited liquidity. The Japanese 'Samurai' market has also lost out because of its inflexibility *vis-à-vis* the Euroyen market.

Then there are the domestic corporate bond markets in the individual countries. This is well-developed in the United States, with a large range of issuers and maturities. The Securities Industry Association reported an average daily trading volume of $13.3 billion in the first half of 1988 in the corporate bond market.

A particular feature of recent years has been the development of the so-called 'junk' bond market. The US junk bond market has been developed essentially since 1982. Before that date most junk bonds were 'fallen angels' – sound companies which had fallen on hard times. Table 15.5 shows that in 1983–5 more than $40 billion of 'high-yield' bonds were issued, compared with an average of $2 billion per annum in the years 1979–82.

Table 15.5 Junk bond issues ($ bn)

1977	1.06
1978	2.13
1979	1.69
1980	2.06
1981	1.74
1982	3.18
1983	8.49
1984	15.78
1985	19.8
1986	45.6
1987	35.8

Source: Drexel Burnham Lambert: *1988 Annual High Yield Market Report.*

Moody's estimate that in 1985 junk bonds accounted for 19 per cent of all new US corporate debt issues. Studies are reported to have shown that the extra yield on such securities more than compensates the investor for the risk of default. However, events in late 1989/early 1990, leading to the collapse of Drexel Burnham, showed the weaknesses of the market. Many of its investors are themselves weak institutions and there is the risk of a chain reaction. Such a chain reaction would obviously enhance the role of the banks against the securities markets again.

The domestic UK corporate market is much narrower than in the USA, as issuers have recently tended to go the Eurosterling route (see Chapter 9). The bulk of purely domestic issues are by property companies seeking very long-term finance and prepared to grant the onerous covenants required by the traditionalist domestic market. There is a large Japanese domestic market (going on for $300 billion) where the most important issues are bank debentures. The corporate bond market has been restricted by the fact that issues had until 1979 to be secured by a mortgage; since that date unsecured issues have been permitted but only on extremely stringent conditions. The German domestic bond market likewise has been dominated by bank and mortgage bank issues, with industrial bonds relatively limited. It is worth mentioning that the Danish bond market is among the ten largest in the world, because of its heavy use of mortgage credit bonds (63 per cent of the market at the end of 1988). These bonds are issued on a tap basis, with original maturities ranging from ten to 35 years, and are considered to be of very high quality – there has never been a default on these bonds.

Finally, there are important markets in a number of countries for private placements of bond issues. These are not offered to the general public and thus have much less liquidity, though they may be actively traded in an informal secondary market. The US private placement market is a large and important source of finance on a long-term basis for corporations and property companies. Recent proposals regarding liberalisation of the SEC's Rule 144a (which restricts trading in private placements) may boost the private market by making it much more liquid.

Likewise there is a substantial Japanese placement market, which includes a subsector called the 'Shibosai' market, for private placements for overseas borrowers. These have tended to be for lower quality borrowers such as Panama and Chile. Germany and the Netherlands also have very important private placement markets, and there is in addition a sizeable Swiss market.

16 Major Equity Markets

As we saw in Chapter 4, the world's major equity markets are, in order of capitalisation, Japan, the USA, the UK, Germany, France, Canada, Switzerland, Italy and Australia. Figures 16.1 to 16.3 show how these markets have grown over the last five years, and also compare them as regards risk and return, capitalisation in relation to the size of the domestic

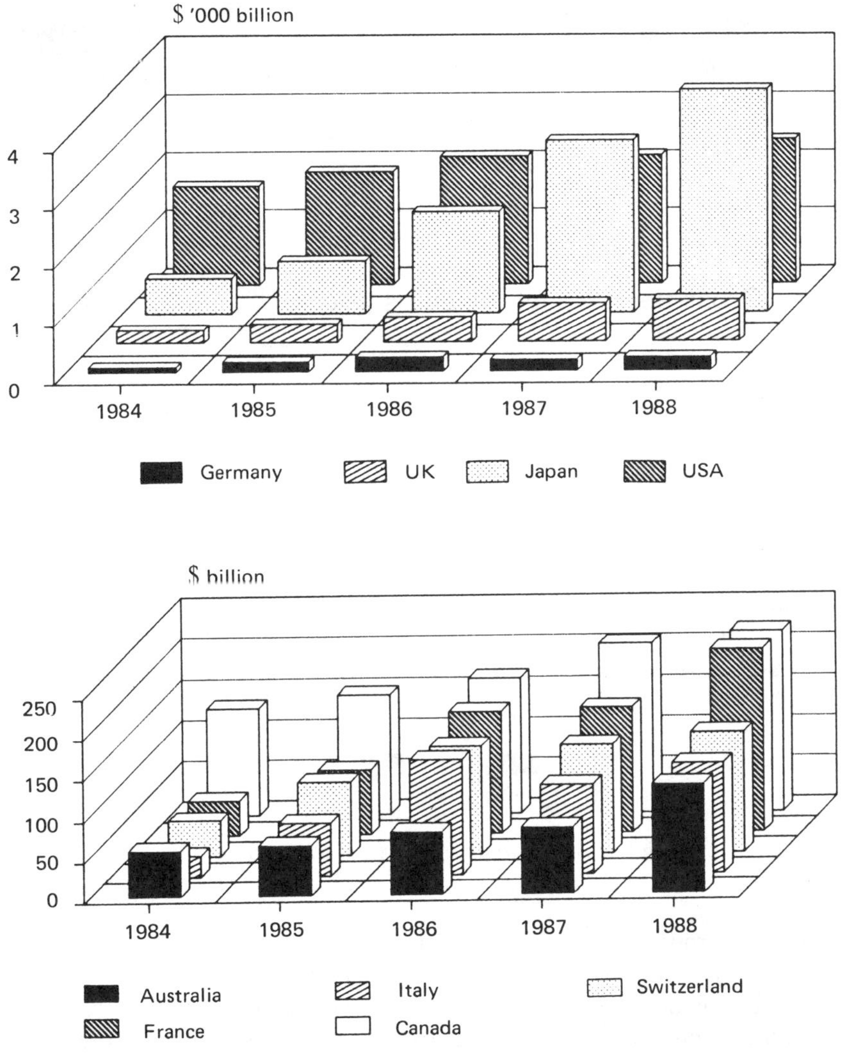

FIGURE 16.1 Market size: $ value of market capitalisation

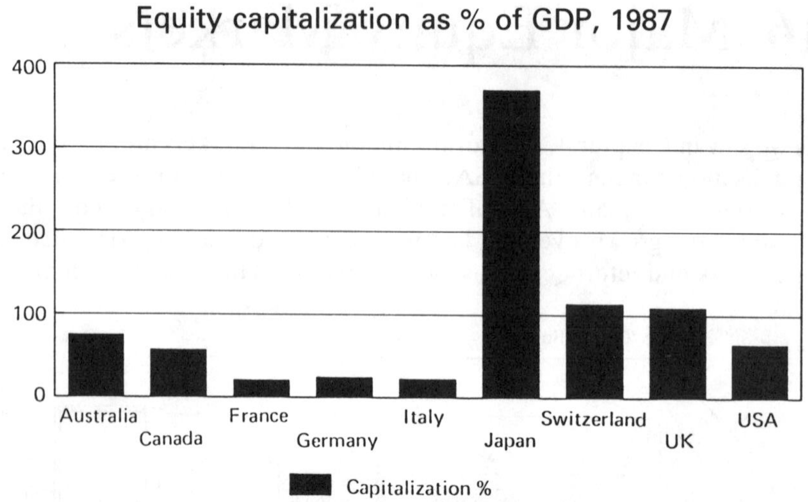

SOURCE: Goldman Sachs, *Anatomy of World Markets*, September 1988

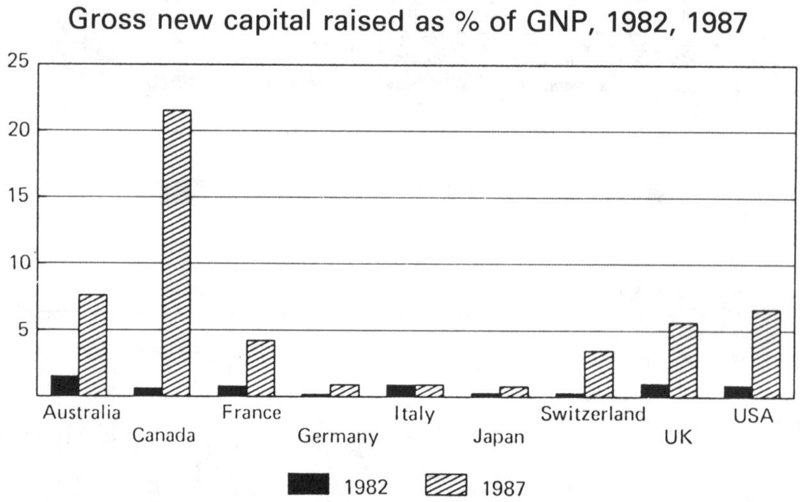

FIGURE 16.2

SOURCE: Goldman Sachs, *Anatomy of World Markets*, September 1988

economy, turnover in relation to capitalisation, capital raised in relation to the economy, and the number of foreign shares listed.

The survey mentioned in Chapter 1 showed that global equity trading is still rather limited, but the main centres are clearly New York, Tokyo and London, with the London market playing an important role. This is partly

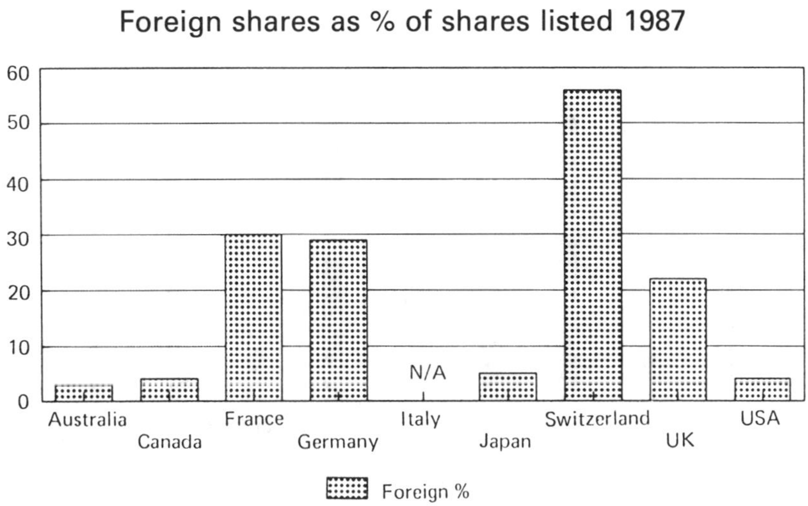

SOURCE: Goldman Sachs, *Anatomy of World Markets*, September 1988

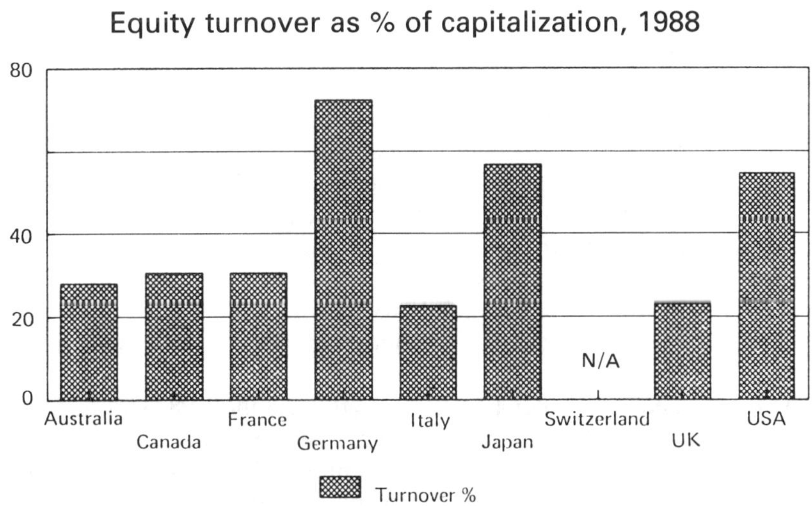

FIGURE 16.2 (*continued*)

SOURCE: Morgan Stanley, Capital International Perspective

built on the fact that it is a key centre for secondary market trading in Eurobonds – as can be seen from the fact that the membership of AIBD council of reporting dealers includes 89 firms from London, compared with six from Paris, five from Amsterdam and Luxembourg, and two each from Frankfurt and Zurich – and on the fact that it is a rapidly growing centre

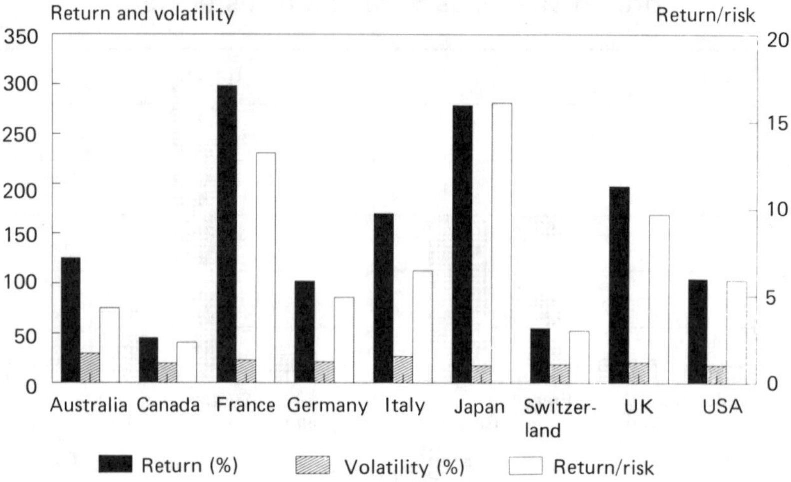

FIGURE 16.3 Risk and return: June 1981–June 1988 in %

SOURCE: Goldman Sachs

for international trading in government bonds, as we saw in the last chapter.

So, given the depth and extent of the London secondary market, it has become a natural focus for international trading in equities. The London Stock Exchange has changed its name to the International Stock Exchange. Its membership merged with the members of the International Securities Regulatory Organisation, which was the body formed by Euromarket practitioners. Its Stock Exchange Automated Quotation (SEAQ) dealing system carries price quotations for 700 foreign stocks. The New York Stock Exchange lists a similar number of foreign stocks in the form of ADRs (see Chapter 4).

As mentioned in Chapter 1, just before the October 1987 Crash, foreign share trading in London had grown 70 per cent over the previous twelve months to a daily volume of £525 ($850) million. It accounted for almost one-third of the volume of trading in the London market. In addition, London had a widespread off-exchange market in international equities, estimated to be about as big as the volume traded on the Exchange; over half the trading was estimated to be done by non-residents.

The bulk of London's trading is in French and German equities, with an active market also in US and Japanese stocks. By contrast, trading on the New York Stock Exchange is largely confined to ADRs (American Depository Receipts – certificates evidencing ownership of shares) – and is a relatively small market, while at the time of the Crash 1.5 per cent of Tokyo's volume was in foreign shares.

INTERNATIONAL COMPARABILITY OF EQUITY MARKETS

Before going on to discuss individual country markets some major caveats should be made. It is not possible to compare equities across countries. Attempts can be made, but the range of differences in accounting and tax regimes, investor valuations, impact of currency expectations and so on mean that the exercise must bear so many qualifications as to be very tenuous. Many attempts have been made, but the assumptions that must be made are heroic.

One interesting recent attempt may be worth discussing in some detail simply to highlight the problems: a paper written by Peter Thompson of BZW (*The Valuation of International Equity Markets*, London, May 1989). The framework used consists of five steps: we adjust for (a) tax systems (imputation systems versus classical systems); (b) accounting differences; (c) the currency in which the earnings from the equity will accrue (and its interest rate structure; (d) inflation differentials; and (e) underlying real growth in retained earnings.

Each of these steps merits a separate book, but will be covered briefly here. Tax adjustments are fairly straightforward. Certain countries, such as the UK and Germany, deem dividends to have income tax deducted at a standard rate. Thus UK and West German dividends need to be grossed up, since price/earnings ratios do not include the full value of dividends under the imputation system. The effect is to push down the UK Market's December 1988 P/E ratio from 10.4 to 9.5, and the German ratio from 15.6 to 13.0. (All Thompson's figures are taken from the Morgan Stanley Capital International Perspective.)

Accounting adjustments (discussed further below) are much more complex. A number of countries (notably Japan) have excessively conservative reported earnings figures – in the case of Japan, because the authorities require reported earnings to be the basis of taxation. (Unlike, say, the US where one set of books is reported to shareholders and another to the tax authorities). Thompson argues that a sensible, rule-of-thumb adjustment for excessively conservative accounting is to adjust by the ratio of cash earnings to reported earnings. Cash earnings figures should be reasonably undistorted, since they have no significance for tax purposes. The December 1988 ratio of cash to reported earnings in the US was 175 per cent and in Japan 313 per cent, suggesting that true Japanese earnings were 1.75 times the reported figure (on the assumption that the US figures are relatively less distorted than other countries' and so should be used as a base). This adjustment would bring down the P/E ratio for the Japanese market from 53.8 to 30.7.

The next step is to consider the currency in which the earnings will accrue, and the associated interest rate structure. Take ten-year government bonds in two different countries. You can get a figure for the amount of currency depreciation built into the market over the long-term. Ten-year US Treasury bonds in December 1988 were yielding about 4.6 per cent more than Japanese government bonds, implying a long-term annual yen appreciation of 4.6 per cent. Thus a US investor in Japanese equities could expect a 4.6 per cent annual 'dividend' from the currency. Such an investor ought to be prepared to expect a higher P/E ratio on Japanese stock – conversely, a Japanese investor would require a lower US P/E ratio to compensate for losing an expected 4.6 per cent per annum on currency.

This raises the question of which currency to use as the base for a global investor. Thompson's argument is that over the long run the Swiss have been closest to a zero-inflation economy. The December 1988 bond yield structure implied a predicted 1 per cent per annum rate of inflation in Switzerland, which is taken as the base inflation rate.

The final step is to look at the underlying growth rate of earnings in relation to return on equity and book value. We begin with some basic definitions. A price/earnings ratio is the ratio of share price to earnings per share. The earnings yield is the inverse of the P/E ratio (abstracting from all tax considerations etc.). Earnings per share (EPS) can be defined as:

$$\frac{\text{Net income}}{\text{Equity}} \times \frac{\text{Equity}}{\text{Shares outstanding}}$$

Put another way, EPS = return on equity (RoE) × book value per share. Similarly, the dividend can be defined as RoE times payout ratio (where the payout ratio equals dividend/RoE). The implied growth in EPS can be defined as RoE times (1 – payout ratio). Finally, total shareholder return is defined as dividend plus implied EPS growth.

Consider now a company with RoE of 8 per cent, book value per share of $100, and a payout ratio of 3/8. Then we know that its EPS will be $8 and its dividend $3. Thus its implied EPS growth will be 5 per cent and total shareholder return 8 per cent = 3 per cent + 5 per cent.

Suppose the company's share price is $100. Then since EPS is $8, we know the P/E ratio will be 12.5 and the current earnings yield is 8 per cent.

Suppose we have another company with twice the return on equity. But it has the same book value per share and the same payout ratio. Then the EPS will be $16. The dividend will be $6 (still 3/8). The implied EPS growth will be 16 per cent × 5/8 = 10 per cent per annum.

Suppose, because of the RoE has doubled, investors bid $200 for the shares instead of $100, then the dividend rate, in percentage terms, is still 3 per cent. The implied EPS growth is 10 per cent. So the total shareholder's return will be 13 per cent. The P/E ratio will still be 12.5 ($200/$16 instead of $100/$8). In fact, of course, investors will bid the shares higher, because of the higher total return; they will be prepared to pay up to $288 for

Table 16.1

Item	*France*	*Germany*	*Italy*	*Japan*	*Neth'ds*	*Sweden*	*Switz'd*	*UK*	*USA*
Cost of assets:									
Historic?	N	Y	N	Y	Y	N	Y	N	Y
Historic + revaluation?	Y	N	Y	N	Y	Y	N	Y	N
Depreciation:									
Straight line?	Y	Mixed	Y	N	Y	Y	Y	Y	Y
Excess depreciation allowed?	N	Y	Y	Y	N	Y	N	N	Y
Long-term investments: >50%:									
Full inclusion?	Y	Mixed	Y	Mixed	Y	Y	Mixed	Y	Y
Long-term investments: 21–50%:									
Equity method?	Y	N	N	N	Y	N	N	Y	Y
Inventory cost:	Mixed	Average	Mixed	Mixed	Mixed	ND	ND	ND	FIFO
Deferred taxes reported?	Y	N	ND	N	Y	N	N	Y	Y
Discretionary reserves used?	Y	Y	Y	Y	Y	Y	Y	Y	N
Currency translation:									
Current method?	Y	ND	ND	ND	Y	Y	ND	Y	Y
Gains/losses taken to current income?	Y	ND	ND	ND	Y	N	ND	Y	Y

Key
Y = yes, most commonly.
N = not commonly used; small number may do so.
Mixed = more than one method widely used.
ND = not disclosed; majority of companies do not disclose method.
Source: V. Bavishi, 'Company Accounts Worldwide', in *Managing Global Portfolios*, Euromoney, 1989.

shares, pushing them to a P/E of 18, since at this level they will receive a comparable total return of 8 per cent.

It cannot be overstressed that the methods used to compare international equity valuations at the present time are extremely primitive. The above approach is given because it is a fairly systematic attempt to grapple with some of the issues, but it is open to a wide range of criticisms. The valuation applied to earnings growth is reminiscent of that used in the USA in the early 1960s to justify the astronomic P/E ratios on the 'nifty fifty' top performing stocks. Belief in indefinite rapid earnings growth can theoretically justify an almost infinite P/E but the reality is that such expectations are rarely fulfilled. Equally, the accounting numbers used in different countries differ widely in quality.

On this latter subject Table 16.1 showing the important accounting differences between some of the major international markets may be of some interest.

THE JAPANESE EQUITY MARKET

Japanese capital markets have always been very tightly regulated. The Tokyo Stock Exchange's trading arrangements were installed after the Second World War under US guidance and reflected that country's laws. The Glass-Steagall divide between banks and securities houses was repeated in Japan. Another legacy was a ban on futures contracts, which has only recently been overturned. Also, the authorities kept rigid control over interest rates and the amount of bank credit.

Of the eight exchanges by far the dominant is Tokyo, with 85 per cent of the business volume. It has two tiers. The first tier includes 1,000 of the most marketable stocks. Of these, the 250 stocks in which trading is most active are traded on the floor of the exchange, using traditional hand signals. The remainder are traded through a computerised system. The second tier has just under 450 stocks of newer growth companies.

The opening of the second tier in 1961 contributed a good deal to the 1965 stock market collapse. The exchange had pressured securities dealers to buy second-tier stocks and hold them during a 1963 sell-off. The largest dealing firm would have gone bankrupt had it not been for a loan from the Bank of Japan, through the creation of a collective lifeboat called the Japan Joint Securities Corporation and its successor institution, the Japan Securities Holding Association.

Membership of the exchanges is limited to securities companies. Depending on what they do they are divided into regular members, special members, and Saitori members. Regular members trade for the public or for their own account. Special members specialise in handling trades in Tokyo or Osaka for orders which could not be handled on regional exchanges. Saitori members may not deal for their own account or with the public. They specialise in handling trades between regular members.

To borrow a Churchillian phrase, the Japanese equity market since the early 1980s has been, for many Westerners, a mystery wrapped in an enigma. Price/earnings ratios of 60 have been common; Nippon Telephone and Telegraph at one stage enjoyed a P/E ratio of over 200 and was valued at more than the entire stock market of Canada. Faced with these valuation levels, many fund managers withdrew from the market, only to be confounded when it continued to rise higher. As a result of these spiralling valuations, the value of the Japanese stock market overtook that of the United States in April 1987, and rose to 50 per cent larger.

Part of the influence on valuations is technical. First, mathematically a low interest rate environment, implying a low discount rate for future earnings, will produce a high P/E ratio. Secondly, conservative accounting practices undoubtedly conceal substantial elements of profits and under-valued assets. Thirdly, there are substantial cross-holdings. These have the following effect: consider two companies each valued at $100, with 50 per cent holdings in each other. To buy both companies you need only pay $100.

Even discounting all these factors, many Western investors found the levels of Japanese valuations hard to accept. Clearly the Japanese economy has performed extraordinarily well. Yet it is equally clear that these astronomic valuations took a great deal on trust, notably a continuation of low levels of interest rates and high earnings growth for an indefinite period. In early 1990, rising Japanese interest rates and the falling yen brought the value of Tokyo's capitalisation back to that of New York.

A single example will serve: Nippon Telephone and Telegraph, which is the largest single stock on the Tokyo market. In December 1988 its market capitalisation of $220 billion equated to that of Canada, or to Spain and Australia combined. The dividend yield was 0.03 per cent, the P/E ratio on forecast 1989 earnings was 123. Although the company has 130 subsidiaries, these need not be included in consolidated accounts under Japanese accounting practice. There is no way of knowing what the company is really worth. Merrill Lynch have estimated that the company's surplus property holdings (telephone exchanges that will be miniaturised) are worth about $17 billion (which is not shown in the balance sheet). The scale of the understatement only highlights the guesswork involved.

The other point of concern for an international investor is that valuations of individual shares are largely controlled by a relatively small group. If a stock is Nomura's flavour of the month it will soar; if it is dropped it will languish. This is of course not unknown in other markets. But the phenomenon is exaggerated in Japan and results in a very strong trend to sector rotation: this month waterfront stocks are the rage, next month it is steels. A related point is the new issue phenomenon, whereby new issues

Japan

EXCHANGES:	Tokyo (83% of volume), Osaka (14%), Nagoya (3%) Fukuoka, Hiroshima, Kyoto, Niigata and Sapporo. Exchange has three sections: First has larger shares (96% of capitalization); second is newly quoted or unlisted shares; third is unlisted shares trading over the counter.
EXECUTION:	By the Zaraba method (open outcry). Must be through member of Japan Securities Dealers Association. All equity is in registered form. Commissions are on a fixed scale.
SETTLEMENT:	Fourth business day after trade. Clearing is through Japan Securities Co. Ltd., subsidiary of Tokyo Stock Exchange.

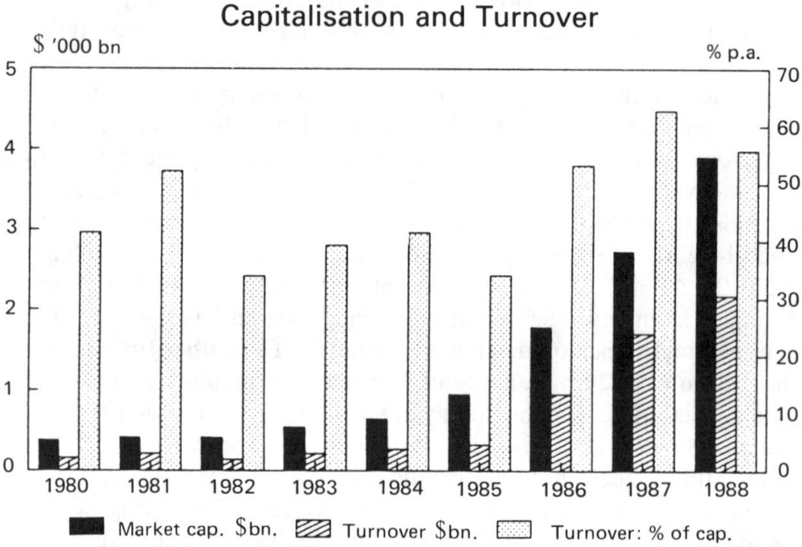

FIGURE 16.5 Japan: exchanges

SOURCE: Morgan Stanley Capital International (Turnover), Goldman Sachs, *Anatomy of World Markets*, September 1988 (Capitalisation)

have regularly gone to a premium, the profits from which have often been used for political purposes. The Recruit Cosmos issue scandal which toppled the then Prime Minister in the summer of 1989 was one of a long series of new issues of a similar nature.

Thus, care must be taken to be in touch with the market. Liquidity in

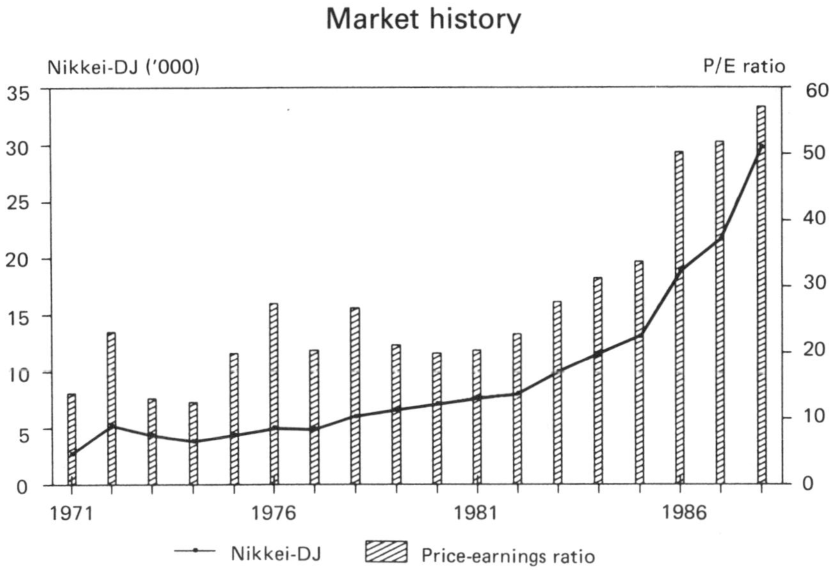

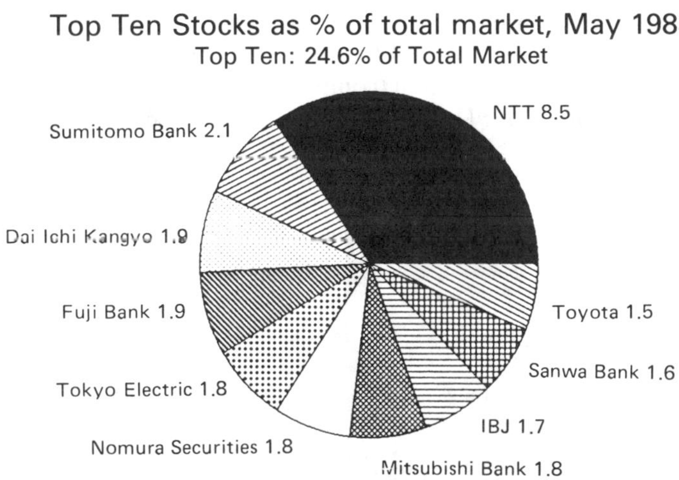

FIGURE 16.4 (*continued*)

SOURCE: Morgan Stanley Capital International

certain stocks is also an issue. It can take a couple of days to get a price in a reasonable amount of stock, even in a stock in the top ten, such as IBJ. Many of the bank stocks are still relatively illiquid. Trading during 1988 for long periods was dominated by the top twenty or thirty stocks; turnover in the remainder was low. This led to volatility, with a 5 per cent price swing during a day being by no means uncommon.

The markets are dominated by the Big Four securities houses (Nomura, Daiwa, Nikko and Yamaichi) which are hugely profitable, helped by the existence of a continuing fixed-price commission structure and a protected environment. As one observer put it:

> 'While this regulatory structure may look formidable, it is of little concern to the securities industry ... At worst, offending branches or departments may be closed down for two or three days, causing a loss of face rather than a loss of income ... While the principle of protecting investors is firmly entrenched at the Ministry of Finance, it believes that the best way to implement this principle is to guarantee the securities houses' continued profitability'.
>
> (S. Bronte, *Japanese Finance*. Euromoney Publications, London, 1982.)

The high commissions are one reason why foreign firms have pressed strongly to be allowed to become members of the Tokyo Exchange rather than splitting commissions with members. In 1982 the Exchange shifted the commission split from 50/50 to 27/73 in favour of the foreign firms. That failed to satisfy them. But the Tokyo Exchange had only 83 seats – compared with 1,366 on the NYSE, and none were for sale. In December 1984 one became available; Merrill Lynch bid for the seat, but it was sold to a Hiroshima firm for $6.6 million (compared with Nomura's $285,000 for a seat on the NYSE in 1981). At last, however, in 1986 six foreign firms were admitted to the Tokyo Exchange.

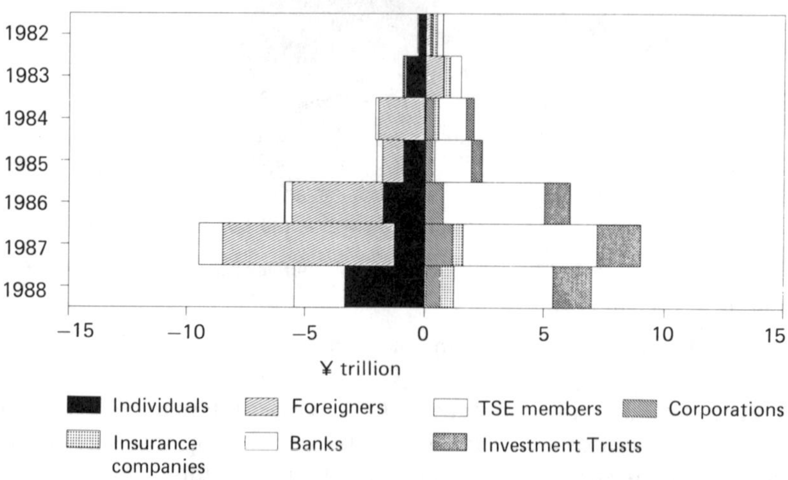

FIGURE 16.5 Japanese stock market transactions, by type of investor
SOURCE: Nomura Securities

A threat to the Japanese securities' firms position in the Tokyo market also opened up from another source in 1986. Deutsche Bank became the first foreign bank to obtain a securities licence in Tokyo, through a fifty-per-cent-owned subsidiary. It has been followed by several others. The Japanese banks are widely thought to welcome the presence of foreign banks with securities licences as 'Trojan horses' which will end in their also being allowed securities licences.

Also in November 1986 large cuts in commission on larger trades were introduced by the Stock Exchange, in response to pressure from large institutional investors. If New York experience is anything to go by, this represents the start of a long struggle towards complete deregulation.

However, the Big Four still reign supreme. Liberalisation has so far made little impact on their position. Of the 45 foreign securities firms operating in Tokyo in the year to September 1988, 39 made losses: the top ten chalked up losses of $112 million between them.

Having said all this, Japan has been a hugely profitable market during the 1980s for international investors, if they held on. Most did not. Figure 16.5 shows how the buying in Japan was led by the banks and investment trusts, with corporations and insurance companies also participating; they bought from individuals and foreign investors.

Important in the market also were the special investment funds (tokkin and kingai) managed by banks and other financial institutions for corporations, which have grown rapidly in recent years (Figure 16.6). The effects of October 1987's events was to change the pattern of funds flow into institutions. Investors have sought more conservative fund management philosophies, as indicated by the fact that funds under management by life

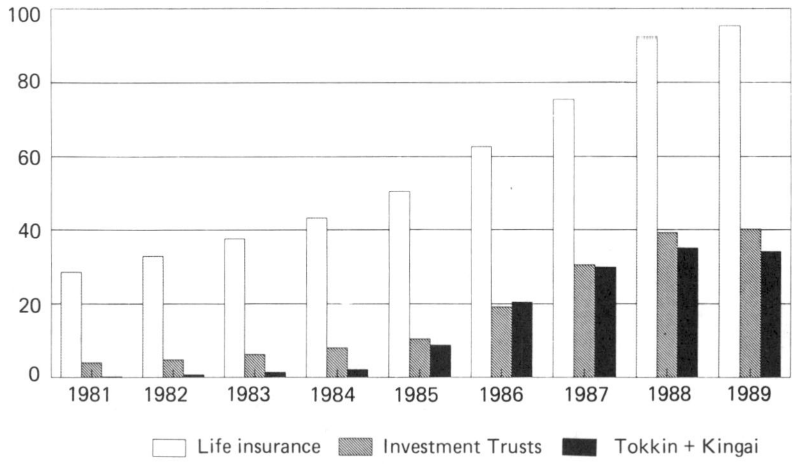

FIGURE 16.6 Assets of Japanese institutions, trillion yen
SOURCE: Nomura Securities

insurance companies have grown strongly, while investment trusts, and tokkin and kangai funds have grown more slowly.

Tax reform has also played a role in directing funds towards life insurance and pension funds, with capital gains taxes now applied to the sale of investment trusts. The Ministry of Finance now places heavy penalties on non-financial corporations that trade actively in stocks; as a result, some corporations are cancelling their tokkin and fund trust contracts. In addition, banks are no longer permitted to count their tokkin and fund trust profits as part of operating income, which reduces their attractiveness to banks.

Despite all the problems and caveats, the importance of Japan to the world is now so great that the international investor cannot afford to ignore the Japanese equity market. What is certain is that in the longer run investment in Japan Inc. will continue to be rewarding.

THE UNITED STATES' EQUITY MARKET

The USA has historically had the most vibrant and largest capital markets in the world, until being overtaken by Japan in 1987. The central market is the New York Stock Exchange, followed by the American Stock Exchange and the National Association of Securities Dealers Automated Quote System (NASDAQ), an electronic over-the-counter market for second-line stocks (and some substantial ones also, such as Apple Computer, Intel and MCI). Important regional exchanges exist also in Boston, Cincinnati, Chicago, Philadelphia and San Francisco.

Then there is the over-the-counter securities market. This is a market between securities houses directly: deals are not routed through the Exchange. It is regulated by the SEC. (All brokers and dealers doing business in the OTC market must register with the SEC. Most of them also become members of the National Association of Securities Dealers, the OTC self-regulatory body.) Trading on the OTC is handled through the National Association of Securities Dealers Automated Quotation system (NASDAQ). NASDAQ started in 1971. It revolutionised the trading quality of the over-the-counter market.

It also put the NYSE under pressure. A study released in April 1972 showed that NYSE spreads on securities that were also traded on NASDAQ were much less than spreads on other securities. After this test, the NASD decided to include exchange-listed securities permanently in the NASDAQ system. As a result, any stock listed on the NYSE can be traded on NASDAQ. The NYSE's share of trade in NYSE-listed stocks fell from 87 per cent in 1978 to 72 per cent in 1986.

Some of this has been because of the success of regional exchanges in attracting business formerly put through the NYSE. But much of it has gone to NASDAQ which has on the whole been very successful. Of a 1979 total of 12.9 billion shares traded on the NYSE, the Amex and NASDAQ, NASDAQ accounted for 28.2 per cent. By 1984, that percentage had grown to 38.2 per cent.

During the 1970s discussion raged over the relationship of the exchanges to the OTC markets, and of both groups to outsiders such as the SEC, investing institutions and the rest of the financial services industry. The role of the SEC, particularly during the 1970s, was that of an activist promoter of a central market system. This was mainly because of concern over the functioning of the NYSE and the specialist.

The role of the specialist is at heart of the stock market system. He has two main functions: that of executing orders given by other members of the Exchange; and that of maintaining fair and orderly markets in the stocks that he services, by dealing for his own account. The execution of orders is handled in two ways: market orders are executed at once and limit orders are entered in a limit order book. When the security reaches the limit, the specialist must execute the trade.

As October 1987 vividly demonstrated, NYSE specialists, with a finite quantity of capital, faced increasing problems in handling the growing volumes traded through the Exchange. A second reason for the SEC to press towards development of a central market system was the back-office crisis of the 1960s. It was felt that automation and linkage of securities clearance and settlement systems would mesh with a national, electronic market system. Finally, there was the example of NASDAQ.

As an alternative, most of the exchanges favoured a national market system that preserved the exchange floors' central role. This was found by developing the Intermarket Trading System which began in April 1978. It was essentially a communications system. It let specialists and flood brokers on one exchange floor transmit buy or sell orders to market-makers on another. If there were a better price on another exchange, the ITS allowed a specialist or floor broker to transmit 'a commitment to trade' to the market-maker on that exchange. The latter could accept or decline.

In 1982 the SEC required the exchanges to permit an automated interface between the ITS and NASDAQ systems. By early 1985, 1,600 stocks were quoted on the NASDAQ National Market System. The present status seems to be an emerging national system consisting of NASDAQ on the one hand and ITS on the other, but the bridge between them remains hampered by the NYSE rule 390 forbidding member firms to deal off the floor of the Exchange.

As is well known, October 1987 saw a major crisis in the US stock market. The extraordinary aspect of this event was how it demonstrated the international integration of the market and at the same time how relatively little actual trading between – and within – the markets took place. The Brady Commission noted that 'only 3 per cent of publicly traded

United States

EXCHANGES: New York (80%), American (15%), Boston, Cincinnati, Midwest, Pacific, Philadelphia
NASDAQ (over-the counter, screen-based)

EXECUTION: Open outcry on exchanges; telephone for OTC
All shares are in registered form. Commissions are negotiable. NASDAQ trades are net.

SETTLEMENT: Fifth business day after trade. NYSE trades clear through National Stock Clearing Corporation
The Depository Trust Company acts as depository for securities of its members.

Capitalisation and Turnover

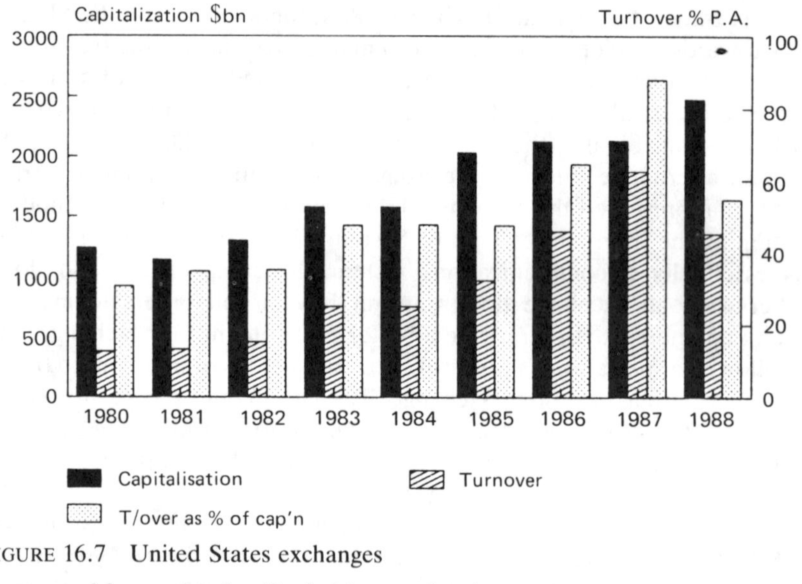

FIGURE 16.7 United States exchanges

SOURCE: Morgan Stanley Capital International

stock in the US changed hands during this period', and the Federal Reserve study referred to in Chapter 1 showed how relatively unimportant international trading in equities was in spreading the crisis.

It would seem that the driving forces behind the Crash were in the first instance the usual influences of any market collapse: excessive previous

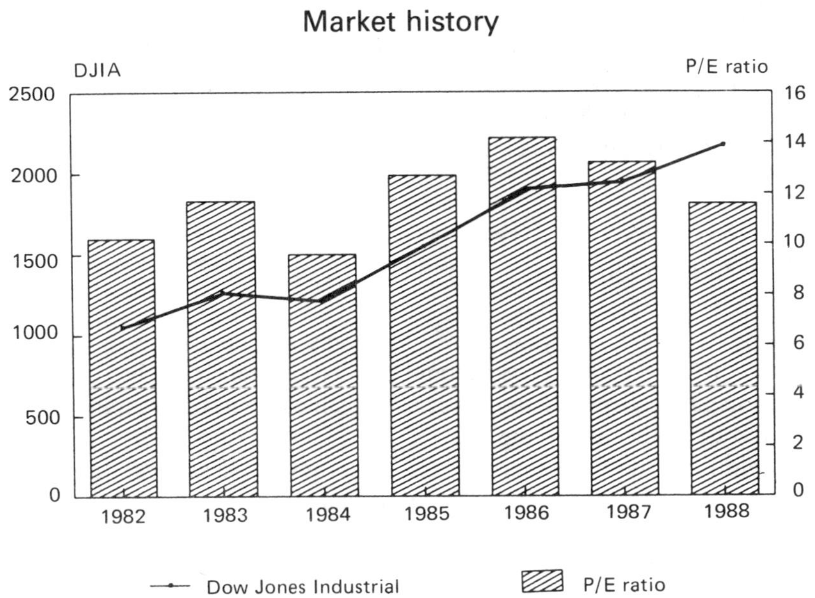

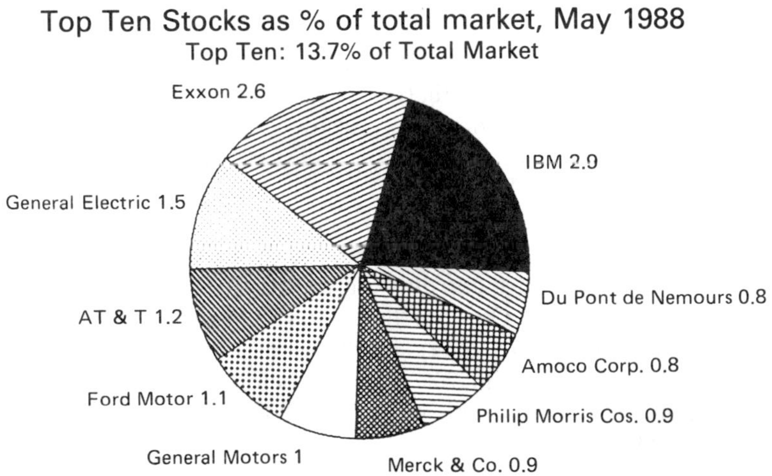

FIGURE 16.7 (*continued*)

SOURCE: Morgan Stanley Capital International

optimism, and underlying economic problems which on this occasion it seemed the politicians were ignoring. Specific problems included poor economic news in the shape of a record US trade deficit, concern over legislation to eliminate tax benefits associated with the financing of takeovers, which led to the dumping of takeover stocks and, once the fall was underway, the triggering of portfolio insurance programmes which followed computer-driven mechanical selling rules. It was this latter which made the speed of the Crash so terrifying and led to the breakdown of links between the New York Stock Exchange and the Chicago futures exchanges, partly because of credit concerns. Under stress, the system's linkages failed.

THE UNITED KINGDOM EQUITY MARKET

Tracing its origins back to New Jonathan's Coffee House in 1773, the London Stock Exchange has become the first to abolish its physical trading floor and go electronic. This drastic move came as part of sweeping reforms referred to as the 'Big Bang'.

Previously, the UK markets for government securities ('gilt-edged' securities) and equities were both controlled by the Stock Exchange. They worked on 'single capacity'. That is, there was a division between stockbrokers and stock-jobbers. Jobbers were market-makers; they could not deal with the public. Brokers dealt with the public but acted as agents rather than market-makers.

The aim was to make sure the firm with which the investor dealt did not profit from the price at which the sale was made. It aimed to protect his interests by getting the best possible price from the jobber, and earned a fixed commission for doing that. This system was replaced by US-style 'dual capacity'. At the same time, outside shareholders were allowed to assume full ownership of stockbroking and stock-jobbing member firms on or after 31 March 1986.

Dual capacity was allowed at the same time as the abolition of fixed commission scales, on 27 October 1986. These reforms – together with the simultaneous halving of stamp duty on securities transactions to ½ per cent – cut dealing costs a lot. On a purchase and sale of £500,000 worth of one of the most heavily traded (alpha) stocks the total cost could now be under 1 per cent compared with 2¾ per cent before 'Big Bang'; the equity commission component of this might be 0.2–0.25 per cent compared with 0.35 per cent on average previously.

The effects of these changes were far-reaching. Brokers, faced with the situation where broking and market-making could be combined, sought partners with large capital resources. The banks and merchant banks recognised an opportunity to make acquisitions to extend their securities activities, and to develop investment banking houses along US lines.

The Stock Exchange opted for a 'competing market-maker system' modelled along the lines of the American NASDAQ system. Its main features are as follows:

(a) All firms are deemed to be dual capacity broker/dealers; several have chosen to remain agents only (James Capel & Co. being a notable example).
(b) All firms are able to deal as principal and/or agent (subject to capital and equity requirements) and to match business between clients subject to disclosure to both parties. Where orders cannot be precisely matched, the firm can deal as principal on the balance.
(c) Firms are able to register as market-makers which requires them to maintain a two-way price on the Stock Exchange Automated Quotations systems (SEAQ). Price spreads are monitored and quotes fed into a screen system.
(d) Clients are permitted access to information contained in Level One terminals only. These show the best bid and offer quotations extracted from the market. Member firms receive the Level Two service which shows the size and price of quotes offered by each market-maker. (In the event there has been some dispute about the size of quotes maintained on the screens, with some firms refusing to show more than minimal amounts on the grounds that others have been taking advantage of the information to piggy-back off their positions).

The final – and unexpected – step in this revolution proved to be the abolition of the trading floor. Although it had been expected that fewer people would use the Stock Exchange floor in the new world, the speed with which trading moved upstairs onto telephones was a major surprise. Within four months of Big Bang, the Stock Exchange announced plans to abolish the physical trading floor (with the exception of the stock options

Table 16.2

	Alpha	*ADRs*	*Beta*	*Camma*	*Delta*
18+	20				
16–17	23				
14–15	33		6		
12–13	32		14		
10–11	17		43		
8–9	6	4	106		
6–7	0	7	192	13	
4–5	1	3	204	504	
2–3				919	24
0–1				1	94
Total	132	14	565	1,437	118

Source: International Stock Exchange, *Quality of Markets Quarterly*, Spring 1988.

United Kingdom

EXCHANGES: International Stock Exchange (London; includes Birmingham, Manchester, Liverpool, Glasgow, Dublin) Unlisted Securities Market; Third Market (for fledgling companies)

EXECUTION: Telephone/screen market (SEAQ). Must be through Stock Exchange member. Commissions negotiable. Most shares are in registered form: physical delivery is normal.

SETTLEMENT: Two/three week account period. Central clearing system called Talisman operated by Stock Exchange

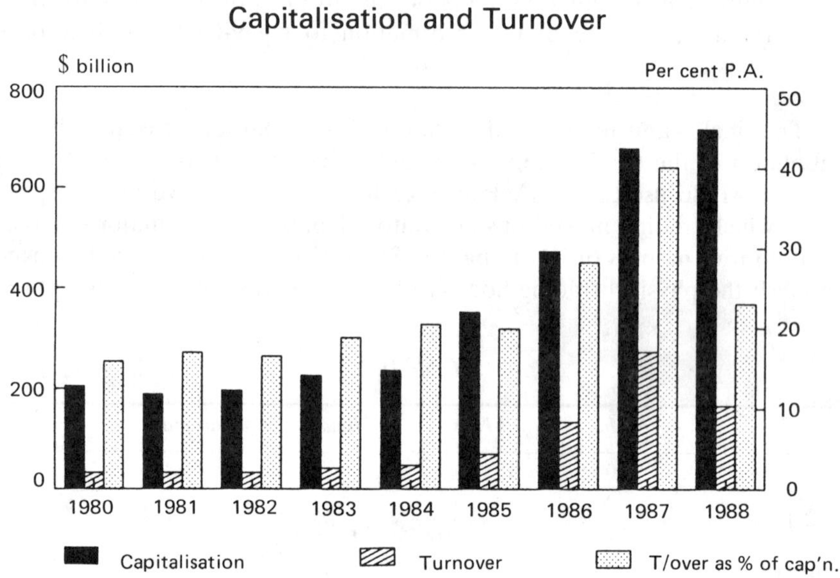

FIGURE 16.8 United Kingdom exchanges

SOURCE: Morgan Stanley Capital International

pit). This triggered a dispute with the New York Exchange, which clung to the notion that its members could only trade NYSE-listed stocks on a recognised exchange, i.e. one having a trading floor. In due course, of course, the NYSE accepted the reality of the situation.

As part of the Big Bang reforms, equities were divided into four

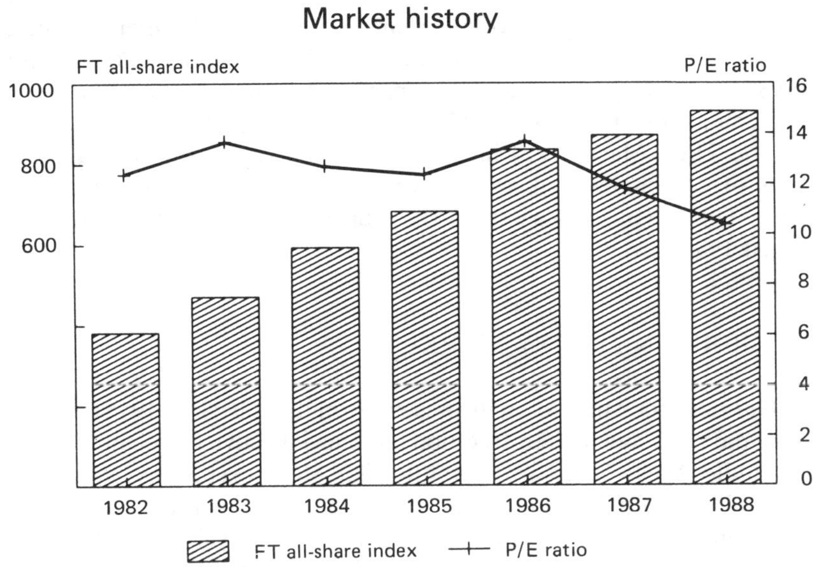

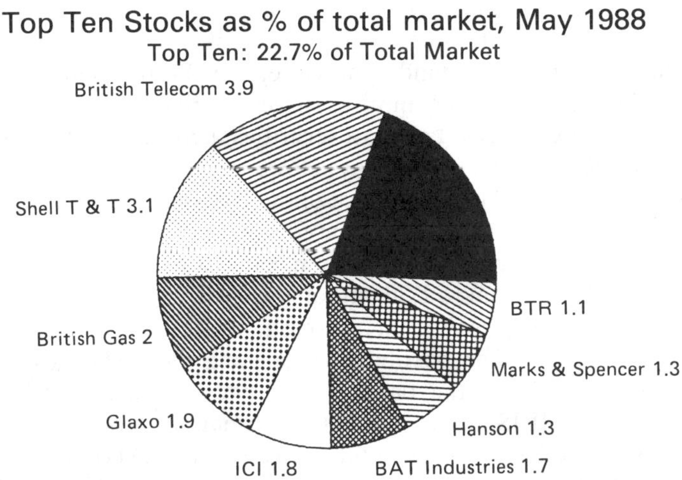

FIGURE 16.8 (*continued*)

SOURCE: Morgan Stanley Capital International

categories: alpha, beta, gamma and delta. Alpha stocks are the largest and most liquid, delta the smallest. A survey in April 1988 showed the distribution of market makers by stock category to be as in Table 16.2. In other words, of the 132 alpha stocks, 17 had ten or eleven market-makers, while 42 of the 565 Beta stocks were in the same position.

In addition to the main Stock Exchange, there are two other exchanges: the Unlisted Securities Market and the Third Market. The USM was set up in 1980 as a means for smaller companies that did not meet the stricter requirements of the Stock Exchange to be quoted and traded. In January 1987 the Third Market was introduced to be a centre for dealings in the shares of companies that are too young or too small to merit a listing on the USM. (In January 1990 the Third Market and the USM were merged.)

THE GERMAN EQUITY MARKET

The German stock market in its present form dates back to 1945 but it is of course part of a much older tradition of financial activity stretching back to the Middle Ages. There are currently eight stock exchanges, with Frankfurt and Dusseldorf accounting for 75 per cent of the market. In addition to trading on the floor of the Stock Exchange there is a substantial telephone market, often bigger than the turnover on the Exchange.

The banks are major players since only banks may take customer orders from institutions and the public; in addition there are two types of brokers. Official brokers (Kursmakler) are appointed by the provincial governments and set official prices. The free brokers (Freimakler) operate independently; they also handle the Geregelter Freiverkehr, a regulated, semi-official market which comprises shares too illiquid for listing or listed on other stock exchanges. For most securities there is a single official price fixed by the Kursmakler once a day. However, trading in the more active shares is continuous. The emergence of the Deutsche Termin Börse (DTB – German futures exchange) has caused some problems in this area. The DTB's operating hours of 10 am to 4 pm contrast with the two hour official trading period (11.30 am to 1.30 pm) on the stock exchanges. But the DTB needed continuous prices from the cash market on which to base its derivative products. The possibility of opening the exchanges for longer hours was rejected by the banks on grounds of cost; they urged the development of IBIS (Inter Banken Informations System) – a system which would feed inter-bank equity prices to the DTB. However, this posed a competitive threat to the Stock Exchange and also raised further questions about the power of the banks over the German financial system. As of the time of writing, the debate continues.

Trading activity in the German market has been held back by the government's turnover tax, which has encouraged some trading to move offshore to London. Domestic institutional involvement has also been historically rather limited partly because, unlike the USA or UK, corporate pensions schemes are typically unfunded or 'pay-as-you-go'. So corporate pension departments are not geared to investing funds with which to pay out pensions. Recently, however, the growth of Spezialfonds, a kind of mutual fund created by insurance companies or corporations which allows them to escape capital gains tax and create hidden reserves, has increased institutional activity in the market. By the end of 1988 it was estimated that the Spezialfonds controlled funds of DM70 billion.

The German stock market has traditionally been thin and narrow, dominated by cartelised cross-holdings. After 1982 a sustained boom and changing attitudes wrought considerable changes. Where, at the start of the 1980s, it was extremely rare for a company to make an initial public offering, the 1983–8 period saw more than 90 such offerings – not large by US or even UK standards but a milestone for the German market. A symbol of the changes is that in 1986 for the first time a formal association of German stock exchanges was set up. Previously fierce regional rivalries had prevented effective cooperation.

Like all markets, the German stock market suffered from the loss of foreign interest following the crash of 1987, but the selling was well absorbed as shown by Table 16.3.

Table 16.3 Supply and demand of equities (m. DM)

	Supply		*Demand*	
	Rights issues	*New issues*	*Domestic*	*Foreign*
1978	3,972	1,578	2,715	2,835
1979	3,635	1,880	4,122	1,391
1980	3,967	2,979	5,850	1,098
1981	3,398	2,117	2,432	3,084
1982	3,525	2,398	5,465	456
1983	3,538	3,731	4,816	2,456
1984	4,123	2,152	2,286	3,992
1985	9,338	1,672	3,796	7,213
1986	13,984	2,412	1,220	15,174
1987	10,119	1,769	13,250	−1,360
1988[1]	2,529	1,560	1,956	2,132

[1]Year to October.

Source: Goldman Sachs.

However, there is still some way to go. Information on German companies is improving but still not of the standards seen in the United States. The law does not require consolidated world-wide balance sheets, for example, but only a balance sheet in which all German activities are consolidated. Also the outstanding 'float' of tradable shares in many companies has been historically very limited due to firm, long-term holdings by banks or individual families.

Germany

EXCHANGES: Frankfurt (60%), Dusseldorf (20%), Munich, Hamburg Stuttgart, Hanover, Berlin, Bremen

MARKETS: Official: Government bonds and large companies
Semi-official: Set up in 1987, replacing an earlier version. Less stringent listing rules.
Over-the-counter: Unlisted stocks and some listed stocks are traded by telephone

EXECUTION: Large stocks trade continuously. Smaller stocks are dealt at a price fixed daily.

SETTLEMENT: Two business days (five days can be arranged). Delivery must be effected through a German bank; settlement is carried out by regional clearing agencies (Wertpapiersammelbanken) or the Auslandskassenverein for foreign securities

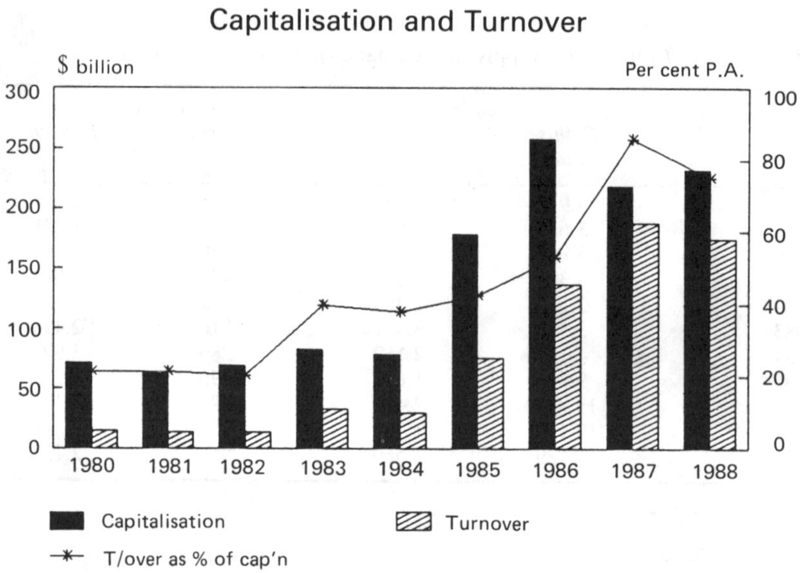

FIGURE 16.9 Germany: exchanges

THE CANADIAN EQUITY MARKET

The three major stock exchanges in Canada are located in Toronto, Montreal and Vancouver. The latter specialises almost exclusively in so-called penny stocks of resource-based companies. There are also ex-

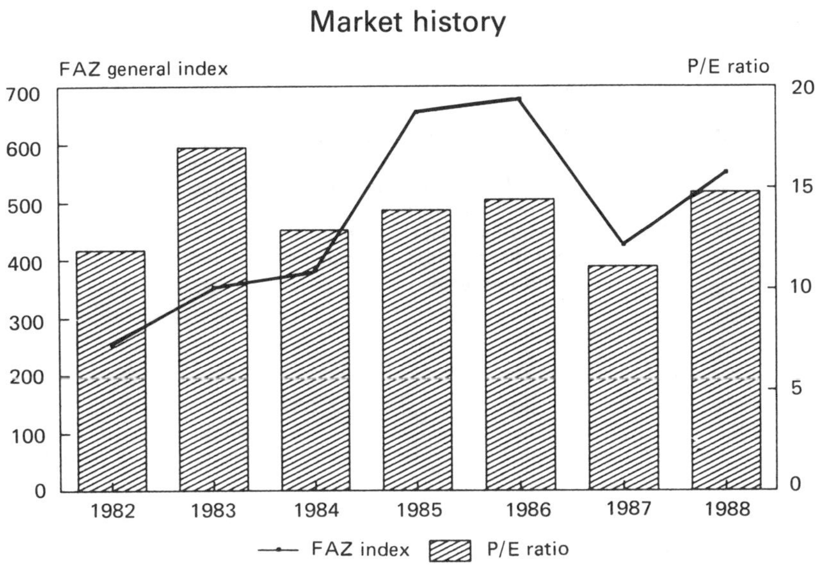

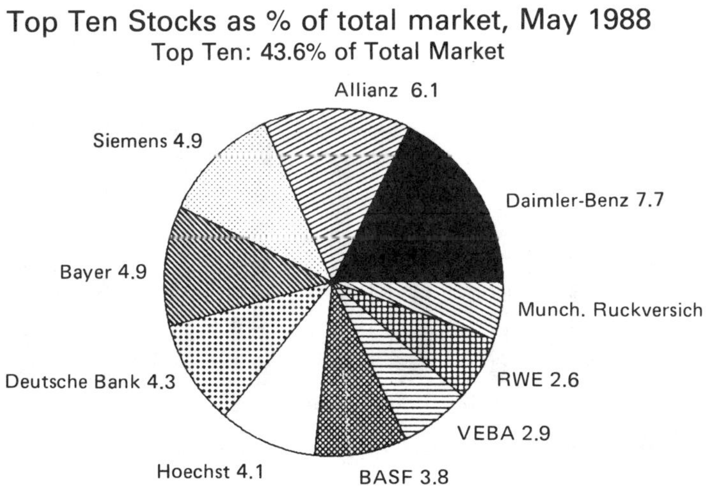

FIGURE 16.9 (*continued*)

SOURCE: Morgan Stanley Capital International

changes in Calgary and Winnipeg. The Toronto exchange accounts for about 75 per cent of the market, Montreal for almost 20 per cent (growing relative to Toronto) and Vancouver nearly 5 per cent. Montreal started an options market in 1975 followed by Toronto in 1976.

The Toronto Stock Exchange (TSE) was founded in 1852 and incorpor-

Canada

EXCHANGES:	Toronto (75%), Montreal (20%), Vancouver (5%), Alberta, Winnipeg. Over-the-counter market trades unlisted shares.
EXECUTION:	On the floor of the exchanges. Must be through member firm. Automated execution for certain kinds of trade. Negotiable commissions. Equity is in registered form.
SETTLEMENT:	Five business days. Canadian Depository for Securities provides automated clearing and custody services.

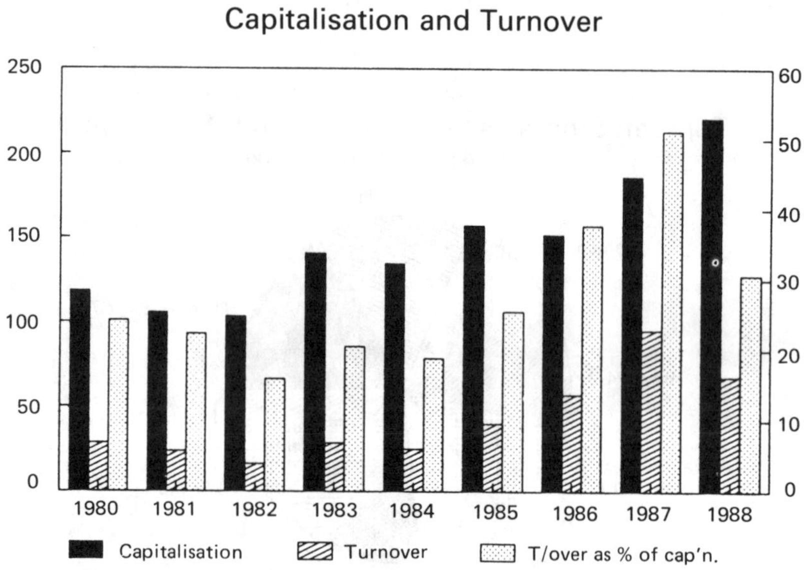

FIGURE 16.10 Canada: exchanges

SOURCE: Morgan Stanley Capital International

ated in 1878. In 1977 it introduced the Computer-Assisted Trading System (CATS) which gave a means of automated trading in a screen-based environment, the first stock exchange to introduce this system. Sixty per cent of stocks listed on the TSE – primarily the less active ones – are traded on CATS. In 1985 the TSE established trading links with the American

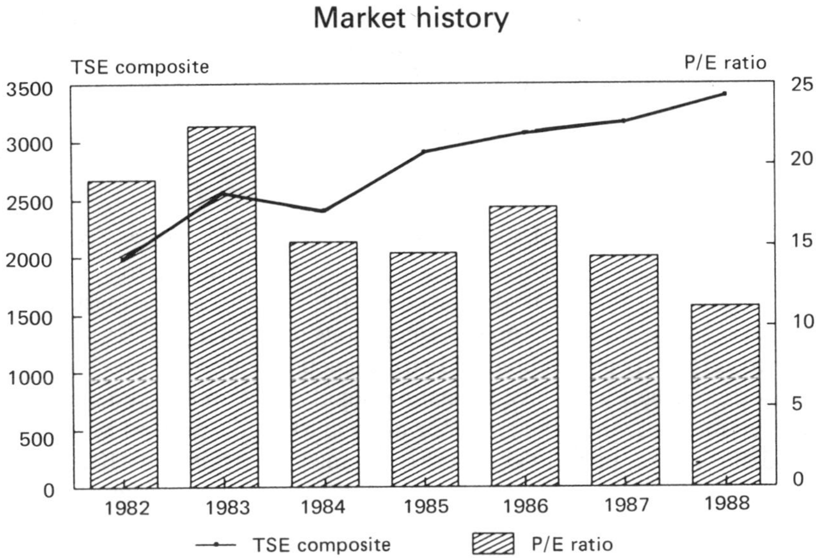

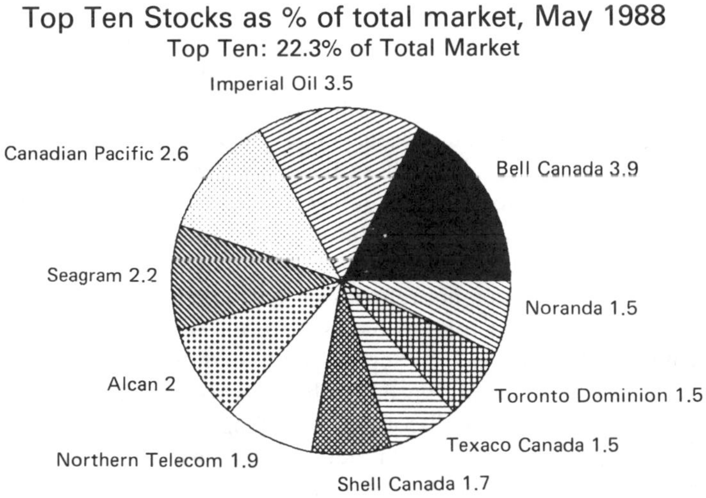

FIGURE 16.10 (*continued*)

SOURCE: Morgan Stanley Capital International

Stock Exchange and the Midwest Stock Exchange. Links were also set up between the Canadian Depository for Securities and its US counterparts, National Stock Clearing Corporation (NSCC).

In December 1985 the Province of Ontario raised the 10 per cent ownership limit on the purchase of security houses by financial institutions to 100 per cent. After twelve months, the decision was ratified by the Federal Government. Canadian banks, trusts and insurance companies were given a headstart by limiting foreign ownership to 50 per cent until June 1988.

THE FRENCH EQUITY MARKET

There are seven stock exchanges in France, but the Paris Stock Exchange handles over 95 per cent of trading volume. All bonds and shares, whether listed or unlisted, must be traded on one of the exchanges. The markets are supervised by the Commission des Opérations de Bourse (COB), set up in 1967. In addition, all trading must be carried out through stockbrokers (agents de change) who have a legal monopoly. Within this system, there are three markets: the official list, or main market; the Second Marché or second market, set up in 1983, where companies need float only 10 per cent of their capital compared with 25 per cent on the main market; and the over-the-counter market, where companies are not required to produce a prospectus nor publish more than the legal minimum of information. The Second Marché, inaugurated in February 1983, has performed successfully and within three years had 180 companies listed on it.

Until recently the equity trading system was rather archaic. Each stock was assigned to an individual broker, who fixed the price sometime between 12.30 and 2.30 p.m. This then remained the price till the next day. During 1988 the market was switched over to a continuous quotation system. At the same time drastic steps have been taken to simplify settlement (see Chapter 17): physical certificates for shares have been abolished ('dematerialised') and replaced with a computerised 'book-entry' system. Options were introduced, from June 1987, on the eleven most actively traded stocks.

As part of the wide-ranging reforms of the French financial system (see Chapter 15) French and foreign banks were allowed to buy into French stockbrokers in March 1987. In September 1988 outsiders were allowed to take 100 per cent control. Faced with intensifying competition – and weakened in some cases by ill-conceived trading on the MATIF (France's futures exchange) where the most notable scandal was the loss by the Stock Exchange itself of Frfr600 million of its investor compensation fund – many brokers sold out to heavily-capitalised outside banks or investments banks.

THE SWISS EQUITY MARKET

The Swiss securities markets, while renowned for their traditionalism, have not been immune either from the winds of change. The Swiss stock exchanges (of which there are eight – the three chief being Zurich, Basel and Geneva) have been run on very old-fashioned lines. Shares were not continuously traded. Instead, prices were established by a Ring, or calling-over system: an Exchange official would call out the name of the stock, after which dealers would make bids or offers until a deal is struck. The procedure takes place once a day for bonds and twice for stocks. In between times, stocks are traded over-the-counter.

The Zurich exchange did not have a full-time manager until 1980; at year-end 1984 its staff totalled six people. The low numbers of administrative staff in Zurich reflects the relative simplicity of the exchange's operations, and the fact that its membership consists entirely of banks. They bring companies to the market, organise the trading, and handle most of the operational functions of the exchange.

Introduction of continuous trading in the bearer shares and participation certificates of 'blue-chip' companies was introduced in October 1986. Testing of an automated transactions settlement system began on the Geneva bourse in November 1986. In May 1988 the Swiss Options and Financial Futures Exchange (SOFFEX) opened with options on eleven shares; after reaching a daily trading average of 10,000 contracts, volume now seems to have settled back down to around 5,000 contracts daily.

Another change has been the development of the 'covered warrant' market. This exploits the fact that Swiss companies have traditionally banned foreign ownership of their registered shares. Foreigners may only buy bearer shares or participation certificates, which do not carry voting rights. As a result of this restriction, bearer shares have often traded at a premium of 100 per cent or more over registered shares, because of foreign demand.

In 1986 BZ Bank persuaded some institutional investors to deposit with BZ Bank 100,000 registered shares of Ciba-Geigy. BZ Bank then issued 100,000 warrants at a price of Swfr350 each, carrying the right to buy the Ciba-Geigy shares for Swfr1,950 each at any time during the next three years (the market price at the time being Swfr1,840). The idea caught on. By September 1989, about 7.5 per cent of all Swiss registered stock was covered by warrants.

In October 1988 Nestlé, which had been severely criticised during its bid for the British confectionery firm Rowntrees for restricting foreign ownership of its equity, announced that it would allow foreigners to buy its registered shares. The price of the bearer shares and participation certificates collapsed and that of the registered shares jumped. To date, few other firms have followed their lead.

THE ITALIAN EQUITY MARKET

Until the early 1980s the Italian equity market was not very active. Trading activity was dominated by the banks, but a number of reforms have livened

France

EXCHANGES:	Paris (95%), Lyons (4%), Bordeaux, Lille, Marseilles, Nancy, Nantes. Three markets: Cote Officielle. Large and foreign companies. Second Marche. Small and medium-size. Marche Hors-Cote. Over the counter market.
EXECUTION:	Cash or forward market. Most trades forward. Automated execution system gradually replacing system of placing orders in pigeonholes. Price movement restrictions: 5% cash, 8% forward.
SETTLEMENT:	Cash: Immediately after trading session. Forward: Last working day of month.

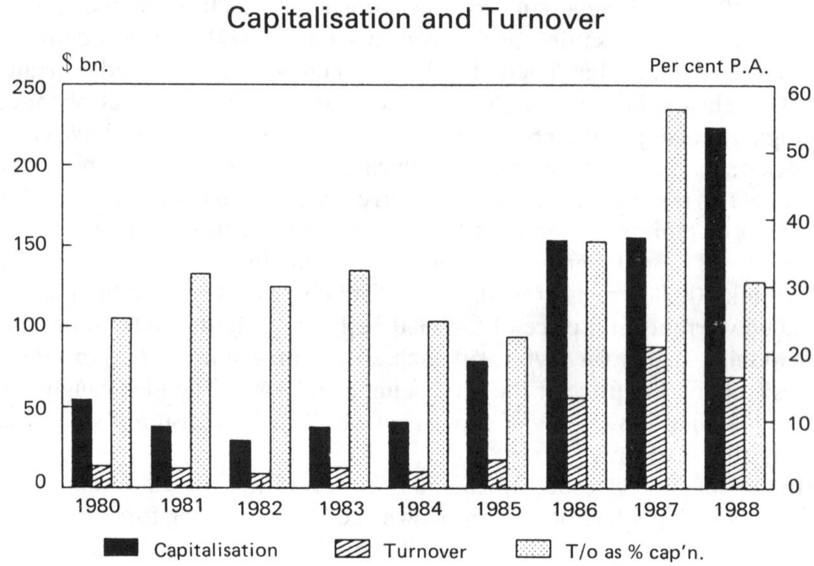

FIGURE 16.11 Canada: exchanges

SOURCE: Morgan Stanley Capital International

it up. The Visentini bis law allowed companies to revalue their assets without incurring capital gains tax, and open-ended mutual funds (unit trusts) were permitted by a 1983 law. This latter reform in particular drove the market upward sharply.

The major exchange is Milan, with secondary exchanges in nine other

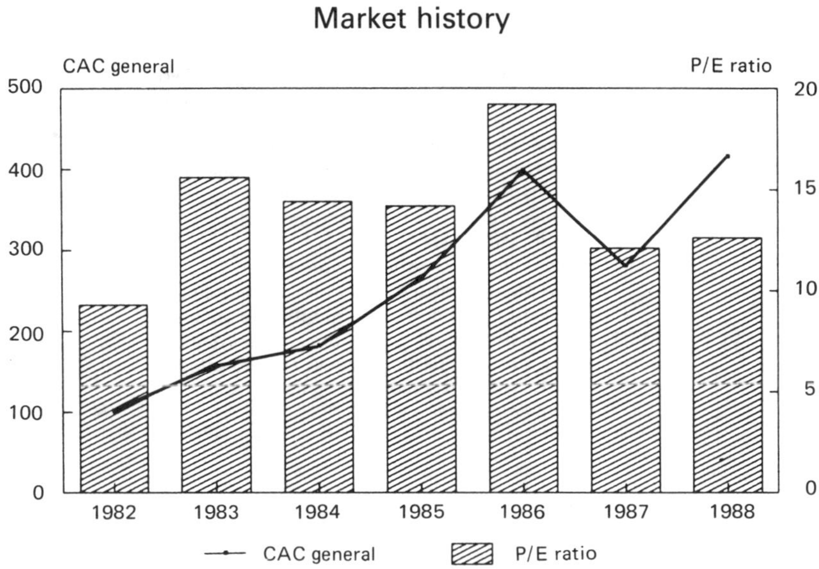

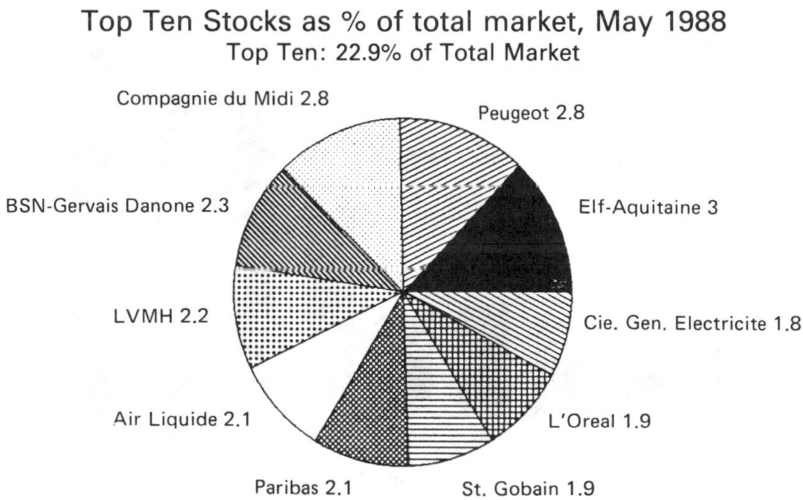

FIGURE 16.11 (*continued*)

SOURCE: Morgan Stanley Capital International

cities. Milan accounts for about 90 per cent of equity volume. Stockbrokers are not allowed to deal as principals, but only as agents. A good deal of trading occurs off the exchange floor. In principle foreigners may trade for cash settlement (three days after trade date) but in practice the Italian market is a forward settlement market. Settlement takes place at the end of

Switzerland

EXCHANGES:	Zurich (60%), Geneva (20%), Basle (10%, Bern, St. Gallen, Lausanne, Neuchatel. Three markets: Official: On floor of exchanges between members. Semi-official: On floor, in unlisted companies Unofficial: Telephone, inter-bank trading in unlisted companies and new issues. Registered, bearer shares and participation certificates exist.
EXECUTION:	Open outcry for official/semi-official markets. 70% of trades are for spot settlement; forward trades up to nine months are possible.
SETTLEMENT:	Spot: within three days. Forward: last day of the month in question. Stocks are deposited in SEGA (centralised clearing house) and book-entry transfers made.

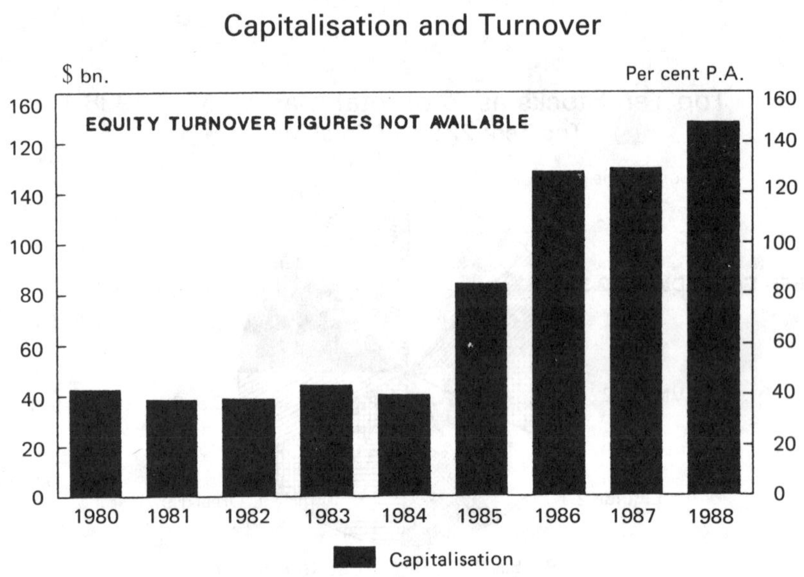

FIGURE 16.12 Canada: exchanges

SOURCE: Morgan Stanley Capital International

the contract period which is usually one month. However, regulations imposed in 1981 by the CONSOB (Commissione Nazionale per le Società e la Borsa) require foreign investors to deposit 100 per cent of the purchase price at the time of the trade (unless the investor is a bank).

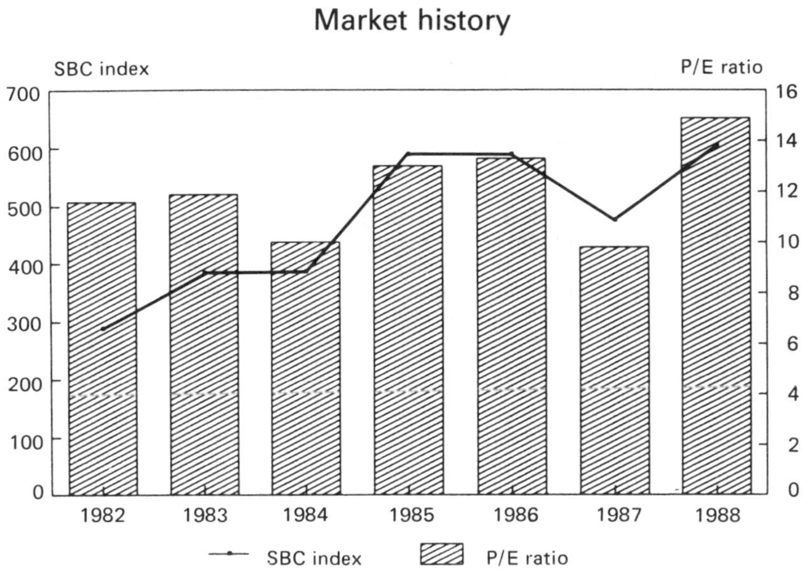

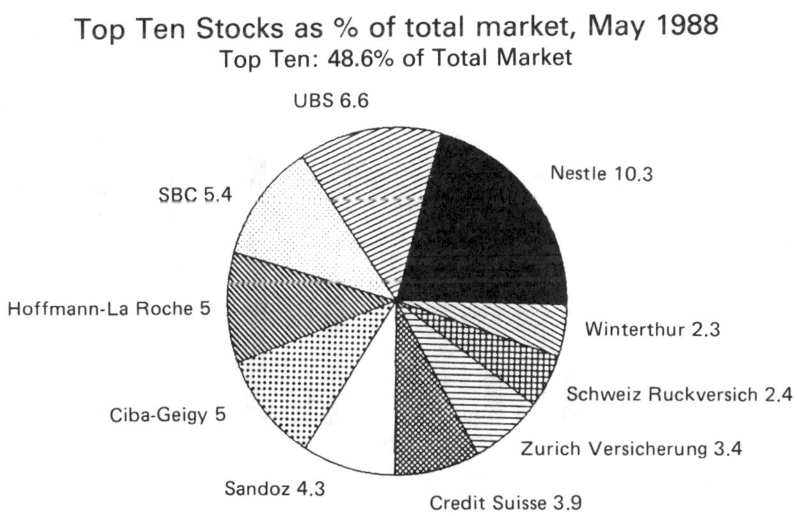

FIGURE 16.12 (*continued*)

SOURCE: Morgan Stanley Capital International

Clearing is handled through local clearing houses managed by the Bank of Italy, linked to a central depository, Monte Titoli. During the rapid growth of the Italian market the settlement system became a shambles – causing severe problems, for example, to the Fiat Euroequity placing (see

Italy

EXCHANGES:	Milan (90%), Bologna, Florence, Genoa, Naples, Palermo, Rome, Trieste, Turin, Venice. There is an unlisted securities market ('grey market'). Common, preferred and savings shares exist.
EXECUTION:	Call system at trading rings. Large amount of off-exchange trading by telephone. All equity in registered form except non-voting savings shares.
SETTLEMENT:	Cash (three days after trade); normally, forward account period runs mid-month to mid-month with settlement in last three days of calendar month. Clearing through Monte Titoli (85% of trades) via book-entry.

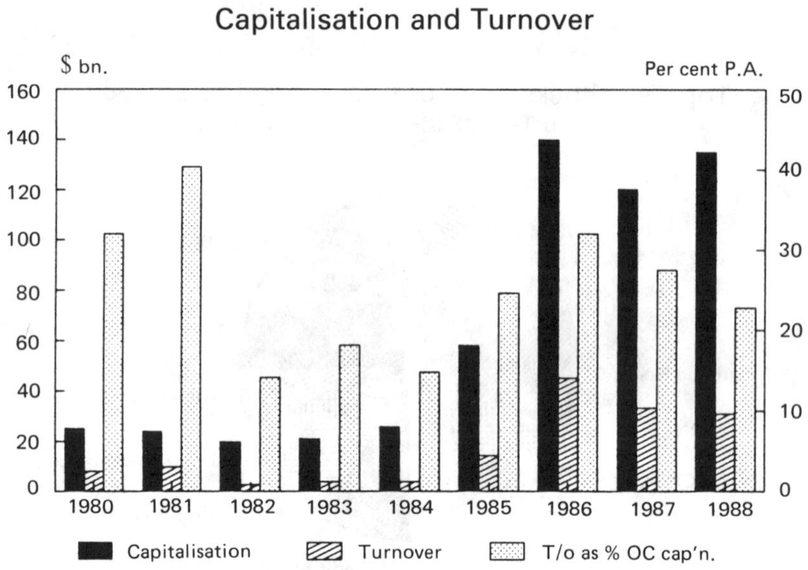

FIGURE 16.13 Italy: exchanges

SOURCE: Morgan Stanley Capital International

Chapter 12) – but the full introduction of the Monte Titoli system seems to have straightened things out somewhat (see Chapter 17).

There is an official second market (the 'mercato ristretto') with 33 quoted shares, of which 24 are banks. Until recently trading in this market was once a week, but it has now moved to daily trading.

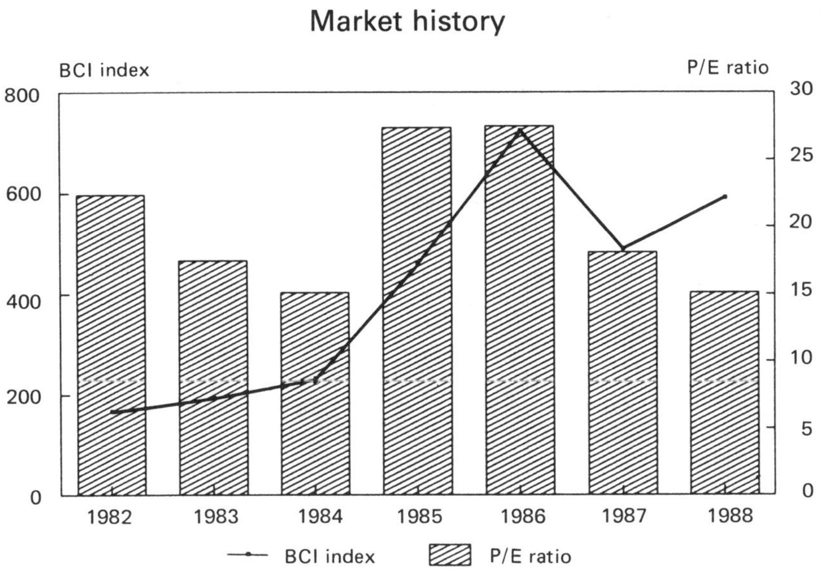

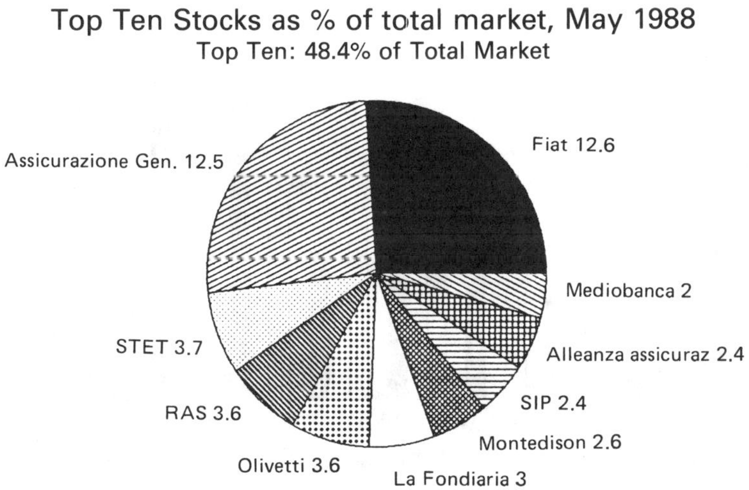

SOURCE: Morgan Stanley Capital International

FIGURE 16.13 (*continued*)

THE AUSTRALIAN EQUITY MARKET

Trading in shares in Australia dates back to 1828 but the Melbourne Stock Exchange first came into existence in 1865; in 1937 the six capital city exchanges (Sydney, Brisbane, Adelaide, Hobart, Perth and Melbourne)

Australia

EXCHANGES:	Australian Stock Exchange (created 1987 from Sydney, Melbourne, Adelaide, Brisbane, Hobart and Perth Exchanges). Main Board Market handles large and foreign shares; Second Board the small unlisted companies.
EXECUTION:	Between brokers at trading posts. Automated trading system in Sydney and Melbourne for 240 companies. Commissions negotiable. Equity is in registered form. Physical delivery.
SETTLEMENT:	Normally five business days. No official settlement period.

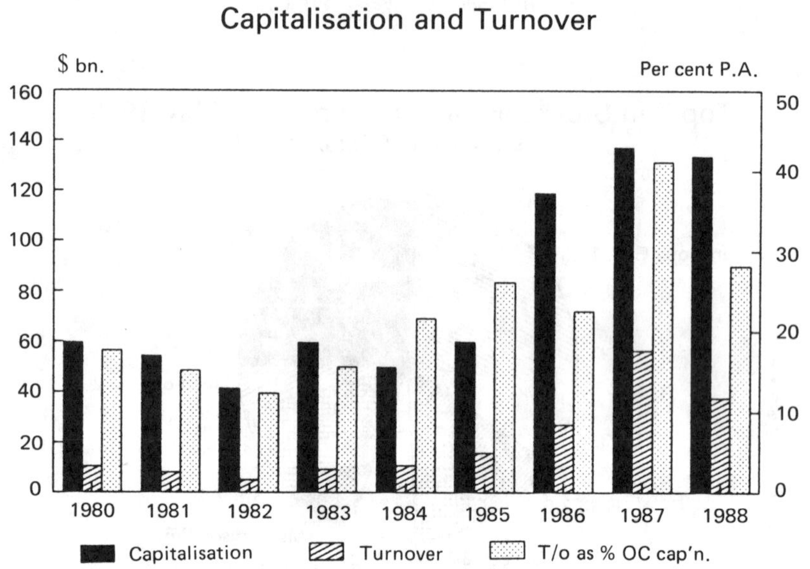

FIGURE 16.14 Australia: exchanges

SOURCE: Morgan Stanley Capital International

formed the Australian Associated Stock Exchanges. In 1984 brokerage commissions were deregulated and stockbrokers were allowed to incorporate and to sell out to outside firms such as banks or insurance companies. In April 1987 the Australian Stock Exchange (ASX) was set up, headquartered in Sydney. At the same time, financial institutions were allowed

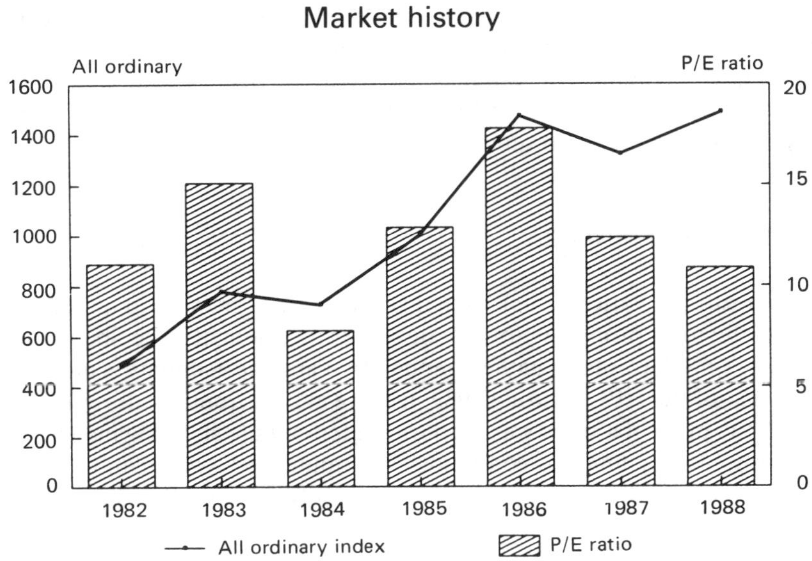

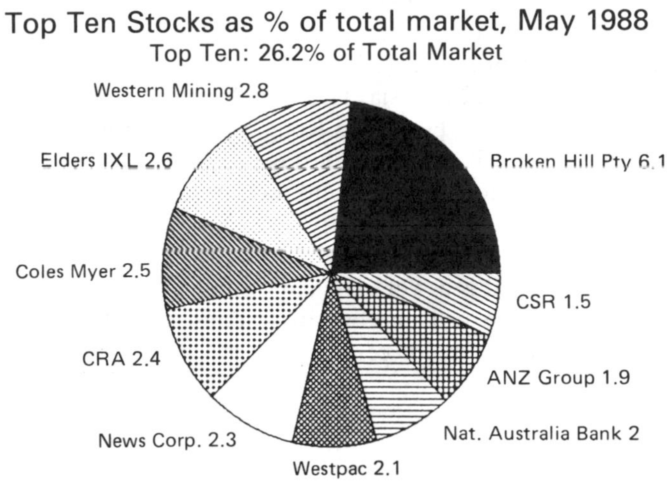

FIGURE 16.14 (*continued*)

SOURCE: Morgan Stanley Capital International

to take up to 100 per cent of stockbrokers.

Most public trading of securities takes place through the ASX or its regional subsidiaries, but there is a Second Market, trading through these subsidiaries, for smaller and previously unlisted companies. There are two execution methods. The conventional system is that orders are placed with brokers who act as agent and who deal direct with one another at specific trading posts on the Stock Exchange floor. Or the Stock Exchange Automated Trading System may be used, in Sydney and Melbourne. Settlement and delivery date for all transactions is normally five business days, though there is no official settlement date (see Chapter 17).

OTHER EXCHANGES

Within Europe various stock exchanges have been growing in importance; one of the most promising for the longer term is thought to be Spain, as the country's modernisation gathers momentum and the economy is integrated with that of the EEC. During 1989, trading moved from a 'call' system – in which the price of a stock was set during a ten-minute shouting match every morning – to a unified, continuous, computerised system modelled on Toronto's order-driven system called CATS (Computer-Assisted Trading of Securities). A National Securities Markets Commission was set up in January 1989 and from July 1989 individual membership of the Stock Exchange gave way to brokerage firms of whom foreigners could buy up to 30 per cent (rising to 100 per cent in 1992).

In the Far East, Hong Kong has traditionally been an important exchange, though its importance is gradually being eroded, first in the face of the relentless rise of Japan, secondly as other markets round the Pacific Rim, such as Singapore, Malaysia, Thailand, Indonesia and the Philippines, begin to grow in stature. For Hong Kong a particular problem is that its performance was much criticised during the Crash of 1987, when the Exchange was closed for four days and the futures market went spectacularly awry. During the 1988 and early 1989 the government worked on a Securities and Futures Commission Bill to bring in an appropriate regulatory body. However, it is as yet early days to see whether the traditionally freewheeling exchange will improve its trading and ethical standards to those expected in other major centres.

EMERGING MARKETS

In recent years some international investors have begun to take an interest in stock markets in countries where such markets have traditionally been rather underdeveloped but which offer long-term opportunities because of the country's economic potential. The risks in these markets are not small; illiquidity and political instability in many countries are notable problems. Also, many of the countries involved restrict foreign investment except through approved investment companies. The definition of this emerging markets group would vary from investor to investor; some would include

Greece, Portugal, Korea, Taiwan and Singapore while others would regard these as part of 'mainstream' markets. Certainly Thailand, the Philippines, India, Malaysia, Indonesia, Argentina, Brazil, Chile, Jordan and Zimbabwe have all at one time or other figured in the 'emerging market' category.

Such a list encompasses markets with enormous variations in structure and performance; no one market could be considered representative. Some are extremely large: Taiwan's $120 billion capitalisation at end-1988 compares with Italy or Sweden. India has almost 6,000 stocks listed – compared with 6,680 in the USA. And the returns can be substantial: in US dollar terms the Brazilian Market in 1988 returned 131 per cent.

Because of its potential economic weight, the Brazilian market is perhaps the one most worth singling out. After all, the country accounts for half of the South American land mass, and is comparable in size to the mainland United States; it has rich resources of minerals, hydroelectric power and rain forest. By 1986 it had become the non-communist world's seventh largest steel producer, and the tenth largest motor vehicle manufacturer; its aerospace industry has begun to develop (albeit behind the shelter of steep tariffs and import controls).

The Rio de Janeiro stock exchange (founded 1845) and the São Paolo exchange (founded 1890) dominate trading. The latter, being centred in the main economic heartland, is the more active, with total trading volume in 1988 (first eleven months) of $9.3 billion compared with $6.0 billion in Rio. Market activity was at its peak in 1986 and fell with the resumption of inflation (and the international Crash of October 1987) – see Table 16.4.

Participation by foreign investors in the Brazilian stock market has historically been small, compared to the sums lent by banks and invested directly in factories and natural resources. This is partly because of cumbersome and restrictive regulations. Foreigners were permitted to

Table 16.4 Brazilian equity market

	Number of listed Co's	*Value traded ($ bn)*	*Capitalisation ($ bn)*	*Turnover (%)*
1980	614	5.3	9.2	57
1981	603	6.2	12.6	49
1982	607	5.9	10.3	58
1983	593	4.8	15.1	32
1984	601	9.7	28.9	34
1985	609	21.8	42.8	51
1986	654	29.8	42.1	71
1987	646	10.1	16.9	60
1988	636	18.2	31.1	58

Source: São Paolo Stock Exchange – BOVESPA; National Commission of Stock Exchanges – CNBV.

Table 16.6

	% change in index	*% change in US$ terms*[1]
1982	64	−17
1983	759	120
1984	442	68
1985	402	52
1986	41	−1
1987	35	−72
1988	1,609	90

1. Using average foreign exchange rate for period.
Source: BOVESPA.

invest in Brazilian securities in 1975, through investment companies organised in Brazil, but restrictions meant that the total invested fell from a 1978 peak of $61 million to $17 million in late 1982. In July 1986 the authorities announced a more liberal regime which by the end of 1988 had attracted about $150 million.

Table 16.5 shows the attractive returns – and the hair-raising collapses – provided by the São Paolo market. The most recent example of the type of incident which can occur was the closure for a day in June 1989 of the country's stock exchanges when a prominent speculator failed to make an $8 million payment in settlement of stock purchases.

EQUITY INDEXES

The measurement of international investment performance is a tricky subject (see Appendix 6) and it has recently been complicated by a proliferation of equity indexes. Investment banking firms have seen the commercial benefits of being associated with an index, first through the prestige/publicity and secondly through being on the inside track for derivative activities such as futures contracts or indexation programmes. Thus we now have the Morgan Stanley Capital International indexes, the Salomon-Russell 1000, 2000 and 3000 Indexes, the FT Actuaries-Goldman Sachs Indexes, the Euromoney-First Boston Indexes and so on. The subtleties of construction differ. The main question is whether or not to exclude those shares which may not be sold to foreigners, on the grounds that it is unfair to judge a money manager against an index he can't duplicate (MSCI do not, FTA-GS do) or to adjust for cross-holdings – long-term shareholdings that it is expected will never, in the ordinary course of events, be traded.

Comparing these indexes is not always straightforward. The Salomon

Russell indexes overlap 79 per cent of MSCI, but only 48 per cent of the FT-A. During 1988 a comparison of monthly returns showed the MSCI index showing consistently better returns in Switzerland, Australia, Hong Kong, Japan and Singapore/Malaysia than the other two. Over the year as a whole, Belgium in the MSCI index returned 48.5 per cent return while in the Salomon-Russell it returned only 28.5 per cent – the effect of takeover speculation in a few major stocks showing up in the MSCI but being diluted in the Salomon-Russell. A further influence was differences between the various categories of share included (e.g. ordinary equities vs preferred), where the MSCI might include two or three types of stock and the Salomon-Russell only one type for each company, choosing the most liquid. Fortunately, these differences, while spectacular sometimes at the individual country level, tend to wash out in the case of regional groupings such as the MSCI Europe and Far East (EAFE) index compared with the Salomon-Russell Europe–Pacific–Asia composite.

Another driving force behind the proliferation of new indexes is the need to create indexes suitable for derivatives. Thus the German Frankfurter Allgemeine Zeitung (FAZ) index, which is updated once a day, is being challenged by the Deutscher Aktienindex (DAX). The DAX is a thirty-share index – more narrowly-based than the FAZ – which was introduced in July 1988. It is an index weighted by authorised share capital, dominated by chemicals (28 per cent), banks (16 per cent) and automobiles (14 per cent). It is updated at one-minute intervals during the day. Although narrower than the FAZ, the DAX accounts for about 75 per cent of the freely floating equity capital of listed German companies, and almost 60 per cent of total market capitalisation.

Similarly, the needs of the financial futures markets in the UK encouraged the development of the Financial Times-Stock Exchange 100-share index (FTSE 100). This is an arithmetic index weighted by the market capitalisations of the constituents, consisting of 69 industrials, 23 financials, and eight others.

For the same reasons of ease of calculation for continuous updating, the MATIF has introduced its CAC 40 which is also designed to provide continuously updated prices for futures and options trading. These areas are discussed in Chapter 7, while index issues are also touched on in Appendix 6.

Part Five
Making the Global System a Reality

17 Clearing and Settlement Systems

The route towards a global clearing system will be rocky, and probably filled with detours. However, it will be an essential step forward for the emerging global capital markets. The risks inherent in the process were vividly highlighted in October 1987; until they are overcome, there must always be a substantial incremental risk to investing internationally. The study by the Group of Thirty (*Clearance and Settlement Systems in the World's Securities Markets*, March 1989) pointed out that the uneven quality of different markets' systems 'could, under adverse circumstances, represent a very serious risk to the world's financial network' (p. iii). This chapter considers some of the essential components of a global clearing system. We begin with the two existing global systems, Cedel and Euroclear.

SETTLEMENT SYSTEMS: EUROCLEAR AND CEDEL

A smooth settlement system is vital to the functioning of any market. Otherwise, participants face escalating credit risks and financing costs. The settlement difficulties of the 1960s led to the foundation of Euroclear and later of Cedel. Euroclear began in 1968 with 50 members. In the twenty years to 1988 that number increased ninety-fold to over 2,500. Turnover in the system in 1988 exceeded US$2,900 billion (Cedel's was $1,700 billion). Securities transactions are settled in over twenty currencies and a wide range of securities can be handled: Eurobonds, foreign bonds, domestic bonds, certificates of deposit, debt and equity warrants and registered securities as well as bearer securities. In recent years, Euroclear has begun to expand into international equity settlement also, processing some 2,000 stocks.

Euroclear was originally set up by the Morgan Guaranty Trust Company of New York. After some criticism in the early years that the system was controlled by a single bank, Morgan decided to reap the goodwill that would be created by broadening Euroclear's ownership and in December 1972, 118 financial institutions subscribed to Euroclear's shares. Morgan Guaranty continues to operate the system under a management contract.

In January 1971 a rival system, Cedel (Centrale de Liveraison de Valeurs Mobilières) started operations in Luxembourg. Eurobond market legend has always held that Cedel was set up as a European (primarily French) challenge to the American bank operating Euroclear, but its founders tended to emphasise first that there should be a clearing system with its own independent organisation and management, and secondly that the formation of Cedel would benefit the market as a whole by providing competition with Euroclear.

After Cedel's foundation, it soon became clear that it would be important to have a 'bridge' between the two systems. In this way a bank which held securities in one system could sell them to a bank with an account at the other. The 'bridge' was set up during 1971–2, although in its early days it was very rudimentary, processing perhaps 60 to 80 transactions per day. An electronic, automated bridge system only became operative in late 1980. (The use of the word bridge was inspired by the 'Pont Adolphe' in Luxembourg, spanning the Pétruse Valley. Daily deliveries of securities had previously to be driven across it between Cedel and the Luxembourg depositary for Euroclear.) Since that date, securities transactions between the two systems have been effected by book-entry transfers on computer. The process takes a day.

Suppose that you bought bonds from a Cedel counterpart, for which the settlement date is day X. As a Euroclear participant, you send instructions to Euroclear to receive securities against payment on day X − 1. Also on day X − 1, Cedel transmits their intended deliveries to the Euroclear Operations Centre. These 'bridge receipts' enter the Euroclear securities settlement processing dated for value the settlement date, day X, starting in the evening of day X − 1.

Today, the bridge handles in addition to ordinary Eurobonds, Swiss franc international issues, domestic and Dutch guilder issues, Samurai bonds, deutschmark bonds, and others. Transactions between the two systems have been helped also by the setting up of the ACE system, a joint project between Cedel, Euroclear and the AIBD, which matches and confirms trades four times a day. It is reported that thanks to ACE only 5 per cent of trades are now initially unmatched.

STRUCTURE OF EUROCLEAR

Euroclear actually stands for a number of things. It is a company (Euroclear Clearance System plc – a UK company whose administrative offices are in Zurich, Switzerland); a cooperative (ECSSC, a cooperative organised under Belgian law with a registered office in Belgium); a system, Euroclear System, which is a clearance system for internationally traded securities owned by the Company but operated under contract by the Brussels office of Morgan Guaranty; and fourthly the Euroclear Operations Centre, which is a separate unit of Morgan Guaranty in Brussels, all of whose employees are employees of Morgan Guaranty.

Euroclear Clearance System plc is owned by 125 banks, financial institutions and dealers, all of which are participants in the System. The company, together with substantially all participants in the System, own the Cooperative. The Cooperative decides all matters of general policy, sets fees, accepts new participants, and determines the categories of securities accepted for deposit in the System, as well as approving new members of the Cooperative.

Euroclear offers its members four basic services: first a clearance service, settling transfers of securities against payment. It includes 'bridges' to Cedel and other clearing systems such as the German Effektengiro. Secondly, a safekeeping service, whereby the securities are physically held at major depository banks in key financial centres. In some cases they are redeposited with domestic clearing systems, such as the Depository Trust Company in New York. Thirdly, an automated securities lending and borrowing service. This allows members to borrow and lend securities amongst themselves. Fourthly, its banking services give members a multi-currency cash clearing in 24 different currencies through the Euroclear Operations Centre.

MECHANICS OF THE SYSTEM

The workings of the Euroclear system can best be seen from an example. Suppose on 4 April we buy US$100,000 nominal amount of General Electric Capital Corporation 7¾ per cent 1991 bonds, for a total amount of $102,668.75 from Large Swiss Bank AG. In line with AIBD rules, the trade will settle for 11 April. Once the deal is done, our operations manager, John Smith, sends instructions to Euroclear by telex, mail or SWIFT or else by EUCLID. (EUCLID is the direct computerised link between system participants and Euroclear's Operating Centre and SWIFT is a computer link between banks.) He advises Euroclear that the purchase has been made, and that Euroclear should accept delivery of the securities to our account against payment from us.

That evening, Euroclear will match our instructions against those of Large Swiss Bank's, to compare the account numbers (and names) of the parties to the trade, the settlement date, the nominal amount, the Security Code Number of the issue traded, the currency and cash countervalue agreed upon. All of these items have to be identical on both instructions – with the exception of the cash countervalue (per AIBD rule number 304, which permits matching on the basis of the seller's amount, provided that the difference is less than or equal to US$500 or equivalent).

Once all instructions have been matched, the system proceeds to the next stage. Unmatched instructions remain in the system until they are replaced by correct instructions or cancelled. The next stage is the 'participants' simulation'. In this process, Euroclear executes all the trades in the system as if they were actually being posted to participants' accounts. When this process throws up situations where members' accounts will be overdrawn through lack of cash, or short of bonds and long of cash through a lack of securities to settle a sale, the instructions are blocked. The blocked deliveries of securities, or blocked purchases, are held in the system until they can be matched off. If at the end of the process they cannot be matched off, they will be posted to members' accounts on a 'failed' basis.

Before proceeding to the posting, however, a final simulation takes place, known as the 'depositaries simulation'. This carries out a similar exercise for physical deliveries or receipts of securities at depositary institutions. Physical deliveries of securities requested by participants are screened to see if depositaries hold enough bonds to arrange delivery, and vice versa. Once this process is complete, the final stage of the daily settlement processing is the posting to accounts and reporting to participants, which normally starts around midnight and is completed around 6.00 a.m.

All of this process takes place during the night before the settlement date. In other words, by the morning of the settlement date, it is too late to do anything about any problems which may have arisen for settlement on that day. Everything must be in the system by the night before: to be precise, by 10.00 a.m. of the day before if information is being sent into the system by mail, telex or SWIFT; or by 17.45 p.m. if being sent by EUCLID.

However, if, say, we were expecting funds into our Euroclear account on Monday, but they had not yet been received, it is possible by arrangement with Euroclear to arrange a 'pre-advice' whereby Euroclear is warned in advance that the funds will be in the system and available before payment on the settlement day, even though they have not yet arrived.

Pre-advices of funds in US dollars, Canadian dollars and Belgian francs have to be received by 10.00 a.m. Brussels time to be given the same value date. Euroclear refers to these as group 1 currencies. Pre-advices of funds in other European currencies, Australian and New Zealand dollars, Japanese yen, and composite currencies (such as the ECU) have to be received one business day before the scheduled value date to be given that value date. These are referred to as Group 2 currencies. Finally pre-advices of funds in 'other' currencies (Hong Kong dollars, Kuwaiti dinars, etc.) have to be received two business days before the scheduled value date to be given that value date. These are referred to as group 3 currencies. The cut-off point is 10.00 a.m. Brussels time.

In addition, Euroclear, through Morgan Guaranty, provides credit facilities to certain members of the system. These are generally secured by securities kept with Euroclear, and can normally be used either as an overdraft, or for borrowing bonds. They can be used for settlement in any of the 23 currencies accepted by Euroclear.

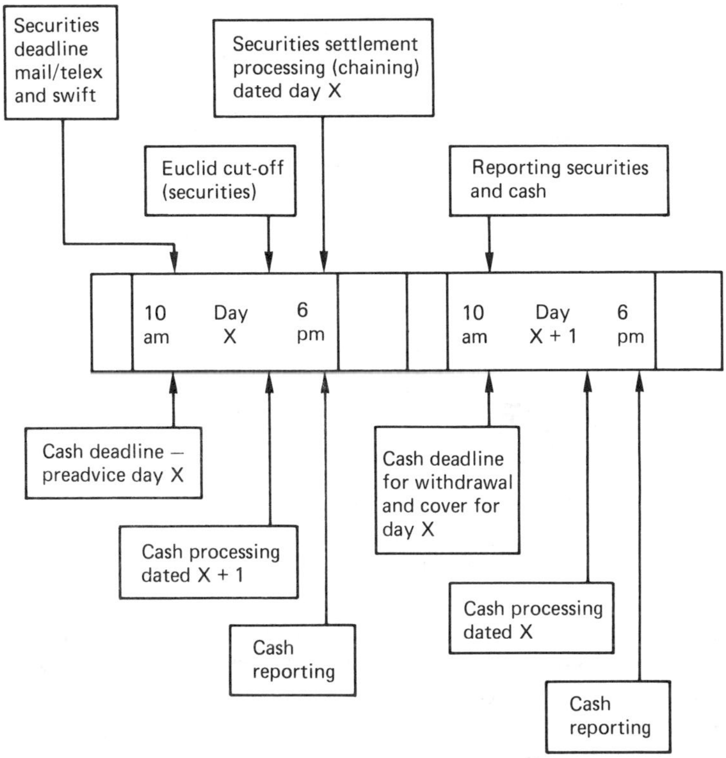

FIGURE 17.1 Euroclear processing of securities/cash

As from April 1986, Euroclear has been accepting internationally traded equities. The distribution procedure and the timing for internationally syndicated equities are very similar to that of Eurobonds. However, unlike with Eurobonds, the new equities are generally deposited with the national clearing system. This deposit allows the domestic portion to be credited to the members of that domestic system while the international portion may be spread between the domestic clearing system and the Euroclear depositary in that country. The equities are credited against simultaneous payment in the Euroclear system. Such equities can be traded with other counterparties in Euroclear for same day value. They are also available for book-entry transactions with Cedel, or AKV, if eligible. Euroclear operates links with domestic markets in a number of countries (see below).

SETTLEMENT ARRANGEMENTS FOR NEW ISSUES

The settlement procedure for new issues uses the same concept of clearance against payment as the secondary market system discussed

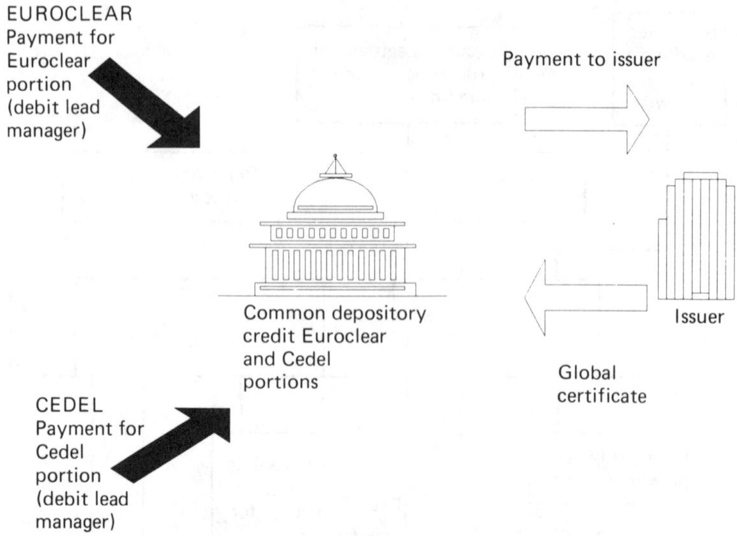

FIGURE 17.2 New issue against payment: closing date

above, but there are one or two points of interest. Distribution and payment of new Eurobond issues are processed through a new issues securities account and a new issues cash account. These are opened on behalf of the lead-manager at each clearance system (Euroclear and Cedel).

Five business days prior to the closing, the lead-manager delivers to each clearance system a complete list of allottees, together with nominal amounts allotted and subscription payments due. Two business days before closing, the details are finalised. On the closing day, before the closing ceremony takes place, the clearance systems debit the lead-manager's cash account and pay the depositary bank for their portion of the issue. On the strength of this, the depositary bank prepares an undertaking to pay the total issue proceeds to the issuer, and attends the closing ceremony, generally in the afternoon.

At the closing ceremony, in exchange for the global bond, the depositary delivers its letter of undertaking, and effectively executes payment to the issuer. When the depositary confirms that this has been done, Euroclear may start the distribution of the new issue to the allottees. This distribution is made during the processing which starts in the evening of the closing day, and is dated for value closing day plus 1.

SECURITIES LENDING

Euroclear also provides a securities lending and borrowing service. This helps prevent failed settlements. For example, suppose that we have bought US$100,000 World Bank bonds from investor A ($80,000) and investor B ($20,000). Later, we sold them on as a single block of $100,000 to bank X. Investor B failed to deliver the $20,000 worth of bonds in time, and so on settlement date, it is impossible for us to deliver the full $100,000 to bank X.

To cover this, we will borrow bonds from the Euroclear programme. To control the risk of speculative activity, Euroclear sets borrowing limits. One borrower may not borrow more than 5 per cent of the outstanding amount of any one issue, and aggregate borrowings by all borrowers of that issue must not exceed 10 per cent. (For convertibles, the corresponding ratios are 1 per cent and 5 per cent.) Typically, borrowers are market-makers or dealers in the Eurobond market. Lenders are portfolio managers and custodians.

Euroclear operates two kinds of services: automatic, and opportunity. Automatic lenders are those who agree to lend all or certain portions of their portfolios, and authorise Euroclear to determine automatically the amount of securities which will be available for lending on a given business day. Automatic borrowers likewise authorise Euroclear to identify their borrowing needs and arrange for borrowings to fill such needs. Opportunity borrowers and lenders are those who from time to time take part in the programme on request.

Lenders do not really take risk when extending loans, since the return of the securities (or the cash equivalent) is guaranteed by Morgan Guaranty Brussels, should the borrowers fail to repay. Lenders are automatically credited with interest proceeds on the securities loaned, as if they had not been loaned, and can keep the collateral value of the securities loaned to secure their credit arrangements. Loans can be recalled at any time, on ten business days' notice.

The mechanics of the operation are that lenders will lend to the 'pool'. Likewise, borrowers borrow from the pool. This ensures confidentiality: a borrower's name is never revealed to any lender, and vice versa. If lending requirements cannot be covered by the available pool, opportunity lenders are contacted with a view to their being included in the pool. If borrowing requirements are below the lendable position from automatic lenders, the loans are allocated amongst automatic lenders first to those whose portfolio exceeds $50 million available for lending, and next to those whose portfolio is smaller.

Lenders of US dollar issues earn 2½ per cent; borrowers pay 3½ per cent. Lenders of Swiss franc, Deutschmark, yen and guilder issues earn 1⅛ per cent, while borrowers pay 2⅝ per cent; all other currencies are calculated at 2⅞ per cent and 3⅜ per cent respectively. Fees are calculated daily on the current market value of the securities lent (plus accrued interest, if any) on a 365 day basis.

LINKS BETWEEN SYSTEMS

As we have seen, the instruments traded in the Eurobond market have their counterparts in domestic markets; inevitably, therefore, a firm trading in one market will often trade in the other.

To do this, it needs to relate to different clearing and settlement systems. A Eurobond house will clear its securities through Euroclear or Cedel. If its traders decide to switch their positions from Euros to domestics, let us say domestic German corporate bonds, this will require a linkage with the German securities clearing system, known as the Effektengiro. The Effektengiro consists of a group of seven regional clearing systems, called Kassenvereine. The Frankfurt Kassenvereine has as a member the Deutscher Auslandskassenverein (AKV). Morgan Guaranty in Brussels, as operator of the Euroclear system, is a member of the AKV. This allows participants in Euroclear to deliver or receive by book-entry securities with other members of the Kassenvereine.

Suppose that the dealers have bought a 5 per cent 1992 bond issued by Commerz Bank. They are bought for settlement on day X, from BHF Bank in Frankurt which is a member of the Frankfurt Kassenvereine. Two days before the new date, the AKV will deliver notice to Euroclear of intended delivery of the securities; if all is in order, Euroclear will accept the delivery, paying out cash, which is then fed back to the AKV.

In some cases, the national clearing system may not be linked to Euroclear, or, alternatively, the counterparty with whom the Eurobond house is trading may not be a member of Euroclear. In this case, it will be necessary to arrange for settlement through the national clearing system.

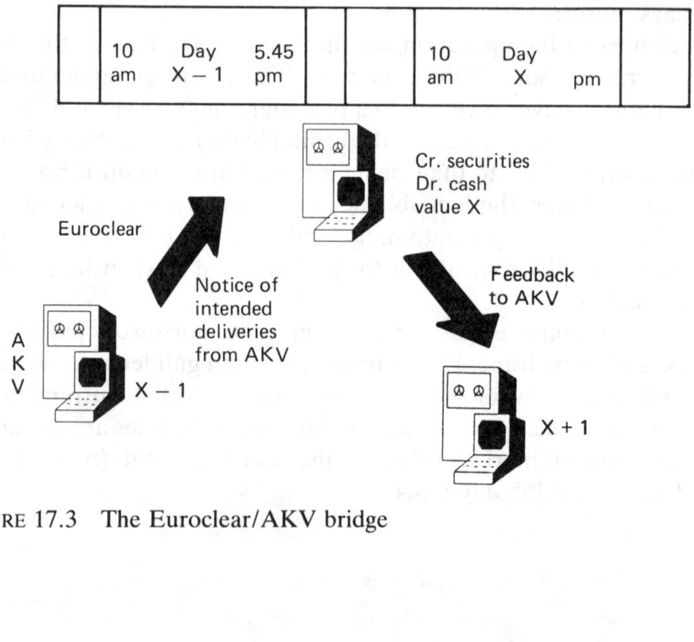

FIGURE 17.3 The Euroclear/AKV bridge

For example, it might be necessary to set up an account with the Depository Trust Company in New York in order to make and receive deliveries of US Treasury bonds which the firm deals in with domestic US primary dealers. A custodian bank would have to be selected, say Manufacturers Hanover, with whom an account would be opened providing membership of the DTC. The house might then buy Treasury bonds, say from Goldman Sachs, and accept delivery of the bonds to its DTC account, while paying Goldman's through the US banking system.

The DTC is the largest securities depository in the world. It was founded by the New York Stock Exchange in 1973, followed in 1976 by the National Securities Clearing Corporation. The two work closely together, the NSCC doing the actual clearing of trades, and the DTC providing the custody and book-entry movements involved in the settlement of transactions. The DTC now has its vaults filled with more than $3 trillion of corporate and municipal bonds and corporate equities. It settles trades worth almost $10 trillion per annum. About 52 per cent of all equities and 70 per cent of all bonds traded on the New York Stock Exchange are on deposit at the DTC.

EQUITY CLEARING AND SETTLEMENT

Probably the largest single hindrance to the growth of international equity trading has been the antique national registration, settlement and clearance systems. The London market is a notorious offender in this respect, but other disaster areas at different times have included Italy, Spain, France and Australia. The combination of poor management in stockbroking firms with the complacent arrogance of self-serving and self-selected ruling bodies in the national stock exchanges lie at the root of the problem, which has been compounded by the growth in trading. It may be worth quoting some heartfelt comments by Colin Grimsey of Chase Manhattan at the Fourth International Symposium of Securities Administrators on Global Securities Investments (May 1988):

> Settlement in a timely fashion . . . is impossible in Australia where there is no official settlement date. . . . We find France to be a difficult market with a settlement failure rate of at least 20%. . . . Italy . . . at one time we despaired of a solution. . . . We have maintained a presence in Madrid for over a year now, and we still are unable to clearly identify how the settlement system works. . . . The United Kingdom . . . backlogs are still sizeable. . . .

A possible solution is emerging through the Euromarket clearing systems. In April 1986 the Euroclear system launched an international equities service, handling a total of 140 equities. By May 1988, it covered over 1,100 securities (counting different classes of the securities as separate issues) and covered Austria, Belgium, Canada, Denmark, Finland, France, Germany, Italy, Norway, Spain, Sweden, Switzerland and the Netherlands. Under this service, trades in international equities and related rights can be settled on the books of Euroclear in any one of the 25 settlement currencies currently eligible within the system.

Simultaneous exchange of cash for equities on Euroclear's books eliminates credit risks and thus allows the market to include participants who otherwise might not have dealt with each other. The same principle applies for book-entry transactions with Cedel and AKV counterparts, when the security is eligible in these clearing systems. Links with home markets exist: trades entailing the receipt and delivery of equities or rights with counterparties outside Euroclear in Canada, France, Germany, Sweden, Switzerland and the Netherlands can be settled against payment in the local currencies. Also, through the New York depository of Euroclear, the conversion of equities into ADRs is undertaken.

The system also offers a service for the distribution of international equity offerings which is designed to meet the needs of lead managers and underwriters of internationally syndicated issues, very similar to the service Euroclear offers for new issues of debt. It offers an against-payment facility for the closing and distribution of such issues. This allows allottees to receive their securities on the day of the closing of the issue, and to deliver these against payment to other Euroclear counterparts with same-day value.

The mechanics involved may be illustrated by considering an American broker wanting to sell shares to a private Swedish citizen. The broker sends his delivery instructions two days prior to settlement date. Euroclear relays these instructions to its Swedish depository, who will in turn verify with the local counterparty if corresponding instructions for receipt have been given. By 'prematching' Euroclear can give timely reporting about unmatched trades, thus reducing considerably the risks of delayed settlement and associated problems.

The cash proceeds from the transaction will be credited to the participant's account the night of the settlement day, for value on the settlement day. For a seller of Swedish equities, a similar process operates in reverse, allowing new equity to be brought into Euroclear for further trading.

Another area of development in international equity trading clearance is via bilateral links, as distinct from the multilateral clearance systems like Euroclear and Cedel. For example, the London Stock Exchange's Talisman system is now linked with the National Securities Clearing Corporation of New York and the Midwest Clearing Corporation of Chicago, as well as providing book-entry transfers for Australian and South African securities.

Table 17.1 Settlement in some frequently traded markets

Market	*Central Depository*	*Dematerialised, bearer or registered*	*Rolling or fixed settlement*	*Time period*
Australia	No	Registered	None	None
Eurobonds	Yes	Bearer	Rolling	T + 5
France	Yes	Dematerialised	Fixed	Month end
Germany	Yes	Mainly bearer	Rolling	T + 2 or 5
Greece	No	Mainly bearer	Rolling	T + 1
Italy	Yes	Mainly dematerialised	Fixed	Month end
Japan	No	Registered	Rolling	T + 3
Portugal	No	Bearer	Rolling	T + 3
Singapore	No	Registered	Rolling	T + 5
Spain	Yes	Bearer and registered	Rolling	Various
Thailand	No	Registered	Rolling	T + 3
UK	No	Mainly registered	Fixed	Two week account
USA	Yes	Dematerialised	Rolling	T + 5

Source: Investment Management Review, January 1989.

Australia

Australia is one of the most difficult equity markets from the settlement point of view. The country consists of seven states, each of which has retained control traditionally over the securities industry within its borders. Each has had its own stock exchange, its own securities industry legislation, and its own stamp duty legislation.

At last, in 1987, the state stock exchanges were united under the banner of the Australian Stock Exchange. But at present Australia does not have a central depository or clearing organisation, nor a fixed settlement period. Trades are settled on a 'best endeavours' basis as and when the seller makes the underlying scrip available to the market.

In theory, a selling stockbroker who has not delivered securities within ten business days of trade may have 'prompt buy-in' action taken against him. In practice, this mechanism is little used. There is also a forty-day delinquent list under which a failure to deliver within forty days results in a fine of A$25, with weekly fines levied at a rate of A$25 for each subsequent week the trade remains undelivered. However, this financial penalty is scarcely terrifying.

To get round some of these problems, a securities depository was proposed in 1986, but had to be withdrawn in the face of opposition which felt it would create a barrier between companies and their shareholders. At the direction of the National Companies and Securities Commission, a consultative committee was set up to evolve a compromise system for uncertificated holding of securities, whereby changes of ownership would be effected electronically.

The proposed system is a 'name on register' approach, known as STARS (Settlement Transfer and Registration System). However, fierce opposition by major listed companies and the implied capital expense of the project have delayed any progress.

Canada

The Canadian Depository for Securities Ltd (CDS) provides depository and clearing services. The normal settlement period for equities and long bond transactions is five business days; short bonds and money market instruments settle on a same-day basis. Buy-ins are possible but rarely enforced. Equity securities continue to be available in physical form, having been neither immobilised (deposited with the Central Depository) nor dematerialised (switched into electronic form). In general, however, the settlement system is reasonably efficient.

France

France has taken the major step of 'dematerialising' virtually all equities. Owners of bearer securities who did not bring them to the banks for dematerialisation will become simple creditors of the issuers and will receive the proceeds from the sale of their shares on the surrender of their certificates. The conversion of physical securities into 'book-entry' holdings in bank or broker accounts required the destruction of about 350 million certificates (2,400 tons of paper)!

During 1989, a computerised delivery against payment system is in the process of being added to the French clearing systems. This should greatly improve reliability of settlement. The leading role is being played here by SICOVAM (Société Interprofessionelle de Compensation de Valeurs Mobilières). It is in the process of developing from a simple depository of securities into a real clearing house.

Germany

The German securities clearing system consists of a central depository and clearing organisation, which is a federation of 'Kassenverein', or 'Wertpapiersammelbanken'. This is a group of seven depository banks for securities, six attached to the eight stock exchanges (Hannover and Bremen are connected to the Hamburg Kassenverein). The seventh is the Auslandskassenverein (AKV). The AKV is linked to Euroclear and Cedel. All government debt, and the majority of corporate debt and equity, is eligible for Kassenverein holding; the major exceptions are registered shares (for example, insurance company shares).

Domestic settlement within Germany is two business days for equities and five days for bonds. The domestic central depository system holds about 80 per cent of all outstanding securities certificates, and there are presently no plans for 'dematerialisation' of other certificates (government and federal agency bonds are already purely book entry).

Italy

The growth of stock market activity in 1985 caused total chaos in the Italian settlement system for securities. However, the development of the central depository for shares and bonds, managed by Monte Titoli SpA, has helped to solve many of the problems. In 1984, shares deposited with Monte Titoli had a nominal value of 510 billion lire. By April 1988 the figure had reached 13,870 billion lire, accounting for 32 per cent of the power value of all listed shares. Bonds deposited with this system rose from 6,135 billion lire in 1984 to 40,234 billion in April 1988.

This progress contrasts with the difficulties in switching from the daily price fixing system to continuous price movement. Consob (the Italian Securities Markets Supervisory Body) proposed in August 1985 the changes needed to introduce continuous trading to the Italian Stock Market. The first experimental phase, covering five shares, started in December 1985; the second phase was put off to December 1986 in the first instance, and by the summer of 1988 had still not been put in place. One of the main difficulties was that, according to Italian laws dating back to 1913, it is the role of the Chambers of Commerce to supervise stock exchanges; considerable difficulties were experienced in getting these bodies to work together. Arrangements in the market have greatly improved, but clearly much remains to be done.

Japan

In certain respects clearing and settlements on the Japanese stock exchange are quite efficient, but in other respects there is still much to be done. The Japanese Securities Clearing Corporation (JSCC), a wholly-owned subsidiary of the Tokyo Stock Exchange (TSE), offers custody services to foreign clearing and depository organisations. However, the development of a new central depository organisation, the Japan Securities Depository Centre (JASDEC) has been on the drawing board since 1984 but is not scheduled to begin operation until 1991, at which point only domestic Japanese equities will be eligible.

Settlement for all trades executed on the TSE is processed solely by JSCC. All of the member brokers of TSE are members of JSCC as well. JSCC's settlement services for its members cover their TSE cash market equity trades (both domestic and foreign), a wide variety of bond trades, and the Japanese government's bond futures contracts. For equities traded in the cash market, settlement procedures are basically carried out under the book-entry system, whereby the JSCC keeps the underlying shares in safe custody. Settlement day comes on the third business day after the trade is executed on the TSE. Failures to deliver account for only about 1 per cent of total turnover.

United Kingdom

The history of developments in UK stock exchange settlement arrangements is perhaps best described by a quotation from *The Financial Times*:

> A 20-year catalogue of bureaucratic fudging, technocratic misjudgment and narrow interest group politics, which has done more than any other issue to threaten London's status as a world financial centre . . .
>
> (Clive Wolman, *FT* 3 April 1989)

Present arrangements centre on the 'account' system, whereby every fortnight (occasionally there is a three-week account) settlement is made of all bargains struck in the previous fortnight. The major benefit of this system is that it allows speculators to trade in equities without having to put up any funds, as a share can be bought and sold within the account.

The major disadvantage is the credit risks implied in the system, which became vividly apparent during the Crash of 1987. (Although recorded credit losses were not enormous, a number of firms had some very worrying moments.) It was this issue which moved the Governor of the Bank of England to suggest that the time had come for London to move to a system like that in the United States, of 'rolling settlements'. Once the account closes, the shares move through a laborious process whereby pieces of paper pass between buyer, seller and registrar.

Discussions over replacing this antiquated system have been running since at least 1966. In 1971 the Stock Exchange approved ambitious plans for Talisman, a computerised settlement system, on which it later backtracked. A limited form of Talisman was introduced in 1979, using a central nominee company (SEPON – Stock Exchange Pooled Nominees) to speed transfers between market-makers.

In 1981 another ambitious leap forward was planned, called TAURUS (Transfer and Automated Registration of Uncertificated Stock). After a temporary suspension in 1984 and again in 1987 because of the pressures of Big Bang, Taurus was scrapped in 1989 when it became clear that it would be hugely expensive to achieve the initial ambitions.

A modified form of Talisman, involving expanded use of SEPON, was preferred. However, this solution itself came under fire, since its full implementation would mean companies would have only one shareholder – SEPON. Without access to sub-registers listing the names behind the nominee company, companies would be in the position of not knowing who controlled them.

A modest step forward in improving the use of Talisman took place in August 1988, with the introduction of Institutional Net Settlement. This is a centralised settlement service for institutional investors, allowing them to settle for many of their bargains with Stock Exchange member firms via one net payment directly with the Stock Exchange.

United States

Clearing in the US market is affected to some degree by the fact that there is a range of exchanges: the major stock exchanges (New York Mid West, Pacific and so on), together with the automated quotation system of the National Association of Securities Dealers (NASDAQ). However, all of these exchanges and markets are linked to two central institutions: the National Securities Clearing Corporation (NSCC) and the Depository Trust Company (DTC).

The NSCC provides three key services: trade comparison and reconciliation; continuous trade netting; daily cash adjustments based on the marking to market of open trading positions. Each day there is a direct

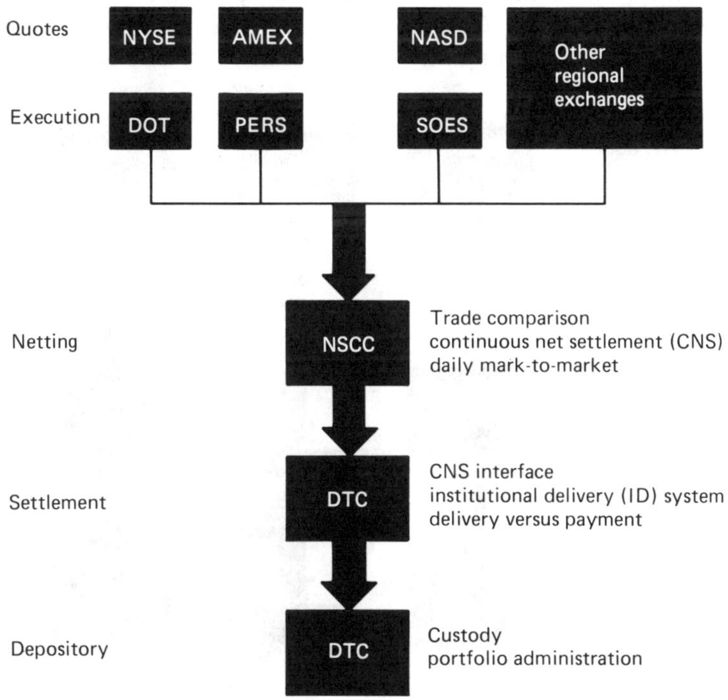

FIGURE 17.4 US corporate stock and bond markets

interface between the NSCC and DTC, which allows the DTC to effect final settlement of net positions from broker-to-broker trading. Also, the DTC is open to major investors through their custodian banks for item-by-item settlement of their individual trades with their brokers. Finally, the DTC operates as the central depository, providing a broad array of portfolio administration services.

To supplement the broker-to-broker clearing services provided by the NSCC, the DTC provides the Institutional Delivery (ID) system in the USA (currently being extended into the International Institutional Delivery – IID – system). ID allows information on a trade to be circulated amongst all parties so that the institutional customer, the selling broker, the buying broker, and the custodians involved can all exchange and compare information electronically. It also automates the settlement process. At this stage IID is seen purely as a confirmation system; automating international settlements will be tackled later. The NSCC is also expanding its international links through its subsidiary, the International Securities Clearing Corporation.

The two other major areas of clearing and settlement involve the government securities market, which has an automated settlement and depository system through the Federal Reserve book-entry system. Because of the scale of exposures of participants to each other, the Government Securities Clearing Corporation (GSCC) has recently been formed. Its aim is to provide netting services similar to those of NSCC.

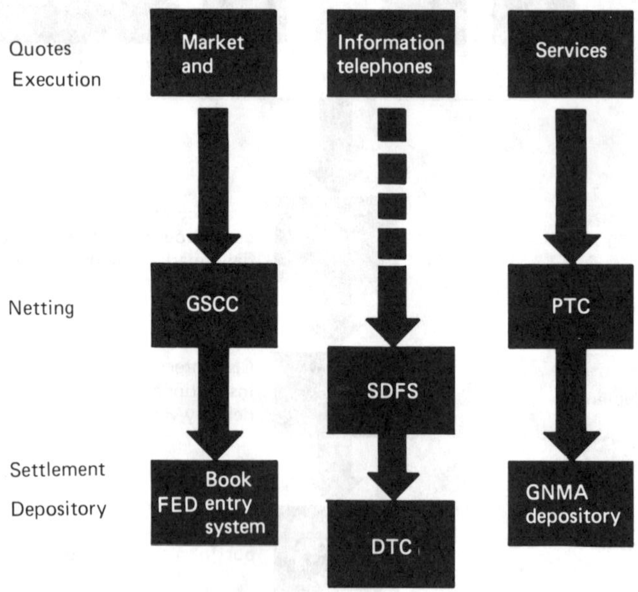

FIGURE 17.5 Other US securities markets

An important new development is the Same-Day Fund Settlement system (SDFS) run by the DTC for money market securities. During 1989, commercial paper is being added to the SDFS. Finally, participants in the mortgage backed securities market are working to build an effective settlement/depository environment for these instruments, in conjunction with the Participant Trust Company (formerly known as the Mortgage Backed Securities Clearing Corporation (MBSCC)).

18 Regulation and the Future of the System

We have looked at some of the issues facing an investor who is thinking of investing on a global basis. Perhaps the biggest is: Where is this global network of markets heading? Will a single transnational system emerge?

In Sam Goldwyn's immortal phrase, 'In two words: im-possible'. There are too many competing national interests at stake, too many differences in regulation, foreign exchange controls and the like. But what almost certainly will happen is a continuation of the present trend. Individual markets, which were isolated islands, will increasingly be bound together by a network of capital flows – if you like, bridges and tunnels such as those in New York that link the island of Manhattan to Staten Island and Long Island.

There will still be delays and blockages at the bridges and tunnels (even tolls, in the form of withholding and other taxes). Individual national markets will still be, as it were, surrounded by the moats and channels of national controls. They will be affected differently, too, by national economic policies. But it will make more and more sense to look at the most closely linked markets as one group, just as the rest of the world considers Brooklyn and Manhattan part of the single entity of New York.

This is already beginning to happen at the industry level; analysts tend to look at Glaxo in relation to Merck and Hoffmann-La Roche as well as Beecham. Increasingly the valuation levels of whole markets – Wall Street versus London or Frankfurt – are being compared, though the example of Japan shows that the process has far to go.

The major force that sets the limit on this trend will be the national regulatory regimes. The Euromarkets are what they are because they have been free from national controls. Stock markets can never have the same freedom. Most companies will be unwilling to relocate their legal headquarters to some offshore location. So their equity shares will still be under the jurisdiction of their headquarters country.

Techniques of trading and placing equity may be influenced by the Euromarkets. But the example of the British pre-emption requirement (under which – unlike practice, say, in the USA – new shares must be offered first to existing holders of shares) and its effect on issues of Euroconvertibles by British companies shows that there are definite limits to the process.

Then, too, governments will always be more keenly interested in corporate equity transactions – which carry with them questions of corporate control – than trading in debt. Finally, the typical individual investing in Eurobonds is already substantially wealthy enough to have little need of government protection. This is not true of individual stock market investors. So the growth of global equity investing alongside global bond investing will be strongly influenced by the interplay of national controls. Of these, probably the most important will be those of the three main international financial centres – New York, London and Tokyo.

NATIONAL REGULATORY SYSTEMS

The USA

The US regulatory system was laid down in the 1930s and has not changed much since (see Figure 18.1). The SEC has oversight of issuing and trading practices in the domestic stock and bond markets, with the exception of the government bond market, where the Federal Reserve is intimately involved. The 'Fed' is responsible for regulating the so-called 'primary dealers', those securities firms who have a major presence in the US Treasury bond market and dealing privileges with the Fed. These include all the major US investment banks. They must report their positions on a continuing basis to the Federal Reserve, which thus has a degree of oversight over their activities.

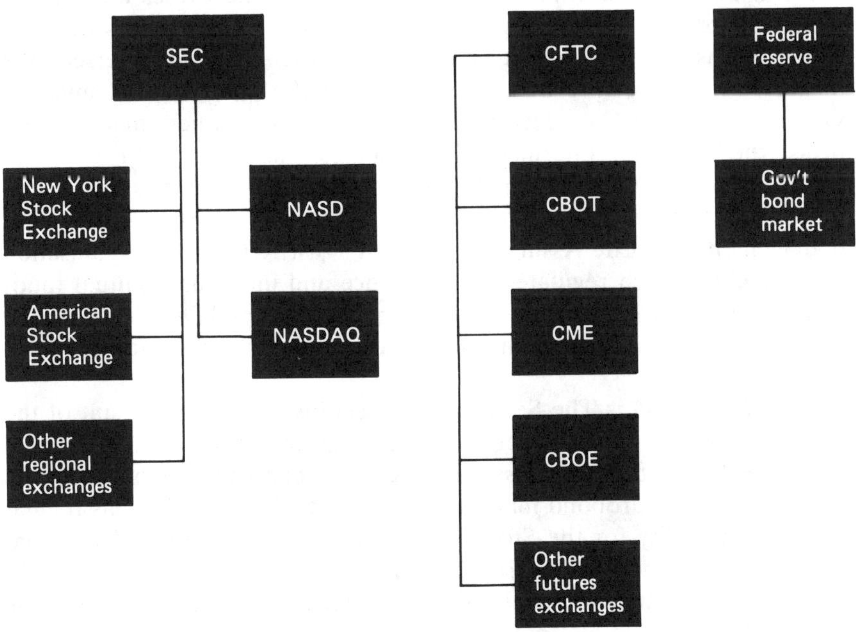

FIGURE 18.1 Regulation of US securities markets

The New York Stock Exchange undertakes detailed supervision of the day-to-day trading activities of its members. It is responsible for ensuring that the system of 'specialists' (firms responsible for making a continuous market in one or more stocks) runs smoothly, while the other regional exchanges perform a parallel function in their areas. The National Association of Securities Dealers supervises the over-the-counter market and its electronic network, the NASD Automated Quotation system.

Another important regulatory body is the Commodity Futures Trading Commission which has oversight of the financial futures markets. These impact on the securities industry through bond futures and equity index futures; there is also the question of options on equities and equity futures. The latter area has been the subject, over the years, of a 'turf battle' between the SEC and the CFTC. In 1981 an agreement was reached between the two that the SEC is the sole regulator of options based directly on securities. The CFTC has exclusive jurisdiction over futures contracts and options on futures contracts.

The UK

The UK system of regulation was transformed in 1986 by the Financial Services Act. This produced an uneasy compromise between the legalistic American approach embodied in the SEC and the traditional flexibility of the pragmatic British method. The Act created a Securities and Investments Board, which oversees the Self-Regulatory Organisations (SROs). These consist of The Securities Association (TSA), which oversees the business of trading in securities; the Investment Management Regulatory Organisation (IMRO), which regulates the large investment management firms; the Financial Intermediaries, Managers and Brokers Regulatory Association (FIMBRA), which regulates smaller securities firms and independent firms selling investments or certain types of investment management; the Life Assurance and Unit Trust Regulatory Organisation (LAUTRO), which regulates life assurance and unit trust (mutual fund) companies; and the Association of Futures Brokers and Dealers (AFBD), which regulates companies in the financial and commodity futures business.

The prime SRO is The Securities Association. This is the result of the eleventh-hour merger between the Stock Exchange and the International Securities Regulatory Organisation which had been set up to look after the interests of the Eurobond market. The Securities Association has regulatory responsibility for the Stock Exchange and the activities of London-based firms involved in the Eurobond market.

The Bank of England remains responsible for supervision of the banking industry, the 'wholesale' money and foreign exchange markets, and the gilt-edged (government bond) market. Because many banks have bought

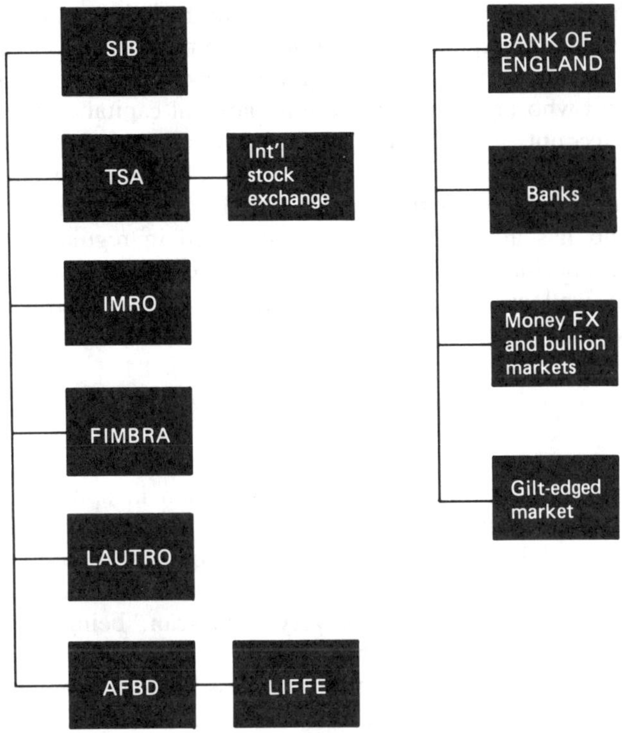

FIGURE 18.2 UK regulatory system

securities firms, the overlap between regulatory authorities is considerable, and a working compromise split banks into four categories. Where a bank has put its securities business into a separate subsidiary, that company is regulated by TSA and the bank by the Bank of England. Where a bank has only very little securities business the Bank will be the supervisor. Where almost all the business is in securities, TSA will be the supervisor. Where a bank has a fairly even split of business, the Bank of England will be the 'lead-regulator' and apply its capital adequacy rules to the banking side. The capital requirements laid down by TSA for the securities business will also be monitored by the Bank.

To begin with, at the behest of the SIB, the whole framework of securities regulation in London became very complex. The first edition of TSA rules ran to hundreds of pages and weighed about nine pounds. Likewise, the IMRO rules were extremely detailed and complex. After a behind-the-scenes revolt in the City, attempts were made by the SIB (under a new chief) to develop a more flexible, practical approach, and the situation now seems to be settling down.

Behind the scenes, the Bank of England has been actively involved in many of the discussions on the development of the industry. The role of the Bank of England in regulating the London capital markets is a diffuse one. The Bank has direct authority over those banks who have bought stockbrokers, and who are active in the international capital markets also for their own account. It is not directly responsible for non-bank members of The Securities Association, who are regulated by the latter body.

However, the Bank has traditionally acted as spokesman for the City of London and has always been deeply involved in regulating all of the various markets in the City – including, for example, the commodities markets as well as, to a lesser degree, the Lloyds insurance market. Informally, therefore, its authority runs throughout the London capital markets.

Japan

The Japanese system of regulation differs again in approach from the British and American methods, being primarily reliant – as in so many other features of Japanese life – on the development of consensus and a pragmatic shaping of legal forms to practical realities. The external legal form of the Japanese system is very American, being the result of American post-war reforms. The most obvious of these is the famous Article 65 which reflects the American Glass-Steagall prohibition of the mingling of commercial banking and securities business.

The main regulatory authorities are the Ministry of Finance and the Bank of Japan. The Bank of Japan is responsible for monetary policy and day-to-day relationships with the banking system. The Ministry of Finance is the more powerful regulator, however, as it licences and supervises all banks, securities exchanges and securities houses. It also licences the Securities Dealers Association of Japan, sets corporate accounting standards, and has a major say in any structural changes in Japan's corporate financing system.

EUROBOND REGULATORS: AIBD/IPMA

The Eurobond market has traditionally been free from regulation by external bodies. However, it has for a long time recognised the need for self-regulation, through the Association of International Bond Dealers (AIBD) and a related group, the International Primary Market Association (IPMA).

The AIBD has its headquarters in Switzerland, but much of its work is based in London, where its Secretariat has offices. Because of the importance of London in Eurobond trading, the impact of the UK's Financial Services Act has been felt upon the AIBD, as on other market bodies.

There were sizeable repercussions. In the early days, the London Stock Exchange was not very interested in the Eurobond market, and left the AIBD more or less to its own devices. The coming of Big Bang and the Financial Services Act changed all this, however, particularly when the AIBD threatened to set up a separate International Securities Regulatory Organisation, in defiance of the Stock Exchange. The resulting compromise produced a merger between the Stock Exchange and the ISRO, called The Securities Association. Its first chairman, Andrew Large, came from the AIBD side of the fence, with Sir Nicholas Goodison remaining as chairman of the newly-renamed International Stock Exchange, under the authority of The Securities Association. In April 1988 the AIBD became a Designated Overseas Investment Exchange under the Act.

Many overseas members of the AIBD objected to this. Securities firms in, say, Finland or Singapore saw no reason to pay large bills for compliance with UK regulations just because the bulk of Eurobond trading activity is located in London. The AIBD endured severe internal struggles, particularly over the development of its TRAX trade confirmation and reporting system. This system had two objectives: to help automate the trading process – critics argued that the ACE system being developed by Euroclear and Cedel was being duplicated – and secondly to provide for a system of reporting information to the AIBD.

By April 1989 all UK members of AIBD were required to be linked to TRAX and to report via the TRAX system all transactions in international securities, as defined by the AIBD, whether or not done with a professional counterparty.

The TRAX system is designed to provide an on-line system for entering transactions; once the trade is in the system TRAX searches its files for the other side of the trade entered by the counterparty, and compares the two. The system provides an audit trail of dealing prices which helped the AIBD convince the SIB that the Eurobond market is reasonably transparent.

The argument put by those in favour of TRAX within the AIBD has been that Euromarket practitioners have to face the reality that regulators are becoming more involved on an international as well as a domestic basis. Certainly, at the global level, regulation of the international capital markets is, in some ways, still in its infancy, at least when compared with the regulation of domestic securities markets and the international banking system. The latter has a well-defined framework operating through the Bank for International Settlements, and the Cooke Committee of banking regulators. As already mentioned, part of the problem is that in the domestic arena the field is a patchwork of criss-cross, overlapping regulatory frameworks.

So, although international securities regulators have begun to work as a group to start grappling with some of the global issues, there have been 'turf' difficulties – for example, in the United States between the SEC and the CFTC. In the UK the Bank of England and The Securities Association have overlapping and differing requirements. Until the various domestic issues have been resolved they have tended to hold up developments in the international arena.

Clearly, however, all concerned recognise the need for regulators to keep pace with market developments. There are likely to be important moves in the direction of stronger international linkages over the coming years. The most likely body to take the lead in this arena is the International Organisation of Securities Commissions (IOSCO) which is headquartered in Montreal, and has 50 members, including the SEC, the SIB and the Securities Bureau of the Japanese MoF.

In 1987 the IOSCO set up a technical committee including members from twelve countries with major securities markets (Australia, Canada, France, Germany, Hong Kong, Italy, Japan, the Netherlands, Sweden, Switzerland, the USA and the UK). Its objective is the exchange of information between members and harmonisation of rules on, amongst other subjects, capital adequacy in the securities industry. The IOSCO does not yet have the authority or standing of the Cooke Committee of the BIS, its banking equivalent, which has been in existence for fifteen years, but it is to be expected that it will develop into a similar position over time.

THE FUTURE OF THE EUROBOND MARKET

Where will the Eurobond markets fit into the global pattern that is emerging? There are those who argue that the Euromarket is dying. Others argue – as I would – that to listen to its members the market has been dying for a long time, yet it survives and prospers. Listening to the recollections of the participants can give one a jaundiced view of history. There is no doubt that times have been hard; 1988 was a year of crisis for the international securities industry. Many firms pulled out or cut back. Salomon Brothers shed large numbers of people in New York, as did many of its major New York peers, while in London Morgan Grenfell and numerous other firms sacrificed their ambitions to become a global player in securities.

Likewise, 1987 was a disastrous year. Sharply rising US interest rates led to the spectacular stock market crash of October, which impelled the financial markets world-wide into a state of panic. Heavy losses were incurred by numerous traders, and job losses in London and New York were substantial.

Of course, 1986 was dire, with a major crisis in the perpetual floating-rate market; 1985 saw serious problems, with the spectacular collapse of the US dollar from its grossly inflated peak in March–April; 1984, too, was a year of crisis, triggered by the collapse of Continental Illinois, which terrified investors world-wide, together with the impact of the removal of US withholding tax; 1983 was a terrible year, with the partly-paids fiasco and the later slump in the straights market which led to FRNs become the major sector for the year; the less said of 1982, the better, with the Mexican crisis capping a long period of rising rates, while 1981 was a grim year, with interest rates rising to 20 per cent; 1980 was terrible, opening with the Soviet invasion of Afghanistan and the sensational volatility of the gold market, while interest rates rose sharply, collapsed, and roared back up again – the volatility caused enormous losses; naturally 1979 was appalling, with huge volatility triggered by the oil price increase and the departure of the Shah from Iran . . .

As can be seen from previous litany, every year has its share of disasters. Yet, through it all, the international securities markets have survived and prospered. There have been, on balance, up years and down years, but the overall growth has continued. It has not lacked its critics, nor its prophets of doom, but the Eurobond market – and more recently the Euroequity market – has shown an amazing ability to survive extreme pressures.

This is not to deny, however, that there are some basic problems. There is the perennial problem of liquidity; the Eurobond market is liquid only in certain segments at certain times. There is a general lack of consistent liquidity. In the market's earliest days, it was accepted that investors would hold bonds to maturity; there was no secondary market. Since then, as we saw in Chapter 10, a secondary market has developed, but its waxing and waning has been fickle, to say the least.

A second, related problem might be called 'fragmentation by innovation'. This problem was particularly notable during 1985–6, when the rapid development of the interest rate and currency swap market led to the creation of a number of specialised issues, designed mainly for Japanese insurance company investors, which never were intended to trade in the secondary market. Equally, the development of the swap market led to the tendency to 'swap driven issues', issues which were badly mispriced in the primary market, but where the issuing house was making so much money on the swap that it did not care. These issues frequently sank without trace in the secondary market. As the range and type of issues diversified, so investors became more confused, and liquidity began to dry up in other sectors.

The phenomenon of swap driven issuance was but part of a wider problem of mispriced deals which became particularly apparent in 1985–7. Tremendous competition between houses, partly driven by the number of firms struggling to establish themselves in the wake of 'Big Bang', and partly by the thrusting presence of a number of Japanese firms intent on establishing themselves by hook or by crook, led to cut-throat competition in pricing of new deals. Issues were brought to market at silly prices. They promptly sank in the secondary market without trace. Underwriters and selling group members sustained continuous losses, and only perhaps the lead-manager, by virtue of the swap, or 'praecipium', could make any money. Investors began to fight shy of new issues, learning all too quickly that the best way to pick up a reasonable priced deal was to wait for it to fall apart in the secondary market and then buy cheaply. During the summer of 1989 various initiatives, led amongst others by CSFB and Morgan Stanley, aimed at reforming syndication methods. It remains to be seen whether anyone can restore order to the syndication process.

Another complication that had to be coped with at this time was the impact of the UK's Financial Services Act. For the first time, a number of the firms in the Eurobond market suddenly had actually to deal with regulators. Cries of pain were heard throughout the City. An enormous amount of time was spent on bureaucratic regulations, weighty handbooks of practice, and interminable argument over fine points of legal detail. The market's response to all of these shocks was, initially, to expand at far too rapid a pace, and then to contract severely. The resulting shakeout has left many fewer players, but probably much stronger ones.

The other lesson perhaps to be drawn from all of this is the impact of technology. Until, say 1980 it was reasonably possible for a firm to set up in the Eurobond market – as indeed in a number of other security markets – with perhaps a few telephones, and maybe a Reuters Monitor. The advent of widespread computerisation with the arrival of the personal computer, coupled with the large-scale firms formed at the time of 'Big Bang' in London, who aimed to compete with the large American and Japanese investment banks, meant that the 'cost of entry' into the market became enormously higher. It was estimated, for example, that one of the top two or three British firms required an income each day of £500,000 simply to cover the cost of opening its doors.

With such huge fixed costs, a concentration in the market became inevitable. The process was a painful one, extending over two years or more, and at the time of writing is not yet complete. Global bond trading activity has increasingly shifted into the government bond markets; these provide transparency and liquidity in a way that is not available in the Eurobond market. Offsetting this, perhaps, will be the impact of changes proposed by the SEC in its Rule 144, which will allow Eurobonds to be sold directly at the time of issue to large institutional investors in the United States, for the first time, without requiring a 90-day 'seasoning'. This should have the effect of broadening and deepening the market, although probably a large proportion of potential buyers of Eurobonds are already involved in the market. However, even if the increase in the number of participants is only marginal, it should help improve liquidity.

INTEGRATING THE MARKETS

The key development of the 1990s will be the continuing process of integrating individual national markets with the Euromarket. Once again, much of this depends on the attitude of the regulatory authorities, and with them the various national exchanges. It has to be said that most of the major stock exchanges have not exactly been the driving force for change.

The NYSE, for example, has never been a modernising influence. It resisted the development of the Intermarket Trading System (an electronic link between the NYSE, the regional stock exchanges, and the National Association of Securities Dealers' Automated Quotation system (NASDAQ)). It forbade its members to trade off the floor of the Exchange, thus emasculating the ITS. It resisted the automation of the limit order book implied by the Cincinnati Consolidated Limit Order Book experiment. Hilariously, it tried to cancel its recognition of the Stock Exchange in London once trading there moved off the floor of the exchange, on the grounds that it was no longer a stock exchange.

However, within its limited conception of the role of a stock exchange, which has been driven largely by the financial self-interest of its members, the NYSE has been successful in generally running a fairly smooth operation – at least since 1968–9, when a major crisis in the settlements area forced the NYSE to move towards automated settlement systems that took shape in the form of the Depository Trust Company and the National Securities Clearing Corporation (see Chapter 17). As long as it is in the interest of its members, the NYSE can be relied on to encourage further development. Whether those interests coincide with the wider interests of international investors is another matter.

There is a similar problem in regard to the Stock Exchange in London, where the settlements system is antique; the roots of the problem here are that, even more than the NYSE, the London Stock Exchange traditionally was a bastion of inward-looking traditionalism. As late as 1971, a leading stockbroker, Graham Greenwell, in a letter to *The Times* resisted the acceptance of women, described the Exchange as a 'private men's club' and declared that it 'is not an institution which exists to perform a public service'.

The arrival of Big Bang in 1986, which swept the Stock Exchange into a shot-gun marriage with the grandees of the Eurobond market, forced a change in view and a wider perspective. A row in early 1989 about the undoing of some of the Big Bang reforms, however, suggested that perhaps the leopard had not changed its spots. Market-makers argued that they should not be required to continue to make prices in large size to other market-makers since this merely allowed the latter to be 'fair-weather traders'.

At the bottom this boiled down to a clash between the established firms, with substantial client bases, and the new entrants, who were mostly foreign firms. The former were reluctant to make prices to the latter, who depended on unloading their positions with other market-makers because they had no clients to bale them out. Though the problem was largely a function of difficult market conditions, there were unfortunate overtones of 'the old London Stock Exchange club' getting together to 'do the foreigners down'.

By the same token, the fact that for years the Tokyo Stock Exchange found itself unable to create enough space for a few foreign firms to become members hardly suggests a dynamic, outward-looking institution. And, as mentioned earlier in the book, a number of trading practices in Tokyo must be seriously questioned. It will be some considerable time before international investors feel truly comfortable that this market's transparency lives up to standards elsewhere.

All of this is not to decry the role of the various national stock exchanges, but to argue that as they have come increasingly under pressure from innovations around the globe they have not necessarily been well equipped to respond. A primary reason for this must be that the very essence of a stock exchange – an institution whose role is to monopolise trading in certain securities and whose members can realise the value of that monopoly by selling their membership seats – is to restrict rather than open the channels of trading. As the fluid, freewheeling Euromarkets move into equity trading on one side, and the multinational trading networks offered by Reuters and Telerate operate a pincer movement on the other flank, the position of the national stock exchanges becomes more and more exposed. Their ability to respond will determine whether they can retain a place in the emerging global securities trading framework.

Appendices

Appendix 1 Major Bond Markets: Statistics and Instruments

The figures given below are by currency, including for comparison the relevant Euroissues. To achieve comparability across markets the figures are given in US dollars; since this distorts time-series comparisons the applicable exchange rates are quoted for those wishing to make the conversion.

UNITED STATES

Table A1.1 US$ bonds outstanding (nominal value, $ bn)

	1981	*1982*	*1983*	*1984*	*1985*	*1986*	*1987*
Government	475	570	707	873	1,038	1,192	1,335
Federal agency (incl.	319	384	452	526	627	802	975
mortgage pools)	129	179	245	289	369	532	672
Municipals	358	395	450	505	640	666	693
Corporate	269	302	340	318	341	411	449
Yankee	28	40	41	39	42	45	47
Eurodollar	40	68	84	109	144	193	218
Total	1,489	1,759	2,074	2,370	2,830	3,309	3,717

Source: Merrill Lynch, *Size of the World Bond Markets: Year-end 1987*, July 1988. Figures exclude convertibles, FRNs and zeros.

Treasury bonds

Issued in the form of notes (up to ten years maturity) or bonds (over ten years). Direct obligations of the US government. Zero coupon bonds are also available under the STRIPS (Separate Trading of Registered Interest and Principal Securities) and CUBES (Coupons Under Book-Entry Safe-keeping). The latter allows holders of stripped coupons to switch them into book-entry form to reduce holding costs.

Agencies

Obligations of US federal agencies that are typically backed either *de jure* or *de facto* by the US government. Major issuers include Government

National Mortgage Association (GNMA – 'Ginnie Mae'), Federal National Mortgage Association (FNMA – 'Fannie Mae'), Federal Home Loan Mortgage Corporation (FHLMC – 'Freddie Mac'), Federal Farm Credit Bank (FFCB), Federal Home Loan Banks (FHLB), Student Loan Marketing Association (SLMA – 'Sallie Mae').

Corporate bonds

Publicly issued corporate bonds must be registered with the SEC. Before 1983 domestic corporate bonds were issued in bearer form, with attached coupons. Since then, most have been issued as registered securities, and, most recently, several bonds have been entirely in book-entry form. Bonds are generally rated by Moody's and Standard & Poor's; bonds rated below BBB are considered below investment grade, commonly called junk bonds – a growing market sector (see Chapter 15).

Specialised types of corporate bonds

These include equipment trust certificates (serial bonds secured in equipment such as aircraft, trucks or rolling stock), collateral trust bonds (secured by a lien on specified assets – see asset-backed bonds below), medium-term notes (continuously offered notes of up to ten years maturity sold in small amounts), deposit notes (banks' counterpart to medium-term notes – they rank *pari passu* with bank deposits).

Asset-backed bonds

The major sector is mortgage-backed bonds, which can be classified into pass-throughs and derivatives. Passthroughs pass through the principal and interest payments on the underlying mortgages to the investor. Three major issuers are GNMA, FNMA and FHLMC. Major derivatives are collateralised mortgage obligations (CMOs) which take the pass-through flows and redistribute them through a trust structure in a way which controls the maturity pattern, and STRIPS, which reallocate the interest and principal payments separately; extreme examples of the latter are interest-only STRIPS (IOs) and principal-only STRIPS (POs). Another important class of asset-backed bonds are those backed by financial receivables such as car loans or credit card receivables; the largest single corporate issue ever made to date ($4 billion) was backed by car loan receivables for General Motors.

Domestic instruments

Classes of assets of little interest to international investors, for tax reasons, include municipal obligations and floating-rate preferred stock. Both categories benefit from special tax treatment which result in very low coupons.

JAPAN

Table A1.2 Japanese yen bonds outstanding (nominal value, $ bn equivalent)

	1981	*1982*	*1983*	*1984*	*1985*	*1986*	*1987*
Government (incl.	364	393	467	478	664	898	1,231
discount bonds)	6	6	8	9	13	20	26
Public sector-related[1]	45	49	59	63	88	118	160
(private placements)	92	94	100	97	128	169	224
Municipal	18	20	22	22	31	39	54
(private placements)	65	62	64	60	73	90	115
Bank debentures	127	132	150	154	206	297	412
Corporate[2]	44	41	41	37	46	58	74
Samurai	11	12	15	17	26	24	41
Euroyen	1	1	2	2	10	30	62
Total	607	649	756	773	1,070	1.473	2,033
Exchange rate used: $1 = ¥	220	235	232	252	200	158	121

1. Excludes NTT.
2. Excludes convertibles.

Source: As Table A1.1.

Government bonds

The majority of outstandings are ten-year bonds; at any one time one issue is the 'bench-mark' (see Chapter 15). A small amount of twenty-year bonds have been issued, and of five-year discount (zero-coupon) bonds.

Municipal and government-guaranteed bonds

Purposes of municipal bonds are controlled by the Local Finance Act. Deficit-financing bonds are rarely allowed. Individual issues must be approved by the council of municipal entities. Only just over twenty entities including Tokyo and twelve prefectural governments may make public issues. Normal maturity is seven to ten years. Government-guaranteed issues (principal and interest guaranteed) include those of Japan National Railway and the Public Finance Corporation; normal maturity is ten years and the coupon is linked to the most recent ten-year government bond.

Corporate bonds

The market is dominated by bank debentures. These are of two types: semi-annual coupon bonds and one-year discount bonds. Individual investors typically take 80 per cent or more of these issues. Other corporate straight bonds have traditionally had to be secured by a fixed charge on the property, though this rule has now been relaxed. There is a large market in convertible bonds, with about $7.5 billion outstanding in 1986.

Samurai/Shogun bonds

Samurai are yen-dominated bonds issued in Japan by non-residents, mainly supranational or sovereign borrowers. Shogun are the dollar-denominated equivalent.

UNITED KINGDOM

Government bonds ('gilt-edged')

Direct obligations of the UK government. Maturity at issue usually five to thirty years. There are some perpetuals outstanding. Some convertibles (i.e. convertible into other gilts) have been issued. There are also (a few) variable-rate bonds, and a range of issues whose interest and principal payments are linked to inflation.

Table A1.3 Sterling bonds outstanding (nominal value, US$ bn equivalent)

	1981	*1982*	*1983*	*1984*	*1985*	*1986*	*1987*
Government (incl.	89	96	109	118	126	132	138
index-linked)	4	8	11	10	13	16	22
Local authority	2	2	2	1	1	0	0
Corporate	7	10	9	9	11	14	19
Bulldog	1	2	3	3	5	5	6
Eurosterling	1	2	3	4	8	12	25
Total	181	171	175	153	207	227	310
Exchange rate used: $1 = $	1.92	1.62	1.45	1.16	1.45	1.48	1.89

Source: As Table A1.1.

Corporate bonds

The domestic corporate bond market is rather limited – recent issuers have tended to go the Eurosterling route. Domestic issues tend to be property company debentures or very long-term industrial bonds; building society bonds have included some index-linked bonds.

Mortgage-backed bonds

These are normally variable-rate, reflecting the UK custom of variable-rate mortgages. Principal and interest payments on the underlying mortgage are passed through to investors who hold pro rata shares of the mortgage pool.

Foreign bonds ('Bulldogs')

Long-term sterling-denominated bonds issued by non-residents, usually supranationals or sovereigns but including some foreign companies.

GERMANY

Table A1.4 Deutschmark bonds outstanding (US$ bn equivalent)

	1981	*1982*	*1983*	*1984*	*1985*	*1986*	*1987*
Government[1]	35	42	47	49	74	116	172
Government agencies	11	12	11	10	15	23	35
Länder	5	5	6	7	11	18	24
Banks[2]	216	223	215	197	268	356	456
Corporate	2	1	1	1	1	1	2
Schuldscheine	196	202	185	165	216	267	328
International[3]	36	35	32	31	48	73	96
Total[4]	305	320	312	293	417	588	783
Exchange rate used: $1 = DM	2.24	2.38	2.73	3.16	2.45	1.92	1.57

1. Excludes savings bonds.
2. Includes mortgage, commercial, specialised and other credit institutions.
3. There is no distinction in Germany between foreign and Euro-DM bonds.
4. Excluding Schuldschein figures.

Source: As Table A1.1.

Government bonds

The German government issues three main types of bond. Bundeskassenobligationen and Bundesschatzanweisungen are short-term (up to six years). The third type of bonds are Bundesrepublikanleihe or Bunds. They generally have maturities up to ten years. The average maturity for government paper is 6.5 years compared to 8.5 years for US Treasuries and ten years for gilts.

Government-guaranteed bonds

Bundespostanleihen and Bundesbahnanleihen are issued by the Post Office and the Railways under government guarantee. There are sixteen special credit institutions in West Germany, of which perhaps the Kreditanstalt für Wiederaufbau (KfW) is the best known. Although these institutions are not part of the government sector, their credit standing is comparable to government-guaranteed issues.

Länder and municipalities

The Länder are the provinces or states making up the Federal Republic. Municipalities' issues are very small.

Corporate bonds

The largest category is bank bonds. They consist mostly of Pfandbriefe (bonds issued to fund mortgage loans) or Kommunalobligationen (bonds collateralised by loans to, or guaranteed by, a public sector entity). The industrial bond sector is very limited.

Schuldscheindarlehen

Not strictly bonds but certificates of indebtedness – private loan agreements between borrowers and banks or other lenders that are resold to other investors with the borrower's permission.

FRANCE

Government bonds

Until 1985 government bonds had no standard form. Thus there were various types of straight bond (bullet, sinking fund or convertible into floating rate) and floating-rate notes (with some convertible into straights)

Table A1.5 French franc bonds outstanding (US$ bn equivalent)

	1981	*1982*	*1983*	*1984*	*1985*	*1986*	*1987*
Government	18	20	22	28	48	74	99
Government agencies	57	61	58	58	87	123	160
Provinces	1	1	1	1	1	1	1
Corporate	21	20	19	20	34	45	63
Foreign	1	1	1	1	2	2	3
Euro-Frfr	2	2	1	1	1	4	5
Total	100	106	104	110	174	252	334
Exchange rate used: $1 = Frfr	5.69	6.74	8.34	9.65	7.51	6.38	5.33

Source: As Table A1.1.

and indexed bonds and zero-coupon bonds: Fond d'Etat Libérés d'Intérêt Nominal or FELINs. The system is now that the French Treasury issues coupon-bearing notes (Bons du Trésor à Taux Fixe et Intérêt Annuel – BTANs) out to five years and bonds (Obligations Assimilables du Trésor – OATs) out to 25 years. There are also some floating-rate OATs. Under the new system liquidity is also enhanced by the fact that existing issues are regularly reopened; the coupon is set at the beginning of the year, and new tranches are sold at a discount or premium as yields fluctuate. The major difference between the BTAN and the OAT is that the legal status of the BTAN is a negotiable instrument, while the OAT is a security; thus the latter comes technically under the legal monopoly of the Compagnie Française des Agents de Change and the bonds are listed on the Stock Exchange; BTANs are not listed and thus trade freely over-the-counter.

Government-guaranteed bonds

This sector, consisting of bonds issued by government agencies, utilities and municipalities that are unconditionally guaranteed by the French Republic, is in fact much larger than direct government debt, but only accounts for about 15 per cent of the trading volume.

Corporate bonds

A substantial market in terms of outstandings but most issues are not actively traded. The major issuers are the banks.

Appendix 2
Bond Market Calculations

This Appendix lays out some of the basic calculations that are involved in bond markets, starting with the Eurobond market and making comparisons with domestic markets as necessary. (A full discussion can be had from 'Yield Calculations', by Paul Fage, published by Credit Suisse First Boston, October 1986). We start with simple bond calculations. It is a temptation to assume that one can just hit the buttons on the bond calculator but it is important to understand the principles on which they work at least. So here goes.

The 'classical' bond is an instrument bearing a fixed rate of interest, called its *coupon*. Valuing the classical bond is simple. Suppose we have a ten-year bond with a coupon of 5 per cent per annum which is paid once a year. Suppose it is issued in denominations with a face value of $100. The price at which it is issued is par, i.e. a price of $100 per $100 face value. So the cash flows are that we invest $100 today and receive back $100 in ten years' time, plus $5 per annum in interest in the meantime:

After 1 year	$5
After 2 years	$5
After 3 years	$5
...	
After 10 years	$105

The price of the bond is the value of the cash flows today. To find that value, we need to understand present value calculations. Present value is found as follows. A sum with a present value of 100 invested today at an annual interest rate of r per cent will yield us $100(1 + r)$ at the end of year 1. At the end of year 2 we will have $100\,(1 + r)^2$ and at the end of year n we will have $100\,(1 + r)^n$. So we can say: 'Future value in year n = present value x $(1 + r)^n$'. Therefore:

$$\text{Present value} = \frac{\text{Future value in year } n}{(1 + r)^n}$$

Another way of saying this is that the present value is the future value discounted back to today at a rate of r. We can make the formula simpler if we put $v = 1/(1 + r)$ because then we have $PV = v^n FV$, where FV = face value.

Now we return to our example. The price of the bond is the present value of all the cash flows given in our example, that is, we have:

$$P = \frac{5}{(1.05)} + \frac{5}{(1.05)^2} + \ldots + \frac{5}{(1.05)^{10}} + \frac{100}{(1.05)^{10}}$$

We can let the coupon of 5 be represented by c and the discount rate by r and we can write $v = 1/(1 + \mathrm{r})$. Then instead of having 5/(1.05) we have c times v and we can write:

$$P = c\,(v + v^2 + v^3 + \ldots + v^n) + 100v^n$$

The expression in the brackets is often known as 'an annuity certain'. Mathematicians and actuaries tell us it can be simplified to $(1 - v^n)/r$ and so we have

$$P = c(1 - v^n)/r + 100v^n$$

which is a convenient formula because it can be calculated in one cell of a spreadsheet.

From this formula we can see that our bond's price is:

$5(1 - 0.952380^{10})/0.05 + 100(0.952380^{10}) = 100(1 - 0.952380^{10}) + 100(0.952380^{10}) = 100$

Naturally, this is because we are discounting a 5 per cent income stream at a discount rate of 5 per cent. The coupon on the bond and its *yield to maturity* or *redemption yield* are the same: both 5 per cent.

What do we mean by the yield to maturity? It is that rate of discount which makes the present value of the bond's cash flows equal to its market price. That is, given today's price, it tells us what the bond will yield over its life, allowing both for the income from the coupons and the change in price. If the bond's price in the market were 90, rather than the issue price of 100, there would be a capital gain of 10 points over the ten years – a bit over 1 per cent per annum – to be added to the coupon and so the yield would be a bit over 6 per cent (actually 6.38 per cent).

So, if the bond's yield to maturity (and hence the discount rate applied to its cash flows) were 7 per cent, then the bond's price would be:

$$P = 5\,\frac{(1 - 0.934579^{10})}{0.07} + 100(0.934579^{10}) = 85.95$$

The formula for yield to maturity given price cannot be given in the same way as that for price given yield since the result must be found by assuming a given yield, finding the implied price, comparing it with the market price, adjusting the yield to a closer estimate, finding the new price, and so on: a process of iteration.

ACCRUED INTEREST

The calculation we made above works for bond prices which are worked out for an exact number of periods to maturity. We were looking at a ten-year bond's cash flows, on the date the bond is issued.

What would the bond be worth, say, three months later? There are two parts to the answer. On the one hand, the bond will have a price which represents the future value of the cash flows at the new market yield to maturity (say 11 per cent). On the other, the seller of the bond has owned it for three months, with no interest being paid: the interest has accrued at a rate of 5 per cent per annum.

To work out the accrued interest we need to consider the exact number of days from the issue date of the bond to date it is being sold. Suppose the bond was issued on 1 March 1989 and is being sold for delivery on 7 June 1989. How many days in this interval?

Suppose that the bond traded is a Eurobond and we want to calculate its accrued interest. To work this out we must use the Eurobond interest calculation convention. This is laid down in the AIBD's Rule 225 which says:

> With the exception of floating rate notes, accrued interest on a contract shall be calculated on a 360 days per year basis (each calendar month to be considered one-twelfth of 360 days, or 30 days, and each period from a date in one month to the same date in the next month to be considered 30 days) from and including the date of the last paid interest coupon or the date from which the interest is to accrue for a new issue, up to but excluding the value date of the transaction.

So in our example the seller of the bond held it for March, April and May – a total of 90 days. They have also held it for six days in June, excluding the 7th of June which is the value date of the sale. (See the section below on value dates for value date rules.) So there are 96 days of accrued interest to consider.

Suppose the seller is selling $10 million worth of bonds. Then the accrued interest due is:

$$\frac{5}{100} \times \frac{96}{360} \times 10{,}000{,}000 = \$133{,}000$$

Rule 225(2) also states that – except for FRNs – accrued interest for the 31st of a month is the same as for the 30th. (FRN calculations are discussed in Appendix 3.)

BOND PRICE BETWEEN COUPON DATES

We have now worked out what the proper accrued interest should be on our bond – in this case $133,000. But what price should the bond itself be? The way we worked out its price before was (relatively) simple, because we were working out the price of the bond on the day of issue. There was no accrued interest to consider, and also, our discount factors were being applied to a round number of periods – ten in that case. Now, three months later, we have to consider a nine and three-quarters year bond.

Hence we have to calculate the price differently. The simplest way to proceed is to find what the bond would be worth on the next coupon date, i.e. nine months from now, if today's rates were prevailing on that date. Then we discount that figure back to today's present value, using the appropriate discount rate.

Step one, then, is to work out what this bond is worth on 1 March 1990 at a yield of 11 per cent. We use our formula again:

$$P = c(1 - v^n)/r + 100v^n$$

Here we have $v = 1/1.11 = 0.9009009$ and so:

$$P = 5(1 - 0.9009009^9)/0.11 + 100\,(0.9009009^9) = 27.69 + 39.09 = 66.78$$

To this should be added the coupon payable on that date, of 5, making a total value on that day of 71.78. Our next job is to discount that back to today, 7 June 1989. To do this we have to use an odd period discount factor. To work out an odd period discount factor we need to do two things: first we take the annual rate of discount and 'decompound' this to a daily basis. Then we 'recompound' back up over the appropriate fractional period.

Here we have a discount rate of 11 per cent per annum as rates have moved up during the three months since the bond was issued. Our first step is to take this down to a daily rate which we do by writing:

$$d = (1 + r)^{(1/360)}$$

where d = daily rate (bearing in mind that the Eurobond market works on a 360-day year). So in this case we have $d = 1.11^{(1/360)} = 1.0002899$. Our next step is to recompound this up over the number of days in the period 7 June 1989 to 1 March 1990 which works out at 264 (24 days in June plus eight complete 30-day months and excluding 1 March 1990). So we must work out:

$$r^* = (1 + d)^q$$

where q = number of days. So here we have $r^* = 1.0002899^{264} = 1.079535321$.

Finally, to put the number back into an annual interest rate, we gross up by the annual number of days:

$$t = (r^* - 1) \times 360/264 \times 100 = 10.8457256$$

So the net result is that an 11 per cent annual rate decompounded over a 264-day period is equivalent to 10.846 per cent annually. For those who prefer the entire process in one formula, it is as follows:

$$\text{Decompounded rate} = [(1 + i/n)^{(nq/360)} - 1] \times 360/q \times 100$$

So now we must discount the price of 66.78 that we worked out for value 1 March 1990, back to today, at the discount rate of 10.846 per cent. We need to find:

$$71.78/(1 + 0.10846 \times 264/360) = 71.78/1.079537333 = 66.49$$

We must also bear in mind that this price of 66.49 includes accrued interest, which we have worked out at \$133,000 per \$10 million, i.e. 1.33. So the 'clean' price of the bond, excluding accrued interest, is 65.16.

DURATION, CONVEXITY AND REINVESTMENT RISK

An important question arises when we own a bond: how risky is it? Setting aside the question of whether the borrower might default, i.e. its credit standing, there is the question of market risk: how volatile the bond will prove to be as interest rates vary. This depends in part on the length of time until the bond matures: the longer this is, in general, the greater the volatility.

The maturity, or date at which final repayment is made, is the traditional measure of the 'length' of a bond or other security. Another measure has been average life, where the loan or security is an amortizing one. Both of these measures are concerned only with the principal amount of the security. They ignore all interim interest flows.

More recently an important concept has been used to give a better measure of the 'length' of an instrument. This concept is called duration. It is important because it is often used in assessing volatility. Another use is when an investor, perhaps a pension fund or life insurance company, wants to measure the 'length' of its assets against the 'length' of its liabilities. Duration is also an important concept for traders, who use it in finding 'hedge ratios'. It measures the weighted average time till cash flow payment. The weights are the present value of the cash flows themselves.

The formula for duration is:

$$D = \frac{\sum_{t=1}^{n} \frac{t.c_t}{(1+r)^t}}{\sum_{t=1}^{n} \frac{c_t}{(1+r)^t}}$$

The top line of this formula is the time until the cash flow is paid, weighted by the present value of the cash flow (i.e. c_t discounted by $(1 + r)^t$. The bottom line is the total of the weights – which is also the total of the present values of the bond's cash flows, i.e. the price of the bond. It is sometimes convenient to write duration in a formula which can be used in a single cell of a spreadsheet. It can be shown (see Patrick Phillips, *Inside the New Gilt-*

Edged Market. Woodhead-Faulkner, 1987) that duration can be written as follows:

$$D = \left(\frac{c}{2}\left[\frac{1 - v^n}{(1 - v)^2} - \frac{nv^n}{1 - v}\right] + 100nv^{n-1}\right)\frac{v}{2P}$$

where D = duration
c = coupon
$v = \dfrac{1}{1 + i}$
t_i = y/200
y = yield on the bond (equivalent to our discount rate r earlier)
n = number of coupon periods to maturity
P = price of the bond

There is another important use of duration, which is in hedging. The measure of duration applied in weighting hedges or arbitrage transactions is called modified duration. It is used because it gives a measure of a security's volatility (and is usually referred to as such in the UK market, rather than as modified duration, which is the US term). The formula for modified duration is

$$D^* = \frac{D}{1 + y/f}$$

where D = Macaulay duration
y = yield to maturity (decimal)
f = frequency of cash flow payments per year

This modified duration is used to estimate the percentage price volatility of a fixed-income security. The relationship is:

$$\frac{\Delta P}{P} \times 100 = - D^* \times \Delta Y$$

where Δ signifies a small change i.e. per cent price change = − modified duration × yield change (in basis points).

From this we can see clearly that a rising yield produces a larger price fall if duration is larger.

This is one of the chief practical uses of duration: as a measure of the volatility of a bond. To be precise, modified duration is a measure of the percentage volatility of the full price (i.e. including accrued interest) of a bond, given small changes in interest rates.

It is important to realise that modified duration as a measure of percentage volatility is only valid for small changes in yield. For larger changes, one must consider the security's convexity. (The term comes from the price-yield curve for a normal bond, which is convex. Mathematically speaking, the convexity is the second derivative of the price-yield curve:

$$C = \frac{10{,}000}{P} \times \frac{\delta^2 P}{\delta Y^2}$$

where P = dirty price of bond (i.e. including accrued interest)
Y = periodic yield (e.g. semi-annual)
C = convexity
δ = signifies differentiation

A less formidable formula which is a practical approximation is to define P*p* and P*m* as the price of the bond if yields rise and fall respectively by one basis point. Then

$$C = 10^8 \times (Pp + Pm - 2P)/P$$

An important formula is that used when we are assessing the return on a bond if rates move. The conventional yield calculation assumes all interest flows can be reinvested at the current yield to maturity. But we might anticipate a fall in rates: we might then want to know the probable yield, allowing for reinvestment of future coupons at a lower rate. That is, we take into account the 'reinvestment risk'.

The formula for calculating reinvestment effect can be derived as follows. We have a bond which as a coupon rate of c per period, current price P, and a term of n periods to maturity. We assume that the coupon income is reinvested at a rate per period of j. Then for \$100 nominal par value purchased the accumulated value at maturity will consist of the sum of the following:

(i) Capital repayment at redemption = 100
(ii) the final coupon payment, $= c$
(iii) the penultimate coupon payment, c, invested for one period at $j = c\,(1 + j)$
(iv) the antepenultimate coupon payment, c, invested for two periods at $j = c\,(1 + j)^2$ . . . and so on until
(v) the compounded value of the coupon n–1 periods before maturity $= c\,(1 + j)^{n-1}$

which all adds up to $100 + c\,\{1 + (1 + j) + (1 + j)^2 + \ldots + (1 + j)^{n-1}\}$.

The series $1 + (1 + j) + (1 + j)^2$ [s2] $+ \ldots + (1 + j)^{n+1}$ can be shown mathematically to be equal to $\{(1 + j)^n - 1\}/j$. Therefore the total value of the bond at maturity is given by the formula

$$\text{Accumulated value} = 100 + \frac{c\{(1 + j)^n - 1\}}{j}$$

This is quite a useful formula as it allows one to assess quickly the impact of reinvestment assumptions. Let's look at an 8 per cent ten-year bond with a yield to maturity of 10 per cent; but we want to consider what its yield to maturity would be, if we assume a 7 per cent reinvestment rate.

First we find its price using the normal method (i.e. our formula above):

$$P = \frac{\frac{8}{2}\left(1 - \frac{1}{1.05^{20}}\right)}{.05} + 100\left(\frac{1}{1.05^{20}}\right)$$

$$= 49.85 + 37.69 = 87.54$$

Next we find what its accumulated value would be on our reinvestment assumptions, using our accumulated value formula:

$$\text{Accumulated value} = 100 + \frac{\frac{8}{2}\left((1.035)^{20} - 1\right)}{.035}$$

$$= 100 + \frac{\frac{8}{2} \times 0.9898}{.035}$$

$$= 213.12$$

So now we know the price we have to pay for the bond, 87.54, and what we think it will be worth at the end of its term, 213.12. All we have to do now is to find the yield, *Y*, in the formula:

$$87.54\,(1 + Y)^{20} = 213.12$$

$$\text{So } (1 + Y)^{20} = 213.12/87.54$$

$$\text{and } Y = \sqrt[20]{\frac{213.12}{87.54}} - 1$$

$$= 9.099\%$$

VALUE DATE RULES

In any bond trade there are two key dates: the trade date and the value date. The trade date is unambiguous: it is the day on which the deal is done. The value date is the date on which the bond is paid for and delivered, and this depends on the individual market.

The Eurobond market has certain standard rules for value dates which are laid out in the AIBD rulebook. The normal value date for a trade is the seventh calendar day following the trade date. Thus a bond bought on the 7th of the month is paid for on the 14th. If the 14th turns out to be a bank holiday in the centre where payment and/or delivery takes place, settlement is on the next business day, without adjustment of accrued interest. If the 14th were also a coupon date on the bond, then the coupon belongs to the seller of the bond and no accrued interest is paid.

For new issues, the value date for settlement of secondary market trades is the business day following the closing of the issue, or seven calendar days after the trade date, whichever is the later.

The definition of business day is laid down by the two clearing systems (Cedel in Luxembourg and Euroclear in Brussels). Most bank holidays in Belgium and Luxembourg are not considered holidays by the clearing systems. Exceptions to this are Good Friday and Christmas Day. (See the information on Cedel and Euroclear in Chapter 17.)

Value date and interest rate calculations used in other markets vary. For example, if one were switching from US$ into DM to buy a DM Eurobond one would have to bear in mind that the foreign exchange market's value date calculations work differently. Full details are given in the author's *Foreign Exchange Handbook* (John Wiley & Sons, New York, 1983) but, briefly, foreign exchange deals and Eurodollar deposit deals are normally done either for 'spot' value (two working days forward) or for the same day in the future month as the spot date. Thus, if today is the 7th, the foreign exchange spot value date would normally be the 9th and the one month forward value date would be the 9th of the next month, when one month Eurocurrency deposits would mature. Deals for a week would be assumed to be 'over spot', i.e. a week from the spot date, unless otherwise specified and so it is as well always to specify the exact date for which one wishes to deal.

Similarly, the US bond market, for example, will normally settle in one of three different ways: 'cash' (delivery next day – normal for Treasury bonds), 'skip-day' (delivery the second business day after the trade) or 'corporate' (five business days after the trade – customary for corporate bonds). In the UK, gilt-edged normally settle 'cash' (next day) and corporate debentures after two days. Equities settle (roughly) fortnightly, on 'account days' laid down by the Stock Exchange.

It is impossible to give all the possible settlement arrangements so the first thing to be said is, always check with the counterparty regarding the value date if the market is unfamiliar to you. Table A2.1 may be of some general help as regards interest rate calculation bases.

Table A2.1 Common interest bases

UK money markets	Annual actual/365
US and Euromoney markets	Annual actual/360
Treasury bonds (US and UK)	Semi-annual actual/365
Eurobonds (AIBD, Continental bonds)	Annual 30/360
Yankee bonds, Federal agencies, US corporate and municipal bonds	Semi-annual 30/360
US commercial paper, bankers' acceptances	Discount basis actual/360
UK bills of exchange, commercial paper	Discount basis actual/365

This is a crude summary because the 'days basis' varies from market to market. There are three main ways:

1. 'Actual' – take the number of days between the two dates. Used in US, UK and Japanese government bonds markets, UK and Japanese corporate and municipal bond markets (but not the US corporate and municipal markets which use (2) below. Note Japan uses simple interest yields – see below). It is also used in France but for domestic trades on Government bonds the normal value date is two business days after trade date and the accrued is calculated up to the calendar day after the trade date (i.e. normally the day before value date).
2. 30-day month – take the number of days between the two dates assuming 30-day months using the following method. The number of days between the dates D1/M1/Y1 and D2/M2/Y2 is given by:

> If D1 is 31 change to 30
> If D2 is 31 and D1 is 30 or 31 change D2 to 30, otherwise leave at 31.
> Then the number of days between dates is given by:
> $(Y2 - Y1) \times 360 + (M2 - M1) \times 30 + (D2 - D1)$

This method is used in Switzerland and the US Federal Agency, corporate and Yankee bond markets.
3. Continental 30-day month – take the number of days using the same formula but

> If D1 is 31 change to 30
> If D2 is 31 also change to 30

This method is used in the Eurobond market, and in the domestic Austrian, Belgian, Dutch, German, and Swedish markets.

The next step is to determine the number of days in the year, because sadly this also varies from market to market. Again there are three main methods:

1. Assume a 365-day year. Used in the French, UK and Japanese government bond markets as also their corporate and municipal markets.
2. Assume a year has $n \times$ days in current coupon period where n = coupon frequency. For example if coupon is paid semi-annually the number of days in the period will range from 181 to 184 and the year from 362 to 368. Used in US Treasury bond market.
3. Assume a year has 360 days. Used in Austrian, Belgian, Dutch, German, Swedish, Swiss, US corporate and municipal markets and in the Eurobond market.

In general, actual/365 and 30/360 produce the same annual interest total, but if the payment is semi-annual there will be slight differences in the half year coupon. To see the differences between 30/360 and actual/365, take a

Table A2.2 Interest payments on different bases: effective annual rate

Formula: Effective annual rate = $(1 + i/n)^n$			
Annual actual/365	10.00	Annual actual/360	10.14
Semi-annual actual/365	10.25	Semi-annual actual/360	10.40
Quarterly actual/365	10.38	Quarterly actual/360	10.53
Monthly actual/365	10.47	Monthly actual/360	10.62

year in which the semi-annual coupon periods are divided into 181 and 184 days. Then on a \$10 million borrowing priced at 10 per cent semi-annual actual/365, the two coupon payments would be respectively \$495,890.41 and \$504,109.58, totalling \$1 million. On the 30/360 basis, they would be \$500,000 each. The annual total is the same, but there is a slight difference in the timing of the flows.

As mentioned above, the US Treasury bond market's day-count basis is not exactly actual/actual. Accrued interest on US Treasury bonds follows the formula N/D × C/F × FV

where N = number of days' accrual
D = number of days in coupon period
C = coupon/100
F = coupon payment frequency (normally 2)
FV = face value.

For example, for \$1 million of bonds traded for value 2 July 1989, coupon payable 15 June and 15 December, coupon rate of 10 per cent:

$$17/183 \times 10/200 \times 1{,}000{,}000 = 4{,}644.81$$

By comparison the UK gilt accrued formula would be N/365 × C × FV.

The effects of the different bases can be summarised as in Table A2.2 which lays out the effective annual rate implied by 10 per cent quoted on various interest bases.

The formula for interest conversion is $(1 + i/n)^n$ where i = nominal rate and n = coupon frequency payment. One of the commonest conversions is from semi-annual to annual. In this case the formula produces $1 + i + i^2/4$ and a simple rule of thumb is:

To Convert semi-annual to annual: Additional basis points are found by squaring the interest rate and dividing by four.

For example, 10 per cent squared and divided by four produces a 25 basis point adjustment to 10.25 per cent.

Finally, interest calculations in Japan are radically different. Issues in the Japanese government bond market are quoted for dealing on a simple yield basis. Thus the price of a bond is found as follows:

$$P = 100 \times [(C \times Y + 100)/(S \times Y + 100)]$$

where: C = coupon
P = price (excluding accrued)
Y = exact number of years to maturity including fractions
S = simple yield.

For example, No. 89 has a coupon of 5.1 per cent and matures on 20 June 1996. Purchasing on a simple yield of 4.77 for settlement on 1 August 1987 (so that the life is 8 years and 323 days or 8.884 years) would give the price of:

$$100 \times [(5.1 \times 8.884) + 100]/[(4.77 \times 8.884) + 100] = 102.06$$

The relationship between simple yield and price is therefore:

$$S = 100 \times C/P + (100/P - 1) \times 100/Y$$

and in our example the yield, given a price of 102.06, would be:

$$100 \times 5.1/102.06 + (100/102.06 - 1) \times 100/8.884 = 4.770$$

The total price payable for a purchase is equal to the sum of the price, as calculated above, accrued interest (coupon/100 × actual days in settlement period/365) and transfer tax, where applicable.

AIBD RULES

The AIBD Rules 221 to 227 on value dates and interest calculations are reproduced below.

Rule 221 **Normal value date**
The value date for a transaction in international securities as regulated by the AIBD shall be the seventh calendar day following the trade date, regardless of any local or generally recognised holidays.

Rule 222 **Special value date**
A special value date may be mutually agreed between the buyer and the seller at the time of dealing.

Rule 223 **Value date on non-settlement day**
Where the value date coincides with a bank holiday in the centre where the payment and/or the delivery is to be effected, the first business day in that centre following that bank holiday shall be accepted by both parties as the date for payment and/or delivery. No adjustment of accrued interest shall be made.

Rule 224 **Value date and coupon due date**

Where the due date of an interest coupon coincides with the value date of a transaction, the buyer shall not acquire such coupon and no accrued interest shall be calculated on such a contract. With the exception of the floating rate notes, in the case of a transaction with a value date on the thirtieth calendar day of the month and a coupon due date on the thirty-first calendar day of the same month, accrued interest shall correspond to the full value of the coupon.

Rule 225 **Accrued interest calculation**

(1) With the exception of floating rate notes, accrued interest on a contract shall be calculated on a 360 days per year basis (each calendar month to be considered one-twelfth of 360 days, or thirty days, and each period from a date in one month to the same date in the following month to be considered thirty days) from and including the date of the last paid interest coupon or the day from which interest is to accrue for a new issue, up to but excluding the value date of the transaction.

Examples of calculations in conformity with rules 224 and 225:

Interest accrues from coupon dates	*Value dates*	*Number of days of accrued interest for*		
		straight and convertible bonds	*floating rate notes*	
			Normal	*Leap year*
	The following year:			
30.11.	28.2.	88	90	90
30.11.	29.2.	89		91
30.11.	1.3.	91	91	92
30.11.	3.3.	93	93	94
30.11.	30.3.	120	120	121
30.11.	31.3.	120	121	122
31.12.	28.2.	58	59	59
31.12.	29.2.	59		60
31.12.	1.3.	61	60	61
31.12.	3.3.	63	62	63
31.12.	30.3.	90	89	90
31.12.	31.3.	90	90	91
	The same year:			
1.1.	28.2.	57	58	58
1.1.	29.2.	58		59
1.1.	1.3.	60	59	60
1.1.	3.3.	62	61	62
1.1.	30.3.	89	88	89
1.1.	31.3.	89	89	90
15.1.	28.2.	43	44	44
15.1.	29.2.	44		45
15.1.	1.3.	46	45	46
15.1.	3.3.	48	47	48
1.2.	28.2.	27	27	27
1.2.	29.2.	28		28

Interest accrues from coupon dates	*Value dates*	*Number of days of accrued interest for* straight and convertible bonds	*floating rate notes* Normal	Leap year
	The following year:			
1.2.	1.3.	30	28	29
1.2.	3.3.	32	30	31
15.2.	28.2.	13	13	13
15.2.	29.2.	14		14
15.2.	1.3.	16	14	15
15.2.	3.3.	18	16	17
28.2.	29.2.	1		1
28.2.	1.3.	3	1	2
28.2.	3.3.	5	3	4
28.2.	5.3.	7	5	6
28.2.	30.3.	32	30	31
28.2.	31.3.	32	31	32
	The following year:			
28.2.	27.2.	359	364	365
28.2.	28.2.	0*	0*	0*

* Seller collects full interest coupon, no accrued interest calculation to the buyer.

(2) With the exception of floating rate notes, accrued interest to a value date on the thirty-first calendar day of a month shall be the same as to the thirtieth calendar day of the same month.

(3) Accrued interest on a contract for floating rate notes shall be calculated on actual days, divided by 360 (or by 365 in the case of a Euro-sterling issue) from and including the date of the last paid interest coupon or the day from which interest is to accrue for a new issue, up to but excluding the value date of the transaction.

(4) No accrued interest shall be calculated where rule 224 applies or where the value date coincides with the date of issue or where a transaction has been concluded at a "flat" price.

Rule 226 **Accrued interest computation – fractions**

In all transactions involving the payment of interest, fractions of a cent equalling or exceeding five mills shall be regarded as one cent and fractions of a cent less than five mills shall be disregarded.

Examples:

$137.625 accrued interest has to be increased to $137.63
$137.624 accrued interest has to be decreased to $137.62.

Rule 227 **Value dates of secondary market transactions in new issues of international securities**

The value of secondary market transactions in new issues of international securities as regulated by the AIBD will be the business day at the recognised international clearing systems following the closing date or seventh calendar day following the trade date, whichever is the later.

MEDIUM-TERM NOTE CALCULATIONS

Medium-term note yield calculations are unique. MTNs have a fixed interest payment cycle that disregards issue and maturity anniversary dates. That is, interest accrues from the date issued, but it is payable on a predetermined semi-annual cycle and at maturity. Hence, as well as a short or long first coupon, there is usually a short last coupon. This has the annoying result that most bond calculators cannot handle MTNs. One must go back to first principles.

An example will show what is involved. Suppose we have an MTN that has a coupon of 7 per cent and we are buying today in the secondary market at a yield of 6.75 per cent. The issue date of the bond was 6 October 1986 and we are buying it on 27 October 1986. The coupon dates are 1 April and 1 October and the bond matures 13 May 1988.

Our first step is to lay out a time-line of the cash flows and days using the MTN's corporate (30/360) convention:

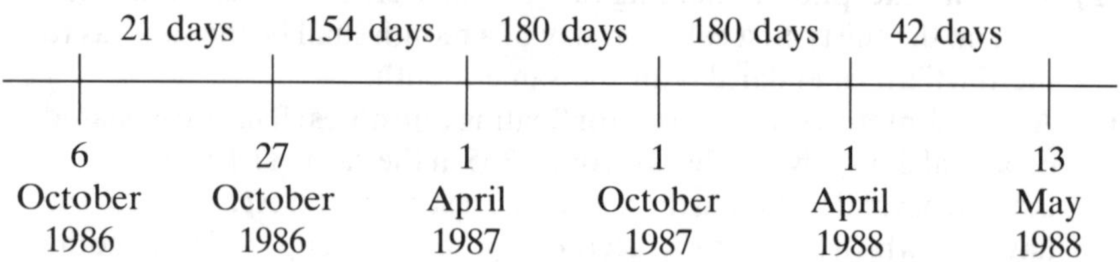

Using this we can set out the cash flows and also measure when they happen, in terms of fractions of periods, for our bond formula as in Table A2.3.

Table A2.3

Cash flow	*Date*	*No. of days (since previous cash flow)*	*As fraction of period*	*Amount*
Accrued interest	27/10/86	21	0.12	0.41
First coupon	1/4/87	154	0.86	3.40
Second coupon	1/10/87	180	1	3.50
Third coupon	1/4/88	180	1	3.50
Final coupon	13/5/88	42	0.23	0.82

To value the MTN we now plug these numbers into the bond price formula:

$$P = \frac{3.40}{\left(1 + \frac{6.75}{208}\right)^{0.86}} + \frac{3.50}{\left(1 + \frac{6.75}{200}\right)^{1.86}} + \frac{3.50}{\left(1 + \frac{6.75}{200}\right)^{2.86}} +$$

$$\frac{0.82}{\left(1 + \frac{6.75}{200}\right)^{3.09}} + \frac{100}{\left(1 + \frac{6.75}{200}\right)^{3.09}}$$

$$= 100.77 \text{ or } 100.35 \text{ excluding accrued interest.}$$

Appendix 3
FRN Calculations and Valuation Formulas

VALUING AN FRN

Each FRN has distinctive trading characteristics. They can be attributed to factors such as differences in coupon spread versus LIBOR, maturity dates and frequency of coupon refix dates. Longer-term FRNs are a relatively less liquid market (because banks, which are major traders and investors in FRNs, tend to concentrate on shorter maturities for prudential reasons). Hence these FRNs as a class tend to be more volatile. The coupon refixing effect means that FRNs that refix quarterly tend to be more akin to true money market instruments, with little price volatility; semi-annual coupon FRNs tend to be more volatile.

There are a number of valuation methods in use; the formulas involved are laid out below. As an example of the differences caused by the various methods, consider Table A3.1.

Table A3.1 Examples of margins

Issue	*Price*	*Simple margin*	*Adjusted total*	*Discounted margin*
Barclays 1990	100.15	15.69	19.77	17.66
Citicorp 1994	100.85	18.2	11.6	14.01
Denmark 2004	100.27	20.95	23.35	21.72
Italy 1999	100.04	16.73	22.15	19.51

Source: Credit Suisse First Boston, *Eurodollar Floating Rate Notes Evaluation Techniques*, November 1984.

Yield calculations on FRNs

There are a number formulas for valuing FRNs. The first of these is the current yield:

$$\text{Current yield} = \frac{C_c}{P_p} \times 100$$

where: C_c = current coupon rate
P_p = flat purchase price.

This is a crude measure, for it implicitly assumes that there will be no capital gain or loss during the investor's investment horizon. Hence, it is effectively a single period calculation, up to the next rollover date of any individual FRN. It also assumes that the FRN really will reprice exactly to par on rollover, which might not be true. Thus a more precise one-period yield measure is the return to coupon rollover date. This is defined as:

$$\text{Return to rollover} = \frac{P_r + (C_c \times D_t/360) - (P_p + A)}{P_p + A} \times \frac{360}{D_1} \times 100$$

where: P_r = estimated rollover date price
D_t = total number of days in coupon period
A = accrued interest on settlement date
D_1 = number of days from settlement to rollover date.

This method of calculation is useful in comparing the potential return of a floater with alternative investments, such as CDs or Eurodeposits. It is less useful in comparing individual FRN issues with one another, since differences in the timing of rollover dates will result in horizons of different lengths.

A common method of valuing FRNs focuses on their margin over LIBOR. Banks, which are important investors in the market, use this to compare the return with that available from a loan priced over LIBOR. The simplest measure (the simple margin) takes the coupon spread over LIBOR and adds to it the amortisation of the FRN's price discount from par over its remaining term to maturity. So we have:

$$\text{Simple margin} = \frac{\left(\dfrac{100 - P_p}{M} + S\right)}{P_p/100} \times 100$$

where: S = coupon spread in decimal form
M = remaining years to maturity.

It may be necessary to adjust for the 'carry' on the FRN. The term 'carry' is defined as the difference between coupon income earned and the cost of finance for the period from settlement to the first coupon refixing date. A note carrying a 20 per cent coupon at a time when LIBOR is 15 per cent will generate a positive 'carry' of 500 basis points. The adjusted simple margin takes account of this one-time carry effect by adjusting the market price, and then calculating the simple margin based on this adjusted price.

So the formula for the adjusted simple margin is the same formula as that for the simple margin, but substituting P_a for P_p, where:

$$P_a = P_p - \left[\frac{\left\{C_c - \dfrac{R_s(P_p + A)}{100}\right\} \times \dfrac{D_1}{360}}{\left\{1 + \dfrac{R_a \times D_1}{100 \times 360}\right\}}\right]$$

where: R_a = assumed average LIBOR rate over remaining life of FRN
R_s = finance rate from settlement date to first coupon rollover date.

The simple and adjusted simple margin calculations ignore the 'current yield effect'. This arises when an interest-bearing security is purchased at some price other than par. The investor earns interest on the par value of the instrument, but when his cost is below par, the current yield is above the coupon. Conversely, when he buys above par, the current yield is below the coupon. The effect depends on the FRN price and the current level of yields as shown in Table A3.2.

Table A3.2 Annual basis-point value of the current yield factor

FRN purchase price	*Coupon rate*			
	5%	*10%*	*15%*	*20%*
99	5	10	15	20
98	10	20	30	40
97	15	30	45	60

Source: Salomon Brothers, *Eurodollar Floating Rate Notes: Techniques for Assessing Relative Value*, January 1982.

Accordingly, the formula for the total margin is as follows:

$$\text{Total margin} = \frac{\left[\dfrac{100 - P_p}{M}\right] + S + \left[\dfrac{R_a(100 - P_p)}{100}\right] \times 100}{P_p/100}$$

Once again, it may be necessary to adjust the purchase price for the cost of carry. The formula for the total adjusted margin is the same formula as that for the total margin, but substituting P_a for P_p.

All of the measures discussed so far are essentially simplifications. The best theoretical measure of the margin on an FRN is the discounted margin, or discounted cash flow margin. This is the margin relative to LIBOR that is necessary to discount the cash flows from an FRN so that the sum of the present value of flows is equal to the gross price of the note. It is necessary to make some assumption about average LIBOR from the next coupon date to maturity, although the discounted margin is not very sensitive to the assumption made.

In principle it is necessary to know the number of days (allowing for weekends and holidays) between each coupon date over the whole of the life of the note in order to calculate the precise cash flows and discount factors that should be used in this formula. A more practical approach is to assume, for all coupon payments except the first, that the payments occur at equal intervals during 365.25 day years.

So the discounted margin (DM) is found by solving the following equation:

$$P_p + A = \frac{C_c}{1 + \left[\frac{(R_s + \text{DM})}{100} \times \frac{D_1}{360}\right]} + \frac{1}{1 + \left[\frac{(R_s + \text{DM})}{100} \times \frac{D_1}{360}\right]} \times \left[\sum_{t=1}^{n} \frac{(R_a + S)h}{1 + \left[\frac{(R_s + \text{DM})}{100} h\right]^t} + \frac{100}{1 + \left[\frac{(R_s + \text{DM})}{100} h\right]^n}\right]$$

where: $h = \dfrac{365.25}{360 \times f}$

f = number of coupon fixes per year

n = number of coupon periods to maturity.

These formulas need some adjustment in the case of a perpetual FRN (see below). The simple margin in this case is equal to the original margin over LIBOR fixed at the time of issue – the quoted margin – since the amortisation of the discount/premium of the note's price to par takes place over an infinite period. The simple margin is, therefore, not a useful way of valuing perpetual FRNs.

The discounted margin (DM) for perpetuals is given by a simplified version of the formula above because the formula is able to use the formula for the sum of an infinite geometric series. It is:

$$P + A = \frac{1}{1 + \left(\frac{D_1}{360} \times \frac{[R_s \times \text{DM}]}{100}\right)} \times \left[C_c \times \frac{100\,(R_a + S)}{R_a + \text{DM}}\right]$$

Appendix 4 Convertible and Warrant Calculations

Certain concepts are relevant in looking at convertible bonds. Table A4.1 sets them out by comparing two hypothetical convertibles.

Table A4.1 Comparative data for Company A and Company B convertibles

	A	*B*
Known data:		
Convertible coupon	10%	11%
Conversion ratio	25 shares	50 shares
Market price of convertible	$900	$1,300
Market price of equity	$28	$20
Dividend per share	$1.5	$1
Call price	$1,050	$1,080
Yield to maturity of comparable, non-convertible bonds	12%	12.5%
Derived data:		
Market conversion price[1]	$36	$26
Conversion premium per common share	$8	$6
Conversion premium ratio[2]	28.57%	30%
Convertible yield – convertible	11.11%	8.5%
Dividend yield – common	5.4	5%
Yield sacrifice on convertible[3]	0.89%	4%
Bond income differential[4]	$62.5	$60
Estimated floor price[5]	$833.33	$880
Break-even time[6]	3.2 years	5 years

1. The price at which the underlying shares can be acquired through the convertible, i.e. for company A, $900/25 = $36.
2. The conversion premium as a percentage of the share's market price – for A, $8/$28 = 28.57 per cent.
3. The yield given up by buying the convertible rather than a comparable non-convertible – for A, 12 − 11.11 = 0.89 per cent. These two items – conversion premium and yield give-up – are a tradeoff for the issuer and the investor. The lower the conversion premium, the lower the coupon the investor will usually be willing to accept and vice versa.
4. The extra income gained from the convertible rather than converting into the equity. A yields $100 in income; it would be convertible into 25 shares yielding $1.50 per share or $37.50, so the income differential is 100 − 37.50 = $62.50.
5. The price to which the convertible would have to fall so as to yield the same as a comparable non-convertible.
6. The time it takes for the purchase premium of common via the convertible to be paid off by the extra yield on the convertible. That is, breakeven time = conversion premium/ favourable bond income per share. For A, it is $8/($62.5/25) = 3.2.

Another way of looking at a convertible is to say that the value of a convertible bond constists of two parts, the value as a fixed-rate bond and the potential value as equity. The value as a fixed-rate bond can easily be found by comparing the coupon on a convertible with a yield on a similar straight. If the borrower must offer a yield of 10 per cent on a straight fixed-rate bond with a final maturity of ten years, and on a convertible the proposed coupon is 7 per cent, the bond value would be 81.6 per cent of the issue price (yield to redemption of 10 per cent). The minimum potential value as equity is the conversion value. This equals the number of shares that each bond converts into multiplied by the market price of the shares.

Analysis of the conversion premium and other data needs to be adjusted in the case of issues convertible across currencies. Take, for example, XYZ (UK) Ltd's 9 per cent convertible US dollar bond issued at 100 per cent with a fixed exchange rate of US\$2 = £1 and a share conversion price fixed at issue of £2.50. Assume that the current exchange rate is US\$1.50 = £1, the current bond price is 90 per cent and the current share prices is £2.25, the conversion premium is found from the formula:

$$P = \left(\frac{MV \times CP \times FR}{NV \times SP \times CR}\right) - 1 \times 100$$

where: P = premium (discount)
MV = current market value of bond in percentage terms
NV = issue value of bond in percentage terms
CP = conversion price fixed at time of issue
SP = current share price
FR = fixed exchange rate
CR = current exchange rate.

Applying this formula to our example we see that:

$$P = \left(\frac{90 \times 2.50 \times 2.00}{100 \times 2.25 \times 1.50} - 1\right) \times 100 = 33.33\%$$

WARRANTS

There are a number of calculations relevant to equity warrants. One is the equity content: the percentage value of the equity entitlement at the exercise price, expressed as a percentage of the face value of the bond. It is expressed as follows:

$$\text{Equity content} = \frac{\left(\begin{array}{l}\text{Number of shares warrant-}\\\text{holder is entitled to}\end{array}\right) \times \left(\begin{array}{l}\text{Exercise}\\\text{price}\end{array}\right)}{\text{Face value of bond}}$$

The capital fulcrum point is:

$$\left(\frac{\text{Exercise price}}{\text{Current share price} - \text{Warrant price}} - 1\right) \times 100$$

and it aims to measure how fast the share price must rise before investment in the warrant is more profitable than direct investment in the underlying shares. This ignores the dividend yield on the shares.

The gross fulcrum point allows for this:

Gross fulcrum point =

$$\left(\frac{\text{Exercise price}}{\text{Current share price} - \text{Warrant price } (1 + Y)^n} - 1\right) \times 100$$

where: Y = current dividend yield expressed as a decimal
n = warrant exercise period.

The valuation of a warrant is a bit more complex in the international markets because of currency questions. But this in itself increases their trading attractions since they can provide a double play on equity and currency. Let's take a typical example.

Suppose we have a US dollar bond issued by Nippon Widget Corporation maturing on 15 March 1992, with a coupon of 2.875 per cent. With it, on issue, is a warrant, with a face amount of $5,000, expiring 3 March 1992, to buy 1,000 shares in Nippon Widget at ¥ 1,135 per share. Thus the exercise cost of the warrant is 1,000 × 1,135 = ¥1,135,000. The yen conversion rate for the warrants is fixed at the time of issue at US$1 = ¥ 167.75. Today's exchange rate is US$1 = ¥ 155 and today's share price is ¥ 1,620.

Clearly the dollar cost of exercising the warrants is ¥1,135,000/167.75 = US$6,766.02. The cost in yen of buying the shares directly in the market today would be 1,000 × 1,620 = ¥1,620,000, and the dollar equivalent at today's rate would be ¥1,620,000/155 = US$10,451.61.

Thus the instrinsic value of the warrant is the market cost of the shares less their cost via the warrant, or $10,451.61 – $6,766.02 = $3,685.59. Let us suppose that the price in the market for the warrant is quoted as 82, i.e. $4,100 per $5,000 nominal. Then the premium on the warrant is the purchase price less the intrinsic value, i.e. $4,100 = $3,685.59 = $414.41.

Is this premium worth paying? There are two ways of looking at this. The crude one is to take the premium paid and see what breakeven share price that implies. Then we decide whether we think the share price will get there or not. Alternatively, we can take a more scientific approach. A warrant is a type of option, and its theoretical price, or fair value, can be found according to options theory. (Although it bears repeating that no matter what its fair value is, the real value is what the other fellow will pay for it or sell it for.)

It is worth noting that the jargon in the warrants market can be confusing for those used to options market terms. The warrant market speaks of 'premium' where the options market speaks of 'time value'. The 'intrinsic value' of the options market is the warrant's 'parity'. The 'gearing' of the warrant is defined as the ratio of the share price to the warrant price. Many warrant traders use this to describe the percentage impact on the warrant of a given change in the share price. The more accurate measure is the options market's delta (change in option premium per $1 change in stocks price).

Appendix 5
Swap Calculations

In this appendix we lay out some detailed examples of swap calculations. They are: (a) a currency swap entailing the exchange of bond obligations – the IBM/World Bank swap of 1981 (although the exact details were never published, the material here draws on an article published by a World Bank official); (b) an issue-driven interest rate swap; (c) an asset swap on a low-coupon ex-warrant Japanese bond.

IBM/WORLD BANK

In 1981 IBM and the World Bank entered into a currency swap. The World Bank, which had issued comparatively little US dollar paper, could raise funds at an attractive rate in the US market. It wanted Swiss francs and Deutschmarks, but had issued a lot of bonds in those markets. IBM wanted to crystallise its foreign exchange gains on some existing Swiss franc and Deutschmark bonds outstanding. The solution benefitting both was for the World Bank to issue a US dollar bond and swap the proceeds with IBM. Details of the transaction have never been published in full; the following outline draws on D. R. Bock's description (*Swap Finance*, B. Antl (ed.), Euromoney Publications, London, 1986, pp. 218–23).

The bond issue was launched on 11 August 1981, settling 25 August, which became the settlement date for the swap. The first annual exchange under the swap, however, was to be on 30 March, the next coupon date on IBM's bonds, i.e. 215 days (rather than 360 days) from the start date.

The first step was to calculate the value of the Swiss franc and Deutschmark flows which were (say) at 8 per cent and 11 per cent per annum respectively. The initial 215-day period meant that the discount factors were 215/360 = 0.597222, 1.597222, 2.597222, etc. Applying the Swiss franc rate of 8 per cent then, the discount factors were $1/(1.08)^{0.597222} = 0.95507746$, $1/(1.08)^{1.597222} = 0.88433099$, etc., as in Table A5.1.

The final terms of the swap were agreed on 11 August, two weeks before the settlement date. So the World Bank bought the Swiss franc and Deutschmark NPV amounts worked out above, using two-week forward foreign exchange contracts. Supposing that these contracts were at Swfr2.18 and DM2.56 per US$, the dollar amounts needed by the World Bank were $87,783,247 to buy the Swiss francs and $117,701,753 for the Deutschmarks, totalling $205,485,000.

Table A5.1

Exchange date	*SFR flows*	*SFR discount factor*	*DMk flows*	*DMk discount factor*
3/30/82	12,375,000	0.95507746	30,000,000	0.93957644
3/30/83	12,375,000	0.88433099	30,000,000	0.84646526
3/30/84	12,375,000	0.81882499	30,000,000	0.76258132
3/30/85	12,375,000	0.75818128	30,000,000	0.68701020
3/30/86	12,375,000	0.70201045	330,000,000	0.61892811
NPV	Swfr191,367,478		DM301,315,273	

It was then necessary to work out the dollar amount of the bond to be issued. Supposing the issue to be at a coupon of 16 per cent with fees of 2.15 per cent (i.e. net proceeds of 97.85 per cent), the dollar amount of the bond issue had to be $205,485,000/0.9785 = $210,000,000. So the final results of the deal look like Table A5.2.

Table A5.2

Exchange date	*Swfr flows*	*DM flows*	*US$ flows*
30/3/82	12,375,000	30,000,000	20,066,667[1]
30/3/83	12,375,000	30,000,000	33,600,000
30/3/84	12,375,000	30,000,000	33,600,000
30/3/85	12,375,000	30,000,000	33,600,000
30/3/86	212,375,000	330,000,000	243,600,000
Discount rate	8%	11%	16.8%[2]
NPV	Swfr191,367,478	DM301,315,273	$205,485,000
FX forward	Swfr2.18/$	DM2.56/$	—
US$ NPV	$87,783,247	$117,701,753	$205,485,000

1. The first $ amount is less because of the partial first period on the bond issue.
2. The yield to maturity on a 16 per cent bond, due 30 March 1988 and bought on 25 August 1981.

ISSUE-DRIVEN SWAP

A $100,000,000 five-year bond is being launched on 1 August 1989, for payment on 15 August. It bears a 9.75 per cent coupon and is being launched at 101.25, with fees of 1.25 per cent. The five-year swap from 1 August 1989 to 15 August 1994 (i.e. a slightly long five-year swap) is at 10 per cent (annual 30/360) versus six-month LIBOR. The swap group is asked to price the swap after adjusting for the present value of the short first payment (see below).

The bond cash flows will be:

15/8/89	$100,000,000 (net of fees)
15/8/90	$9,750,000
15/8/91	$9,750,000
15/8/92	$9,750,000
15/8/93	$9,750,000
15/8/94	$109,750,000

Now the swap cash flows will be, allowing for a short first period ('stub period') of 1–15 August 1989, on which we assume the LIBOR is fixed at, say, 7.25 per cent:

15/8/89	$106,944.44
15/8/90	$10,000,000
15/8/91	$10,000,000
15/8/92	$10,000,000
15/8/93	$10,000,000
15/8/94	$10,000,000

We need to find the net present value of the stub payment of $106,944.44. This is going to be earned by the swap group; it can be spread back out over time to push up the swap rate paid to the issuer.

To find the present value of the stub payment we must use the correct discount rate. This is the swap rate, but it is decompounded to turn it into a rate applicable to a fourteen-day period. The decompounding formula is: (a) convert rate to an annual effective rate; (b) take down to a daily rate; (c) compound back up over the number of days involved; (d) deduct 1, then gross up by 365/number of days to a percentage rate. Here we have the swap rate already at an annual effective rate of 10 per cent. We take it down to a daily rate: $1.10^{(1/365)} = 1.0002611579$. There are fourteen days involved: $1.0002611579^{14} = 1.003662423266$. So we now deduct 1 and we have $0.003662423266 \times 365/14 = 9.54846$ per cent.

That is, a 10 per cent rate decompounded down to a fourteen-day period is equivalent to a 9.54846 per cent rate over that period. We now use this rate to discount our stub payment of $106,944.44 over fourteen days. This discounts back to $106,554.1, i.e. about 10.6 basis points on the principal amount. These 10.6 basis points need to be spread out over the five years, making due allowance for the time value of money.

This is done by using the PMT function on a HP12C or Lotus spreadsheet to answer the question, what annual payment over five years at 10 per cent extinguishes a loan of $106,544.1? The answer turns out to be $28,108.72 if we spread the lump sum over five years. (To be truly exact it should be over five years and fourteen days but the computations then would be rather tedious.) That is, the swap rate of 10 per cent can be adjusted up to 10.028 per cent say 10.03 per cent. It may seem a lot of work for three basis points, but swap traders have to fight for every point!

A LOW-COUPON EX-WARRANT JAPANESE BOND SWAPPED INTO FLOATING RATE

Today is 13 December 1988. We own a $100,000,000 five-year ex-warrant bond issue bearing a coupon of 2 per cent. The price of the bonds is 69.73 for a yield (AIBD basis) of 9.98 per cent. It is proposed to sell the bonds to X Bank who will buy the bonds at par and in exchange pay us the 2 per cent coupon annually. In exchange, we will pay twelve-month LIBOR (twelve-month LIBOR is used here for simplicity) + 30 basis points. To cover ourselves, we do a swap in the market at 9.55 per cent (AIBD basis, against twelve-month LIBOR). Our cash flows look like Table A5.3.

Table A5.3

	Pay to swap market	*Receive 2% coupon from X*	*Pay 30 bp spread to X*	*Net*
13/12/89	9,550,000	2,000,000	300,000	7,850,000
13/12/90	9,550,000	2,000,000	300,000	7,850,000
13/12/91	9,550,000	2,000,000	300,000	7,850,000
13/12/92	9,550,000	2,000,000	300,000	7,850,000
13/12/93	9,550,000	2,000,000	300,000	7,850,000

The key to valuing this deal is the net present value of the swap flows. If we revalue at 9.98 per cent, which is the yield on the low-coupon bonds, on the grounds that in theory we can invest funds at that rate, the NPV of the stream of swap losses is $29,772,886.53. On the bond side, we buy the bonds at 69.73 and sell them at par, for a cash gain of $30,270,000. The difference is $497,113.47 which when spread back out over five years at a rate of 9.98 per cent per annum is equivalent to an annual payment of $131,070 or roughly 13 basis points.

What has happened is that there was a profit margin of 43 basis points between the underlying yield on the bond and the swap rate paid to switch into a floating rate. That margin has been split into 30 basis points to X Bank and 13 basis points for ourselves.

The example is simplified by ignoring interim six-monthly payments which would normally occur as the market tends to use six-month LIBOR, and if any other interest rate is used for the net present value calculations, e.g. the swap rate, then the symmetry of the deal disappears.

Appendix 6
International Bond and Equity Portfolio Measurement Issues

CHOICE OF INDEX

Multi-currency investments pose a number of problems which do not really arise in a single-currency portfolio. Performance measurement in particular raises a number of issues. Of course, performance measurement even in a single currency is not completely straightforward. Some of the questions that arise are:

— which index best represents the universe of investment opportunities we are interested in?
— what risk is implied in that index? e.g. its duration (if a bond index) or its industry/geographical concentration if an equity index.
— is the index accurately measured?

Let us start with an investor confined to, say, US dollar bonds. In a way, the question is straightforward. One sets a bench-mark target, such as the Shearson Lehman Government and Corporate Bond Index (SLGC) plus a spread. Then one aims, by judicious selection of bonds and astute trading in and out of the market, to beat the bench-mark.

But as one looks more closely, questions arise. Generally, the purpose of the index is to measure the universe of opportunities. It is the range of assets open to the naive investor who makes no selection but buys everything. Yet in practice, this is not true. Every index ends by being a selection. Many securities, both in bond and equity markets, are illiquid and difficult to trade in or even to price. They are usually excluded. Practicalities of computing the index usually mean that the sample included is relatively small – especially for derivatives indices such as the DAX or the CAC40 which have only 30–40 shares included.

Then, too, a bond index will not normally be consistent over time. Swings in issuance change its mix. During 1978–83, for example, Treasury bonds rose from 39 per cent to 53 per cent of the SLGC Index; the average credit quality of the index changed. The durations of the components also change; from 1974–88 the overall duration fell from over 6.5 years to just over 4 years and back up to 5 years. More fundamentally, the concept of the duration of an index is dubious.

The reason that yield volatility is different for different maturities. Take a five-year bond with a duration of 3.9; the duration is about four times that of a one-year bond. So, *for a given change in yield*, the five-year bond will move about four times as much as the one-year bond. But five-year yields are usually less volatile than one-year yields – say 60 per cent as volatile. So in fact five-year bonds' relative volatility is 60% × 3.9 = 2.3 times that of the one-year bond. Simply calculating the duration of all the bonds in the index and averaging them does not give a good picture of the riskiness of the index – or of a portfolio.

Then again, by comparison with the SLGC, the Shearson Lehman Aggregate Bond Index, which includes mortgage-backed, is subject to even wider changes: during 1980–7, the mortgage sector grew from 5 per cent to 25 per cent of the index, but the maturities of the mortgage sector were very volatile, ranging from 18 years to five years. By the same token, the convexity of this index compared with the SLGC will be different.

There are even problems with perhaps the most widely-used index of all, the S&P 500. One would expect to be able to measure this accurately. Yet an article in the *Wall Street Journal* (26 January 1989) points out that the S&P 500 in 1988 rose by 16.34 per cent, 16.61 per cent or 16.94 per cent on a total return basis, depending on whether you use calculations from Salomon Brothers, Standard & Poor's, or Bankers Trust. Factors such as when dividends are considered to be received – on declaration date or payment date – can affect the numbers, and in this case the difficulty is that historically Standard & Poor's never saw it as part of its role to provide an authoritative calculation of total return on its index. Thus there was room for different interpretations to become acceptable.

Then, too, between 1984–89, 24 per cent of the S&P 500's component companies disappeared in the US wave of corporate restructurings. The effect has been to tilt the S&P to more aggressively managed, 'growth' stocks, with smaller market capitalisations. Of the new entrants to the index 58 per cent had market capitalisations of under $1.5 billion compared with 38 per cent for the index as a whole.

So the choice of index is fraught with complications. Yet it is crucial, not simply because one wants to measure oneself against the right bench-marks, but also because there is an inherent tendency for any investor, or investment manager, to 'home in' on the index. Unless one has a very strong conviction, there is a natural tendency to invest in securities that tend to replicate the index.

Next comes the actual measurement of performance against the index. This is a subject which has generated endless controversy. First, there are questions about the actual calculation of performance and the attribution of that performance to contributory factors – discussed below. Then the question of how far attention should be paid to risk as against return. How should risk be measured? Over what time horizon should performance be measured? Against what bench-mark should performance be compared – i.e. the appropriate market or set of markets, including any adjustment for tax, regulatory or other restrictions? Against what 'universe' of competing investment managers or investment funds should peer comparisons be made?

Each of these subjects merits a long treatise. But in most cases the relevant issues are highly specific to the investment fund in question. One fund may be greatly concerned about withholding taxes and indifferent to whether it holds futures. Another may have a good double taxation treaty network which reduces withholding tax worries but may have a tax authority (as in the UK) which has not yet come to the view that futures are part of a legitimate investment portfolio. Thus their choice of bench-mark and investment guidelines would be quite different.

GLOBAL BENCH-MARKS

Once one begins to invest internationally, the choice of bench-mark becomes even more confusing. A number of firms, such as Salomon Brothers, now produce global government bond indices: the attraction of this is that it represents the 'minimum-risk' index. On the other hand, there are some government bond markets, such as the Japanese, which are unattractive to foreign investors in many countries for withholding tax reasons. Then there are indices which are confined to the Eurobond market: should one confine oneself to them?

Then, too, there is the question of currency hedging: should one target a hedged index, or an unhedged one? Is it more appropriate – particularly for global equity management, where at the time of writing Japan accounts for over 60 per cent of the non-US index by market capitalisation – to take a weighted average of country indexes, weighted say by GDP, than the more normal market-weighted indexes?

For global equity investors, probably the most common bench-mark is the Morgan Stanley Capital International (MSCI) World Index. The MSCI indices aim for 60 per cent coverage of the total market capitalisation of each market. A representative sample of companies with the same industry profile as the universe is included in each index. Individual country indexes exclude investment fund companies and also locally-listed shares of companies not domiciled in that country.

Only those stocks with sufficient liquidity to be available to international investors are included. As far as possible, companies whose shareholdings are affected by cross-ownership by another company of more than 50 per cent, or other dominant shareholders, are avoided. MSCI estimate that in total cross-ownership occurs in less than 5 per cent of the MSCI indexes. One difficulty in adjusting for cross-holdings is in deciding which shareholdings are long-term, and thus likely to count as cross-holdings, and which are purely trading positions which could break up soon.

The indexes have been calculated weekly since 1970 and daily since 1972. The MSCI World Index includes securities (such as Swiss registered shares) which are not available to the international investor. To meet this problem the MSCI World Free Index has recently been introduced, including only those shares available to foreigners. Similarly, the Europe and Far East (EAFE) index is paralleled by an EAFE (Free) index.

For UK and some European investors a more common index is the FT-Actuaries-Goldman Sachs-Wood Mackenzie World Index, introduced in March 1987, though daily pricing of the indexes started on 31 December 1985. The FT-A index covers about 2,400 stocks in 36 countries, which account for around 70 per cent of world market capitalisation. The FT-A excludes shares which are not available to foreigners.

In any event, the choice of index will be affected by the investor's objective. For example, a global property and casualty insurance company whose estimated risks are approximately 60 per cent US$ and 40 per cent non-dollar will want to distribute its assets accordingly. A US pension fund, which is investing internationally purely to diversify, might be 90 per cent dollars, 10 per cent non-dollars. It will probably tend to choose a US index for its US portfolios, and a non-US index for its non-US portfolios. The global insurance company, investing on a global basis, might well prefer a single, global index.

TIME-WEIGHTED RATE OF RETURN

Accordingly this Appendix is simply concerned to lay out the basic calculations for performance measurement in an international context. We begin with the simplest case: a purely domestic portfolio. Appropriate measurement of performance here requires an accurate measure of return which is unaffected by cash flows into or out of the fund during the period being measured. This is provided by the time-weighted rate of return.

Consider ABC Corporation's equity, purchased for \$100. At the end of Year 1 it pays a dividend of 11 per cent – \$11 – and its value in the market has been bid up to \$128. Then the total return earned on that equity is the 11 per cent dividend plus the 28 per cent capital gain or 39 per cent. In Year 2, however, the company stumbles. No dividend is paid, and the share price falls to \$110. Total return is −14.1 per cent. Now let us consider a portfolio which has been invested only in ABC. There are three possible measures of return: (1) the internal rate of return of the cash flows; (2) the annual average rate of return; (3) the time-weighted rate of return.

The definition of the internal rate of return (IRR) on an investment which yields a series of cash flows is as follows. It is the rate which, if used to discount future cash flows back to today, makes their present value equal to the sum of the investment. The IRR generated by an investment of $100 on Day 1, a cash dividend of $11 at the end of Year 1, and realisation of the investment for $110 at the end of Year 2, is 10.52 per cent per annum. But the key assumption made in the IRR calculation is that intervening cash flows (e.g. the dividend at the end of Year 1) can be reinvested at the IRR. In our example this is not true. So the IRR's usefulness is limited.

To drive the point home, take the example of two investment management firms, X and Y. We plan to give $10,000,000 to each firm to invest on our behalf. But because of cash flow constraints, we can only invest $15,000,000 today. So we give $10,000,000 to X and $5,000,00 to Y; we give Y another $5,000,000 at the end of the year. Both firms follow an identical investment policy. They invest all assets (including dividends received) in ABC Corp.'s shares.

So X buys 100,000 $100 shares of ABC stock today, and the $1,100,000 received at the end of the year is invested in 8,594 (say) more shares at $128. At the end of Year 2 we have a portfolio of 108,594 shares at $110 each, worth $11,945,340. We took no cash income – since we reinvested the dividend – from the portfolio, so the IRR stream consists of an investment of $10,000,000 and a return of $11,945,340 in two years: the IRR of that stream is 9.29 per cent.

Now consider the portfolio in the hands of Y. They invest $5,000,000 in 50,000 shares and receive a dividend of $550,000 which is invested in (say) 4,297 shares at $128. They also invest the $5,000,000 we give them at the end of Year 1 as their second tranche of funds, at $128, buying 39,062 shares. At the end of year 2 we have a portfolio of 93,359 shares worth $10,269,490. The IRR on an investment of $5,000,000 in Year 1, $5,000,000 at the start of Year 2 and a return of $10,269,490 is only 1.78 per cent.

Both X and Y followed identical policies. But because Y was only half invested in the good year, and full invested in the bad year, their portfolio shows an IRR of 1.78 per cent compared with 9.29 per cent for X – who did exactly the same thing but was given the money at a lucky time. Hence the IRR is not a very good measure of performance.

The annual average rate of return or arithmetic average is also unsuitable. In our case we have a total return of 39 per cent in Year 1 and −14 per cent in Year 2; thus the average will be 12.5 per cent (39% + [−14%])/2. But in practice this is simply an arithmetical concept: it has nothing to do with investment return. Take a simplified example: suppose no dividends are paid by ABC in either year. The stock price starts at $100, as before. Suppose now its price falls to $50 at the end of Year 1 and then doubles back to $100 in Year 2. We started with $100, and we end with $100, and we got no dividends. Therefore in real cash terms, our investment earned nothing over two years. But the measured return was −50 per cent and +100 per cent for an annual average of 25 per cent. Hence the meaninglessness of the arithmetic average rate of return (ARR).

The geometric, or time-weighted rate of return (TWRR) provides the only satisfactory answer to the deficiencies of the IRR and ARR. Effectively the TWRR takes the percentage return in each period and compounds them. The formula involved is:

$$\text{TWRR} = [(1+r1)\ (1+r2)\ \ldots\ (1+rN]^{1/N}$$

where $r1, r2 \ldots rN$ are the returns for each of N periods. In words: take the return for period 1, expressed as a decimal (e.g. 0.075 for 7.5 per cent), add 1 to it, multiply by $1+r2$ etc. The result of all that multiplication will be the worth of 1 unit invested during the N periods. To express that as an annual (or more exactly a periodic) rate, we take the Nth root.

In the simplified example just quoted, there was a return of −50 per cent and +100 per cent: expressing these as decimal factors, the time-weighted return would be $[(1 - .5)\ (1 + 1.0)]^{\frac{1}{2}} - 10$. Or, to go back to our original example of ABC, we had a return in Year 1 of 39 per cent; in Year 2 of −14 per cent. Thus $100 would grow to $139 at the end of Year 1; but that $139 would shrink to $119.5 at the end of Year 2: a return of 19.5 per cent over the two years. To convert this to an annual rate we raise 1.195 to the power of 1/2 (i.e. in this case the square root) to get a TWRR of 9.32 per cent.

It might be helpful to summarise our various results so far in a short table:

Table A6.1

		Year 1	*Year 2*
ABC share price at start of year		100	128
Income at end of year		11	0
ABC share price at end of year		128	110
Total return in year		39%	−0.14%
Cash flow	*IRR*	*X*	*Y*
Year 0	−10,000,000	−10,000,000	− 5,000,000
1	1,100,000		− 5,000,000
2	11,000,000	11,945,340	10,269,490
IRR	10.52%	9.29%	1.78%
TWR	9.29%		
ARR	12.50%		

Summarising, this table shows that given our assumptions for ABC (initial stock price $100, dividend of $11 paid in Year 1, stock price rising to $128 and then falling to $110 with no dividend paid in year 2) a portfolio invested totally in ABC would show three different internal rates of return (10.52 per cent if we assume that the dividend income can be reinvested at the IRR; 9.29 per cent in the case of X where all the funds were invested for the good year; 1.78 per cent for Y who missed the good year but were fully invested for the bad year). The average rate of return would be 12.5 per cent, but that has only arithmetical meaning rather than practical. The time-weighted rate of return is 9.29 per cent.

The concept of TWRR is a fairly simple one – most of the elaboration above came from the need to show that TWRR is the most appropriate measure. All it says is, at the start of Year 1 we have \$1 invested; it grows by $r1$ per cent so at the end of the year we have $1+r1$; in the second year it grows by $r2$ per cent, so at the end of Year 2 we have $(1+r1)(1+r2)$, and so on. Then to get the annual growth rate we take the Nth root.

But the concept gets a little more messy when we look at a large number of cash flows in short periods. An example would be if we want to work out the return earned on an operating cash account where there are a large number of cash inflows and outflows. A useful formula in this context is

$$\text{TWRR} = \frac{\text{Net change in fund}}{\text{Opening balance + cash flows weighted by time invested}}$$

$$= \frac{\text{F} - \text{S} - \Sigma\text{Ci}}{\text{S} + \Sigma\text{PiCi}}$$

where F = final value of fund
S = starting value
Σ = sign meaning 'take the total of all items'
Ci = cash inflows and outflows
Pi = fraction of period from date of cash flow to end of period (for example, if the cash flow occurred on Day 1, Pi=1; if half-way through the period, Pi = 0.5 etc.)

Table A6.2 shows the fourth quarter flows across an operating account. We start with an opening balance of \$3,700,124; we receive various kinds of income, pay out operating expenses for the company, and receive the payment of an inter-company loan. At the close of the quarter (31 December being a Saturday in this year) the account – including accrued deposit interest due to be credited to the account – stands at \$32,000,413. What return has the account earned? Applying the formula quoted above we arrive at R=0.01926 or 1.93 per cent during the quarter – an annual rate of about 7.72 per cent.

ANALYSIS OF PERFORMANCE

We have now established how we should measure the return earned by a portfolio during any given period. The question naturally arises: how was this return earned? By brilliant stock picking, or because the market as a whole performed well? In a single-currency, single-sector market the

Table A6.2

Date *Inflow* *Time-weighted flow*		*Cash flow period*		*Fraction of cash*
		Ci	*Pi*	*PiCi*
Opening balance	3,700,124			
25 Oct dividend income		146,215	0.98507	144,033
31 Oct coupon income		720,941	0.89552	645,619
01 Nov coupon income		1,189,505	0.88060	1,043,952
15 Nov coupon income		1,000,000	0.67164	671,642
17 Nov operating expenses		(727,883)	0.64179	(467,149)
01 Dec coupon income		5,804,906	0.43284	2,512,571
05 Dec operating expenses		(1,000,266)	0.37313	(373,234)
20 Dec sale of rights		2,460	0.14925	367
30 Dec repayment of intercompany loan		21,016,680	0	0
30 Dec coupon income		151,731	0	0
Closing balance (including accrued)	32,000,413			
ΣCi (sum of cash flows)	28,148,588			
ΣiCi (total weighted flows)	4,177,801			
m (days in period)	67			
R	0.01926 = 1.926%			

answer can be quickly found. Suppose the whole stock market consists of industrial conglomerate companies – say 100 of them. We invest in say 20. Suppose our portfolio rose 7 per cent last year and the market rose 10 per cent, then we have underperformed because of poor stock selection, by 3 per cent.

Now suppose the market is expanded by adding 100 banking shares, whose aggregate market value equals conglomerates – that is, the market is half conglomerates and half banks in terms of market value. Suppose, as before, the conglomerates rose 10 per cent, but the banks fell by 10 per cent. Suppose as before our portfolio returns 7 per cent. If our portfolio were invested only in conglomerates, then our sector selection has been good but our stock selection has been poor. On balance, though, we did well to return 7 per cent when the market as a whole returned nil (+10 per cent industrials and −10 per cent banks). Conversely if we were all in bank shares our sector selection was terrible but our stock selection brilliant.

The issue becomes more complex when we include foreign markets since they bring in a currency effect. How do we handle all these factors? The following approach is similar to that adopted by most international performance measurement firms. *We can make two kinds of analysis: absolute, and relative. Absolute breaks down the portfolio's performance into its different sources. Relative analysis compares this absolute performance with some bench-mark* – be it an index, or a universe of competing investment managers.

To show how the approach works, let's imagine we live in a two-country world. The countries are Home and Abroad. The currency of Home is the

Home and the currency of Abroad is the Abroad. We live in Home, so our portfolio is measured and reported in the Home. Suppose each country has two companies: an industrial conglomerate and a bank, called Home Industries, Home Bank, Abroad Industries and Abroad Bank.

Suppose our 'benchmark' is an index which is divided equally between the four equities. That is, for 100 units of Home (H100) invested in the index, we have H25 in Home Industries, H25 in Abroad Industries, H25 in Home Bank and H25 in Abroad Bank. Suppose that we now set up a portfolio of our own which is in fact an index fund – its composition exactly matches that of the index.

To start with suppose we are measuring performance over a quarter, and that during this first quarter there is no change in the exchange rate between the Home and the Abroad. Suppose all four stocks appreciate by 4 per cent during the quarter. Then in each case H25 invested in the stock grows to H26 at the end of the quarter.

We are interested in the contribution made by each sector (or each stock in our simple example). The formula for this is Sector (or Stock) weighting/100 × Return on stock. In our case each contribution is the same: 25/100 × 4 = 1 per cent. Each stock has contributed 1 per cent of the 4 per cent total return on the portfolio. Since we started with H100, each stock has contributed H1 to the growth, and the total portfolio grows by H4 to H104.

This simple example has been laboured to make a particular point. It might be tempting to argue that to arrive at the total portfolio return in a given period the contributions of different areas should be multiplied together. Multiplicative comparisons are suitable for time-series work, as we shall see. But in this case, what would happen if we were to link the contributions together multiplicatively? The argument would be: each stock contributed 1 per cent performance. We would write $((1.01) \times (1.01) \times (1.01) \times (1.01)-1) \times 100 = 4.0604$ per cent. Instead of showing a 4 per cent return the multiplicative method shows 4.06 per cent.

The discrepancy increases with the number of sectors into which we divide the portfolio. If we have ten stocks each contributing 1 per cent, the additive method will show 10 per cent but the multiplicative method shows 10.46 per cent – nearly ½ per cent difference. Thus where we are putting together the components of a portfolio in a single period, the multiplicative method is unsatisfactory, although it is appropriate where we are measuring relative performance, as we shall see below. *In any one period, returns are added together.*

The next step is to relax the assumption that our portfolio is the same as the index. For the next quarter, let's go hog-wild and dump all our Bank stocks – Home and Abroad. But to our horror, we find that at the end of the quarter the prospects of emerging recession have depressed industrial sector stocks which fell 5 per cent and boosted banking stocks by 5 per cent. Still there has been no change in the exchange rate. What is our portfolio return, and how does it compare to the index? If we had stayed with the bench-mark index, our results would have looked like this:

Table A6.3

	Weight %	*Return* %	*Contribution* %
Home Industries	25	−5	−1.25
Home Bank	25	5	1.25
Abroad Industries	25	−5	−1.25
Abroad Bank	25	5	1.25
Total return			0

Our portfolio would have been weighted 25 per cent in each stock, with negative and positive contributions offsetting each other for an overall return of nil. But our theory of an industrial revival led us to this:

Table A6.4

	Weight %	*Return* %	*Contribution* %
Home Industries	50	−5	−2.50
Home Bank	0	5	0
Abroad Industries	50	−5	−2.50
Abroad Bank	0	5	0
Total return			−5

Clearly we underperformed the index. It is at this point, in comparing with the index and more especially in making these comparisons over periods of time, that the multiplicative method becomes appropriate. For here we have a situation in which our portfolio shrank from 100 to 95, while the index remained constant. Now suppose in the next period that at last our industrial theory comes sensationally right: the banks fall back 5 per cent but industrial stocks rise 20 per cent. What happens to our portfolio and the bench-mark?

Our two stars each contributed 10 per cent return to our portfolio for a total return of 20 per cent (note that the multiplicative method would have shown a return of 21 per cent). By comparison they only contributed 5 per cent apiece to the bench-mark, which was dragged down by the banks, for a total return of 6.875 per cent. (Note that the different relative performance of the stocks in the previous period has altered their weights in the index.)

By how much did we outperform? The temptation is to reply 20−6.875

Table A6.5

	Currency change	Weight in %	Return % (local)	Return % in Home	Contribution in %
Portfolio					
Home Industries		50	20	20	10
Home Bank		0	− 5	− 5	0
Abroad Industries	0	50	20	20	10
Abroad Bank	0	0	− 5	− 5	0
Total return (additive)					20
Total return (multiplicative)					21
Bench-mark					
Home Industries		23.75	20	20	4.75
Home Bank		26.25	− 5	− 5	−1.3125
Abroad Industries	0	23.75	20	20	4.75
Abroad Bank	0	26.25	− 5	− 5	−1.3125
Total return (additive)					6.875
Relative return: portfolio/bench-mark					12.2807

= 13.125 per cent. Combined with a previous underperformance of 5 per cent, that would give a cumulative outperformance of 8.125 per cent. But in fact this is not so. The reason is that the portfolio sizes to which these percentages apply are different. In the first period, we started with H100 and lost 5 per cent, so our portfolio ended at H95. By contrast the index earned a nil return, starting at H100 and ending at H100. So our 20 per cent gain in the second period applies to a smaller portfolio than if we had held the index. At the end of the second period our portfolio has risen to 114 (a 20 per cent gain on 95), while the index has risen to 106.875 (a 6.875 per cent gain on 100). If we were measuring relative performance by the additive method, that would imply an outperformance of only 7.125 per cent (114−106.875), rather than 8.125 per cent. And obviously, over periods of time, as different stocks' performance drifts apart, this distortion will tend to increase.

It is for this reason that we must use multiplicative (or index) methods over time, and additive methods within a period. Within a period, the value of shares involved is constant. So the additive method is accurate. But over time they rise or fall. So the bases to which the percentage performance is applied will change. So we must express relative performance in index (multiplicative) terms.

That is, we measure percentage performance in each quarter as if we started with 100. At the end of the first quarter our portfolio was worth 95 while the index was worth 100: our relative performance was thus $(95/100-1)\times100 = -5$ per cent. In the second quarter, H100 invested by us grew to H120 against H106.875 invested in the index, so our outperformance is $(120/106.875-1)\times100 = 12.28$ per cent. Our cumulative performance over the two quarters is measured by chain multiplying them: $((1-5/100)\times(1+12.28/100)-1)\times100$ = 6.67 per cent. That can be confirmed by comparing the final cash values of the portfolio and the index (114 vs 106.875). The relative performance is $(114/106.875-1)\times100 = 6.67$ per cent.

IMPACT OF CURRENCY

So far we have assumed that there is no currency change. Now let us assume that in the third quarter Abroad's currency rises by 15 per cent against the Home. Suppose for simplicity that all stocks rise 10 per cent in local currency (i.e. before converting back into Home terms). What happens?

Here we have to consider a new factor: the impact of currency. This impact is multiplicative: because we are changing quantities. One way of looking at this is to draw the combined returns in a diagram, Figure A6.1. Suppose we invest \$100 in a German equity. Suppose at that time the exchange rate is such that it costs \$0.50 to buy one Deutschmark (i.e. DM2.00 per US\$). Thus the German share price is DM200 per share. During the quarter, the equity rises 10 per cent to DM220, and the Deutschmark rises 5 per cent to \$0.525 (i.e. it now costs more dollars to buy Deutschmarks). Our investment is now worth DM220 = \$220 × 0.525 = \$115.50. We have gained more than 15 per cent: the 0.50 per cent difference represents the foreign exchange gain of 5 per cent on the equity gain of 10 per cent. The diagram shows this visually. The horizontal axis is

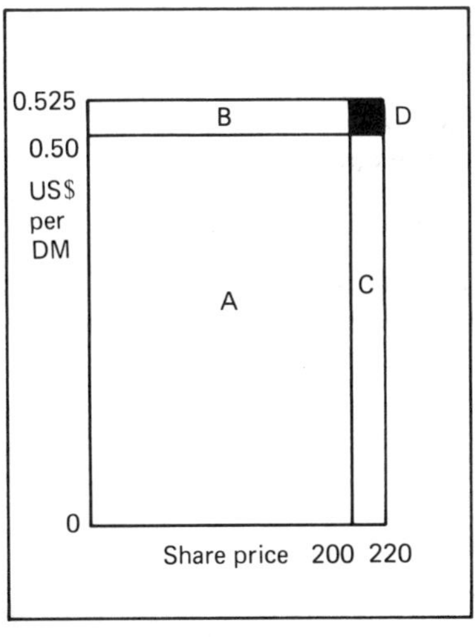

FIGURE A6.1

Table A6.6

	Currency change	Weight in %	Return % (local)	Return % in Home	Contribution in %
Portfolio					
Home Industries		50	10	10	5
Home Bank		0	10	10	0
Abroad Industries	15	50	10	26.5	13.25
Abroad Bank	15	0	10	26.5	0
Total return					18.25
Bench-mark					
Home Industries		26.667	10	10	2.667
Home Bank		23.333	10	10	2.333
Abroad Industries	15	26.667	10	26.5	7.067
Abroad Bank	15	23.333	10	26.5	6.183
Total return					18.25
Relative return: portfolio/bench-mark					0

the local equity price. The vertical axis is the exchange rate. Area A in the diagram is the initial dollar value of the holding ($100 = DM200 × 0.5). Area B is the pure currency gain: by construction, its area is 5 per cent of A's. The shaded area, D, is the currency gain on the equity gain.

Clearly, if we were simply to add the currency in our performance measurement, we would be leaving out Area D. Hence the reason currency is a multiplicative factor. Bearing this in mind, then, what has happened to our performance against the index?

In our case we now have our portfolio 50 per cent in Home Industries, which appreciates by 10 per cent, and 50 per cent in Abroad Industries, which also appreciates 10 per cent in Abroad terms but gives a further 15 per cent in the appreciation of the Abroad against the Home. Allowing for the exchange gain on the equity gain, our total return on Abroad Industries is 26.5 per cent and the portfolio as a whole returns 18.25 per cent. In the case of the index the assets are of course more evenly spread, though the pattern of past events is showing up in the drifting of the weights. Note how the weights have changed again, with the Industries stocks appreciating 20 per cent from the 23.75 weights and the Banks weakening 5 per cent from the 26.25 level. Both sets of weights are divided by 1.06875 to normalise the total weights back to 100. That is:

$$\text{New weight} = \text{Old Weight} \times \frac{(1+\%\ \text{rise in stock})}{(1+\%\ \text{rise in index})}$$

$$\text{E.g. } 23.75 \times \frac{1.20}{1.06875}$$

The differing impact of local currency return and foreign exchange gains means that each stock now makes a different contribution to the index, with Abroad Industries giving 7.07 per cent of the index's total 18.25 per cent performance. Of the two stocks benefiting from foreign exchange gains it is the more heavily weighted. The weakest performance comes from Home Bank – lowly weighted and adding no foreign exchange gain. As it happens, both the portfolio and the index are 50 per cent exposed to changes in the Abroad, and since all stocks returned 10 per cent in local currency, both the portfolio and the index appreciate by 18.25 per cent in this quarter. Hence our relative outperformance is nil.

ATTRIBUTION ANALYSIS

Having analysed the contributions of individual stocks to total portfolio performance we can now begin attribution analysis proper, which aims to explain how much of the portfolio's return has been achieved from currency exposure, local market movements and investment selection. The method for this is as follows:

Currency contribution = category weight × currency change
Market contribution = category weight × bench-mark TWRR in local currency terms
Selection contribution = category weight × portfolio TWRR relative to bench-mark TWRR

For example, 50 per cent of our portfolio is exposed to a 15 per cent currency change; so the currency contribution is 0.50 × 15 = 7.5. Likewise, the market contribution for our portfolio is 0.5 × 10% + 0.50 × 10% –

Table A6.7

	Currency	*Market*	*Selection*	*Weighted contribution*
Contributions: portfolio				
Home Industries	0	5.00	0.00	5.00
Home Bank	0	0.00	0.00	0.00
Abroad Industries	7.5	5.00	0.00	12.87
Abroad Bank	0	0.00	0.00	0.00
Total return (add.)	7.5	10	0	
Total return (multi.)				18.25
Contributions: benchmark				
Home Industries	0	2.67	0.00	2.7
Home Bank	0	2.33	0.00	2.33
Abroad Industries	4	2.67	0.00	6.77
Abroad Bank	3.5	2.33	0.00	5.92
Total return (add.)	7.5	10	0	
Total return (multi.)				18.25

10% (that is, all of our portfolio was invested in stocks which rose in line with the 10 per cent rise in bench-mark stocks). Similarly, because all of our holdings moved exactly in line with the bench-mark, the contribution of our stock selections is nil.

Notice that the returns are added within categories. To combine them we multiply. Thus we have, for the index, a currency contribution of 7.5 per cent and a market contribution of 10 per cent. To find the combined index return we would write $((1.075 \times 1.10)-1) \times 100 = 18.25$. It has been argued that the weighted contributions can be linked by chain multiplication to produce the index but in this case this would yield $((1.0267 \times 1.0233 \times 1.0677 \times 1.0592)-1) \times 100 = 18.816$ which is significantly out. (In fact this approach would entail multiplying factors which have already been multiplied in calculating the weighted contribution, hence the distortion. See the Mathematical Supplement to this Appendix.)

Finally, we can compare the attribution analysis for our portfolio to that of the bench-mark. Just as in analysing relative performance, the index or multiplicative approach is appropriate for this process. By using the index approach we can compare performance over a series of periods on a consistent basis, which we could not otherwise do. Since our interest is in comparisons with the bench-mark, the relative contributions will in each case be calculated against the bench-mark. Thus for any given currency the contribution of the currency is measured not in terms of its change against the base currency but in terms of its change relative to the total contribution of currency movements to the bench-mark. The market contribution is measured relative to the total market contribution to the bench-mark, and so on. Thus we can write:

Relative currency contribution	=	difference in category weights	×	currency change of local currency vs base currency, relative to total benchmark currency contribution
Relative market contribution	=	difference in category weights	×	benchmark return in local currency, relative to total benchmark market contribution
Relative selection	=	category weight	×	portfolio TWRR relative to benchmark TWRR

For example, suppose the Abroad rose by 15% against the Home. Suppose the effect of all currency changes on the benchmark was 7.5%. Thus the relative currency contribution of Abroad Industries would be (Portfolio weight in Abroad Industries − benchmark weight in Abroad Industries) × (change of Abroad vs. Home relative to total benchmark currency contribution) i.e. in the case of our example (Tables A6.6 and A6.7):

$$\frac{(50 - 26.67)}{100} \times \left(\frac{1.15}{1.075} - 1\right) \times 100 = 1.63\%.$$

Applying this produces the following:

Table A6.8

	Currency	*Market*	*Selection*	*Weighted contribution*
Home Industries	−1.63	0.00	0.00	−1.63
Home Bank	1.63	0.00	0.00	1.63
Abroad Industries	1.63	0.00	0.00	1.63
Abroad Bank	−1.63	0.00	0.00	−1.63
Total return (add.)	0	0	0	
Total return (multi.)				0.00

From this we can see that by being exposed to Home Industries, which is denominated in a weak currency (the Home) we gave up 1.63 per cent of performance relative to the bench-mark, while by not holding Home Bank we gained similarly. Since all stocks rose by the same amount as the bench-mark, there are no market or selection effects to consider.

Our next step is to consider these effects and at this point it may be useful to introduce a further level of analysis used in some cases: *we will split the market effect into two components, the country effect and the sector effect*. That is, if the Hong Kong market rises 15 per cent and we have 10 per cent of our portfolio in Hong Kong there will be a total Hong Kong contribution in our portfolio of 1.5 per cent. But our portfolio will be invested in various stocks in Hong Kong which can be classified into sectors – industrials, banking, and so on. We might want to measure the contribution made by our selection of sectors in which to invest as well as the contribution made by stock selection within the sector. For our purposes we will assume our investments are in Industrials and Banking stocks. In principle one could subdivide further into finer classifications, e.g. industrials could be subdivided into textiles, chemicals, paper and so on, and they in turn could be subdivided. The method outlined here could be used to do this but there soon comes a point where the wood can no longer be seen for the trees: too fine a classification would create a mass of individually unimportant numbers.

The method to be used is as follows. We have at the moment the Weighted Contribution of each stock which is produced by multiplying Currency × Market × Selection contributions – e.g. for Abroad Industries the currency contribution was 7.5 per cent, the market contributed 5 per cent, and stock selection 0 per cent so we have Weighted contribution = ([1.075 × 1.05 × 1.00] −) × 100 = 12.875%. We want to subdivide the market contribution into Country and Sector. *We start by working out the increase in the country index in local terms. Then we define the Sector contribution as the percentage outperformance or underperformance of that sector relative to the Country increase.*

Table A6.9

	Currency change	*Weight in %*	*Return % (local)*	*Return % in Home*	*Contribution in %*
Portfolio					
Home Industries	0	8	11	11	0.88
Home Light Industry	0	2	6	6	0.12
Home Bank	0	7	− 7	− 7	− 0.49
Home Savings Bank	0	9	5	5	0.45
Abroad Industries	10	12	9	19.9	2.39
Abroad Light Industry	10	11	9	19.9	2.19
Abroad Bank	10	10	5	15.5	1.55
Abroad Savings Bank	10	9	5	15.5	1.40
Foreign Industries	7	8	5	12.35	0.99
Foreign Light Industry	7	7	5	12.35	0.86
Foreign Bank	7	8	5	12.35	0.99
Foreign Savings Bank	7	9	5	12.35	1.11
Total return (additive)		100			12.43

Suppose the Hong Kong market rises 15 per cent. Suppose the Banks sector rises only 7 per cent. Then the Sector contribution would be defined as $(1.07/1.15 - 1) \times 100 = -6.96\%$. That is, the Hong Kong banking sector underperformed the Hong Kong market by 6.96 per cent. Within the banking sector, we would then look at the contribution of our stock selection as the residual outperformance of the portfolio's stocks relative to the sector.

To give a concrete illustration, let us consider a new world, which has in it three countries (Home, Abroad and Foreign – so that we can compare the effect of two currency changes) and two sectors, Industrial and Banking, each of which has two stocks: we add in a Light Industries and a Savings Bank for each country.

Here we have a portfolio with 8 per cent in Home Industries, which returns 11 per cent and thus contributes 0.88 per cent; we have 11 per cent of the portfolio in Abroad Light Industries which returns 9 per cent but also benefits from a 10 per cent rise in the Abroad and so returns 19.9 per cent in Home terms and contributes 2.39 per cent to the portfolio, while we have 9 per cent of the portfolio in Foreign Savings Bank which rises by 5 per cent but benefits from a 7 per cent rise in the Foreign to produce 12.35 per cent in Home terms and a contribution of 1.11 per cent.

Now we have the bench-mark (Table A6.10). Note that the total weight of the bench-mark by country is the same for each country (we have 26 per cent in Home, so does the bench-mark; likewise 42 per cent in Abroad and 32 per cent in Foreign) but only our Foreign holdings are exactly in line with the bench-mark. All Foreign returns are identical; in Abroad, individual stocks within a given industry all return the same. It is only in Home that all the individual stock returns are different. Thus our Foreign returns will show a pure currency and country effect, with no sector or stock

Table A6.10

	Currency change	Weight in %	Return % (local)	Return % in Home	Contribution in %
Bench-mark					
Home Industries	0	5	11	11	0.55
Home Light Industry	0	6	6	6	0.36
Home Bank	0	7	− 7	− 7	− 0.49
Home Savings Bank	0	8	5	5	0.40
Abroad Industries	10	9	9	19.9	1.79
Abroad Light Industry	10	10	9	19.9	1.99
Abroad Bank	10	11	5	15.5	1.71
Abroad Savings Bank	10	12	5	15.5	1.86
Foreign Industries	7	8	5	12.35	0.99
Foreign Light Industry	7	7	5	12.35	0.86
Foreign Bank	7	8	5	12.35	0.99
Foreign Savings Bank	7	9	5	12.35	1.11
Total return (additive)		100			12.12
Relative return portfolio/bench-mark					0.28

selection impact. Our Abroad returns will also show sector effects, but no stock selection effects since all Abroad stock returns are identical within sectors.

We start by breaking out the country and sector returns in local currency. Each sector is a weighted average (weighted by bench-mark weights) of the stock returns in that sector, so we have:

	Home		*Abroad*		*Foreign*	
	Industry	*Banks*	*Industry*	*Banks*	*Industry*	*Banks*
Sector return	8.27	−0.60	9	5	5	5

Clearly, in Home and Abroad, industry was the place to be. As mentioned, elsewhere all sectors returned the same because all stocks returned the same. From the weighted average of each country's sector returns we arrive at the country returns:

	Home	*Abroad*	*Foreign*
Country return	3.15	6.81	5

Now we can proceed to the attribution analysis, beginning with the absolute contributions of the portfolio.

Let's look at Home Industries. There is no currency effect because Home is the base currency. The Home market returned 3.15 per cent; we have 8 per cent of our portfolio in Home Industries, so the country contribution is 8/100 × 3.15% = 0.25%. The Industry sector of Home

Table A6.11

Portfolio attribution	*Contributions to portfolio by:*				
	Currency	*Country*	*Sector*	*Stock selection*	*Weighted contribution*
Home Industries	0	0.25	0.40	0.20	0.85
Home Light Industry	0	0.06	0.10	−0.04	0.12
Home Bank	0	0.22	−0.25	−0.45	−0.49
Home Savings Bank	0	0.28	−0.33	0.51	0.46
Abroad Industries	1.2	0.82	0.25	0.00	2.28
Abroad Light Industry	1.1	0.75	0.23	0.00	2.09
Abroad Bank	1	0.68	−0.17	0.00	1.52
Abroad Savings Bank	0.9	0.61	−0.15	0.00	1.36
Foreign Industries	0.56	0.40	0.00	0.00	0.96
Foreign Light Industry	0.49	0.35	0.00	0.00	0.84
Foreign Bank	0.56	0.40	0.00	0.00	0.96
Foreign Savings Bank	0.63	0.45	0.00	0.00	1.08
Total return	6.44	5.28	0.06	0.22	12.37

returned 8.27 per cent; it outperformed the country return by $(1.0827/1.0315 - 1) \times 100 = 4.96\%$ so the weighted sector contribution is $4.96 \times 8/100 = 0.40\%$. Home Industries' stock outperformed its sector, by $(1.11/1.0827 - 1) \times 100 = 2.52\%$ so the weighted selection contribution is $2.52 \times 8/100 = 0.20\%$. The combined weighted contribution is got by multiplying all the factors:

$$([(1 + 0/100) \times (1 + 0.25/100) \times (1 + 0.40/100) \times (1 + 0.20/100)] - 1) \times 100$$
$$= [(1 \times 1.0025 \times 1.004 \times 1.002) - 1] \times 100 = 0.85\%.$$

For comparison, let's look at Abroad Bank. We have 10 per cent of our portfolio in the stock; the currency rose by 10 per cent, so there is a currency contribution of 1 per cent. The country rose by 6.81 per cent so its contribution is $6.81 \times 10/100 = 0.68\%$. The industry, however, underperformed the country index, rising by only 5 per cent, so its weighted contribution is negative (if you invested in Abroad you wanted to be in industrials not banks) to the tune of $[(1.05/1.0681 - 1) \times 100 \times 10/100 = -0.17\%$.

For the bench-mark there is a similar process, except that by definition all stock weightings are at the bench-mark weightings and so there is no stock selection effect. (Table A6.12)

The next step is again to do a relative attribution analysis. For example, compared with the index, we were 3 per cent overweight in Abroad Industries (we held 12 per cent of our portfolio in it as against the index's 9 per cent). The Abroad currency was stronger (+10 per cent) than the total currency contribution to the bench-mark of 6.44 per cent and so there was a positive relative currency effect of 0.10 per cent. The Abroad stock

Table A6.12

Bench-mark attribution	*Currency*	*Contributions to portfolio by:* *Country*	*Sector*	*Stock selection*	*Weighted contribution*
Home Industries	0	0.16	0.25	0.00	0.41
Home Light Industry	0	0.19	−0.21	0.00	− 0.02
Home Bank	0	0.22	−0.25	0.00	− 0.03
Home Savings Bank	0	0.25	−0.29	0.00	− 0.04
Abroad Industries	0.9	0.61	0.18	0.00	1.71
Abroad Light Industry	1	0.68	0.21	0.00	1.90
Abroad Bank	1.1	0.75	−0.19	0.00	1.67
Abroad Savings Bank	1.2	0.82	−0.20	0.00	1.82
Foreign Industries	0.56	0.40	0.00	0.00	0.96
Foreign Light Industry	0.49	0.35	0.00	0.00	0.84
Foreign Bank	0.56	0.40	0.00	0.00	0.96
Foreign Savings Bank	0.63	0.45	0.00	0.00	1.08
Total return	6.44	5.28	−0.50	0	11.50

market rose by 6.81 per cent, again exceeding the country contribution to the bench-mark of 5.28 per cent, so there is a positive country contribution. The sector rose by 9 per cent, outperforming the total bench-mark return net of currency and country contributions, so there is a positive sector contribution. Because all stocks in the sector returned the same, it didn't matter which you bought, and so there is no stock selection contribution.

Notice that the overall currency and country contributions net to zero because our country portfolio weightings match those of the index, while we have a positive overall contribution from sector and stock selection.

Table A6.13

Relative attribution	*Currency*	*Contributions to portfolio by:* *Country*	*Sector*	*Stock selection*	*Weighted contribution*
Home Industries	0.18	−0.06	0.18	0.20	0.14
Home Light Industry	0.24	0.08	−0.24	−0.04	0.04
Home Bank	0.00	0.00	0.00	−0.45	−0.45
Home Savings Bank	−0.06	−0.02	−0.03	0.51	0.40
Abroad Industries	0.10	0.04	0.32	0.00	0.46
Abroad Light Industry	0.03	0.01	0.11	0.00	0.15
Abroad Bank	−0.03	−0.01	−0.06	0.00	−0.11
Abroad Savings Bank	−0.10	−0.04	−0.19	0.00	−0.34
Foreign Industries	0.00	0.00	0.00	0.00	0.00
Foreign Light Industry	0.00	0.00	0.00	0.00	0.00
Foreign Bank	0.00	0.00	0.00	0.00	0.00
Foreign Savings Bank	0.00	0.00	0.00	0.00	0.00
Total return (multi.)	0.00	0.00	0.08	0.22	0.29

FIXED INCOME PORTFOLIOS AND ASSET ALLOCATION

So far, it has been assumed that the portfolio is entirely in equities. The principles outlined here are equally applicable to fixed income portfolios, in the sense that it is possible to take the total return and break it up into components while comparing these with the bench-mark. Clearly, however, the individual components would normally be different. Since, in general, a bond is a bond is a bond, whether it be issued by a chemicals firm or a bank, the more important question is the degree of investor protection (i.e. the credit quality) and perhaps the bond's structure (for example a collateralised mortgage obligation or a zero coupon bond as against a straight industrial bond). Hence the analysis of fixed income portfolios would normally concentrate on breaking the portfolio down into, say, currency, interest rate, sector/credit quality and selection effects.

The operational mechanics of this process closely resemble the equity performance measurement process described above. The currency contribution is clearly handled in an identical manner. The interest rate effect can be found by measuring the 'pure' effect of interest rate changes in the form of the change in yield on a specified government bond or group of bonds during the period. (A technical difficulty with fixed-interest performance measurement as against equities is of course the effect of time: whereas equities are in principle eternal, bonds move closer to maturity with each period. Thus the interest rate calculation would have to be for a constant maturity.) This would be the equivalent of the equity country contribution. The sector/credit quality return would be found from the percentage out- or under-performance of individual sectors, as with equities, and the selection effect would be found as a residual, as before.

So far, we have implicitly assumed that all portfolios are either entirely equity or entirely fixed-income. Further complications arise when a portfolio can be invested in either type of asset: there is then an asset allocation or timing effect to be considered in addition to the other sources of return: how well timed were switches from one asset to another?

Within an equity portfolio, for example, investment managers may decide to hold cash. They may do so either by retaining the cash in local currency accounts – thus proceeds of German equity sales might be placed in a DM call account – or by holding a central pool of cash in the home currency, say in US dollars. In the former case, the asset allocation issue is one of how well timed moves into and out of the country's equity market are. In the latter case, there is the extra layer of currency timing to take into account: was the switch back into the central pool well timed?

There are several ways of handling the asset allocation/timing issue. One method, which has the merit of relative simplicity, is to treat the cash held in each country as if it were a holding of shares in a company which is not included in the equity bench-mark: Cash Ltd. We can then treat it just as we treated all the other stocks. Since holdings of cash are a positive decision not to hold the country index which is the bench-mark for that country, our performance measurement will consider Cash's return relative to the country bench-mark – just as we would for any other stock. The appropriate sector bench-mark will be the return by a suitable cash or fixed income index. Our actual return relative to these bench-marks will show the contribution earned by asset allocation/timing decisions.

Table A6.14

	Currency change	*Weight in %*	*Return % (local)*	*Return % in Home*	*Contribution in %*
Portfolio					
Home Industries	0	8	11	11	0.88
Home Light Industry	0	2	6	6	0.12
Home Bank	0	7	− 7	− 7	− 0.49
Home Savings Bank	0	0	5	5	0.00
Home cash	0	9	4	4	0.36
Abroad Industries	10	12	9	19.9	2.39
Abroad Light Industry	10	11	9	19.9	2.19
Abroad Bank	10	10	5	15.5	1.55
Abroad Savings Bank	10	9	5	15.5	1.40
Abroad cash	10	0	5	15.5	0.00
Foreign Industries	7	8	5	12.35	0.99
Foreign Light Industry	7	7	5	12.35	0.86
Foreign Bank	7	8	5	12.35	0.99
Foreign Savings Bank	7	9	5	12.35	1.11
Foreign cash	7	0	5	12.35	0.00
Total return (additive)		100			12.34

This is the situation that would have arisen in the last case if instead of leaving a 9 per cent weighting investment in Home Savings Bank we had decided we didn't like the look of the stock and had sold out, putting the proceeds in cash, which during the period earned a return of 4 per cent. By comparison, let us assume that the appropriate cash and fixed income index against which we choose to measure our cash's performance returned 5 per cent – we were not very successful at investing the cash. As a result our total return fell by 9 basis points. Our other country holdings remain fully invested in equities, though for completeness we have shown the base currency returns assumed. The performance of the bench-mark is of course unaffected, since the cash holdings have a zero weighting in this equity bench-mark index:

Table A6.15

	Currency change	Weight in %	Return % (local)	Return % in Home	Contribution in %
Bench-mark					
Home Industries	0	5	11	11	0.55
Home Light Industry	0	6	6	6	0.36
Home Bank	0	7	− 7	− 7	− 0.49
Home Savings Bank	0	8	5	5	0.40
Home cash	0	0	5	5	0.00
Abroad Industries	10	9	9	19.9	1.79
Abroad Light Industry	10	10	9	19.9	1.99
Abroad Bank	10	11	5	15.5	1.71
Abroad Savings Bank	10	12	5	15.5	1.86
Abroad cash	10	0	5	15.5	0.00
Foreign Industries	7	8	5	12.35	0.99
Foreign Light Industry	7	7	5	12.35	0.86
Foreign Bank	7	8	5	12.35	0.99
Foreign Savings Bank	7	9	5	12.35	1.11
Abroad cash	7	0	5	12.35	0.00
Total return (additive)		100			12.12
Relative return: total portfolio (inc. cash)/bench-mark					0.20

We still outperformed relative to the bench-mark, but not by as much. What did the switch into cash imply for the attribution analysis? We start by adding up the appropriate bench-mark returns for countries and sectors, including the new sector Cash in each country:

Bench-mark returns:	*Home 3.15%*	*Abroad 6.81%*	*Foreign 5%*
Industry	8.27	9	5
Banks	−0.60	5	5
Cash	5	0	0

We held 9 per cent of our portfolio in Home Cash, and if we had held that in the Home equity index it would have returned 3.15 per cent, so Cash's return includes a country contribution of $9/100 \times 3.15 = 0.28\%$. The Home Cash sector outperformed the Home market, and hence there is a sector selection contribution of 0.16 per cent. But because we did not manage our cash very well, there is a negative 'stock' selection effect of 0.09 per cent. All in all, the switch to cash produced a positive weighted contribution of 0.36 per cent.

The bench-mark attribution analysis is unaffected since the cash components do not figure in the bench-mark. The relative attribution reflects the fact that the Home currency effect was negative (a return of nil compared with the total currency contribution to the bench-mark of 6.44

Table A6.16

Portfolio attribution	*Contributions to portfolio by:*				
	Currency	*Country*	*Sector*	*Stock selection*	*Weighted contribution*
Home Industries	0	0.25	0.40	0.20	0.85
Home Light Industry	0	0.06	0.10	−0.04	0.12
Home Bank	0	0.22	−0.25	−0.45	− 0.49
Home Savings Bank	0	0.00	0.00	0.00	0.00
Home cash	0	0.28	0.16	−0.09	0.36
Abroad Industries	1.2	0.82	0.25	0.00	2.28
Abroad Light Industry	1.1	0.75	0.23	0.00	2.09
Abroad Bank	1	0.68	−0.17	0.00	1.52
Abroad Savings Bank	0.9	0.61	−0.15	0.00	1.36
Abroad cash	0	0.00	0.00	0.00	0.00
Foreign Industries	0.56	0.40	0.00	0.00	0.96
Foreign Light Industry	0.49	0.35	0.00	0.00	0.84
Foreign Bank	0.56	0.40	0.00	0.00	0.96
Foreign Savings Bank	0.63	0.45	0.00	0.00	1.08
Foreign cash	0	0.00	0.00	0.00	0.00
Total return	6.44	5.28	0.55	−0.38	12.25

per cent) as also was the country effect (a return of 3.15 per cent compared with the bench-mark return, net of currency, of [1.1212/1.0644 − 1] × 100 = 5.34%). The sector effect was positive, since the Cash sector at 4 per cent outperformed the country index at 3.15 per cent. Our poor cash management meant a negative selection effect of 0.09 per cent. Hence the relative attribution for Home Cash is −0.54 per cent from the currency effect, −0.19 per cent from the country effect, 0.25 per cent from the sector and −0.09 per cent from selection for a net contribution of −0.56 per cent.

If we had cash in several currencies and we wanted to analyse our cash management separately it would be possible to take a subtotal of the Stock Selection component; if we wanted to assess the role that cash as a whole played in the portfolio (i.e. our asset allocation decisions) one would take a subtotal of the weighted contributions column.

Much more could be written about the measurement of performance and attribution analysis: for example, much attention is paid by certain clients of investment managers to analysis of the manager's style (e.g. 'low-capitalisation' or 'earnings-momentum' or 'low P/E' or 'value-driven). The measurement of the manager's performance then would include an assessment of the extent to which he/she deviated from this announced style, and why. Such an assessment is often done by constructing a 'normal portfolio', usually agreed with the manager, of stocks that he might typically be expected to hold. The performance would then be measured against this normal portfolio, rather than a normal equity index bench-mark (or indeed fixed income bench-mark for bond managers). The above discussion would still be applicable but the bench-mark would now be the 'normal' portfolio.

Table A6.17

Relative attribution	*Contributions to portfolio by:* *Currency*	*Country*	*Sector*	*Stock selection*	*Weighted contribution*
Home Industries	−0.18	−0.06	0.18	0.20	0.14
Home Light Industry	0.24	0.08	−0.24	−0.04	0.04
Home Bank	0.00	0.00	0.00	−0.45	−0.45
Home Savings Bank	0.48	0.17	0.21	0.00	0.86
Home cash	−0.54	−0.19	0.25	−0.09	−0.56
Abroad Industries	0.10	0.04	0.32	0.00	0.46
Abroad Light Industry	0.03	0.01	0.11	0.00	0.15
Abroad Bank	−0.03	−0.01	−0.06	0.00	−0.11
Abroad Savings Bank	−0.10	−0.04	−0.19	0.00	−0.34
Abroad cash	0.00	0.00	0.00	0.00	0.00
Foreign Industries	0.00	0.00	0.00	0.00	0.00
Foreign Light Industry	0.00	0.00	0.00	0.00	0.00
Foreign Bank	0.00	0.00	0.00	0.00	0.00
Foreign Savings Bank	0.00	0.00	0.00	0.00	0.00
Foreign cash	0.00	0.00	0.00	0.00	0.00
Total return	0.00	0.00	0.57	−0.38	0.19

However, hopefully the above sketch of the main problems and issues will be of help: but it is incomplete in two important areas to which we now turn. These are the impact of derivatives and the all-important risk part of the risk-return equation.

IMPACT OF DERIVATIVES

So far we have confined ourselves to the analysis of portfolios holding only what might be called the 'classical' types of asset – equities and bonds or cash. Many investors now also use derivatives, either to improve returns or to reduce risks. What impact do these have on the performance measurement process? We begin with financial futures.

In one sense financial futures do not make a large difference to the performance measurement process, provided that they are not used to gear up the portfolio. That is, provided a, say $5 million position in Treasury bond futures is backed by a $5 million cash or cash-equivalent holding. In this case, the futures position is simply another asset which generates a combined return of the interest earnings on the cash or cash equivalent position plus a capital gain or loss on the futures position (allowing for interest earned, if any, on the initial or variation margin deposits). As such, bond or foreign exchange futures resemble cash positions in the bond or foreign exchange markets, except of course that their return will differ by the amount of basis (see Chapter 7 on futures).

The only complication that arises is in reporting the asset distribution of the portfolio: traditional software will report the cash holdings that back the futures position, but not the futures, since they are not in fact assets but are an off-balance-sheet position – a contingent asset or liability. Generally speaking the simplest approach here is to introduce a dummy contra account which shows the futures holding and allows the true asset distribution to be analysed.

One performance measurement firm (Frank Russell) for example recommend the following procedure:

(1) When a futures contract is opened, the relevant asset class should be booked a purchase amount equal to the equivalent physical value, or contract value, of the futures. This amount will be considerably in excess of the amount of deposit required to open the futures position, which is the only cash payment actually required. The asset class 'Liquidity' should correspondingly be reduced by the contract value, of which a small part represents the cash paid for the deposit and the balance represents a book entry transferring from 'Liquidity' to the asset class of the futures.

As an example, consider a long position in SPI futures newly opened at a price of 1512.0 in the month of January. The asset class is 'Australian equities', and the contract value is A$151,200 (A$100 times the index). For the month of January, the data form should report this event as:

Australian equities – Purchases	A$151,200
Liquidity – Sales	A$151,200

Note that the deposit amount of A$6,000 is not separately recorded on the data form (although it no doubt will be in the manager's accounting system).

(2) For futures contracts still open at the end of a month, including the initial month, the market value supplied should be the contract value at that time. The 'Liquidity' market value must be adjusted for the net transfer to futures.

To continue our previous example, if the futures price at the end of January had risen to 1518.50, then the market value of 'Australian equities' would include A$151,850 for this contract. The market value of 'Liquidity' will include the closing cash balance, and this must be reduced by A$151,200, being the contract value when opened. Note that there is no need to adjust this amount for the A$6,000 deposit which would have been paid when the contract was opened, the assumption here being that deposits are also classified as 'Liquidity'.

(3) Each month that the futures contract is open, even if only for part of the month, interest earnings on futures deposits and on the amount of 'Liquidity' transferred to the futures asset class must be calculated and transferred between asset classes. The amount of interest is most easily

calculated using the average cash rate for the month, although a more accurate calculation would separate futures deposits from other liquidity assets. Interest is calculated as the average cash rate multiplied by the number of days the contract was open multiplied by the contract value at the time of opening.

For our SPI example, if the contract was open for 20 calendar days and the average cash rate for the month was 15 per cent, the interest would be calculated as:

$15/100 \times 20/265 \times A\$151,200 = A\$1,242.74$

and reported as:

Australian equities – income	A$1,243
Liquidity – income	–A$1,243

(4) When the futures contract is closed out, the transfer to the futures asset class made under (1) above must be reserved, but at the close-out futures price (or delivery price, if the contract should go to delivery).

To complete our SPI example, if the contract is closed out during March at a price of 1480.30 (thus generating a loss) then the reporting should be:

Australian equities – Sale	A$148,030
Liquidity – Purchases	A$148,030

The net effect of reporting entries (1) through (4) above is that the profit (or in our example, the loss) on the futures contract, being the difference between the opening and closing futures price, is modified by the interest earned on deposits and on the cash transfer attributed to the contract. Simultaneously, the base for determining the rate of return will be the equivalent physical value, rather than just the deposit value of the contract.

Frank Russell: Australian Investment Fund Performance Asset Class Reporting Form Completion Instructions.

OPTIONS

Options positions, however, represent a quite different situation from futures. Here for the first time we have an asset class of a totally different kind. To see why, let us take a simple three-currency portfolio of cash. For simplicity we assume that the cash earns no interest – these holdings are managed simply for speculative gain or loss on the currency movement. Let's assume that we have invested $1 million in US$, in DM and Yen, at exchange rates of DM2.00 and ¥140. We have also bought put options on these currencies at those strike prices. (We assume that the purchase of the options is free of charge – we are not considering returns at this point. We also assume that the options are either over-the-counter options written to us by first-class banks of undoubted standing or else exchange-traded options on an Exchange whose clearing corporation's credit is undoubted.)

Tables A6.18 and A6.19 show the effects of a sharp weakening of the foreign currencies. At DM2.70 and ¥210 per dollar our portfolio's value has fallen to $2,407,407. However, if we have puts on the full amount of the currency holdings at the current strike the portfolio's value is unchanged. (See below for the implications.)

Table A6.18

DMk	2.7	2.6	2.5	2.4
Yen	210	200	190	180
US$	1	1	1	1
DM holdings	740,740.74	769,230.77	800,000.00	833,333.33
Yen holdings	666,666.67	700,000.00	736,842.11	777,777.78
US$ holdings	1,000,000	1,000,000	1,000,000	1,000,000
Total	2,407,407	2,469,231	2,536,842	2,611.111

Table A6.19

DMk	2.7	2.6	2.5	2.4
Yen	210	200	190	180
US$	1	1	1	1
DM holdings	1,000,000	1,000,000	1,000,000	1,000,000
Yen holdings	1,000,000	1,000,000	1,000,000	1,000,000
US$ holdings	1,000,000	1,000,000	1,000,000	1,000,000
Total	3,000,000	3,000,000	3,000,000	3,000,000

RISK

Our firm recently hired John Gunslinger, a recently-qualified MBA who after studying our portfolio recommends that 100 per cent of our funds be invested in Humungous Bets Ltd, a recently quoted Hong Kong registered casino operator. Rumours that Humungous is controlled by a syndicate formed by the Mafia, the Medellin drugs cartel and a Chinese Triad gang have failed to prevent a sparkling 70 per cent per quarter return on the stock over the last 12 months. Why should we not do this? Nothing in our performance measurement so far would militate against it. We need a measure of the risk of the portfolio.

There are various ways of looking at risk. The traditional Modern Portfolio Theory measure of risk is the standard deviation of returns from a stock or portfolio. The standard deviation of the portfolio will be lower than the individual standard deviations to the extent that the holdings are not perfectly correlated (see the discussion on efficient frontiers in Chapter 8 for the formulas involved) – the portfolio risk is reduced by diversification.

A refinement of this approach was introduced by the so-called Capital Asset Pricing Model which segments the standard deviation into two parts: 'systematic' and 'unsystematic' risk. Systematic risk is, as its name implies, risk affecting the system as a whole – a good example might be a political revolution, which would affect all the securities of a particular country. Unsystematic risk is that part of total risk which is unique to a firm or industry. As such, it can be 'diversified away' – while systematic risk cannot.

An equity's sensitivity to systematic risk is measured by its 'beta'. Beta is, in technical terms, the slope of the stock's characteristic line (the line which shows how the equity moves for any given change in the total market). An equity with a beta of 2 is expected to rise or fall 10 per cent if the market rises or falls 5 per cent. Shares with high betas are often called 'aggressive' while those with low betas are often called 'defensive'. The portfolio as a whole will also have a beta – a measure of its overall riskiness of defensiveness.

Reduction in risk will normally imply reduced return, and so the question arises of how much return per unit of risk we get. To answer this question William Sharpe devised a measure called the Sharpe ratio which is defined as the ratio of the risk premium earned by the portfolio to the total risk, that is, the extra return per unit of extra risk. The formal definition is:

$$S = (Rp - R)/\sigma$$

where
Rp = return on the portfolio
R = risk-free rate of return
σ = standard deviation of portfolio's returns
S = Sharpe ratio

A related but different approach was taken by Jack Treynor who related the portfolio's return to its 'systematic' risk. Here we have

$$T = (Rp - R)/b$$

where
b = beta of the portfolio as a whole
T = Treynor ratio

The main problem with all this is that these measures are fundamentally flawed. Standard deviation is a symmetrical measure: a profitable surprise is treated as adding to risk, just as much as a loss-making surprise is. Intuitively, one thinks of risk as risk of loss. Of course, risk is normally two-way, and so the standard deviation is a fair approximation. It is a truism that normally to make a big profit one must accept the risk of a big loss. But the effect of options is different. We still take a risk – we will spend a lot of money on premiums, and if the options do not pay off, the money is gone. But the sacrifice shows up in reduced portfolio return, not in increased risk, if risk is defined as the chance of loss of portfolio value.

If one has all the assets of the portfolio in cash and options, properly structured, there is no risk of a negative return: the lowest possible return will be zero (less the premium cost). The two-way risk definition is no longer appropriate. Suppose that we have in the past held a cash portfolio of identical structure to that shown above, but only in cash. It will exhibit a standard deviation that results from the historical standard deviations of past currency movements allowing for their correlation. Normal performance measurement would treat this as the portfolio's risk. But now we introduce put options on the currency holdings. The past standard deviation is no longer an adequate measure of future risk. We need a projected risk.

One possible solution to this dilemma is to define risk of an optioned portfolio as the standard deviation of all past negative movements. However, it is not intuitively clear that this is a meaningful measure of the risk: for example, if the entire portfolio has been invested in a stock which has been rising steadily and has now peaked, measured risk would be nil. This would be accurate if the portfolio were protected by an at-the-money put but not if the put were out of the money.

There seems to be no clearly defined answer and certainly none which would be automatically calculated. In theory perhaps the best measure of risk would be to calculate the portfolio's valuation on the basis of a 10, 20, 30, 40 and 50 per cent (say) fall in all asset values. Using different degrees of movement would allow for the possibility that the portfolio's puts might only kick in after say a 15 per cent fall. A refinement might be to weight these price changes either with estimated probabilities or else with figures derived from historical volatility. One could then calculate a weighted average probability of loss. This entails some subjectivity in the estimate of probabilities, of course. An 'objective' measure might be a scatter diagram showing the portfolio's total return plotted against negative and positive changes in all asset values.

Another aspect of the impact of options on risk assessment is that a portfolio containing options will also cause problems in reporting the asset distribution. It is customary to consider the asset distribution of the portfolio in considering its riskiness: but, as an example, consider a portfolio which is invested totally in an S&P 500 index, hedged with at-the-money S&P 500 puts. If equity prices fall, the portfolio will act as if it were invested in cash. If they rise, as if it were invested in equities. Is the portfolio 100 per cent in equities or 100 per cent in cash? Another example: consider the portfolio of currency holdings outlined above. Most traditional investment software will report the portfolio to be invested one-third in DM, one-third in yen, and one-third in dollars. But it could be argued that it is also invested 100 per cent in dollars.

There seem to be at least two ways of handling this problem: one is to prepare two asset distribution reports, one on the assumption that the options are exercised and one on the assumption they are not. This is simple and straightforward, but rather clumsy and possibly could cause some confusion. A related approach would argue that the exposure to options should be reported differently depending on whether the portfolio has bought or sold the options. Where the options have been sold – say call options on equity stocks – the equity stocks should be transferred to an 'Options portfolio' at the option price. This separates the performance of the two instruments.

In a recent study prepared for the London Traded Options Market, the consulting actuaries Baron & Woodrow argue for two measures of the performance of futures and options. The first, 'contingent exposure', measures the exposure to a market that the portfolio would have, contingent on the derivative contract being exercised. The second, 'differential exposure', would measure how the portfolio would perform if small differences occurred in the value of the underlying markets/stocks. The two concepts are identical for futures contracts. For options contracts, they would vary according to the direction of movement.

Another approach would be more sophisticated but would certainly cause confusion unless those involved have a clear understanding of options (although if they didn't of course they should not be involved). This would be to 'delta-weight' the asset distribution. (See the discussion in Chapter 7 for the definition of delta – the sensitivity of the option's value to a change in the price of the asset). If the option is at-the-money the delta is normally 0.50 or thereabouts – which in a kind of way makes intuitive sense since there is a 50/50 chance the option will be in-the-money at expiry. So in our currency example, if the DM holdings were protected by an at-the-money put with a delta of 0.50 you would show half of the optioned assets in dollars and half in Deutschmarks.

As the option becomes more in-the-money (i.e. the DM weakens and the dollar strengthens, in our example) the delta rises and so does the probability of the option being in-the-money at expiry and the proportion shown held in dollars would also rise, until when the option is very deeply in-the-money and delta is 1 your portfolio would be shown 100 per cent in dollars.

In conclusion: perhaps enough has been said to show that there are many different ways of looking at performance. It is not suggested that the above treatment is comprehensive, or indeed necessarily appropriate for every investor. Different users of information will want it presented in different ways, which may be of more help to them than the methods discussed above. As Kipling wrote:

> There are nine-and-sixty ways of constructing tribal lays
> And – every – single – one – of – them – is – right!

MATHEMATICAL SUPPLEMENT

This section lays out what we have been talking about in mathematical notation. We begin by defining

$\sum_{i=1}^{n} w_i$ as meaning 'add up $w_1, w_2, \ldots w_n$'

Next we define the parallel concept in multiplication:

$\prod_{i=1}^{n} w_i$ as meaning 'multiply $w_1, w_2, \ldots w_n$'

Now we consider a portfolio consisting of m stocks which are affected by the n factors. We define w as the weight in the portfolio of the ith stock. We define f_{ij} as the impact of factor i on stock j. One of those factors is the impact of the exchange rate. For convenience we will call this factor number 1. That is, f_{Ij} is the impact of a change in the exchange rate in which stock j is denonominated on stock j's return in Home currency terms. (If there are several exchange rates involved the size of the factor will vary according to the currency.) We define the return on stock j in local currency terms as r_{Lj} and the return in Home terms as r_{Hj}. Clearly we can put, for stock j denominated in currency i:

$$r_{Hj} = r_{\text{Lj}}\,(1 + f_{1i})$$

What is the total return, R, of the portfolio? It is the return in Home terms of each stock, weighted accordingly to its share of the portfolio.

$$R = \sum_{j=1}^{m} w_j r_{Hj} = \sum_{j=1}^{m} w_j\,(1 + f_{1j}) r_{Lj}$$

The local currency return on stock j is itself determined by the impact of the other factors upon it. Thus:

$$r_{Lj} = \prod_{i=2}^{n} (1 + f_{ij})$$

Substituting, therefore, we can write:

$$R = \sum_{j=1}^{m} w_j \prod_{i=1}^{n} (1 + f_{ij})$$

Now we return to the attribution analysis. We want to set this up so that the return arrived at by totalling the contribution of the stocks is the same as that from totalling the contribution of the factors and this can be done if the totals are arrived at by multiplying, not adding, the elements. The contribution by stock j to the portfolio is:

$$\prod_{i=1}^{n} (1 + w_j f_{ij})$$

and the contribution by factor i to the portfolio's return is:

$$\prod_{j=1}^{m} (1 + w_j f_{ij})$$

The combined total return of the portfolio, which we will call C, can be found in two ways: either from the contributions of all the stocks, or from the contributions of all the factors. If we multiply all the stock contributions (i.e. going horizontally in the tables used earlier), we have

$$C = \prod_{j=1}^{m} \left\{1 + \prod_{i=1}^{n} (1 + w_j f_{ij})\right\}$$

We can arrive at the same result by a different route by multiplying together all the factor contributions (going downward in our tables):

$$C = \prod_{i=1}^{n} \left\{1 + \prod_{j=1}^{m} (1 + w_j f_{ij})\right\}$$

It will be remembered that we found the total portfolio return from the contributions of individual stocks as follows:

$$R = \sum_{j=1}^{m} w_j \prod_{i=1}^{n} (1 + f_{ij})$$

It is clear that C and R are not identical. But it would be useful to be able to break up R, which is the actual measured return on the portfolio, into the component elements as measured by the attribution analysis which yields C. An appropriate way to do this would be to scale down the components of C by the ratio R/C.

Index